Beyond the Fields—World Travels

Beyond the Fields— World Travels

Autobiographical Memories

LouCelle Nelson Fertik

VANTAGE PRESS
New York

I dedicate this book of memories to:

My grandmothers: Laura Jaathun, who left her home and family near Stavanger, Norway, at age twenty-one, came to America, married Lewis Larson in 1889, and farmed near Holmes, Iowa, raising nine children, instilling in them the love of family and the work ethic; and Caroline Furuseth from Oslo, Norway, born in 1858, arrived as a small child with her parents and sister, married Oliver Nelson in 1877 and farmed near Goldfield, Iowa, raising five children. Grandma Laura and Grandma Lena and fourteen aunts and uncles and their spouses showered me with love and an understanding of my immediate world.

My parents, Albin and Tillie Nelson, who supported all my dreams.

My three brothers—Al (Doc), Bob, and Orin—my cousin-brother Wayne, my sister Carol, and their spouses—they truly have been kindred spirits.

My sixteen nieces and nephews and their families, who have given me so much pleasure and love—as though they were my own.

My friends and students, too numerous to individually name, who have warmed my heart and made my days so satisfying.

My other families through marriage, the Goldens and the Fertiks.

The Music-Makers of the world, especially two teachers: Maxine Berkhimer Dwyer, who filled my sixth-grade year in country school with music and theater; and Alice Peters Riley, my high school choral teacher, who made music my main focus during those four years, encouraging my music interest, which led to a major in music in college.

Ruth Hanson, who shared my "around the world" sabbatical with me.

People of many countries, of many races, of many religions, who have "touched me" with acts of thoughtfulness and kindness.

Birds and animals that made my traveling much more interesting, and in some cases, extremely exciting.

Uncle LeRoy (Dr. LeRoy Larson) and Aunt Margaret, who made the printing of this book possible.

Contents

Introduction   ix

Part I.   Born Alive (1923)
1. Iowa, 1923 3
2. Minnesota, 1942–1944 17

Part II.   Teaching in Winter; Travels in Summer (1944–1951)
3. Teaching Music in Public Schools 21
4. Summer Adventures 26

Part III.   Overseas Teaching: Japan and Germany (1952–1958)
5. Teaching in the Army Dependent's School in Tokyo, Japan, 1952–1954 51
6. Teaching in the Army Dependent's School in Heidelberg, Germany 73

Part IV.   Long Island, New York, and Travels (1958–1978)
7. Marriage and Teaching in Roslyn 91
8. The Demise of Two Lives 100

Part V.   Traveling the World (1970–1978)
9. Historical Cultural Tour of Southeast Asia, Summer 1970 105
10. Nairobi, Kenya, Summer 1972 111
11. Larson-Jotten Ancestry Book, Autumn 1972... 120
12. Sabbatical to Study Music and Culture around the World, 1974... 123
13. Istanbul, Turkey, Winter 1976 166

Part VI.   In the Shadow of the Best
14. Special Music Moments, Special People.......... 183

Part VII.   Living in India (1978–1982)
15. Teaching at the Woodstock School, 1978–1982   203

16. Bus Tour around India, Winter 1978–1979 211
17. Tibetans in Exile, 1978 224
18. Houseboat Holiday in Kashmir, Summer 1979 236
19. Ladakh, Summer 1979 253
20. Birthday Trip in the Himalayan Foothills,
    March 22, 1980 263
21. Music Conference in Poland, Summer 1980 ... 266
22. Kuwait, Winter 1980 272
23. Pakistan and Sri Lanka, Winter 1980 278
24. Darjeeling, Summer 1981 282
25. Bhutan, Summer 1981 291
26. Bharatpur Bird Sanctuary, Winter 1981 303
27. Rajasthan, Winter 1982 307
28. Pony Trek in Nepal, Winter 1982 315
29. Change of Plans, Spring 1982 323

Part VIII.   Retirement and Travels (1983–)
30. Marriage and Travels 327
31. A Strong Stand on Education 333
32. My Iowa Home—Three Pine Farm, 1993 337

Part IX.   Epilogue
Tributes 343
Countries I Have Visited (1948–1998)............. 345
Uncle LeRoy's Letter about Dr. Sabin, 1993 .. 347
Post-Polio Syndrome 349

Introduction

What happened to all those years? I am now retired and in my seventh decade of this thing called *Life* on Planet Earth. I grew up on a farm in Iowa; my ancestors were all Norwegian. In high school I knew I wanted to spend my life teaching choral music and thought it would be good to teach in various states so I could learn about the different areas of our country. In my wildest dreams I never thought I would teach music in other countries . . . or that the love of my life would be international travel . . . or that I would be the Miami Regional Director of the U.S.–Tibet Committee . . . or I would marry twice.

How did it happen? Why did it happen to me? As I look back it seemed one good thing after another happened. As each offer came, I accepted the challenge. In retrospect, it was the correct decision.

This is the story of my adventure in life—always in the shadow of the best!

I
BORN ALIVE (1923)

Happiness is not a picture which is painted with a few bold sweeping strokes. It is rather a delicately wrought mosaic whose intricate pattern is composed of many small pleasures and interests. The people who continually manufacture little harmonious pleasure pieces of experience get real joy out of living.

—Anonymous

1

Iowa, 1923

As our small rented boat approached tree-covered Crescent Island's shore in Kenya in Africa we noticed there was no dock. When we landed, our native Kenyan boat operator, and Jim, an American man, moved several large stones for the five women and one boy to step on so we would not get our shoes wet. We saw waterbuck and impala on the island and had seen five nearly submerged hippos not far from the water's edge. Jim helped me up the steep, rocky embankment to the level path. The others strolled rapidly down the trail, but I decided to stay in that area to photograph the numerous birds, my reason for making arrangements for this side trip to a bird sanctuary island on our four-day safari to Lake Naivasha.

From a distance Jim yelled to me, "I think we are going to a bird blind—you better come." I hurried to catch up. I looked ahead, then to the right, and was absolutely stunned to see the head of a young lion coming over the crest of a grass-covered small mound. I screamed frantically to my friends, "There's a lion." (They later told me they thought I was joking.) Soon a second young lion came into view! I could not run; there were no trees nearby to climb; I was beside myself with fright. Then Jim saw the two lions and shouted, "Freeze." I was so happy to hear that word—it was the only thing I *could* do. The others watched from a distance and Jim kept saying, "Down boy, down boy" in a very calm voice. I don't know what it did to the lion but it surely had a quieting effect on my wildly beating heart and shaking hands. I stood perfectly still, all the time looking just above the head of the first lion who was now slowly walking down the narrow trail towards me. Thoughts raced through my head. Would he bite? Where would he bite? Was this the way my life would end? (People say that one's life races through the mind just before they die; I realized that wasn't happening to me.) Perhaps there was a chance I would live.

What was I doing here on this island in Lake Naivasha in Kenya anyway? I was one of two hundred students and teachers accepted to study at the American Institute for Foreign Study's summer school, in

1972, connected with the University of Nairobi, Kenya. It was my first trip to Africa and I had looked forward to the summer with great anticipation. We already had been on a ten-day safari visiting Ngorongoro Crater, Tsavo National Park, lived in a tented camp site at Tarangire Park (when I took a shower in the canvas enclosure open to the sky, I knew I was "Ava Gardner"). We had seen extraordinary wildlife including lionesses and cubs resting or sleeping in the shade of acacia trees, a lion and lioness mating, watched seven alert lionesses observing a wildebeest herd when suddenly the one perched on a rock dashed forward accelerating with every step to make the kill. Always the safari van had enclosed me and I was without fear. Now I was standing on the ground right in the animals' environment, and the lion was getting so close he was sniffing my right knee. Then he slowly circled me and ambled down the trail in front of me. I barely had enough energy to call out, "Please come help me." The lion heard my pitiful sounds, turned around for more investigation. I thought, *Now what?*

From the middle of the island, an African with a pail in each hand strolled on another path. Both young lions saw him and hurried over, swishing their tails from side to side. At that moment we all realized these two were not really wild lions . . . how tame do lions get? The man gave each lion a huge chunk of meat and watched carefully as they ate.

By this time I was ready to collapse, so Jim carried me back to the boat. In a short time I felt stronger, and we discussed the situation. Without knowing it, I had done one thing wrong, one right. I should *not* have gone off by myself to photograph birds; I should have remained with the group. As the lion walked toward me I never looked him straight in the eye (that means confrontation) but looked above his head. That was the correct response, even though I didn't realize it at the time. Why had I insisted that Jim go with us on our little bird-watching afternoon boat trip? What was it—ESP on my part? Perhaps! I was so thankful he was there.

When our party of seven had left the lodge after lunch the school official had said, "If you are not back by 6:15 a boat will come searching for you at your own expense." We arrived back at the Lodge seconds before the deadline! Word of my experience spread like wildfire, and I had to tell the story over and over all weekend. One friend said to me, "Joy Adamson, move over." Of course I tried to find out why we weren't warned about the lions on a bird sanctuary island. Why were they there?

Were they part of the "Born Free" film project? No one could or would answer my questions. I will never know.

This was not the first time my legs had been "sniffed" and by a much bigger danger than a young lion. When I was seven years old I got that dreaded childhood disease, poliomyelitis. Our family had visited our cousins in Colfax, Iowa, for a few days. Both young children were not feeling well. My mother and her sister discussed this, finally deciding Aunt Lue would do more checking. When we got home, she phoned to say the doctors confirmed that K.J. did have infantile paralysis (polio) and suggested we go to the doctor for shots, which we did. There was a serum made from the blood of people who had had polio; that was what was given to us in 1930. My older brother remembers how sore his buttocks were, so we took small pillows to school for more comfortable sitting. After a few days the soreness subsided—but I got the disease. My mother said I was in the bathroom and couldn't stand because my legs were so weak. Then she knew!

I was kept in isolation in the bedroom at the top of the stairs. The local M.D. who had given us the shots was called and said I should lie perfectly still and not move. My father had a cousin who was an osteopath—he was also called. Dr. Royal Nelson said I should be massaged and moved frequently. For three days these two doctors saw me and gave my parents conflicting opinions on my care. They had to make a choice. As I look back, I believe this may have been one of their most difficult decisions in their fifty-one years of marriage! They chose Dr. Royal. He drove the twelve miles from Humboldt to the farm every day for ten days to massage my muscles and move my legs and arms. I do remember one night when he had been phoned to come quickly. My mother kept looking west through the window for the bright car lights, softly crying. My illness must have been difficult for her because my sister was born in August, 1930 (I came down with polio on Dec. 7, 1930), and I had a three-year-old brother and a ten-year-older brother. Dr. Royal taught my father how to massage my muscles, to do it several times a day. I have been told I was paralyzed to my neck but gradually my legs were the only affected part, especially the left leg, which was weak and has an ankle drop.

The large windup Victrola was placed in the room; however, there were only two records: "Beautiful Ohio" and "Moonlight and Roses." What I should have had were symphonies, concertos, operas—but that was not to be until years and years later.

After a time I started to crawl, mainly using my arms to pull myself along the floor; my legs were too weak to be of much use. I was like a baby learning to walk all over again. Through the massage I could later walk holding onto chairs or the large dining room table. Since it was winter I did not go to country school, but books and lessons came home with my oldest brother and I was able to advance to the next grade the following year. I was carried whenever we went out to visit. Finally a stationary bicycle was placed in the basement and someone helped me on it and I pedaled to regain strength in my legs. When the weather became sunny and the snow had melted my father gave me a push on the bike on the gravel road in front of our house and I rode down the road where my brother was standing. He stopped me, turned the bike around, and I pedaled back to my father—he stopped me and turned me around for another ride. By the time September 1931 came, I would be helped on the bike by my father, then pedal the half-mile to school with him watching. If I fell off during the ride, he would get in the car, come to me, and put me on the bike (it was quite a long time before I could get on the bike without help).

During this inactivity, I began to take piano lessons through the mail—a Kansas City Music Company had a series of sixty lessons. One lesson came with information, a song to learn to play, and a sheet of questions. I sent back the sheet filled with correct answers, I hoped. In a few days that paper came back graded and corrected, with the new lesson. What a way to learn to play the piano! In spite of it, I grew up to major in music and taught choral music for thirty-eight years.

Sister Elizabeth Kenny of Australia, born in 1880, treated her first polio patients in 1911. In the 1930s, there was a polio epidemic. She disregarded the idea of splints and no movement, the usual way victims were treated, in favor of hot, moist packs to relieve the spasms and tightness of the muscles and moving the affected limbs for "muscle reeducation." In the 1975 book by Victor Cohn titled *Sister Kenny, the Woman Who Challenged the Doctors,* she is quoted as saying, "Infantile paralysis is a damnable thing; it leaves the child neither dead nor alive." She finally came to the U.S. in 1940 and did her work in Minneapolis, where she was called "healer from nowhere" and "angel from the Outback." She met our president, Franklin D. Roosevelt, also a polio victim; a movie was made of her life with Rosalind Russell playing Sister Kenny, opening in New York in 1946. In spite of much opposition from medical doctors, her method of hot packs and muscle reeducation had won. I have always wondered if Dad's cousin, Dr. Royal Nelson, had heard of her radical treatment back in 1930, or did he know massage and movement were best? I surely have been grateful for the decision my parents made that fateful day in December when they chose Dr. Royal instead of the other doctor.

Now you know why I couldn't run when I first saw the young lion in Kenya fifty-two years after my bout with poliomyelitis. Who knows what my life would have been like if I had not had polio; however, I *did* have it. These are the memories of my life.

My birth certificate states my name and only two other words, "Born alive." No time, no weight. The date was March 22, 1923. Our new farmhouse had been built in 1922 and they moved in just before Christmas of that year. There were four upstairs bedrooms, a sleeping porch the width of the house, a small room used for a nursery or playroom, a bathroom and a hall. Downstairs were the living room with a fireplace at one end and French doors opening into the sunporch, a hallway or front entrance with more French doors opening to the dining room, a rather small kitchen (later my father always said in his next house he was only going to build a kitchen because that is where everyone gathered on cool and cold days), a closet with the hot water tank off the kitchen and the back steps and entrance. Of course, there was a full basement with a cistern for rainwater from the gutters, a coal room, a room for the canned food and storage for vegetables from the garden, a furnace room, and a huge washroom. This beautiful new house was waiting for me to arrive. . . . I loved that house on the flat prairie land with a thick grove of trees to the north and a line of cottonwoods to the west and fields all around.

When I was three I found a small container on a stump in the backyard, so I began to drink the contents only to find out it was kerosene. I had to drink cream to counteract the liquid (I was told this story). As a child I loved to wheel the doll buggy with a mother cat dressed up in doll clothes. We had such good times together. Then at age five I got diphtheria; the doctor told me I got it from my precious cat. I have always wondered if that were possible—or was it just conversation with a child? To this day I don't like cats. Was there a connection with my cat and the "big cat" in Kenya? I wonder.

Growing up on a farm gave each child many opportunities with chores for every age: gather the eggs from the chicken house; keep the woodbox filled with cobs and wood for the kitchen stove; set the table for meals and later clear the table and wash the dishes; help milk the cows and feed the hogs for the boys and help with the cooking and cleaning for the girls. We all learned responsibility, gained respect for the larger family unit, and were happy to help wherever it was needed.

As a child my environment was new and there for exploring, listening, and learning. Dusk descended when the chores were almost finished and peace and quiet settled on the people and animals at Three Pine Farm: the sounds of the night, the bright stars so close I could almost pluck one from the sky, the moon large and round as it came up over the horizon in the east. We tried to see the "man-in-the-moon" (much later in Japan it was the "rabbit-in-the-moon"). Sometimes our dog barked and was answered by another dog from a nearby farm, frogs croaked in the small creek, insects buzzed. Morning brought the soulful call of the mourning doves, later the meadow larks, the robins, and red-headed woodpeckers. If a rooster crowed Mother said company was coming and we got busy with chores before they arrived (rather good psychology on her part; it worked). The neighbors, the small towns, the weekly visits to grandparents' homes, country school with one teacher teaching all eight grades gradually enlarged my world.

There was that wonderful invention, the Delco! In our new home we always had electricity; however, we made it by having a Delco. In the evening either we could listen to the radio by lamplight or we had lights and no radio. It was impossible to have both because of the pop, pop, pop, sound of the Delco in the radio. When everyone got into bed I held my breath to see if the pop, pops would stop when the last persons shut off the light. Many times the Delco would continue to pop because somewhere on the farm a light was still on. It always seemed to be in the hayloft in the barn, and my oldest brother would have to get up and walk quite a distance to the barn to shut off the light. I wonder if he was ever scared as he went out in the dark?

How I enjoyed hearing Mom tell the story of one buggy ride with her brother, Joe, when a buggy passed them at night with a man groaning, making their horses run so fast a box of hats was thrown on the road, so they turned the buggy around quickly to retrieve them and raced to their farm home. It was a scary story, and Mom told it with much emotion. My mother also memorized dramatic readings for programs at Evergreen, a community association. The one of Saul in prison with the rays of light coming through the narrow window was so sad; the Norwegian newcomer reading "Lena on the Telephone" was very funny and made everyone laugh.

In the autumn I would walk home from the country school and hear the sound of the corn hitting against the side of the wagon as men hand-picked corn. Sometimes pheasants would quickly fly away making a whirring sound with their wings. Everything was so quiet, any man or animal sound was loud. If a plane flew overhead, everyone ran outside to watch it. The boards on a bridge were loose and every car that rumbled across was heard.

Winter on our farm in Iowa was *cold*. The French doors into the dining room were closed and we used the kitchen and dining room; heat was shut off in the rest of the house. I took a flat iron all wrapped up in towels and placed it between my bed blankets but I was still cold. Sometimes it would be a hotwater bottle. In the morning I would rush downstairs to dress in front of the cookstove Dad had fired up before going out to do the chores. The best seat in the entire house was getting all curled up in the woodbox beside the stove. Toward spring there generally was a shoebox under the stove with the "runt" of the pig litter. One could hear those little squeals now and then, and when you looked at those little pigs they were always shivering.

Christmas Eve was always the coldest of all. We all had to get into a cold car and drive the four miles to our country church. How rewarding it was after we got there. We were all dressed in our very best and gave our little recitation or song with our class, heard the minister give his beautiful talk about baby Jesus, and finally received a little box of Christmas candy from our teacher. The happiest Christmas was getting a small piano with one and a half octaves; my brother received a rolltop junior-size desk (both from our parents).

What a thrill when spring finally came after the long, cold, snowy winter and I could roll my long underwear up above my knees and roll down my heavy stockings. There was much work to be done to get all the planting done in the fields and the garden and even more work when vegetables in abundance were canned. We had a few apple trees but several mulberry trees. When the berries turned purple, all available canvasses were gathered and laid under the tree. Someone climbed up and shook the branches. The berries fell onto the material spread beneath. We picked them up, ate a few, put others in pails and were stained with juice. What a fun time for the family. We canned mulberry sauce and had mulberry pies. I also helped cut up fat into small squares for rendering into lard and canned the meat. When summer was over, my mother's pride and joy was going to the basement into the "fruit room" where all the shelves were filled with the bountiful harvest of the summer—jar after jar, ready to be used during the winter. Her special song she often sang was, "Everybody works at our house, nobody sits around." We heard it often and we all pitched in and helped. All I can remember was *praise* for those jobs we did. Some of them must have been done poorly but all we ever got was praise! (My very first paid job at home was picking potato bugs off the potato plants, getting one penny for every one hundred bugs.)

I always liked it when Dad got out his violin and played for us. Generally it was, "Oh, we got a pig in the parlor"; it sounded mighty good to my ears. He also yodeled very well and played the ocarina ("sweet potato"). Sunday afternoon, after naps and before beginning chores, Dad would get the fire going in the kitchen stove, put the black popcorn popper filled with corn on it and fix a huge bowl of popcorn for all. Was it ever good with all that melted butter! He also bought a bushel of delicious apples each autumn and stored them in the basement. "An apple a day keeps the doctor away" was his philosophy. If there were coconuts in the store he would buy one and treat us with this delicious coconut milk and small pieces of fresh meat from a faraway place.

Sunday morning we always dressed in our best clothes, put on hats and gloves and went to church arriving just in time for the 9:30 A.M. service (once a month it was at 11:00 A.M.); the farmers had to finish the chores so early. After visiting with a few friends at church, we would stop at Grandma Nelson's home for a short time. I enjoyed going into the "closed up" parlor and looking through the stereoscope at the few cards with photos of faraway places. Grandma always had a yellow cake or a jelly roll for us to sample, always with egg-white frosting. She was so prim and proper in her dresses with lace at the collar . . . and she was always seventy-two years old (her husband had died at that age, before I was born).

After dinner on Sunday, we often drove to look at hogs—Spotted Poland purebred hogs, since that was the kind my father raised and showed at County Fairs. Sometimes we visited friends who spoke only Norwegian. I couldn't understand what was said and I didn't care to listen and learn; however, one of those families had a small stringed instrument, like a zither, and I always got to play it, a real treat. Some

Sundays we drove the ten miles to Grandma Larson's home for a short time. She always had special cookies for us.

Each summer I got to spend a week there. It was such fun to help her feed the little chickens and goslings in the chicken coops along her front yard. I was scared stiff as the geese flew at me and hissed. A cousin, K.J., visited Grandma the same week, and we always planned a musical program to be given the following Sunday when our parents came to get us. Aunt Gladise still lived at Grandma's, and it was fun to watch her get ready for a date—I had never seen so many cosmetics or eyelash curlers. The big clock in the dining room ticked so loud it was hard to fall asleep on the couch below. Grandma washed clothes out in the wash house. She had to move the stick back and forth on the wooden machine for the many loads and then hang them out on the line to dry. What hard work this must have been for a woman who immigrated from Norway in 1888, married and had nine children. What a warm, kind, loving grandmother. Grandpa was always tinkering down in the machine shed by the water tank and pump so I didn't see much of him even though I spent much time playing house on the large rock in the back yard; sometimes K.J. and I called it our castle.

The most memorable Christmas at Grandma Laura's was when we had to leave our cars on the main road and transfer to a sled pulled by horses for the last two miles. We snuggled down under the horsehair blankets to keep warm. What an exciting ride. When we got to the warm, cozy house we sat down with other aunts/uncles/cousins for a delicious meal. Later we walked into the parlor where a real Christmas tree was lighted with small burning candles. What a memory that is!

In our dining room a cage hung from a rod in the east window with a beautiful yellow canary. He sang and sang until we came downstairs one morning and found him dead. That was a real tragedy for a small child. I also remember looking in a robin's nest built low in a tree and seeing the bald heads and wide-open mouths of three babies waiting for a worm or insect from their mother. It was a strange and memorable sight. As an adult I became a bird-watcher and have spent many hours enjoying and identifying birds in sanctuaries around the world. One never knows where early experiences will lead.

Oats ripened in the fields; men would cut it, then pile the sheaves of grain into shocks. This was hard work in the heat of the day so Mom and I would prepare a big jug of cold lemonade and cookies or sandwiches and drive out to the field so the men could have a short rest with

11

refreshments. Later came the threshing of the oats with all the neighbors joining together with their horses and wagons, the large threshing machine, going from farm to farm to thresh. The women were also busy preparing the big meal for all the men, fifteen or twenty of them. When they came to our farm, Grandma Nelson and Wayne's wife, Mable, always were there to help with the meal—potatoes, vegetables, usually Mom made Swiss steak, bread, relishes, and of course, pie for dessert. We younger ones fixed the washing area under the shade of a tree in the backyard with basin, water in pails, mirror, soap, towels . . . and did other small errands. Usually it was a two-day affair and everyone was busy inside and out. Finally when all the farms had their oats threshed, a watermelon feast occurred at the home of the farmer having the highest yield of oats. Everyone in the families attended, enjoying the delicious juicy fruit and thankful another year's crop was gathered. (Later, combines took the place of threshing machines so this interesting farm tradition disappeared.)

The Evergreen Sporting Association was a community organization with many activities throughout the year. There were two sides, the Red and the Green, with captains to head each side. Points were given to individuals in many ways and each person tried to get the most so they would become the high man/high woman or high boy/high girl. There were evening programs: dramatic and humorous readings, debates, instrumental solos and duets, vocal solos and duets, quartets, choruses, etc. Judges were usually teachers from the local schools and they decided who got first, second, third. How we practiced to try to get first place! There were summer picnics with potluck dinners in the park with races, ball throws, broad jumps, etc. From the annual report of ESA on February 15, 1917, this is what my father had received the previous summer: 100-yard dash: third; high jump: second; broad jump: first; pole vault: first; hop, step and jump: 4th; men's ball throw: first; hammer throw: first; entry of wheat: first. From a program in January, 1917, Dad got second in a vocal duet and second in a man's quartet. The magazine *The Wallace's Farmer* of July 2, 1926, written by W. E. Drips, states:

Albin Nelson, president of ESA besides being a farmer, is also an all-around athlete. Nelson, although he is nearly forty, can put a shot over 35′ and broad jump with the best of them. At the annual picnic of the association last week he showed the youngsters he was still full of pep by taking 2nd in the 100-yard dash, defeating 20 others, all younger.

Nelson has been showing the boys his stuff for several years. Back in 1910 while competing for his team in the association he took first in the high jump and broad jump. . . .

A two-day short course was held at the large country school with women bringing baked goods, canned goods, sewing, embroidery, and quilts. The junior girls also brought items for their categories. Men took animals for judging to three farms across from one another. Men and women came from Iowa State College at Ames to judge—telling them why one was better than another. All the points were counted for individuals and the sides to see who had won. The losing side had to plan a banquet for the winning side. It was a special event, which was enjoyed by all. Gifts were presented to the individual winners. I was the winner for the junior girls' division in 1932 and received a sterling silver spoon engraved "ESA 1932." I still have this treasure from my youth.

I can't say enough about ESA and what it did for our community and for me. I was not afraid to stand up and sing or play piano in front of an audience; I learned to do embroidery and cook; I was a participant, sometimes a leader, sometimes a follower. ESA was probably the biggest "plus" while growing up. How thankful I have always been that I was part of it!

Special "visitors" came to our door to sell their wares. I don't know if they walked all the way from town or left their transportation down the road and walked a short distance to our house. We called them "peddlers." One man had a sack of goodies—embroidery threads, needles, ribbons, etc. To me they were pure magic when he put the contents of his bag on the dining-room table. Many years later I wondered about him and mentioned it to my brother Bob. He suggested he might have been a Lebanese man from Fort Dodge. I phoned and found out that three brothers had indeed come to this area and did walk to farm homes to sell their wares, later going by horse and carriage. The son of one of these men had become the mayor of Fort Dodge! That is what our wonderful United States is all about. Another peddler was the "broom man" and Mom would buy a new broom from him every year. Later there was the "Watkins man" who arrived by van with spices and bottles of vanilla, almond, and lemon flavors, the three Mom would buy.

In a grove about a mile west from our home, Gypsies would often camp for a few days. How I wanted to visit them and learn about their lives. My parents would never let me do that and said, "They steal children." That would scare off any child, for sure, but it only increased my interest in them and their lifestyle. (With all my travels and wanderings I often feel like a Gypsy; I have a very dear friend from New York who has lived and danced all over the world; she is my "Gypsy sister."

Smells. I enjoyed coming home from school to find the house full of neighbor women having a club meeting or helping Mom quilt. The smell of coffee filled the house as well as the ground meat-pickle-mayonnaise filling on freshly made rolls. Way back in my mind I remember a pancake supper with neighbors present. Some man, trying to sell pots and pans, came and cooked pancakes for all. Of course, the homemade bread freshly made was the most memorable smell. We also churned butter. Mom was so proud of the fact she only ran out of butter once—when we had a hired girl, so it wasn't Mom's fault. The smells of a clean house—polish, wax, varnish during spring housecleaning. Wonderful scents in this beautiful farm home.

On December 19, 1935, my youngest brother, Orin, was born. What a surprise that was when Dad told us, when we came home from school, that we had a baby brother and that he had been born with one arm and hand. The left arm was off just above the elbow (probably the umbilical cord had somehow cut off the circulation so it didn't develop). What a shock this was for everyone. The winter of 1935–36 was the worst, with snow piled high above buildings; tunnels had to be made to get from one to the other. Orin was often ill; I was too, with terrible pains in my abdomen. The doctor would be called, driving on the main road and met by Dad in a horse and sleigh for the last mile. I had these pains off and on for years and no one knew what caused them. (Between my junior and senior year in college they were so bad I was hospitalized for a gallstone operation. Everyone had said I was too young to have gallstones. Finally in 1955 an army doctor told me I had them because I had spent so much time in bed during polio. I asked him why someone hadn't told me that. He answered, "They didn't know then.") How I suffered with those excruciating pains!

In 1937 Mom gave me a five-year diary, which I faithfully filled with each day's activities. March 6, 1938, states that Orin was sitting on the table and pointing to his left arm said, "Arm broke off." He was a little over two years old then. (He grew up, graduated from college, married, built a garage for his house, later rebuilt an old house, enjoyed riding motorcycles, is an excellent mechanic, was a county auditor for several years and is now the manager of a nursing home where he can put all his talents to use.) Everyone in our family was encouraged to do whatever they wanted to do and praise was always given for any accomplishment. We never heard the word "No."

High school brought me music! I learned to play the oboe and became a band member. We had excellent music teachers, especially our vocal music teacher, Miss Peters. Our mixed chorus, girls' chorus, and girls' sextet were highly rated in programs and contests. I was in the sextet and we often sang at clubs, church programs, and other events. Probably that one group made me want to be a music teacher more than any other. For those four high school years, music was my life! I also sang contralto solos and played piano solos in yearly contests, even winning so that I could go to the state contest in Iowa City. Once the judge for my solo was the famous Howard Hanson, president of the Eastman School of Music and one of our esteemed American music educators and composers. One year our girls' chorus won the state contest and we went to the national contest in Minneapolis.

Another world opened to me in high school when I corresponded with a pen pal in Vienna, Austria, Maria Luise Likar. Through her letters I had a glimpse of that city of music-making by Mozart, Beethoven, Schubert, and the Strausses and was offered an intimate idea of a place far away from the Iowa prairie. We both took piano lessons and enjoyed classical music and concerts; she liked movies and some of the same movie stars I liked: Nelson Eddy, Jeanette McDonald, Tyrone Power, Myrna Loy; she liked opera, especially Richard Wagner's operas, and so did I. We were about the same age, but she had her own dressmaker and often asked for pictures of clothes from magazines so they could be copied for her. Most of my clothes were hand-me-downs, which my mother adjusted for me. We sent each other little gifts (I still have those she sent me). Some letters contained magazine pictures of places and of Hitler (I have wondered if she sent them so her letters would get through to me without problems). Her first letter arrived November 1937. Her last letter arrived the spring of 1939 after her birthday telling me she had received new furniture for her personal living room and some new clothes. She also said I should save the stamp; "It might be valuable someday." The next letter I wrote was returned to me and stamped "Address unknown." I was devastated! Whatever happened to my friend in Vienna? I have since written to the American embassy in Vienna asking them to find out about her; the answer came back, "We can't find out." Every time I have been to Vienna I have tried to find out about

15

her—to no avail. It was a very sad day for me to end the correspondence with a friend so far away . . . it made the march of Hitler across Europe very real.

Our family did have a few trips. Once a year we would all drive to South Dakota to visit my mother's sister, Aunt Clara and her family, four hundred miles away. We left at 4:00 A.M., had a picnic lunch in a park along the way and arrived in time for the evening meal. Once, during Depression days, a hog was loaded in a crate and tied to the side of the car. Somehow it got out and everyone scurried around trying to find it. Yes, it was found and crated and we continued on our way. (In the 1930s during the dust-bowl days, three of their children spent two summers with us in Iowa.) We got to know our cousins very well and always enjoyed the visit at their home; Mom loved to see her oldest sister.

My father enjoyed fishing. There would be day trips with neighbor men to Spirit Lake or Lake Okoboji and a weeklong trip to a northern Minnesota lake. He certainly deserved those peaceful and carefree days away from all the farm chores and work. Much later, my brother Doc and his family of three invited Mom and Dad and me on a fishing trip to the canoe country between the U.S. and Canada. Everything we would use that week had to be brought in on the two boats—food, tents, fishing equipment, etc. That was one of my most memorable family vacations. The peace, the quiet, the cry of the loons, the occasional deer that walked by our campsite; Doc's small dog was always with us so the bears would smell the animal and stay away; the smell of bacon frying as we awakened in the cool dawn (Virginia and Doc always had the breakfast ready) were a few of the memories. Once when I was fishing in the boat with Mom and Dad, my fishline got caught in a branch in the water—I thought it was a branch, but when I finally pulled it free there was a ten-pound walleye on the hook. Yes, we brought it in the boat and got it to our camp safely. What a fabulous week in the wilds of North America!

2

Minnesota, 1942–1944

During the 1940s my oldest brother, Doc, was in veterinary school at Iowa State College in Ames, Iowa. During the summer he had to work and was not at home. I took his place and drove the tractor and cultivated corn in the fields. As I did this day after day I often would do vocal exercises. No one heard me; it was a perfect place to do two things at once. With him in college, I spent my first two years at Eagle Grove Junior College, coming home on weekends. There were no music courses but I did complete the required college courses, making it possible to take the music courses at St. Olaf College in Northfield, Minnesota. Gas was rationed by then and food stamps were required for certain items, such as sugar. There were very few men in classes; however, men from the V-5 Naval Pre-Flight Cadet Corps had their training at St. Olaf, using Mohn Hall for their residence. I had to move from Mohn to Agnes Melby Hall into a room meant for two but used for three. Classes began at 7:50 A.M. About the same time the "Star Spangled Banner" was played for the flag ceremony for the cadet corps. If students weren't inside their classroom building by that time, we would have to stand still until it was finished. What a rush to avoid this and get to class on time.

In spite of gas rationing I did attend the Minneapolis Symphony Orchestra concert in the city once. My parents came to visit one Sunday, driving the two hundred miles and arriving before I was even out of bed. We enjoyed a delicious picnic in the Northfield Park. Excellent teachers with real dedication made my two years at St. Olaf most memorable. My best friend was Doris Braithwaite, also a music major, and we did a lot of studying together. When we graduated her mother and my mother arrived for the special event—we were happy the four of us could spend the day together.

I could go on and on about childhood memories while growing up on Three Pine Farm. How did I know when I was so bored with all the Norwegian talk that I would visit Norway many times and find extraordinary relatives there? How did I know that someday I would live in countries where rice was the most important food? (I never liked rice at

17

home.) How did I know that these roots in Iowa were the beginnings for my travels around the world? What a privilege to have been part of the Albin and Tillie Nelson family!

After my first year of teaching, Dad said there were forty acres next to our farm and he thought I should buy the land. Thoughts in my head told me I didn't want to be involved because I didn't want to have to stay for plowing and planting and harvesting. He hadn't expanded his idea; therefore, I really didn't know what he had in mind. My answer was, "No." That was the last I heard about buying Iowa land. I used my money for traveling and learning about a bigger world. After all, my birth certificate only had the date, year and the words "Born alive"!

II
TEACHING IN WINTER;
TRAVELS IN SUMMER
(1944–1951)

Travel was the beginning of a passion . . . for identifying myself with people who were not my own and whose lives were governed by ideas alien to mine.

—V. S. Pritchett

3

Teaching Music in Public Schools

Gilmore City, Iowa, 1944–1946

My teaching experiences began in Gilmore City, Iowa (twenty-four miles from my home), called the limestone capital of the state. I arrived there in September 1944 and taught in former stores, the town theater, and church basements. Why? The entire school had burned the previous year. One teacher had gone back into the burning building to see if any students were still there. The automatic doors closed while she was inside and there was no escape: a tragic experience for everyone in the small town.

My first job was during World War II—with my first check, I bought a bicycle with three gears and found it was a good way to get around town. Often on Saturdays I would pedal to a nearby lake for a picnic with friends.

The very first program I was involved with was first graders singing songs for their parents. They were lined up behind me as I introduced the songs. I turned around and two little boys were shoving and pushing each other, so I asked them "Why?" One boy said, "Miss Nelson, you told *me* to stand there." The other boy had been absent the previous day and had stood in the other boy's spot—and he was going to get it back no matter what happened. Quite a lesson I learned from them!

The high school had an excellent wrestling program and they needed a room for practice. It was decided to dig out the dirt under the stage of the theater and build a room there. At night a tarp was placed over the open area. Some music classes were held in the front of the theater. In the evening movies were shown, and the popcorn smell permeated the whole place the next morning. Music books were kept on a desk, and I began noticing the book bindings were peeling and ragged. I gave speeches about this to all the classes and said they should be very careful with books and take good care of them. Several days later we found out that rats got into the building through the opening under the stage; they couldn't get out and were hungry, so they ate the binding and glue from the music books. It wasn't the students. The fifth grade class was housed

21

in the Baptist church basement. One day I was busy teaching them a new song when oranges and apples started rolling toward me. What a surprise that was. The teacher and class had decided to have a "Fruit Roll" and at a given signal they all let their fruit roll. In my thirty-eight years of teaching this was the only time it happened.

Manson, Iowa, 1946–1949

After two years of teaching music all over town, I accepted a position in Manson, another small town about fifty miles from Eagle Grove. An excellent music program had been in progress for years; it was a real joy to have choirs and small ensembles of such high quality. We received many awards at the contests and often performed at functions around town. One year Manson was the host school for the area music contest. What a lot of work was involved in setting it up. At the same time many students had mumps and daily there were new cases. The night before the contest, my neck began hurting very much, but I said to myself, *It can't be . . .* I would try to sleep, then turn on the light and check my neck in a mirror, then try to rest. After this routine most of the night, I finally burst out crying, knowing I did have mumps! One of the most difficult phone calls I ever made regarding teaching was to the high school principal the next morning telling him my news. He couldn't believe it—I couldn't believe it. The following two days I was suppose to accompany eighteen soloists and small ensembles and direct three large groups: boys' chorus, girls' chorus, and mixed choir. Somehow, other accompanists were found and another director took over the choral groups. After the postings of the ratings on the bulletin boards, students would rush to my bedroom to report on the outcomes. I really did feel a part of the events—but in a most unusual way. Everyone had carried on with style and persistence.

Another time the elementary students prepared a simplified musical version of "Hansel and Gretel." This time it was measles. Both children who played the leads got measles and the entire production was postponed until the fall semester of the following year.

My three years in Manson were filled with many wonderful moments, not just disasters. Talented students abounded there and music making was an integral part of the community life. In fact, there was a freckled-face, red-haired girl in first grade who grew up and married my youngest brother. No, I can't forget Manson.

Boone, Iowa, 1949–1952

I was then offered a music position in Boone, Iowa, involving high school and junior college choral music, so I accepted. This town was near Ames, with a huge college, and Des Moines, which had several auditoriums for guest musical performances. As an extension of music in Boone High School, often a bus or cars were driven so we could attend the Metropolitan Opera spring tour performance as well as concerts by soloists, such as Marian Anderson and Nelson Eddy. During the years I have had many students tell me they saw their first opera with me. At Boone we had an excellent boys' quartet, Dick-Harold-Bill-George were the first four. They sang almost every week at a function in town. Often we included Mary Ellen Dowd, a student who aspired to be an actress; she would recite a poem or a reading. (Later she became Me'l Dowd, was in movies and Broadway plays, including "Camelot.") One of the quartet, Richard Hughes, now teaches voice to aspiring concert and opera singers in New York City.

My first year in Boone I lived in a room in a large house about seven blocks from school. Now I wonder why I chose that place; how did I get to school, especially in winter? I had no car. The following year I stayed at the YWCA right across from the school and a park. That was an excellent choice. My last year I stayed with an elementary music teacher, Ruth Hanson, in her lovely home filled with antiques and treasures. She and her brother Myron, his wife, Eleanor, and their three children—Bob, Mary Carol, and David—were just like family to me. Years later, whenever I am in Iowa I always make a visit to these very special friends in Boone.

For three years everything went extremely well with teaching music. Then I saw a notice on the bulletin board about teaching overseas in the army schools. I applied and was accepted. Teaching music in Iowa had given me excellent training and I was most grateful for the fine music students and supportive administrators I had known.

23

Interlochen Music Camp, 1945 and 1947 Summers

After my first year of teaching I decided to attend Interlochen National Music Camp in northern Michigan. Mom and I got on the train near home to Chicago where she visited her college friend, Ethel, and I continued by train to Interlochen. I enrolled in the university division and lived in a small two-room cabin with twenty other young women from many different states. We each had an orange crate for our few possessions. Uniforms were worn at all times: blue corduroy knickers, blue blouse, blue knee-length socks, red sweater. For concerts we changed to a white blouse. Each division of the music camp wore uniforms, each slightly different.

I attended lectures, receiving credit for them at the University of Michigan, sang in a choir and had piano lessons. Every day was filled—when I didn't have a class I could attend rehearsals of other choirs and learn from their conductors. What an opportunity to learn more of the choral repertoire! Most students rehearsed under trees; however, there were piano studios for practice. Recitals and concerts were presented every weekend. There was so much music everywhere that at the end of the fifth week, some of us went to Traverse City and spent the day fishing—for some peace and quiet.

During this time the unions would not let professors teach here. There were many organized rallies with the burning of an effigy of Petrillo, the union leader, before we sent Dr. Maddy, the founder of Interlochen, to Washington, D.C., to fight this ruling. Also, no student had a car. My small-ensemble teacher, from Chicago, had a car and would drive four or five students in the evening to surrounding areas. The evening I was invited to go, we were on a hill looking over the bay while three sturgeon were slowly swimming below us. He told us to look at them so hard and long that we could take them out of our mind's eye and see them whenever we wanted to. What a helpful lesson that was; I have tried to follow that advice in all my travels. We also saw the northern lights in many colors and designs. (I haven't seen them for years; where are they now?)

August 1945 arrived and with it the news of the end of World War II. Our university choir had rehearsed the beautiful "Requiem" by Fauré, sung in Latin. We sang that at the concert commemorating the end of World War II. When we finished singing, I walked alone to the nearby lake and sat on a rock thinking about all those who would not come

24

home, about the wounded and maimed, so thankful it was all over and all involved could now go home to their families and loved ones. (Little did I know then that nine years later I would visit both Hiroshima and Nagasaki and see firsthand the results of the atomic bombs which ended the war.)

I developed a boil under my right eye and had to go to the dispensary. While I was there a man told me he would drive me to Traverse City to see a doctor there; however, I declined his kind offer. Later I found out he was the father of several children at the camp, including a son in the university division; his wife also spent the summer there. Since I felt Interlochen was quite expensive I wondered how he could afford it, only to find out he was Mr. Delacorte from New York and the owner of Delacorte Press. How I wished I had accepted his offer to see a doctor in Traverse City.

I learned so much at Interlochen, I enrolled the summer of 1947 too. What a wonderful place with quiet and stately pines all around. As a child at home I listened as often as I could to the daily radio program, "Music Box," 7:30–9:00 A.M., from Iowa State College at Ames and heard the classical repertoire for instruments and voice. Saturday afternoon I heard the Metropolitan Opera broadcasts sponsored by Texaco—the two summers at Interlochen made these radio music programs come alive! I also made lasting friends from all over the United States, learned from excellent teachers, and sang in choirs with fine conductors. (The first ISME, International Society of Music Educators, conference held in the United States was at Interlochen in the 1960s. Of course, I attended with my husband and a niece, Linda, who later majored in music.)

4

Summary Adventures

University of Oslo, Norway Summer School, 1948

While in Manson I became a friend with Betty Almen, an English teacher who lived there but taught in a nearby town. We decided to apply to the 1948 summer school for Americans at the University of Oslo in Norway. Her background was Swedish and mine was Norwegian—it should be the perfect place to learn about our ancestry. We were accepted and made our plans. My Aunt Irene was an experienced driver; Mom decided to go, as well as Esther, a friend from Manson. On June 7 the five of us packed our Ford V-8, tied my trunk on the top for the ten-day sightseeing trip East. We stopped in Chicago to see my sister, Carol, and her friend Miriam, both nurse's aides for the summer at Lutheran Deaconess Hospital. We stayed at the Palmer House, had a tour of Chicago sights, then the two girls joined us for dinner at the Empire Room where the guest performer was Hildegarde. After a wonderful night's sleep in our suite of rooms, followed by breakfast, we had the valet bring the car. Mom immediately looked in the glove compartment for the "kitty money," $48—each of us had put money in it for gas money. Of course, it was gone! We got the house detective and a policeman who took us to the hotel authorities but to no avail. It was a sad lesson we learned at the beginning of our trip.

After the two-hour delay we continued on to Ann Arbor and the University of Michigan; Greenfield Village in Dearborn; Niagara Falls on the Canadian side; Tanglewood Festival grounds, empty, but the caretaker let us see the music bowl and shed and the formal gardens; Boston; Concord and the writer's homes; and New York, arriving June 16, ten days after we left Iowa. It had been a good trip with laughs, a few problems, and memorable sightseeing.

The day in New York City was spent on a tour, then shopping, and the matinee Broadway performance of *Mister Roberts* with Henry Fonda. The play had been written by Thomas Heggen and cousins of his were members of my church in Iowa. Mom was really looking forward to the play and telling the Heggens about it later, however, the language was so filthy she decided she would say nothing about it. In the evening Betty and I accepted the invitation from International House to meet others going to Oslo Summer School.

Next day Esther took us all out to lunch, after which we drove to Pier 95 to embark on the S.S. *Marine Jumper,* a converted troop transport. We said our good-byes with kisses and tears and left Mom, Aunt Irene, and Esther to find their way back to the Midwest. Betty and I boarded the ship, found our cabin no. 53 (not so bad, not so good), got our luggage, then went on deck to meet other students. We saw Anker from the evening before and he came over to talk. He was from Brooklyn and told us about the landmarks as our ship pulled out. We even saw his mother waving a red coat from a Brooklyn park. He kept talking and talking and we missed supper (we had not heard the bell for the first sitting). The dining room manager took pity on us and let the three of us eat with five Norwegians later. Bedtime arrived with twenty other girls in the cabin—a smelly, hard canvas bunk, not enough covers, light on all night (why?), and the ship rolled slowly from side to side with creaks everywhere. Ten days of this—we got used to our *Marine Jumper.*

Breakfast was at 7:30 (first sitting), followed by student orientation later. We were introduced to those in charge of the summer school and told: 111 students were going to Fontainebleau Art and Music School near Paris, 215 to Oslo, and 15 to Switzerland. The library books were kept in ''some lockers in that corner of this recreation room on D deck''; the piano was ''in a white box in that corner of this room''; there were cards and games available and space for dancing. Often in the evenings there were movies. Our group had classes in Norwegian; we chose a choir director, Al Griffin, a black American with a beautiful voice and a fine musician; we all learned the Norwegian national anthem, ''Ja, vi elsker dette Landet'' (Yes, we love this land of ours); and the international student song, ''Gaudiamus''; we had lectures on what to expect at the summer school. There was also time to make new friends, go sunbathing on deck, and rest. Some days were gray—gray sea and sky mixed in fog and spray . . . nothing is as gray as that scene! This led to a storm and a rolling sea with such monotony—a slow 1-2-3-to-the-left followed by a slow 1-2-3-to-the-right—on and on. A monotony that insisted on continuing no matter how much I wanted a level foundation. A step one place generally took me to a wall or a table. Three of us went up near the gun turrets and saw waves gray-blue turn into aqua as they rose with white snowbanks blowing off the tops by the strong wind. The air was icy cold against our faces and ears, and our feet got wet. The rolling sea tossing our ship to and fro made me want to sing, "I Love Life" or perhaps Brunnhilde's "War Cry" from Wagner's opera would have been more appropriate. Sounds were many: the ship strained and creaked, the fog horn blew every few minutes, waves were pounding and hitting each other, the loudspeaker blared, the ventilation system kept blowing air, and someone tried to play piano. I felt so helpless knowing I could do nothing about what was happening, and my thoughts turned to the fateful day the *Titanic* hit an iceberg—the GIs on this transport during World War II with their false hilarity trying to entertain each other yet knowing there were mines, submarines, and enemy planes in these same waters—storms do subside and calm does descend on passengers and ocean alike. What a lasting impression of my first storm on the ocean!

Everyone had a lecture about England and France because students were getting off there. The lecturer stated, "We haven't come to like or dislike, but we have come to understand. Plymouth and Le Havre are bombed cities, people have to stand in line for everything, the air raid shelters became a community life during the war." We were told of the hardships after the war, the education, the sports, on and on. One evening a movie on Plymouth was shown; knowing we were near made it even more significant. At 5:30 A.M. the next morning the loudspeaker said, "All persons docking at Plymouth will leave within the hour." I quickly dressed, went outside to watch and was greeted by the first birds we had seen for days, sea gulls, and a black hazy outline of land. On getting closer I saw the most beautiful shade of green. Yes, land. Then I saw cows on a hillside, trees, a small village with Plymouth directly in front of us and the tender *Sir John Hawkins* coming for the passengers. A gangplank was laid across the tender and ship tied together. It took three hours to transfer the trunks into the baggage nets. In the meantime I left for a breakfast of cantaloupe, rolls, bacon and eggs, and coffee. I was warmed up by the tasty food and went on the upper bridge to wave good-bye to friends leaving. I thought of Browning's poem, "Oh, to be in England, now that April's there, And whoever wakes in England . . . " It wasn't my time—yet.

Later that same day as we approached Le Havre, France, we saw many porpoises for the first time as we stood on the upper bridge watching our ship enter the harbor. Here there were buoys, ringing bells, and flashing lights as we zigged and zagged around the bombed and twisted ship hulls to our dock. Along the dock were several ships painted gray; along the shore were gray buildings. One huge structure was standing with sky showing through every glassless window. I saw a church steeple, then emptiness, then more church. An apartment house had crumbled walls and a clothesline between two sections with clothes hanging on it. A car, a bike, but not a sound anywhere, neither from the students on the ship or those on the pier. There was the light of the welder's torch, a few French berets on men watching from shore and our pilot boat. This was my first view of what war had done to a harbor and a town! Gradually more men came into view wearing knickers, shirts, boots, and berets. People on our ship started throwing oranges, tobacco, gum, candy, and cigarettes to the men over there. Betty and I each threw a chocolate bar—a man caught mine, then took out a photo of his small daughter and pointed to it—I knew she would get the gift. I have never enjoyed a chocolate bar more! Many items landed in the sand or water and I wondered how they could "down" their pride and dignity and accept what we threw. I later realized I didn't know much about that terrible word *war*. One small boy was bulging with fruit and candy and would, no doubt, make quite a bit of money from his trip to the dock that day. For the rest of that day it was very quiet as we pulled out of the harbor to continue on our way to Norway. We had all been affected by the sight at Le Havre.

Sunday, June 27, 1948, was the end of our Atlantic voyage of eleven days. We packed as we arose, had breakfast, and I went to church and sang in our choir—"Steal Away" and "Fairest Lord Jesus." Lunch was a delicious baked-ham meal; I then went on deck to watch Norway come into view. At first there were faint outlines of land; as we progressed farther up the fjord we saw homes, towns, and villages. I was most impressed by the color of the houses—red, yellow, rust, blue, green, purple—all brightly painted with a Norwegian flag flying in front of each home surrounded by tall green pines. People were waving hands, a white cloth, anything, on both sides of the fjord. We really were being given a royal welcome! At 4:00 P.M. the voice over the loudspeaker announced there would be southern fried chicken for all. Did students ever move from the bridge, the sun deck and go below to eat. At 5:15 our ship entered Oslo proper and came to the dock. Since we arrived a day early, there were only a few people with bouquets of flowers tied with ribbons for the person they expected on the ship. I looked for my cousins, Osvald and Bertha, but everyone looked the same. Having never met them, I gave up. We waited for the officials to come aboard to welcome us, then we all sang, "Ja, vi elsker," the "Star Spangled Banner," and the international student song. We formed a line to go through passport clearance, exchanged money for krone, walked down the steep gangplank and *touched Norwegian soil!* We found our baggage and went through customs. I was worried about all the wrapped gifts my Grandma Laura and Mom had sent in my trunk for relatives but there was no problem. Someone took only a package of gum.

A bus finally came to take us to Blindern Student's Hall. As we drove through Oslo I noticed that everything was so clean and neat, narrow streets, and the few people around were all walking. Arriving at Blindern we saw three buildings with formal flower gardens—what fragrance filled the air. Norwegian students were there to help us with trunks and bags. Betty and I shared room 418. There were closets and drawers—hurrah! No more living out of suitcases. On the windows were blackout curtains, because it stayed light so long. (Sometimes we would forget to pull them down and would wait until it got dark before retiring for the night. We soon learned to use those curtains.) Gracemarie, our good friend, lived in the adjoining room. We were all happy to be settled in our new home for six weeks.

Our meals were eaten at the cafeteria in the new science building of the University of Oslo, a short walk from our room. The next morning we slept late, so our first meal consisted of meat, potatoes, and prunes with vanilla sauce for dessert. The summer school brochure stated: "While there is no longer a shortage of basic foods in Norway, Americans must remember that items like bacon, eggs, certain fruits and fresh vegetables are scarce, while citrus fruits are not available. In general the menus and serving will be Norwegian." (Looking back on the food, I remember we had one egg a week, only dark bread, goat cheese, cauliflower, potatoes, and whale-burgers. I did get so hungry for American food after a few weeks, I went to the American embassy and looked at food pictures in American magazines. It helped. I had some chocolate bars and ate one of those each week.)

The first afternoon there was a welcome party for the American students hosted by the city of Oslo at a bathing beach. Friends found the correct station then the ferry and arrived for bathing (undress and dress on the shore), lots of sunshine, people everywhere, an orchestra, drinks, songs, dancing. This was where I finally met Osvald and Bertha, two of my relatives. Betty knew some Swedish, so she translated what they said and with their few English words we got along fine. How good it was to meet them.

The following day we were officially welcomed to the University of Oslo at the *aula* (university auditorium), which had fourteen murals by the famous Norwegian artist Edvard Munch on the walls. The chancellor of the university welcomed us, saying we were the second group to attend, the first group was in 1947, and even though Norway had not yet reached the pre-war normal, we would be provided with the best possible facilities and materials. "Welcome to Norway! Welcome to our university!" Our choir sang two numbers, followed by more speeches. Later in the evening the American students welcomed the Norwegian students. Betty and I talked with Lillemor, a very interesting Norwegian girl from Oslo. We hoped we would get to know her better (we did). We also hoped we would be able to bring some friendliness to the people here who welcomed us with outstretched arms.

The next day classes began. Students could choose from several courses. This was my schedule: 7:30–8:15 breakfast; 8:45–9:45 General Survey of Norwegian Culture (required); 10–10:50 Elementary Norwegian; 11–11:50 Government and Politics of Norway; 12–12:50 Norwegian Music; 1–1:30 lunch; 2:00 Museum visits, field trips, etc., days and times to be arranged; 5:30–6:30 dinner. In the afternoon, if we didn't have a required trip, we could go downtown, shop, wash clothes, sleep (we seemed to need lots of sleep), visit with friends, or go to the movies.

My relatives, Rev. Osvald Grandborg and his wife, Edel, were wonderful to Betty and me. They lived near Oslo and often came in their small car to take us to their home or to a restaurant for *smorbrod,* cake and coffee. Bertha Hegre was a home economics teacher and lived in Askim, outside Oslo. She often came to visit us. We appreciated so much all their help in showing us the special sights in Oslo—Holmenkollen, Oslo Town Hall, Frogner Park with all the Vigeland statues; all the meals they shared with us; we attended church with Osvald where he was the pastor, and so much more.

July 4, Sunday: In all countries, the American Embassy has open house for the Americans who live or are visiting that country. So it was on this day in Oslo. Betty and I enjoyed the "American" look inside the embassy and in the garden where a buffet table had many platters of cookies, American ice cream, and punch. It was interesting to see the Americans with their pancake makeup, lipstick, costume jewelry, nylons, and newly set hair. I already had gotten used to the fresh look of the Norwegian women. What a contrast.

One weekend Betty and I caught an overnight train for Stockholm, Sweden. The train stopped at Lillestrom for ten minutes and my relatives, Osvald, Edel, and Sissel (their daughter), were on the platform to visit with us; beautiful scenery of valleys, pines, rivers, clouds—quiet beauty everywhere. We tried to sleep in our nice compartment but with the conductor yelling the name of each station all night and a person snoring in our area, it was difficult. I looked out the window at 1:30 A.M. and saw it was light; however, the mist covered the wheat fields and towns. Upon arrival in Stockholm we walked to three hotels with no available rooms; the Continental Hotel had one, we signed in and found a chaise lounge, a small table, and two good beds with lots of covers and soft pillows. We slept for two hours before venturing out to see the shops—woolen sweaters and socks to match, vests, glassware, handicrafts of all types—the shops all seemed filled. In the open-air market we bought fresh fruit, we had so little at our school cafeteria. For dinner we had *smorgasbord,* followed by pork chops with tomato sauce, vegetables, and ice scream with strawberries. How delicious it all tasted! We spent the evening at Skansen's, a large park with orchestras, restaurants, many old buildings, and people everywhere with fellows calling out to us, "Hi, flicka, snakke til." (Hello, girls, come and talk to us.) We didn't; we continued on our way. When it was time to leave we walked partway to our hotel, then stopped at a quaint cafe with heavy wooden beams on the ceiling and beautiful woven mats on the tables, and enjoyed cake and coffee. That short rest stop gave me a wonderful, lazy, heavenly feeling and made me grateful to be alive. Why was I so blessed! Back in our room, we cut the cantaloupe with a water glass and ate the pieces with a glass—Betty leaning over the silver platter and I over the wastepaper basket so juice didn't get on the carpet. Here we were in Sweden, a very progressive country, eating fruit in such a primitive way—we laughed so hard we thought we would choke.

The next day, Sunday, we boarded a train to Uppsala to see the thirteenth-century cathedral, Old Uppsala with kings' burial mounds and an eleventh-century cathedral, a king's castle, the university library with the Silver Bible, one of the oldest—and much more. Back in Stockholm we got on a sightseeing boat for a tour, saw a variety show in a theater, and boarded the packed train at 10 P.M. We were separated the entire train trip—I sat on my suitcase in the entryway for most of the night until a Swedish man found a seat for me. My neck and bones never had been so asleep or felt so crooked.

Our music class was taught by Professor Dr. Sandvik, who traveled all over Norway recording songs sung by locals before radio had reached the faraway places and influenced the natural native melodies. One of the best music classes I have ever had was the day a woman from Telemark, dressed in her traditional dress, sang "Cow Calls." Each cow had a name and a call or melody. When she sang the call that cow would come from the herd to be milked, then the next one and so on. She also sang lullabys—the woman had never heard any other tunes, only those she made up and from her local area. What a unforgettable musical moment. (In ISME in 1968 at Interlochen I met and shook hands with another musician and composer who traveled all over Hungary collecting songs—Zoltan Kodaly.) As soon as summer school was over, Professor Sandvik would continue his walk and search for more natural and native Norwegian melodies.

On Karl Johansgate, Oslo's main street, my favorite restaurant was located—Blom, the Artist's Restaurant. It was decorated with plaques, paintings, sketches, and sculptures commemorating great artists like Ibsen, Munch, Toulouse-Lautrec, Charles Chaplin, Kirsten Flagstad and others. In the nineteenth century it had been a stable with many features kept when it became a restaurant in the twentieth century. It was rich in art and culture, cozy and intimate, and we often went there for coffee and cake.

A sign-up sheet on a bulletin board told of an upcoming "whaling weekend"—the first seventy-five names on the sheet would go. Betty and I immediately signed up even though no one seemed to know what to expect; we did notice several teachers' names on the list—perhaps it was special. We packed a small case with *no* dressy clothes on Saturday, July 17, and went to the ferry, which took us on a morning trip to Tonsberg, where we changed to the old train with oil lamps. The train ride was rough (square wheels, we joked) and arrived at Sandefjord located on an arm of the Oslofjord. Once there our luggage was taken off and placed in trucks and the seventy-five of us walked to a museum. We were greeted by a seventy-foot-long whale hanging from the ceiling (at first I thought it was a Viking ship). It was a whaling museum and the best one of its kind. The shelves were filled with books about whaling and whales; pictures were on the walls of ships and in glass cases were musk ox, penguins, polar bears, seals, and walrus; harpoons of many varieties were displayed; model of ships and many trophies were evident. This museum had been presented to Sandefjord by our host for the weekend, Lars Christensen, in honor of his father, Christen Christensen, who had the first steamship as the first modern whale factory ship in 1903. He also invented the electric harpoon. After the museum tour I went in the car with Ingrid and Lars Christensen and another couple to the dock (the road was rough) where the students boarded small yachts for a short trip to the *Torshavet,* a whaling factory ship in drydock, our floating hotel for the night. Our luggage was there, but first we were all invited to the dining room for *smorbrod,* coffee and cake. It was delicious and so plentiful we all thought this was our supper. Our room, 218, was meant for four but only Betty and I occupied it. There were maple bunks in the wall, dresser and drawers, varnished floor—it made our *Marine Jumper* look rather insignificant. We rested, washed, went on deck for choir rehearsal, then toured the ship—the radar equipment room, the whale factory area—and saw the huge open area where the whale was hauled into the ship, kitchen, bakery, etc. I decided then that my next trip must be to Alaska; my next study must be whales.

Once again we walked down the temporary steps on the gangplank on the side of the Torshavet to a boat which took us to the Christensen mansion near the water's edge, where we walked on a concrete footpath edged with flowers to the patio entrance where each of us was welcomed by Ingrid and Lars Christensen. Inside we met some of their other seventy-five guests including Mrs. Bendix of the Bendix Corporation and Lars Christensen, their son. Some of the memories of the house are: a swimming pool with colored lights on the bottom; a lion skin on a wall Lars had shot in Africa as well as a deer head, rhinoceros head, wild boar head and others; three fireplaces; flowers everywhere; original Edvard Munch paintings around the walls in the dining room; a collection of swords on a wall; beautiful furniture everywhere; a six-piece orchestra for music and dancing. The program consisted of welcome speeches by our host and hostess, our choir sang three selections; more speeches—when I got teary-eyed during one of them the tenor behind me whispered, "Don't let it throw you." I knew for sure I was Cinderella in a fairylike setting.

We were invited to the dining room, where two long tables were covered with food of all kinds: turkey flown from Africa, ham, salmon, rare roast beef, lobster, shrimp. mushroom-meat cups, potatoes, lettuce salad, cauliflower, carrots, cheeses, crackers, breads, olives, pineapple, tomatoes, fish molds, and so much more. What a feast for students who had been given whale-burgers and dark bread at our school cafeteria. Of course, all the time everyone's glass of wine was kept full. Later, after much good conversation, dancing by some, and more speeches, we were invited to help ourselves to the dessert tables: bowls of fresh gooseberries, strawberries, raspberries, plums, grapes, ice cream, and highly decorated whipped-cream cakes. What a variety we enjoyed with our coffee.

All too soon the evening came to a close with our choir director, Al, singing, "Auld Lang Syne" so beautifully. As we left at 11:30 we walked down the path with lighted candles on either side singing, "Good Night, Ladies" and "Good Night, Gentlemen" we gazed at our floating hotel with every light shining brightly across the water. We got in the boats and waved good-bye to those on shore. I had never been so royally entertained before and probably it will never happen again. As we settled down for a good night's sleep, I said to Betty, "And we never brought our dressy clothes for this fantastic evening—no one else did either." I guess it didn't matter.

The following morning we were awakened by seven bells, dressed, went to a huge breakfast on the ship at 8 A.M., and left the ship for the last time at 9:15. As we left, Consul Lars Christensen handed each of us three postcards of the whaling factory ship and a small, round, pewter container with the cover having a raised whale across the top and an engraved map of Antarctica with tiny engraved ships, whales, and penguins. (What a visible lasting gift to remind me, years later, that this perfect weekend really did happen.) Buses were waiting to take us to the Kings' burial mound for a lecture, then to the railroad station where we sang to our host, "For He's a Jolly Good Fellow". (Lars participated in four Antarctic whaling expeditions and a strip of land there is named in his honor; another strip is called Ingrid Christensen Coast.) During World War II Lars was financial attaché in the Norwegian embassy in Washington. It was said that after the war he brought trainloads of shoes for Norwegians because of the devastation caused by the Nazis. What an honor for me to have met this special couple—a-once-in-a-lifetime experience!

We still had three weeks before the end of summer school, and we made the most of our time by visiting the Bygdoy Folk Museum; the ships' museum—*Viking, Fram* (the only ship to reach the North and South Pole), and *Kon Tiki*; Akershus, a castle from the fourteenth century

35

where Nazis shot forty-three Norwegians and where Quisling, the Norwegian traitor, was shot, and many more interesting sights. One weekend we went to Lillehammer, where we attended a wedding in a stave church; visited the home of the famous writer, Bjornson; and left a note in the mailbox of Sigrid Undset, another writer, saying we enjoyed her books very much. It was cold because we were farther north and at a higher altitude. We stayed in a youth hostel and were each given one blanket. Because we were so chilled Betty and I decided to sleep in one bunk (it felt as though we were sleeping on a stone) with all our clothes and sweaters on. I remember waking in the middle of the night telling Betty not to snag my nylon hose . . . one of the coldest nights I have ever experienced anywhere in the world. . . .

Our choir recorded several songs that were later played on the radio. Al, our director, sang two solos and I was his accompanist. The embassy had a party just for our students' group and our choir sang for that event. I was so happy our choir was so good and had such a fine conductor. Often students were asked about the Negro problems in United States; all we had to do was tell them we had chosen a black conductor—that was how we felt about them, living proof right there in their country. The choir surely had many opportunities to perform in Oslo and was a real asset for our summer school.

One day when several of us were listening to each other play piano, I played Brahms' "Lullaby." A big husky fellow from California asked me to play it over and over. Then he told me this story: "That piece always calms me, mostly when I am in love. When I was seventeen I loved a girl but didn't think I was good enough for her so I joined the service. I bought a music box with Brahms' 'Lullaby' and listened and wrote many poems, but the girl married someone else—I gave the box to my sister. When I die I want to just play and hear that music. I could very easily cry when it is played!" A story spoken by a huge fellow studying criminology.

Eddie Cantor happened to be in Oslo—someone invited him to speak to the American students and he graciously came. He made us laugh, he made us think as he stood before us in his gray suit, checked shirt, and blue suede shoes. It would be good if people saw more of this side of Hollywood.

Days were now filled with last-minute shopping, sightseeing, visiting homes of Norwegian friends who lived in Oslo or nearby, sunbathing (the sun doesn't shine often and when it does everyone is out-of-doors to enjoy it) and swimming—and studying for final exams in each subject. Our last evening of school was spent at Lillemor's home with her parents, brothers and much conversation about immigration, drinking problems, World War II, as we enjoyed *smorbrod*, "sweet" cookies (most cakes and frosting were not sweet because of the food restrictions), and tea. We were taken back to our room at Blindern by her brother in a red fire brigade open touring car, from 1930. What a way to go. (We planned to meet Lillemor in England the following summer—and we did.)

We had to pack three different ways—trunk for the hold of the ship, ten-day trip to visit relatives on the west coast of Norway, and for our return trip on the *Marine Jumper*. I couldn't believe the summer school was over with afternoon graduation exercises at the university *aula* with speeches. Our choir sang: "Let Down the Bars, O Death," "Battle Hymn of the Republic," and "Auld Lang Syne." Our class presented a purse of money for the King's fund to the Rector of the university so that a Norwegian student could study in America. The successful summer school had come to an end!

A taxi took Betty and me to Osvald and Edel's home for good-byes; then Osvald drove us to the railroad station. Betty went to Sweden to visit her mother's cousin; I boarded the train for the west coast of Norway for visits with my numerous relatives there. After an all-night train ride, I was met in Stavanger by Bertha (she had gone on ahead and made the necessary arrangements with relatives making sure I met everyone in their own homes), Muelfrid (Grandma Laura's niece), and Margrette, Bertha's niece. In every home we had *smorbrod*, coffee and cake—some days I ate as many as five or six times. Bertha took me to her brother Olaf who lived in his parents' home; Marie (who died in 1944) was Grandma Laura's sister. Then we visited another brother, Magnus, and his one-and-a-half-year-old daughter, Marit. Bertha accidentally spilled some flower water on her leg and she cried so hard she turned blue in the face. (In 1990 when eighty-one Americans flew to Norway for a reunion with two-hundred relatives, I happened to sit beside Margit at the Sunday banquet and reminded her of that early incident.) Grandma's brother, Lauritz, died in 1945, but I was happy to meet his widow, Brita (eighty-two), and three sons, Jacob who showed me his family tree going back to 1405 (when Mom and I did the family book in 1972, he gave us so much help); Magnus, who had been to America and helped build our house in 1922; and Lars, an engineer, who looked so much like my Uncle LeRoy. Another brother, Tom, had moved to New York, and when I arrived back there he met the *Marine Jumper*. Grandma's sister, Therese (eighty-three), lived alone in an old house; everywhere I looked there were pictures of the families in America—Laura's family, Josephine's family (another sister who went to America) and Carrie's family (Josephine's daughter). Therese's daughter, Birgit, was there as well as her daughter, Margot, who spoke English, a great help. We had *lefsa,* cookies and cakes with coffee. Later we visited Theresa's son Sevart's home. His sister, Maren, also was there. Because Margot and I could speak together, Birgit invited me to their home too, and I learned so much more about life and school here. Boletta was Grandma's youngest sister (seventy-eight), and she lived with her daughter Muelfrid. I stayed at this home for a couple of nights and enjoyed so much getting better acquainted with them. I remember being taken to the attic and seeing several large pieces of meat drying from a line. Boletta's son was Osvald, the minister in Oslo who had helped me so much. Another daughter, Pauline, was married to Peter Fjetland and had nine children. They all spoke English very well, which helped my visit. One night they had a dinner party for most of their children and spouses, Aunt Boletta, Muelfrid and husband, and me. After a delicious meal we visited and Pauline played the guitar while we all sang—this went on until 2 A.M. What a beautiful evening with relatives in Stavanger. I awoke the next morning and found a plate of fruit Pauline had placed on a table next to the bed. Such hospitality. Boletta's other son, Emil, had moved to Iowa, and he and his family often visited my family.

At each home we met the spouse of the person mentioned in the story and their children. I surely felt I had a better idea about my relatives across the ocean; however, all the time I kept wishing that Grandma Laura could have been there instead of me. When she left in 1888 she had been so seasick on the ship she never wanted to cross the ocean again. I felt so honored to have met her two sisters and one sister-in-law and even though we couldn't speak the same language their smiles and the twinkles in their eyes told me much. In 1914 my Grandpa Lewis had bought two tickets for a return trip but Grandma refused to go, partly because of the young children, and Grandpa took his daughter, Luella, age fourteen, to visit the relatives. No others from America had visited until I arrived in 1948.

After seeing the sights of the area and the Jotten farm of Grandma's family, I boarded a small ship for Haugesund, north of Stavanger. Peter and two daughters drove me to the dock where I found other relatives, all with presents for Grandma, my mother Tillie, and me. What a lovely surprise and farewell. I hoped I would see these newfound relatives again very soon. They had showered me with hospitality, love, and friendship—how I wished Grandma Laura had been there too.

When I arrived in Haugesund, a Norwegian carried all my luggage off the gangplank amidst cars, baby carriages, trucks. At the bottom a man called my name, "LouCelle?," and I looked at him and answered, "Soren?" We hadn't seen each other since 1930 when he went back to Norway after working on our farm as a hired man for a few years. Mom had written him saying I would arrive on August 16, and he was there to meet me. We went to his home on Haraldsgaten, met his wife, Petra, daughter and son, and enjoyed *smorbrod*—we talked all afternoon. I gave them the presents: soap, sugar, dried beef in jars. Olaug, the young daughter, received a barrette, and her mother immediately cut off her braids for the new short look from America. Soren told me many stories from my childhood, things we had said and done. A professional photograph of the three of us, Joyce, Bob, and me, was prominently displayed on a living room table. How good it was to be with Soren and his family.

The following morning Soren and I took the package Mom had sent with me to give to Kristen Haaste, Grandpa Lewis's youngest brother, eighty years old, who lived on the family farm and house. I was hoping I could board the small boat; however, the captain told us the boat went in the evening, stayed there all night, and came back in the morning. Kris lived there alone, wasn't too well—I decided I better not go. I sent the package with the captain and two days later we talked to him. Yes, Kris had gotten the parcel, saying, "Ya so, Ya so." I never met him. He died in 1950.

Soren, Olaug, and I sometimes rode bicycles and saw the important sights in Haugesund. We visited Dagmar, Grandpa's sixty-four-year-old niece, who had a cat on her shoulder as we talked in her small home and ate doughnuts and coffee. We toured a fish canning factory, two-thousand cans of fish an hour. Petra gave me some fish pudding (*fiske* balls) to take home to Mom. Soren sent a gift to my oldest brother, Joyce, because Soren had known him best. The days had been spent reminiscing; once Soren said he wished we could talk all night about Iowa and his memories from there. Just when I got reacquainted and acquainted with family or friends, it was time to move on. (I did see them again in 1955 when my parents visited me in Germany and we traveled by car to Norway—they enjoyed seeing everyone.) No, my Grandma Laura never got back to Norway before she died in 1959, at age ninety-two.

A bus trip from Haugesund took me to Odda through thirteen tunnels—a herd of goats was in one. We had a rest stop at a hotel and I asked for the ladies' restroom. The man answered "Ikke forstor English." I said, "Water closet?" and he answered, "Oh, you mean toilet." After Odda we had rain, four more tunnels, then a valley with hundreds of fruit trees—pear, apple, and plum. Along Sorfjord we saw the mountains, snow, waterfalls. The people's backyard was the mountain and their front yard was the fjord. How could they possibly live there? At Kinsarvik we changed to a ferry, which took us to the other side of fjord to Kvandal, where we boarded another bus and saw more fjords and a beautiful valley where men and women were cutting the hay and grass with scythes, then gathering and placing it across wires attached to posts, for drying. I had often seen pictures of this scene and was thrilled to actually see it! Valleys don't last long in this country, and soon we were up on a mountain with hairpin curves and waterfalls. How can such a road be constructed and repaired?

By the time I arrived in Bergen on the west coast I was exhausted from the trip—ups and downs, sharp curves, gorges, tunnels. I finally found a hotel with the help of the Bergen tourist office. In the morning the manager brought waffles and coffee to my room after 9 A.M. What a nice way to begin a rainy day in Bergen. (They say if a child in Bergen isn't born with an umbrella that is the first gift the child receives—so much rain there.) The middle of the town has a market where I saw huge fish, little mackerel, crabs still alive, boxes of shrimp—another area had vegetables, another flowers of many colors and kinds. The funicular took me to the top, where I could see all over Bergen as I enjoyed my trout lunch, served by a waitress wearing her Hardanger national dress. A sightseeing tour included Troldhaugen, Grieg's home near Bergen. A narrow winding path led me to the rather plain house where I visited three rooms—his traveling trunk and purse in the hall; the dining room had photos, dishes, and furniture; the living room had his grand piano and his red monkey mascot he always carried with him on tours. (A visit another year included a piano concert and I sat on the couch in that room.) His composition hut was down by the water's edge; when I looked in the windows I saw his piano and desk. Nearby was a cliff where Edvard and his wife, Nina Grieg, are buried.

How thrilling it was to visit the home of Norway's greatest composer. I had often played his piano solos, especially "Wedding Day at Troldhaugen." In 1955 when I took my parents here, my father said, "Do you suppose Grieg ever fished in the bay here?" I answered rather rudely, "Dad, you don't talk about things like that. This is a sacred spot." After we signed our name and address upon entering the house and were outside going to the composition hut, the caretaker yelled, "Who is the man from Iowa?" My father said he was as he walked toward him. The Norwegian had worked on farms in Iowa many years ago and wanted to know all about prices of the grains, the tractors and how things were there now—what a good visit these two "farmers" had at Grieg's estate. Yes, I felt very ashamed and apologized for being so arrogant.

On that tour we stopped at an eleventh-century stave church back in the woods. Here I saw the small window where lepers came to talk with the pastor, but they could not enter the church.

In the evening I was invited to the home of Thorbjorn and Karen Amundsen (Karen was Grandpa's sister's daughter's daughter). I learned so much from them because they spoke English. During the conversation I was taken to a window in their living room where they had seen the first German ships come into Bergen when they invaded Norway—a memory I won't forget. Karen inherited the property at Haaste. (On other trips I visited Haaste and saw the house where my Grandpa Lewis was born—and the windowpane where he scratched his name, "Lauritz," with a diamond before leaving for America in 1886.) My two days in Bergen, a cosmopolitan and friendly city nestled in the mountains, facing the North Sea, had been most interesting, except for all the rain. Again it was time to move on.

I boarded a train for Oslo. Breakfast on the train was *smorbrod* that we made ourselves—tomatoes, herring salad, fish balls, meat, cheeses, jam, breads, and lots of coffee—the cost was sixty-five cents. Afterwards I settled at a window to enjoy the magnificent scenery—mountain plateaus with patches of snow, barren rocks, small lakes, clouds and sun, a few houses, animals, and stops to let others board the train. Again, I counted tunnels between Bergen and Oslo—the number was 151. Sometimes they were snow tunnels made of wood and concrete to keep the snow off the tracks. I also wondered why I had insisted on taking a day train! For lunch I had potatoes, halibut with cream sauce, and cantaloupe. Dinner at 7 P.M. was a meat patty, fried potatoes (the first fried ones), bread and jam, and coffee. Summer-school students boarded the train at Gielo and I heard their stories of their days in Trondheim.

Early evening we arrived in Oslo. Osvald and Edel were there to meet me, but they had sad news. Their eight-month-old daughter, Elizabeth, had pneumonia and had almost died the week before but was a little better now. What a shock. Betty already had arrived from Sweden. We stayed at Edel's all night, sleeping on two couches in the living room, but we heard Elizabeth every time she cried. The next day we took the other two daughters, Sissel and LivJorunn (seven and three years old) to a park, hoping that would help the parents.

Our last evening in Oslo we met Lillemor at a theater and saw Ibsen's *Peer Gynt,* using Saeverud's music instead of Grieg's . . . very modern music and a fantastic performance, mainly because of the staging. What a perfect climax to a perfect summer! When we came back to Osvald's we were told Elizabeth had been taken to the hospital. The next morning we wrote our thank-you note and good-byes on a paper, since Osvald and Edel were at the hospital. Bertha and Lillemor helped us with our luggage and bags in the taxi and at the ship. Lillemor gave us apples and five red and yellow roses: Bertha had already given me two of her paintings for Grandma and Mom. Everyone was waving white handkerchiefs and Norwegian flags as the Americans said their last good-byes. Yes, we were all teary eyed. What a summer it had been for me, my first one in Europe, and I hoped with all my heart it would not be the last.

The *Marine Jumper* was our home again for the twelve-day Atlantic crossing—some very stormy days, some calm days. Resting, eating, talking, making new friends, and so the days followed one another. When the canteen opened I bought fifteen Nestle chocolate bars (I was so hungry for chocolate), one of the American favorites I had missed. August 30, a Monday, was the first day of school in Manson, Iowa, where I was teaching but here I was in the middle of the Atlantic instead. When we arrived in New York we each had thirty dollars for our two-day bus fare and food. My relative Tom met us and asked us to stay in Manhattan with him and his wife; however, since we were already late for school, we left on the first crosscountry Greyhound bus. September 6 we arrived back home after ten weeks in Europe. What a great way to spend the summer of my life—a quarter of a century!

During the school year I gave many talks about my summer abroad, often taking the high school girls' sextette along to sing Grieg's "My

Johann'' and other Norwegian songs, dressed in white blouses with embroidered red vests and black skirts. A few of the programs were a mother-daughter banquet at a Lutheran church in Humboldt; a banquet at a Methodist church in Fort Dodge; a Catholic Women's Society at Manson; and the PTA at Manson. Not too many were traveling abroad in those days, and everyone seemed genuinely interested.

Europe, Summer 1949

Betty and I boarded a ship for Europe in 1949. (We had written to Norway and Sweden to ask about jobs; the answer came back we could be maids in hotels only. We were teachers and decided we would teach during the school year and travel during the summer.) We arrived at Cork, Ireland, where a tender came to the ship to take those going ashore, including some Irish nuns going back to visit. They began singing and others joined in, making us feel like one big family. I had no idea that I, a Norwegian-American Lutheran, would encounter such a welcome! We had reservations at a Cork hotel, however, our ship arrived a day early and there was no room. Twenty of us slept on the floor of the lobby with our luggage tucked very close beside us. When the cleaning woman came to vacuum the carpet at 7 A.M. we all had to get up. What a beginning for that summer.

We went to Blarney and kissed the Blarney Stone, got on a train for Dublin and met Hugh, a Dubliner. He said he would be our guide in Dublin, and we took him up on his offer. Never did we see a city so thoroughly. Hugh's tour included a visit to a school where everything was taught in Gaelic; a play at the famous Abbey Theater; a concert at a radio station where his friend, Tomas, was the soloist (we all went out for coffee afterwards and I learned more about the music business in Ireland); a session of the government in progress. On Sunday I attended a service at the Dublin cathedral and was so thrilled with the choir made up of boys, I stayed for all three masses (my first experience). There were many more experiences with these friendly people. Looking back on travel, the visit in Ireland had to top the list!

In England we stayed in youth hostels—we each had our own sheet sleeping sack, an army pan that folded over and fastened, with our cutlery inside, and a tin cup. We bought the needed food along the way with English food stamps we requested upon arrival. The Lake District had very little water—lack of rainfall. We asked the manager of the hostel where we could wash our hair; he answered, "In the lake." After helping to clean the hostel everyone had to leave by 9 A.M. and couldn't return until 5 P.M. We left with our bathing suits, shampoo, and towels and walked to the lake. The water was wonderful; so was the sun. We stayed there for most of the day. A huge water blister developed on my upper arm and I didn't feel well, perhaps a slight sunstroke. Betty helped me to a small hotel and the manager was so kind he let us sit in the parlor. He even brought us hot tea and said it was much better for us than a cold drink. When a busload of tourists arrived, he asked us to go upstairs to a guest room to wait until the hostel opened. What hospitality when it was most needed!

We met Lillemor, as planned, in Glasgow, Scotland, and traveled together for several weeks. In Inverness I heard a strange sound—music several blocks away. I quickly found the source—bagpipes playing for Scottish dancers at a festival. I listened and watched; another first with bagpipes. (In 1969 and 1970, my niece Linda was a dancer with the Sottish Highlanders at the University of Iowa and then was the drum major of the group. I flew from New York to Iowa one weekend to see her strut as the leader. Yes, I was a very proud Aunt Lou that day!) We wanted to go to Edinburgh but the train wasn't going when we wanted, so we began hitchhiking, something I had never done (Betty had while in college). People only had petrol if they *had* to travel and we felt safe, riding in the backs of trucks and cars. They would take us to the youth hostel and wait until they were sure there was space for us. When we told them how kind and helpful they were, they always replied, "This is return lend-lease." Once in Wales we were on our way to a castle. A man stopped for us, later asking if he could go with us because he had always wanted to see that particular castle. Of course, he could—after all, it was his country.

In England we were waiting for a ride in the country when we saw beautiful trees in the distance, got out our cameras, and took photos. Almost immediately policemen arrived and asked why we took the photos, who we were, and other questions. It turned out there was an army camp in the trees, and they thought we were spies! After talking to us they realized we were innocent tourists and they left. We were shaking from this close call.

In London we would go to the theater and get a number for the evening's performance. Instead of us staying in the queue all day, the number was placed on a stool in the line and we explored the city. We came back in the evening, found our matching numbers and sat on the stools until the ticket office opened. Quite an ingenious way of doing things. Remember, this was only four years after the end of World War II—it was different then.

Betty and I flew across the English Channel and continued hitchhiking. In Belgium we rode with a woman driver and both of us were *so* glad to get out of her car—she was a fast driver and we felt unsafe. In Amsterdam a diamond merchant gave us a lift for a short distance. In Luxembourg two men picked us up. They said they had a plane and would fly us to our next country. After a few miles Betty and I looked at each other, telling the men to let us out now—we weren't sure about that promised plane ride. All the other rides were fine and we got all the way to Bellinzona, Switzerland. There I bought a ring watch because I enjoyed wearing unusual rings. I put it on and forgot to take it off when I washed my hands. Water got under the crystal, so back to a jewelery shop, saying, "Aqua" and pointing; he took care of the problem. I was more careful after that. It was another interesting summer and very different from the previous one.

Canada, Summer 1950

The summer of 1950 Betty and I took buses to the Gaspé Peninsula area. A church cookbook I bought included—as the first recipe—Braised Moose. We ate lobster often; went to the top of a lighthouse; saw the high waters at the Bay of Fundy; became acquainted with a family involved with lumber and enjoyed their hospitality; saw the opera *Tales of Hoffman,* by Offenbach, in Saint John, New Brunswick—our lodging was in a cozy attic room in a private home. We fished for cod with three hooks on each line, often reeling in two of three fish. We were in Quebec City when I received word my Grandma Nelson had passed away—a sad day. It was another wonderful summer exploring our neighbor Canada.

Europe, Summer 1951

Betty and I wanted to visit other countries in Europe and two teacher friends wanted to go with us. By now we knew "the ropes," but Lois

Crim and Gerri Rolland had never been there. At the end of the ship crossing we had decided that after our visit to London we would go separate ways with Betty and Gerri together and Lois and me. It turned out to be a good plan; on a certain date we would meet at our reserved hotel in Paris. The highlight of our stay in London was July 4, when we joined hundreds of others to line the streets near Saint Paul's Cathedral and watched the American service men and women march; the Queen, Princess Elizabeth, and Princess Margaret slowly waved a as they passed by in a carriage; the Duchess of Kent, Winston Churchill, and many others as they went into Saint Paul's. Just as the Queen arrived at the steps the long trumpets with banners hanging from them played the fanfare high above the entrance. This service was commemorating America's war dead with the supreme commander in Europe, general of the Army Eisenhower, handing over to the cathedral authorities a roll of honor of the 28,000 men and women of the United States forces who died in the war in military operations launched from the United Kingdom. The roll was an illuminated manuscript bound in red leather and was the joint work of American and British craftsmen and artists: a gift from the United States. Its resting place is in the American Memorial Chapel at Saint Paul's. I was so glad I could see a little part of that auspicious ceremony. (Mrs. Eisenhower, Mamie, was born in Boone, Iowa, the town where I was presently teaching—it was good to see her in London.)

Lois and I boarded trains on the Continent and I remember seeing wounded men in Germany, without an arm, an eye, whatever; cigarette stubs were quickly picked up from the ground or sidewalks; many cities had been badly bombed. Heidelberg had not been bombed and we enjoyed a wonderful weekend in that university town with the castle on the hillside. We spent several days in interesting and unusual Venice, Italy. We roamed the canals, the plazas, and saw the hundreds of pigeons in Saint Mark's Square. As we rode in the train to another Italian city, Lois looked at her blouse and saw drops were falling on it. She looked up at the storage rack and saw a wine bottle had tipped over. the Italians around us were concerned and began sharing their food with us; it soon became a happy energetic Italian-American party.

The four of us met in Paris on the appointed day, seeing the sights for several days. We had stored our extra baggage in Paris and all had arrived at our hotel except Lois's bag. If she left without it, she knew she would never see it again, so she got in a taxi and went to the storehouse to look—of course, it was there. She was so happy and we finally left on our ship for the U.S. On board were five Polish men leaving their home-land for their dream of living in America. We all became good friends and helped them with their English and told them what to expect in their new country. Lois was an excellent ballroom dancer and one of the Polish men was too. They danced so beautifully together every evening. When we arrived near New York City their first dream was to see the Statue of Liberty. We stayed up all night to show them this symbol of freedom. It was the only time I had an opportunity to be with immigrants who were coming to live in our great country! I do hope they realized their dreams.

III
OVERSEAS TEACHING:
JAPAN AND GERMANY
(1952–1958)

Bend with the bamboo.
                              —Japanese maxim

5

Teaching in the Army Dependent's School in Tokyo, Japan, 1952–1954

After teaching in Iowa for eight years, I applied for a music position with the Army school for dependents' children, hoping that I would be assigned in Europe. After filling out many forms, I finally had a personal interview in Cedar Falls, Iowa, where approximately twenty five other music teachers were interviewed that same day. The interview went extremely well and I was pleased with it, but didn't expect to get accepted. However, on May 5, 1952, I received a letter stating that I *had* been accepted—but for Japan. I knew so little about Japan, only three words: Mount Fuji, geisha, Ginza. This was not the time for me to say "no" to learn more about another part of our world so I sent a telegram saying that I accepted the position . . . somewhere in Japan. (One was never given a final assignment until you were actually in the country.)

What a busy summer that was. My sister got married on July 14 and asked me to be her maid-of-honor at her large church wedding. Everyone knows what a wedding entails. Friends kept telling me that I hadn't seen the United States yet why would I want to go to another country? My answer was always, "The opportunity is here and I want to take advantage of it."

A small booklet from the civilian personnel department of the Army told me how to prepare for an overseas assignment:

> You have been selected for a specific job overseas. Some of your friends and most of your family may think you're a little bit out of your mind but others envy you the privilege of serving in the important overseas program and at the same time having the opportunity to travel. There are many applicants for oversea positions and you have reason to feel proud that you have met the selection requirements. No matter where you are scheduled you must be prepared to accept conditions as you find them. . . . You will be quartered with other people and will have to adjust your habits and make the best of situations which may be trying. Keep your sense of humor working fulltime and you may have

51

some interesting anecdotes to tell later about your companions and experiences.

In addition to the two pieces of hand luggage you may take 350 pounds of baggage which will be stored in the hold of the ship and will not be accessible to you. Your baggage must be sturdy, durable and securely locked.

Do not leave home until you are advised to do so by your processing station. They will receive your port call and will arrange for your travel to the proper port of embarkation. All reservations will be made for you and tickets will be furnished.

You are not allowed to take more than $50 in U.S. cash into most overseas commands; you will be wise to convert $100 more into traveler's checks or postal money orders. This will give you $150 to carry you until your first pay which may not be for approximately three weeks after you arrive overseas. Also have sufficient funds to pay incidental expenses enroute. [There were many more instructions but these few were the gist of the brochure.]

The day I was told to report, August 5, finally arrived, and my parents drove me to Omaha, Nebraska. A new kind of life began for me. I took the oath, was told of the seriousness of the situation, and was fingerprinted. I waited from 3:30 P.M. until 1:40 A.M. when I boarded a Pullman on the City of Portland train for Seattle, my port of embarkation. The ticket cost $73.81—paid for by the Army. Two hours later our train stopped for a long time. Later I was told that at 3:30 A.M. the train had run over a woman near Grand Island; we had to wait for an hour and a half for the coroner to arrive before the train could continue. A rather sad beginning for my new adventure.

After a sleepless night with much bouncing around in the upper berth, morning finally arrived. Breakfast made me feel like Mrs. Astor, and I wondered what I had done to deserve all this! The day was spent finding others on the train also going to Japan, getting acquainted, watching the scenery go by . . . Wyoming seemed to be covered with sagebrush; Utah had so many sand hills; the Columbia River Gorge had people fishing salmon with spears from the dam. Later we saw the results of the timber and lumber business and the logs rolling into the river. At Portland we had to change trains for Seattle. We got aboard the "Train of Tomorrow" where each coach was different. There were four Vista Dome cars; one was a restaurant, and each was unusual and beautiful.

Seattle at last. The brochure told us to proceed to the New Richmond Hotel via a military bus. This hotel was near the railroad station and pier so it was not in a good section of town, with characters around. That same night there was an open house on the *General Gaffey,* the flagship of the Pacific. Rumor had it we might go to Japan on it. We went aboard and saw the troops' quarters, the mess hall, the engines, radar, etc.

The brochure said: "You are responsible for having your hold baggage delivered to the port. You will have about three days [I was there five days] in Seattle and your expenses will be app. $3.50 a day for room and $4.50 for food."

Part of each day was spent in orientation and the rest of our shots (I had to have a tetanus shot) and immunization papers had to be in order. Then we could tour the city, visit friends there, attend movies or concerts in the Civic Center. The orientation sessions contained information about conduct on the ship, living in a different country, etc., etc. Terms were explained that were new to me: off-limits, script, billet, PX, etc.

August 12—our sailing day. Up at 5:30 A.M.; luggage in the lobby at 6:15; breakfast at the Olympic Hotel at 6:30; 8:15 each one waited in the lobby until her/his name was called. We had to walk in a certain order and sit in an assigned seat on the military bus. The bus filled and we drove off toward the pier. We saw the troops also moving but we still didn't know if we would go on the *General Howzie* or the *General Gaffey.* At 9:30 we went aboard the ship and it *was* the *General Gaffey!* Hip hip hurray! As we departed a band was playing as the troops, wives, and children of men already in Japan, officers, and civilians milled around, each with their own thoughts . . . sad to be leaving our country and wondering what new experiences awaited us in the Orient. We were finally on our way.

Ship travel was not new to me since I had gone to Europe on ships the summers of 1948, 1949, and 1951. I was happy that the movement of the ship on the ocean waves never made me seasick, but our first night on the *General Gaffey* was rough and rocky; many others became ill. I find ship travel very relaxing because I can spend the time as I choose: sitting on the sun deck, reading, talking to friends, playing shuffleboard, sleeping, eating, whatever. I did get involved in directing the choir and played for the church services aboard so there were rehearsals. On Sunday there was a service for civilians at 9 A.M., and at 9:50 an MP led the twelve choir members and myself down through a maze of stairs, and men and crew, to the recreation room on C deck for their service. The troops were wearing fatigues, some were sitting on chairs, some standing, others were sitting on the floor. Our choir sang two songs, "The Heavens Resound" and "I Would Be True" and Chaplain Spence led the service. As we left, all the men had risen on both sides of the aisle as we filed out and up. Later Chaplain Spence told us many of the men had said they didn't know the choir would be that good. For me, this was an unforgettable experience!

Crossing the International Date Line is a time for breaking the monotony of a voyage. That day we went from Sunday to Tuesday. Whatever happened to Monday that week? (Later this was a good question to ask young nieces and nephews.) One rule for the day was the left pant leg must be rolled above the knee. At 2 P.M. the ceremony was held on deck for King Neptune's Court, with a queen, mermaid, and a royal baby (a huge fat man). Twenty-five officers, troops, and teachers had received summonses for the ceremony. They were blindfolded and walked on mustard, eggshells, and spaghetti; catsup and mustard was rubbed into their hair; they got the hot seat, and finally walked a plank into a tank of water. Two of my teacher friends had received summonses and had gone through the line of "torture." Everyone was enjoying the entertainment and laughing and joking with those in the line when all of a sudden water came from all directions and everyone got soaked! Yes, forty-plus years later I still vividly remember the first time I crossed the International Date Line!

Part of the entertainment was a variety show. I accompanied several soloists and sang in a women's quartet. It was so hot and humid that the floor of the lounge and dining room were wet, but we kept on rehearsing in spite of the heat. Again, the show was given for the troops down in C deck. It was so hot down there that all the men were naked to the waist. A spotlight was on the performer; a captain acted as M.C. Performers sang songs such as: "The Girl that I Marry," "Walkin' My Baby Back Home," "Basin Street Blues," "You Made Me Love You," "All My Love," "Pagan Love Song," and "Wunderbar." There were jokes of all sorts; one was about a three-year-old at 9 P.M.:

> Come det me, I'm fru. Come det me, I'm fru,
> Who took me out of my nice warm cot
> And put me on this cold cold pot
> To make wee-wee whether I want to or not. . . .
> Come get me I'm fru (noise)
> I thought I was fru!

We also did the variety show for the civilians and another for the children aboard.

The last night aboard we had the captain's dinner: shrimp cocktail, delicious steak with vegetables, French pastries, nuts, the works. The meal was excellent but the heat had been almost intolerable for the last days. Finally, at 10:30 we saw a lighthouse beacon. Land, at last, after eleven days on the Pacific Ocean.

August 23: We were awakened at 5 A.M. and saw that fog surrounded our ship. After breakfast at 6:00 we stood on deck and watched two pilot boats, freighters, steamers, a junk far in the distance, other fishing boats with sails, and finally the breakwater and a lighthouse. (We had been told that there would be no picture-taking here and if anyone tried, their camera would be confiscated.) One time I counted twelve huge ships; never had I seen a harbor with so much activity. This was Yokohama, Japan.

We finally pulled into the pier where an army band was playing. All the wives aboard were looking for their husbands; children were trying to find their daddies. Those of us who had no one to meet them just looked at all the soldiers on the pier with corsages and presents for their loved ones. I finally left and went into the lounge where all the teachers were. Soon, three people called roll: one female major yelled, "Sound off," and called us in various sized groups. I was called in the last group of approximately twenty-five and told we were assigned to Tokyo (from the beginning I felt that was where I would be teaching). I was busy with my things and carefully listening to words from those in charge, when I looked another direction and there stood a friend from the States. I couldn't believe my eyes. I walked over and said, "What are you doing here?" He told me he had been stationed in Korea for a year and was now in Japan. He had pulled strings to get on board to meet me. (This was the first of seeing many former friends in Japan. Many were in Korea and would come to Tokyo on R and R. They would call and we'd go to dinner or a concert or show. Once I was in a line to cash my paycheck and a former student of mine was in the same line. Even though I had crossed a wide ocean, I never felt far from home because of these chance encounters.)

The newly arrived civilians walked to the military bus headed for Tokyo and a most interesting ride. My eyes were glued to the window, where I saw strange and curious sights. People were everywhere; I had never seen so many crowded together. There were shacks along both sides of the road we wouldn't keep animals in. None of the houses had paint. Special gates were in front of each shrine. Even though the road was very bumpy we could hear the tap-tap-tap and clopping of the Japanese wooden *geta* (shoes). Most women were wearing kimonos; many had children tied on their backs with a wide sash. Whenever the men had the urge to urinate they just stood with their backs to the traffic and relieved themselves. The multitude of impressions came as our bus rapidly sped toward Tokyo. It seemed I was observing a circus or carnival and at the end of the day everyone would disappear. Inside the bus we laughed, we talked, we pointed, we whispered, we shed tears, we were silent. . . . This country was to be my home for at least two years, the length of my contract.

Traffic became heavier as we finally arrived in Tokyo and the Osaka Hotel, a very large building used for housing 600 DACs (Department of Army Civilian Women), not far from the old Imperial Hotel, the palace, and Hibiya Hall (concert hall). I found the room assigned to me, but inside were two Oriental women eating food with chopsticks. I quickly went to my friend's room and said in a disgusted voice, "I thought this was housing for American women." She told me, "They are American women, probably from Hawaii or California." Yes, that was the case.

After getting settled I wanted to go to the Ginza to see what Tokyo at night was like. Down to the lobby to the information desk where I said, "Where is the geisha?" I meant Ginza. What a confused beginning day in the Orient.

I finally got to bed, but the overpowering heat and humidity made sleep difficult, even with two floor fans moving the air. Then I remembered the photos in newspapers during World War II of Japanese men with a sneer on their face and the flaps of their caps pulled down over their ears, and I was scared. Something told me that I would never live through the night; someone was sure to take a long sharp sword and decapitate me. . . . Then outside I heard the soft quivering sounds of a flute playing a song over and over. With these delicious sounds the tension and stress of the day disappeared and I slept. Next morning I asked about the music and was told it was a *soba* (flute) player announcing his arrival on his night route selling hot soup from his cart. If a Japanese was interested he or she went out and bought a bowl before retiring. What a great idea.

For two weeks I had to wear the few clothes from my carry-on suitcase because my 350 pounds of baggage had been taken to the city of Osaka instead of the Osaka Hotel in Tokyo. I tried to purchase a few blouses on the Japanese market but that was impossible; they were too small. A friend of mine had a worse story to tell. She was packing to go to Japan; her daughter was packing to go to college. When Mildred's luggage arrived in Japan it was her daughter's and her daughter got hers. Many months passed before the correct luggage arrived. How about that surprise halfway around the world?

Our first high school meeting was held on Sept. 5, 10:00 A.M. The school, Grant Heights, called the Narimasu American School, was approximately one hour by military bus from the center of Tokyo where I lived. The bus arrived at the Osaka Hotel at 7 A.M. and in one hour we were at the housing area where the school was located. Our duty hours were from 8 to 4; we had to be in the classroom at 8:30. School was over at 3:15 and we again took the military bus at 3:30. Teachers' meetings were held before school began; we had no afterschool activities because of traveling back into Tokyo.

At the combined Tokyo teachers' first meeting, Major Spreng, the school superintendent, told us, "We are workers here to carry out *his* thoughts." *His* meaning the commanding officer of Far East education. We were introduced to the school nurse; the assistant director of the Tokyo schools; the one in charge of civilian personnel who talked about the correct channels and the chain of command, to notify the Red Cross in case of an emergency, our annual leave would be thirteen days per year, etc. All the speeches presented made me realize how different teaching within the army framework would be from my previous teaching experiences. One statement was "If you ask something unreasonable, you will become aware of it." Another said, "I will be truthful without being too revealing . . . telling you the bitter with the better."

Registration for the high school students began. Since I was the high school choral and band teacher, I told those in charge of registration that any students who wanted to sign up for music should go to the music room so I could hear them sing if they wanted to be in chorus; to find out the instrument played, how long, etc. Hours went by and no students came. I finally went back to the registration desk realizing that in the Army school one did not get choir and band students that way. What a big surprise for me! As the year progressed I found out that a student could be in class today and gone tomorrow because fathers were often transferred or their duty would be up and they would go back to the States. When I realized this, I taught what I could each day; I never knew

57

for sure who would be in my class tomorrow. When one is training trios, octets, sextets, and choirs and a band to perform for audiences, you, the reader will begin to understand my problem. Somehow we managed. The letters quoted here will tell the story better than I can.

American Red Cross
Tokyo Army Hospital
8059th Army Unit
APO 1052
26 December 1952

Dear Miss Nelson:

On behalf of the patients at Tokyo Army Hospital Annex, we wish to express our appreciation for the very fine singing done by your Narimasu choral group at the Annex Saturday, 13 December.

The patients' first taste of carolling for the Christmas Season was a refreshing and stimulating one. All aspects of your program from the Christmas Story, in narration and in song, to the informal octet numbers were a success with the Annex patients.

Please extend to all members of the choral group our sincere thanks for their generous contribution of time and enthusiasm, so necessary for the morale of boys far away from home during the holiday season.

A Happy New Year to all of you!

Very sincerely,
Field Director, Margaret M. Ryan

* * *

The American Red Cross
Office of Field Director
Volunteer Services Headquarters
Tokyo Area APO 500
16 January 1953

Miss LouCelle Nelson
Music Teacher, Narimasu High School
Grant Heights
APO 500

Dear Miss Nelson:

Reports from the three hospitals in Tokyo and American Red Cross staff in hospitals in Korea are that 1952 Christmas was truly Christmas! Some of the patients have joyfully expressed amazement over all the good cheer and gifts brought their way during the holidays. We are proud of you and your group and wish to convey heartfelt appreciation for your contribution to the success of this program.

As you perhaps know, the Military and American Red Cross are responsible for providing only the basic comfort items for U.N. Servicemen patients. It is Community Services' job to coordinate the efforts of individuals and groups on a volunteer basis to furnish the gifts and warm human interest to make the boys feel less far away from home and family.

We decided that there was no more convincing proof of the wonderful spirit of the Tokyo Community than the December monthly report which is prepared for the Tokyo Field Director's Office and Red Cross Theatre Headquarters. We hope also that you will accept it as many, many thanks for your part in a job well-done!

Your sincerely,
Mrs. Tristan E. Beplat, Chairman
Community Services to Hospitals

* * *

Narimasu Elementary
Headquarters Camp Tokyo
Tokyo American School Division
APO 613
30 April 1953

Dear Miss Nelson:

May I again congratulate you and your fine choral group on the splendid program which you rendered to our children on 28 April 1953.

The choir evidenced fine points of choral technique and enthusiasm for singing. I can appreciate the time, effort and training which you have given to make such a program possible. Please extend to your students our compliments and our thanks.

Very sincerely yours,
Ruby Ruth Bartley
Specialist in Music Education

*   *   *

American Red Cross
13 May 1953
Dear Miss Nelson:

We wish to express our thanks again to you and to the students of Narimasu High School for providing the patients at Tokyo Army Hospital with entertainment. Your program was one of the best performances we have had in our lounge. Many of the patients have expressed wishes that you will soon return for a repeat performance.

Thank you again for thinking of the patients at this hospital in such a wonderful way.

Sincerely yours,
Field Director, Margaret M. Ryan

*   *   *

Tokyo American High School—Narimasu
Headquarters Camp Tokyo
APO 613
3 June 1953

Dear Miss Nelson:

The Senior Class of '53 Narimasu High School wish to thank you for helping to make our baccalaureate and commencement exercises a wonderful occasion in our lives.

> Raymond D. Gay
> President of Senior Class
> Narimasu High School

But this is getting ahead of the story.

Soon after I had been assigned my music room, I wanted some changes in the room. Several Japanese custodians (I don't remember their official name) were cleaning the room; I told them where I wanted the furniture placed. Immediately they all stopped working and stood like statues. They would not continue until the head custodian came and I told him what I wanted done; he then gave the orders to those under him. My mistake—I had neglected to use the chain of command.

Several months later the music room was moved to a Quonset hut in the courtyard. This was a better place for our small band rehearsals, which were sometimes loud. There were two other Quonset huts nearby, one used by the sixth grade class. The teacher of that class came to me at lunchtime and said, "I wish you would stop practicing the 'Star Spangled Banner.' " I couldn't imagine why we should stop so I asked her why. She said, "Everytime you practice the song I have to tell my students that we must stop whatever we are doing and stand up until you finish." I said, "You only stand up if you are in the same room when it is performed." I couldn't believe a teacher wouldn't know that! The brochure from the Army had said, "Keep your sense of humor working fulltime and you may have some interesting anecdotes to tell later about your companions. . . ."

The teaching-for-a-day with not too many plans for long-range goals became easier for me. The students were industrious, bright, talented, studious, traveled, and wonderful to teach. The weeks went by rapidly, as though I were still in America; however, the two hours each day on the military bus made me realize this WAS a very different culture and way of life. What sights I saw: people opening their small stalls, babies tied on the backs of grandpas or grandmas, rag men beginning their collection for the day, priests with their begging bowls, groups sitting around the hibachi (charcoal burner), men pulling honey-bucket carts, shrines with activities, markets; the scenes never stopped. For two school years I had the privilege of seeing ordinary people's daily lives. Almost four decades later these scenes are still etched in memory.

Many of the staff learned the Japanese language; my interests were with music opportunities. I joined the Tokyo Madrigal Singers. The Japanese director had studied in England and was excellent. We rehearsed often and sang at many functions. The most impressive was the coronation service (for Queen Elizabeth II's coronation in England) at Saint Andrew's Church. We sang "Zadok the Priest" by Handel; the same song was sung in London at the actual event. The Englishmen wore their uniforms, many medals and ribbons, some with a sword in the scabbard. This was at 11 A.M. on May 31, 1953. At 2 P.M. the same day the baccalaureate service for the senior class was at Saint Luke's Chapel with some of my groups singing. What a busy day in most unusual circumstances.

For special performances I sang in the Tokyo Chapel Center Choir. In December 1952 we performed *The Messiah* by Handel. Many of the singers were Japanese. Thoughts were vivid when I remembered that on December 7, 1941, in Fort Dodge, Iowa I was also singing in the chorus of the same work when news of the bombing of Pearl Harbor reached us. During intermission that was all we could talk about; we could hardly believe it. Now, eleven years later here I was in Japan singing the same great oratorio. Strange. . .

Because I lived in the middle of Tokyo, near the Imperial Hotel (recently torn down and a tall Imperial Hotel built) designed by Frank Lloyd Wright and earthquake-proof, near the Hibiya Hall (a concert hall), it was possible to attend concerts, recitals, and shows often: Russian Ballet, *Elijah* (oratorio) by Mendelssohn sung by 500 voices (Japanese), famous operatic stars such as Helen Traubel, piano recital by Walter Geiseking, Princeton Seminary Choir, Horace Heidt show, *Madame Butterfly* opera (what a perfect setting), Isaac Stern violin concert accompanied by the NHK Symphony Orchestra, International Ice Show, Louis Armstrong show with Oscar Peterson and Gene Krupa, DePauer Infantry Chorus (I attended all four of their performances), Budapest String Quartet, Tagliavini (tenor), Josephine Baker show, Jascha Heifetz violin recital, Globe Trotters, and Aqua Show with Mickey Rooney and Margaret

O'Brien, Mrs. Eleanor Roosevelt narrating *Peter and the Wolf,* Xavier Cugat's Band . . . only a few examples of the great variety in programs available to me. I attended all of them.

There were the traditional Japanese productions to attend: Kabuki, begun in the latter half of the eighteenth century, the most popular drama for the Japanese reflecting contemporary life. Only men performed in Kabuki and some did the female impersonations. The 2–3 hour play included music, dancing, elaborate costumes, sometimes masks, heavy makeup, and superstars. The audience would shout the name of a favorite actor; there was nothing "shy" about those Japanese who attended Kabuki! Often people ate lunch during the play. During the Kabuki season I attended as many Saturday performances as possible and was fascinated with each one. Noh plays reached perfection in the fourteenth century and survive unchanged from an ancient culture. Each actor wore a carved wooden mask and a beautiful brocade costume. A very, very slow lifting of the foot and placement on the floor could symbolize a long space of time. Everything about Noh seemed so slow and deliberate; I did not have the background to understand or enjoy it. Noh was a "no." Bunraku or puppet theater began in 794 and was raised to a dignified dramatic art in the late seventeenth century. Three men, heads covered with black cloth, acted in unison for each puppet. One man controlled the expression on the puppet's face and right arm and hand; one controlled the left arm, hand and any props it carried; another moved the legs of this very large puppet, perhaps the easiest job. It takes approximately thirty years to become an expert. Each puppet is two thirds the size of a human being. Talking and instruments told the story.

Sumo wrestling began approximately A.D. 200 and is steeped in tradition. The 200-to-365-pound professional wrestlers wear only loincloths; their hair is slicked down with linseed oil in a topknot. With much ceremony they try to push each other out-of-bounds or down. A most unusual entertainment, but enjoyable.

The tea ceremony is very formal, usually held in a teahouse surrounded by landscaped gardens. In this demonstration on preparing and serving green tea only the most beautiful receptacles are used by the hostess as the guests watch each slow and careful move. *Fodor's Guide 1989* states, "An aesthetic experience designed to help achieve a profound understanding of life's basic tenets through serenity and harmony." The first time I was invited to a tea ceremony we were all given small cakes as well as tea; however, one of the guests accidentally dropped her cake. We were all so embarrassed. This was a formal-formal occasion and one did not do anything to detract from that, even accidentally. In 1985 my husband and I were in Tokyo. A tour of the city included a tea ceremony. Many were already in the tea house when we got there so I sat next to the *tokonoma,* a special place of beauty in the room. After the tea was made, whisked into a frothy drink, and poured into an exquisite tea cup, she brought it to me . . . because I was sitting in the place of honor beside the *tokonoma.* I thought what a lovely bonus for the help I had given to the Japanese during my teaching days thirty-five years earlier! (The other guests drank tea which had been made in another room.)

The public bath house was typically Japanese, a form of relaxation and pleasure, and communal, like a social gathering. The huge pool was for soaking only, not for washing. Before getting into the bath one washed with soap and rinsed oneself. Usually the sexes had separate areas or pools. Yes, of course I tried the public bath and found it very relaxing.

The Japanese did not often invite friends to their homes but rather entertained them at a restaurant. Usually shoes had to be removed and slippers were provided. Once I was invited by a teacher to visit his Japanese artist friend and Korean wife. They had recently moved into a new, charming, small home with a metal roof. Soft rain was hitting the roof making a pleasant sound as we four sat on the floor around a low table and ate tempura lotus root among other foods I had never tasted. What a memorable evening of friendship, conversation, and delicious Oriental cuisine.

Again, in 1970 I found myself in Tokyo and my dear Japanese friend Mary, from my teaching days there, invited me to spend the weekend at her home in Chofu, a suburb of Tokyo. As we got closer to her home via public transportation, she told me she had to phone her mother to tell her the time of our arrival. After meeting her charming mother, I was told the *ofuro* was heated for me so I could bathe. That was the reason for the phone call. The *ofuro* was a round wooden "barrel" filled with water. I soaped myself, rinsed off, and climbed into the delicious hot water to relax after a very busy day in Tokyo. What an experience! Because I was the first guest they had had in their home, both mother and daughter were afraid that something was not quite right, that I was too cold, or too hot, etc. Such tender loving care I received in that home. My gift from them was a cotton (yakata) kimono made by Mama-san. I still have it and often wear it. My friend Mary has often visited me: in

Long Island, in Miami, even on my family farm in Iowa when relatives from Norway were also visiting. It was a perfect time for an "East-Meets-West" party—all because I had been a teacher in the army schools in 1950s.

I shall never forget June 13, 1953, a very special day for me, when I shook hands with one of America's most distinguished citizens, Mrs. Eleanor Roosevelt. She was traveling in Japan for some days and a garden party for invited guests was included in her itinerary. She was seated beside her daughter-in-law in the receiving line. What a thrill for me to take a photo of her and actually shake her hand!! Franklin Roosevelt had had polio, yet he became the President of the United States. He was my role model, and I told myself that if he could attain such heights, I, who had also had polio as a child, could accomplish any goals I set for myself. He was my inspiration; his wife was his eyes, and ears, as she traveled around the world for him. How happy I was that our paths finally crossed.

Music Activities of Narimasu Army Dependent's High School, Tokyo, Japan, 1952–1953

Miss LouCelle Nelson, Director

December 13, 1952.............................. One-hour concert in the recreation room of the Army hospital annex. Fifty students participated in giving the Christmas story in narration and song. We also caroled in the halls and some wards.

December 17, 1952.............................. Junior High Chorus caroled in the halls and some wards at the 8167 Army hospital from 7:30–8:30 P.M.

December 19, 1952.............................. Music Christmas Program at the Grant Heights Theater at 2:00 P.M.

1953

January 26... The Boys' Octet, Girls' Trio, trombone and trumpet soloists performed at the Camp Drake Service Club.

February 4... Small groups performed at a School Assembly

February 15 .... The Boys's Octet, Girls' Trio, trombone and trumpet soloists and a baritone solo by Bill Fleming presented a program at the Tachikawa Air Base Service Club at 7:30 P.M.

March 16... Boys' Octet, Village Band, and Trio performed at the PTA program.

March 19... Girls' Triple Trio presented a fifteen-minute program at the Christian Women of Tokyo Retreat at the Grant Heights Chapel.

March 27... Twelve members of the school band furnished the music for the Red Cross Western Sock Hop.

April 2	The Boys' Octet and Village Band performed at the Far East Principal's Banquet in Yokohama.
April 25	The Mixed Chorus of 70 students, Octet, Trio, Triple Trio gave a one-hour concert at the Tokyo Main Hospital at 2:00 P.M.
April 26	The Village Band, Boys' Octet, Trio gave a one-hour program for the elementary students at 1:00 P.M. in the elementary auditorium.
April 30	Junior High Variety Show to pick the three best acts for the Senior High program. Twelve acts were judged.
May 8	Boys' Octet sang between acts of the Senior Class Play at Grant Heights Theater.
May 9	Mixed Chorus gave an hour concert in the Tokyo Army hospital annex at 2:00 P.M. Because of bus trouble from the bases only thirty students were present.
May 20	Boys' Octet and Girls' Trio made a tape recording at the NHK Building from 12:00–1:30.
May 20	Boys' Octet sang at the Lettermen's Banquet at Grant Heights at 7:00 P.M.
May 21	The tape recording made on May 20 was played over the air on Bessie Gray's program at 9:45–10:00 A.M.
May 24	Senior High Variety Show for the entire student body at 1:00 P.M. Eighteen acts appeared.
May 31	Massed Choir sang at Baccalaureate at the Saint Luke's Chapel.
June 3	Girls' Chorus and Boys' Octet sang at Commencement at the Grant Heights Chapel.

The music events for the school year 1953–1954 were much the same as those listed for the previous year. I felt there was no need to list all of them. Students were talented and worked very hard making the melody, harmony, and rhythm of the music as perfect as possible. For two years we did make beautiful music in far-away Japan.

New Year's Day, 1954

On New Year's Day the Imperial Palace grounds were open to the public; people could cross the moat and see the Emperor and family standing on the balcony of the Imperial Household Building. I decided to join the crowd but first I had to walk to the main Army dispensary to have a doctor check my very sore throat and prescribe medicine for the pain. After finishing with the doctor I sauntered back to the Imperial Plaza filled with people: Japanese, old men and women, young women and a few young men, babies tied on the backs of their mothers or grandmothers; some Americans: soldiers and civilians. I walked a few steps into the plaza. Very soon I was carried forward by the crowd; my feet were *not* touching the ground! This was extremely scary for me since I had had polio and my balance was not very good. The throng kept moving toward the narrow Nijubashi Bridge over the moat. Finally someone stepped on the back of my shoe and off it came. What a dilemma I was in then. Somehow I got over to the wall, trying to catch my breath as I stood on one shoe. Then I saw an American soldier and yelled to him, "I lost my shoe. If you find it, please bring it to me." When the crowd crossed the bridge the plaza near me was nearly empty. I noticed many kinds of Japanese footwear on the ground; it was reassuring to know I was not the only one to lose a shoe. Soon, the soldier came running toward me with his arm held high clutching my lost shoe. What an act of kindness; I hope he knew how grateful I felt.

What to do now? There was no way I could retrace my steps because the next wave of humanity was fast approaching the bridge. I was weak and on the verge of tears from the experience but knew I had to continue forward. As I stood there thinking about the mess I was in, there came a teacher from my high school making his way to the bridge. I shouted to Bill and he came over. I told him my problem and asked him if he would help me through the palace grounds. What a relief to take the arm of this six foot, two inch, strong American who escorted me the rest of the way! I was much too worn out to enjoy the landscaping, trees and bushes but we did pause in front of the balcony where the Emperor and his family were standing. (Before the war he was considered divine and no one dared look at him; after the war this changed and Japanese came from all over Japan to show their respect and see him.)

We arrived safely at the other gate of the palace grounds and I was none the worse for my "shoe experience." An hour after I had been in the plaza, the people thought the guards were closing the bridge for good so there was a stampede to cross the bridge. In that rush, some Japanese stumbled and fell. Others fell on top of them. It was our American soldiers, also sightseers, who saw the impending disaster, so they surrounded the pile of bodies by stretching their arms and linking hands so no one else would fall and get trampled. When the plaza was finally cleared there were sixteen Japanese dead from that stampede.

How grateful that I had only lost my shoe for a short time. A very important lesson was learned that day. Never go where there is a huge crowd. No repeat experience of "walking-on-air" for me!

Two special music festivals occurred while teaching at Narimasu. We invited the Seigakuin High School Chorus to join our chorus and spend the day at our school. Dr. Nakada was the guest conductor. Our chorus learned three Japanese songs in Japanese and they learned three American songs in English. The day of the festival we rehearsed these in the morning. Our home economics classes had prepared American food for lunch and I remember watching the Japanese students trying to eat with a fork instead of the usual chopsticks. That was only one of the many firsts that festival day. In the afternoon the assembly program for the entire school opened with the singing of both national anthems, followed by each school chorus singing two numbers. The assembly program ended with the combined choirs singing in Japanese and English. It was a beautiful day, integrating two cultures and learning about each other through music.

The other festival was on a Sunday: the International Music Festival of Yokohama. Many Japanese groups performed; the Narimasu Boys' Octet was entered from our school. What a day of music making! Como. Matthew C. Perry had entered Japan in 1853, which opened Japan to the West; Yokohama became the foreign trading post. One hundred years later, to commemorate this event, the Yokohama Music Festival occurred. "My" boys' octet won one of the beautiful prizes, an embossed bronze vase on a wooden stand. Under the base of the vase is Japanese writing in gold telling of this event. There were eight boys in the octet and one teacher, so they graciously gave me the prize.

Every Friday Japanese teachers had made arrangements with the Japanese Education Office to visit our American school and learn more about American teaching methods. A group of ten or so would come to the classroom while we teachers went right on with our regular classwork. I was always glad to see them and hoped they received ideas for their own teaching. There seemed to be few libraries in Tokyo at this time, and I remember Japanese students reading books as they patiently stood in line, for hours, to finally be admitted into the library for an hour or so. Such diligent students.

Japan has earthquakes, and we often felt tremors. One late evening when I was in bed in my room at the Osaka Hotel I could hear the rumble in the windows and felt the bed move. I quickly turned on the light (we were told never to do that) so I could see the time on the clock and watch the swinging light hanging from the ceiling. This was a strong quake and lasted longer than most. When it subsided many of us went into the communal bathroom to talk to others about the experience. Some carried a favorite item they didn't want broken, but one woman, a secretary, said, ''I knew my time had come. I had been drinking so I came to brush my teeth. I didn't want to be caught with a whiskey breath.'' What an interesting and revealing gabfest . . . in the middle of the night . . . in a communal bathroom . . . in Tokyo. . . .

The music activities in school and away from school were many and kept me very busy, but I still had time for lessons in flower arranging from Mrs. Tamara. She taught a group of us in a room in the Osaka Hotel, bringing with her the flowers we should arrange, usually in a low flat bowl. In Japan, flower arranging (Ikebana) is a fine art with the arrangement symbolizing heaven–man–earth. We would spend much time in placing the uppermost twig at just the right spot; the blossom as man; the lowest twig or leaf as earth. Often there was only one flower or bud in the arrangement. Mrs. Tamara was a talented and kind teacher and we became good friends. (When I was visiting Japan in 1970 she invited me to her home. Later she visited me when I lived on Long Island and she was on an Ikebana tour of Europe and the U.S.)

I was so contented and happy and felt I could stay in Japan forever. My teaching was going so well, I was involved in so many different parts of the Japanese culture, and I had many interesting Japanese and American friends. However, several teachers had asked for a transfer to schools in Europe, but their transfers hadn't come through. I decided I had better ask for a transfer when my two-year contract was up, knowing I would probably have to stay in Japan for another two-year contract. To my surprise, on February 4, 1954, Mr. Hoffman, the high school principal, walked into my classroom saying I had been accepted to teach in Europe. My answer was, "But I don't want to leave Japan." He said, "You don't have to." Now what? Decision-making time. If I didn't accept, perhaps it would be years before I would get another transfer. I didn't really want to leave this fascinating country. I knew being in Europe with all the operas, symphony orchestras, etc. would be better for my career in the future than staying here and learning more about the koto, samisen, and Kabuki. After much soul searching, the answer came to me. Yes, I would transfer. I still had almost five months before departing Japan. I would use my remaining time wisely.

It was Samuel Johnson who wrote, "The use of traveling is to regulate imagination by reality, and instead of thinking how things may be, to see them as they are." Often on Saturday several teacher friends would take a train to a nearby village and spend the day exploring. If I didn't do that, I would spend the day in a Japanese department store looking at the various departments: brocades, kimonos, dishes, bamboo items, whatever. One Christmas holiday I flew by CAT to Hong Kong and Thailand with other teachers. On an Easter holiday four friends flew to the south and visited Hiroshima and Nagasaki; I also visited Kyoto, Nikko, Sendai, Gifu, Kamakura. Teachers seemed to make the most of working in another country, taking advantage of all the opportunities for travel and learning. I am forever thankful for the privilege of teaching in the Army Dependent's Schools.

In 1954 the senior class of Narimasu High School dedicated the school annual to Crown Prince Akihito. The foreword states, "During the past year, His Imperial Highness toured North America and Europe. He toured countries as a gesture of friendship, and in the theme of our annual we represented in symbols some of these countries: America, France, Switzerland, Italy, Japan, Spain, and England."
The actual dedication reads:

> To His Imperial Highness the Crown Prince of Japan
>   because he has done much to promote goodwill
> and friendship between his own and other countries;
>   because of his interest in the academic pursuit

of youth in other parts of the world
  because his thought and ideas on international
affairs are much the same as our own
  We, the Senior Class of Narimasu High School in 1954
dedicate this annual to the Crown Prince Akihito.

Now, thirty-five years after the dedication to a young Crown Prince, he has become Emperor Akihito of the new Imperial era of *Hei Sei,* or "achieving peace," after the death of his father, Emperor Hirohito in February, 1989.

The closing of a school year is very busy, and when one is leaving a faraway country it is even more hectic. There was last-minute shopping, many farewell parties, and packing (even though the Army did the final packing in huge crates, we had to have all our items ready by a certain time). The Junior-Senior Banquet was on Friday evening, June 4; Baccalaureate was Sunday, June 6, at Saint Luke's Chapel; and Commencement was Wednesday, June 9, at Grant Heights Chapel Center. Music groups sang at both events; school ended on June 11. On Saturday, June 12, my hold baggage was sent; Tuesday, June 15, I had to get clearance from school, TAS, Camp Drake, payroll section, Hardy Barracks, OPS, and dispensary. Wednesday, June 16, I got on an army bus at my Osaka Hotel where I had lived for two years, at 8:30 A.M. and drove to Yokohama and the port; at 11:00 A.M. I was on the USNS *Mitchell.* We sailed at 3:00 P.M. What a frantic twelve days it had been. Many tears were shed as I left Japan knowing I probably would never return and waving to many friends who had come to see me off.

We soon found out the USNS *Mitchell* would sail to Korea to pick up more troops. Several of us decided that when we got there we would rent a car with a driver and tour Pusan for a couple hours. That was not to be. We docked at Pusan on June 18 and left on the 19th but no civilians were allowed to get off the ship. (I finally got to Korea in 1970.) On board I was again involved in helping with shows for the troops and civilians. On July 1 we arrived in Seattle after a relaxing and smooth voyage. After a train trip to Iowa to visit my family and unpack the many crates that finally arrived, I went by train to New York and spent a few days doing the necessary army routines at Fort Hamilton before embarking for Europe.

6

Teaching in the Army Dependent's School in Heidelberg, Germany

We arrived in Bremerhaven, Germany and were told our new assignments. Mine was Heidelberg, Germany! I realized then I had hoped for an assignment to Munich, where so much was happening in the music world. I said to myself, after all, I had already spent a weekend in Heidelberg in 1951 and felt I knew all about that university town. (What a stupid thought. After four years there, I still didn't know all about Heidelberg.)

First I was given a room in a small hotel downtown but later was moved to the BOQ very near the American High School on Mark Twain-strasse. The BOQ was comfortable; a door opened into a hall with two rooms and a shared bathroom between. When the other room became empty my dear friend Ellen Oppler, whom I knew from Tokyo, moved there. It is good to have a friend so near. Each of the four floors had a kitchen with one stove and two refrigerators, or was it two stoves and one refrigerator? Milk from cartons was often taken and we didn't know why; several of us were talking in the kitchen when another girl came in and said, "I always take milk from an unopened container; then I know it is fresh." Another time I had bought chicken to serve to guests but when I went to get it from the refrigerator, it was missing. I was very upset. That same day my friend Virginia Porr went outside to her car and her car was missing. I quickly forgot about the chicken! There were so many quaint cafes and restaurants in Heidelberg by the Neckar River we often ate out.

Since I had taken flower arranging in Tokyo I wanted to have flowers in my room. I found a florist shop and chose a couple of blossoms and some interesting leaves for the heaven–earth–man Japanese-type arrangements. When I went to the clerk to pay she said "No" to what I had selected and answered, "Ein bunch." Oh my, it *was* true that East is East and West is West and never the two would meet! Forty-plus years later her words still ring in my ears.

The school building was large and new (1950). My music room was spacious, sometimes used as a small assembly room, with windows on two sides. There was one problem: it was next to the railroad tracks. After several weeks of teaching I decided to count the trains that chugged by—in one day. Yes, the number was high: sixty-five. Imagine getting interrupted that many times while teaching. We survived.

In Heidelberg High School besides Boys' Chorus, Girls' Chorus, and Mixed Chorus, several small groups were organized: Nonettes, Eight Teens, Heidelettes, and Four Counts. These ensembles were often asked to perform at various clubs and organizations connected with the Army, as well as German schools and clubs. It was such a joy working and making music with these talented students.

Army personnel inspected the school, including the auditorium, where they found wooden risers on the stage. Wood was against the fire regulations, so they took away the risers. The next week was our big concert with a chorus of approximately sixty singers. During the song, "One World," and just as we sang the words, "One world built on a firm foundation," students began to wobble as the makeshift risers almost gave way. What a scary moment. The program finished without a total collapse.

One Christmas the chorus was singing a concert for a German school audience. We had been on stage quite a while, where it was very warm. One boy in the front row began getting glazed eyes and as I watched him, still conducting, I mouthed the words, "Are you all right?" He didn't respond. Soon he stiffened and fell on the piano keys in front of him. He had fainted. I continued conducting the song "Silent Night" in German until we finished. Someone came and took him off stage. Later when I phoned his home to check on him, he was on the second phone and said, "Is that why my nose is so sore?" No serious damage; only a vivid memory.

I felt students could learn much by attending performances by professionals. Since I had to go to the ticket office for my ticket, I would buy several other tickets for faculty or students. The most tickets were ninety-nine for a concert by the Vienna Boys' Choir. One teacher friend always tells me now (forty years later) she remembers me as the teacher with an extra ticket. Through the years many students have told me they attended their first concert with me.

USAREUR American High Schools presented an annual music festival each year, usually in Frankfurt, Germany. Choirs and bands came from different Army schools in Germany: Berlin, Bremerhaven, Frankfurt, Heidelberg, Kaiserslautern, Munich, Nuernberg, Stuttgart, Wiesbaden, Wuerzburg; and one chorus came from Paris, France. There was a

THE FIFTH ANNUAL MUSIC FESTIVAL

USAREUR AMERICAN HIGH SCHOOLS PRESENT

——— FRANKFURT·GERMANY ———

13 May 1955 20.00 hours

PROGRAM

John Rider, Band Conductor   Edwin Willson, Choral Conductor

Band
Star-Spangled Banner

Light Cavalry Overture	Franz von Suppé
Deep River Rhapsody	Harold L. Walters
March: Normal	Harold Bennett

Mixed Chorus

Gloria in Excelsis	Wolfgang A. Mozart
Jesu, Joy of Man's Desiring . . .	Johann S. Bach
Bless Ye the Lord	Ippolitof- Ivanof-Wilhousky
Beautiful Savior	Arr. by F. M. Christiansen

Girls' Chorus

Ave, Maria	Vittoria-Scott
Shoes	Manning-Foss
Come to the Fair	Easthope Martin

Band

New World Symphony	Anton Dvorak
March: Event of the Day	G. E. Holmes
Teddy Bear's Picnic	Bratton-Yoder
Il Relicario (Paso Doble) . . .	Padilla-Walters

Boys' Chorus

Brothers, Sing On	Edvard Grieg
Kentucky Babe	Adam Geibel
Ole Ark's a-Moverin	Arr by Noble-Cain

Mixed Chorus

Holiday Song	William Schuman
No Man Is an Island	Whitney, Kramer-Ringwald
Soon-Ah' Will Be Done	William L. Dawson
Cindy	Arr. by Harry R. Wilson

Band and Mixed Chorus

Battle Hymn of the Republic	Arr. by P. J. Wilhousky

ACKNOWLEDGEMENTS

The Dependents Education Organization is indebted to Major General Richard W. Stephens and his staff for making this Music Festival possible. The excellent facilities that have been provided are greatly appreciated.

The interest and cooperation of the American Forces Network in rebroadcasting this program is likewise appreciated.

The students and teachers are indebted to Miss Gay Long, Art Teacher of the Frankfurt High School, for the fine decorations at the Music Festival each year since the first concert in 1951.

guest conductor for band and another for chorus. Rehearsals were during the day; the concert was in the evening for the public. This festival was the highlight of the music program in the high schools.

The list of the chorus and band members for 1955 follows:

Heidelberg High School

Arvo E. Lohela, Principal

LouCelle Nelson, Choral Director
John Rider, Instrumental Director

Chorus

James Arthur
Dale Ballard
Donald Bates
Duke Beker
William Bracey
Beverly Brooks
James Brown
Rudy Bush
Shirley Cannon
Lynne Cantrill
Carol Cheney
Oakley Chemey
Bobbie Clayton
Monica Crown
Sylvia Cottingham
Larry Coulson
Virginia Curry
Carol Epperson
Shirley Fladeland
Mary Fugh
Dale Garvey
Marie Grider
Robert Hester
Yvonne Houston
Chris Hughes
Kenneth Ishoy
Josephine Johnson
Steve Johnson

Thomas Keyes
Elaine Koup
Marilyn Krohn
Richard Lacey
Judy LaFogg
Terry Langley
Anne Longley
Paul MacDonald
Katie McNair
Gloria Mason
Craig Morris
Mary Murphy
Raymond Nagy
LaVonne Newman
Nyla Nielson
Virgil Parker
Edward Post
Linda Redd
Judy Rhea
Rebecca Sadler
Ruth Shinn
Donna Steel
Carolyn Storke
Mary Thompson
Norma Ulander
Wayne Urban
Dale Wade
Judy Wright

Band

Charles Ackembom—Cornet
Betty Alien—Clarinet
Larry Banks—Cornet
Cherri Bowers—Drums
Betty Brandon—Clarinet
Theodore Cannon—Cornet
Jean Carson—Clarinet
Lewis Clements—Trombone
James Crews—Trombone
John Delk—Cornet
Joan Dickson—Alto Saxophone
Marshall Hammer—Baritone Saxophone
Fred Diercks—Cornet
Leon Hawkins—Bass

Karen Heinlein—Flute
Sandi Johnson—Clarinet
Betty Kelly—Clarinet
Richard Martindale—Trombone
Marilyn McKay—Cornet
Betty Meaders—Clarinet
Douglas Nickolson—Cornet
Sandra Reynolds—Clarinet
James Richards—French Horn
Marsha Rider—Clarinet
David Schubert—Cornet
Barbara Siler—Clarinet
James Sloat—Clarinet
Michael Sordelet—Tenor Saxophone

Each year graduation ceremonies were held in the Heidelberg Castle, begun as a fortress in the 13th century, ruined by war in 1689 and 1693, with restoration slowly continuing since then. This castle on the hillside overlooking the Neckar River is one of the most beautiful and historic in all Europe. What special memories come to mind for students and faculty of the Heidelberg American School!

Musical opportunities were so abundant in Europe I wanted to take advantage of as many as possible. I was a member of ISME (International Society of Music Educators). Music educators belonged to this organization from forty countries. In 1955 the weeklong conference was held in Lindau, Germany, and Zurich, Switzerland. Since I lived only five hours by train from the cities it would be held, I asked my "chain-of-command" if I could leave school a few days early to attend ISME. The request went from one to another but the answer was "No." They felt I was needed at graduation since some of my ensembles were performing. Of course, I agreed with them, but felt very badly I had to miss this world music conference—only five hours away. (Finally, I did attend ISME at Interlochen, Michigan: 1966; Perth, Australia: 1974; Warsaw, Poland: 1980; and Eugene, Oregon: 1984.)

I became a member of the Heidelberg Bach Verein, rehearsing one evening each week. Everything was sung in German, as well as all directions from our conductor, Herr Hubner. Several times a year we gave programs for the public. Singing German as it should be was a real challenge for me—but most rewarding.

77

A friend, Hermene, and I had German lessons once a week from a wonderful teacher, Frau Gassner, and the three of us became very good friends. One year when I came back from a Christmas holiday, she had had the piano from her home moved to my BOQ room to use during my stay in Heidelberg. What a thoughtful Christmas gift! (My other piano gift was from my parents in 1944 when I graduated from St. Olaf College and received a beautiful grand piano!) When Frau Gassner went to the United States later to visit her "students" from the East Coast to the West Coast, she came to Iowa to visit my parents and me.

Germany had concerts by orchestras, organs, and recitals and opera performances in most towns. Schwetzinger, the former summer residence of the Palatinate's Prince Carl Theodor, near Heidelberg, had a festival of music each spring. (When Mozart was a little boy giving concerts throughout Europe, he played in the lovely theater there.) Several of us went to see the opera *The Turn of the Screw* by Benjamin Britten. Before the opera began we ate at the outdoor cafe near the theater ordering the specialty of spring, Spargel und Schenken (asparagus and ham). At the next table were the English composer Benjamin Britten and the great English tenor Peter Pears, who had the lead in the opera. How we wanted to talk with them—we decided not to disturb them since they were involved in the evening's performance.

Farther west of Heidelberg was Mannheim. The opera house had been bombed during World War II and a new one had been built. I was one of several teachers lucky enough to get tickets for the opening performance and gala. That was a most memorable evening for me: an American music teacher teaching in Germany. I often went to the Mannheim Opera, because the productions were excellent. Once I attended a Sunday afternoon opera there and later went backstage to talk with an opera singer I knew. He said, "How did you get tickets? This performance is for German children." I didn't know the answer—I had just gone to the ticket window and bought a ticket.

I bought a new Volkswagen for $1250 and could drive to performances in nearby cities such as Wiesbaden, Stuttgart, and Frankfurt, taking friends who loved music as I did. Several times I attended Bayreuth's Festival to witness Wagner's operas. Wagner had designed the opera house and I was surprised at the wooden seats we sat on even though everyone was formally dressed. (He knew that wood was best for acoustics.) Once during intermission I got to say a few words to Richard Wagner's grandson, Wieland Wagner. (When in college many of my reports were on Wagner and his music.) Yes, it was with much pleasure that I finally got to Bayreuth!

Europe had many travel opportunities for me, too. My favorite jaunt was getting into my VW (now named Mel-D-Ray for three very special students) after a busy teaching day and drive for an hour or so on my "woodchopper's road" over the Heidelberg hills, through small villages, beside narrow crystal clear brooks and back to Heidelberg. This was peace, quiet, and relaxation at its best.

During my first winter holiday in 1954, I joined a group for a two-week tour by chartered plane to the Holy Land and Egypt. Jerusalem was a divided city so we were limited in what we saw. In Jericho I looked down at the walls that had been destroyed; I saw where Jesus was born in the stable in Bethlehem "according to tradition"; and much more. We were in Damascus for three days, then flew to Cairo, Egypt. Many in our group bought large articles, and when I wanted to buy a huge brass tray and a camel saddle, our pilot said the plane could hold no more big items. What a disappointment. Why didn't he say at the beginning each of us could buy two or three big items? It didn't seem fair to me. Of course, I rode a camel, "Telephone," around the pyramids, all the time the camel owner asking for "baksheesh": I rode a donkey going from one tomb to another in the Valley of the Kings. When I was resting on the terrace of a hotel in Luxor with the Nile flowing by, I decided I would retire to that very spot and give piano lessons! Aren't those silly thoughts and dreams precious?

When our plane was taking off from the Cairo airport it slid off the concrete onto the sand. We had to deplane and were told it would be several hours before we could leave. An Egyptian came up to us saying he could smell out cobras; would we be interested in going with him to find one? With nothing else to do some of us decided to take a chance. We walked and walked out in a garden, then a field until he finally stopped and told us he smelled a cobra. He moved around in a circle and sure enough, he picked up a live cobra on his stick. Yes, I am sure he had "planted" it there hoping some gullible tourists would let him be the guide. It turned out to be a pleasant way to spend some unexpected free time and makes an interesting story.

I invited my parents to visit me in Heidelberg the summer of 1955. They discussed the invitation but had not decided; however, my mother immediately made herself a new housecoat in case they decided to go. They decided they would go because Dad had always told Mom he would take her to Europe someday. They drove to Montreal, left their car there and boarded a ship to Bremerhaven, where Mary Clemons and I met them in her VW. What a good time the four of us had visiting relatives in Norway and seeing the sights. We stayed at a hotel in Bergen and had a huge buffet breakfast. Mom wrote all the items in her notebook (almost forty) and the manager came to her and asked what she was doing. Mom told her that she wanted to tell her friends at home about the foods. The manager said, "Oh, you will advertise for us?" Even though Mary was not related (she was a teacher at Heidelberg, too), she was welcomed with open arms at all the relatives' homes in Stavanger, Haugesund, and Oslo. We also drove into Sweden, Denmark, and back to Heidelberg. Before they came I had written to see where they wanted to visit; Dad wrote back he wanted to see Paris. We spent a weekend there, and the first item he bought was a French beret, which he wore every day. (He had not been in World War I and had heard so many stories from neighbors who had been in the war that he wanted to see Paris for himself.) We went to the "Follies" and saw Josephine Baker, the lead singer-dancer.

I was one happy daughter those days while I showed my parents highlights and they met many of my friends. It was a lifelong dream for them and for me too.

Another teacher, Ann Brookins, had a beautiful white Buick and often invited me for weekend trips. Everytime we passed the border, the guards made up some excuse to detain her. We finally found out why—she was a tall, good-looking black woman. They had not seen a black woman before and wanted a closer look. One time we drove to a small village in Austria where the townspeople were performing the "Passion Play." Ann had been there before, and we stayed in the home of the girl who played the part of Mary and her brother who played the part of Jesus. The mother did the cooking, and we were invited to eat all our meals with the family. She was an oldfashioned large woman who exuded friendship and hospitality. Ann and I enjoyed those delicious meals outside in the garden with all the family members—of course, we also were pleased to see the Passion Play and two friends as leads. When I accepted Ann's invitation to accompany her on a weekend trip I never knew where or what unusual experiences we would have. (Years later when she went to Nigeria to teach, she stayed with us in New York before we took her to the ship for the trip to that African country.)

My winter holiday in 1955 was spent on a bus trip to Spain and Portugal. Three experiences come to mind. After a few days a problem developed in the engine of the bus. One of the drivers would have to hang on the the outside of the back of the bus and hold some wires together so the engine would work—we arrived very late in the evening at our hotels. One of the popular songs was "I Could Have Danced All Night." We changed the words to "I Could Have *Ridden* All Night": that was our theme song the rest of the trip. In Seville arrangements were made for our group to see Gypsies dance the flamenco, a vigorous, rhythmic dance with clapping. From my early days I had heard that Gypsies stole; when I dressed that evening I left my rings, earrings, beads, and watch at the hotel. We arrived at the Gypsy cave, were shown our seats, and thoroughly enjoyed the fascinating stamping, clapping, and vocal sounds from the men and women dressed in long elaborate dresses. At the conclusion of the program as we were all showing our appreciation with much applause, one of the women came over to me and pointed at my coat. Somehow I knew this would happen—but I had left all my jewelry at the hotel, so why was she pointing at me? I looked down at the coat lapel and saw the Christmas artificial corsage pinned there. She wanted it so she could put it in her long, glossy, black hair. Yes, I gave it to her—I had no choice!

In Barcelona I left the group and flew by myself to the island of Majorca to see the monastery where Chopin and Mme. George Sand had spent a winter in the 1830s. It was a cold, wet winter and the cell was ill-heated and damp, so Chopin became very ill. I was pleased to see his piano and a few compositions on it and happy I could make this pilgrimage in honor of this great Polish composer and pianist. (In 1980 I did attend a concert at his birthplace Zelazowa-Wola, a small village near Warsaw, Poland.)

Yugoslavia Tour

The summer of 1956 a friend, Dorris Quinn, and I boarded a bus in Switzerland for an organized tour of Yugoslavia. Three weeks before we left, Tito had opened the borders to his country; therefore, our bus tour was the first one into this interesting area. After a stop at Lake Lugano and Trieste, we arrived at a grand old Victorian hotel on the Adriatic. We were the only tourists—tourists were new, so the waiters kept staring at us, causing them to spill things. There were no bellhops; American army blankets were on the beds; each of us got one quarter of a napkin to use at each meal.

There were only four Americans on the bus: a WAC, a young man fresh from an African trip, Dorris, and me, civilians working for the Army in Germany. The others on the tour were from France, Switzerland, Germany, and Holland. The following morning we set off down the Adriatic coast on a two-lane dirt road over rocky cliffs high above the sea. Often men on the work crews on the road would hitch rides on our bus. The passengers sometimes had to get out of the bus while the driver maneuvered over rough places. Once the road was not wide enough at the cliffside and men poked down wooden pegs and filled in the space with rocks over which the driver drove like mad to the opposite side. Later when we went down to visit waterfalls we had to get out while the driver went back and forward around a hairpin curve. The last time a bridge had been bombed the officials were afraid to let the loaded bus across—we got out and walked while the bus zoomed across. This was on the way to Sarajevo.

We came to other waterfalls and were told they would someday be a national park. That was also the place which had a restroom—a shed with a hole in the floor suspended over the falls. We usually made rest stops between cities "out in the clean nature" as our excellent guide would say: "Ladies go up the hill, gentlemen go down."

Our trip continued on a road twisting and turning around the cliffs. We stopped at Split and visited a museum. Mostar was where we saw the place where people claimed to have seen visions. Several days later we arrived in Dubrovnik for some days. They were shooting a movie, as the industry was just discovering what a great location it was. The old ship from the movie was in the harbor—also sharks, so my friend skipped swimming.

There was no cooperation trying to get to Mass as they were all communists (our guide pointed that out to us), but when Dorris finally got to a church it was packed and people were even sitting on the altar. The WAC really had a time and caused some difficulties as she went to Mass every day. She said she was given a very hard time every time she tried to find out where the Mass was held.

Dorris and I attended the opening night of the Sixth Music Festival with the Dubrovnik-Belgrade Philharmonic Orchestra playing Tschaikovsky's Violin Concerto and Beethoven. During the concert a cage was opened and white doves were released—symbolizing freedom and peace.

What a poignant moment! In Dubrovnik we visited the oldest pharmacy in the world; however, I think it has been bombed in the recent conflict. We also went to Centinje on the Albanian border at Lake Seutari in Montenegro. We visited the castle of the King of Montenegro, and the guide for our tour was the current prince, who was allowed to live there—as a guide. The king had been known as the "grandfather of Europe" because Victoria was the "grandmother." He had seven daughters and married them all to royals. We crossed the Bay of Kotor but were not allowed to take photographs. Too bad, because we saw a car being ferried on two rowboats.

The most cars we saw in one day were fifteen and that was at Zagreb. There was only one paved road going from Belgrade to Bled, Tito's summer home. We didn't drive on the paved road until we were headed out of Yugoslavia.

Our next stop was Sarajevo, where I stood in the footprints of the man who shot the Grand Duke and started World War I. People were dressed in their traditional clothes with men in baggy pants, shirts, and vests and women in long dresses with interesting jewelry. A visit to several markets showed us vegetables and fruits available to them. We saw a bearded old man washing his feet outside a mosque near many small shops with brass and wood items. In the country the bus stopped at a school where many people were gathered. We talked to them and they asked if we were from Detroit or Buffalo because they had a relative there and would say, "Do you know him/her?" They were so happy to talk with some Americans . . . and they offered us some of their *slivovitz.* One child held up his Mark Twain book.

Dorris got sick on the way to Zagreb and how startled the hotel clerk was, with no English, when she tried to tell him she had to throw up. She also remembers the caves and having to translate (English) for the Yugoslavian guide trying to make an English cockney accent understood. Dorris has often reminded me that halfway through the trip, when we went up and down those mountains every day, I finally told her, "Dorris, do you think we can go through another day like today?"

Memories of another time—almost forty years ago, when Yugoslavia was opening to outsiders, I was one of those who had a glimpse of this varied and interesting country and its people. When I read the papers today and see the destruction of very old cities that can't be rebuilt or replaced, the farms and villages destroyed, and the heartaches of those people, my heart aches also. I pray that the "white doves of peace and freedom'' I saw released in 1956 will soon become a reality in that entire region.

Summer 1957—Car Trip to Norway, Finland, and Sweden

Another teacher friend, Virginia Porr, and I decided to drive my VW to the top of Norway, then drive down through Finland and part of Sweden. We bought many tins of soup, vegetables, meat, and fruit from the PX and loaded them in the backseat. We also bought a small camp-stove for heating the items for lunch. Breakfast came with the room; we would buy dinner in the evening and would stop for lunch at a waterfall or scenic spot and enjoy the fresh air of Scandinavia. Our supplies would be augmented with bread and rolls from bakeries, cheeses, and fresh fruit. I never had read many of the great classics—a trip to our school library helped me. I took ten books, such as Goethe's *Faust,* which I planned to read at beautiful locations along the way. This was a great thought on my part but rather strange. (I read fifty pages of *Faust* and was so tired from driving all day, I needed my rest at night—there was never time to read at those scenic places. The project soon vanished; the books went back to the library unread.)

We drove to Oslo, where we met some relatives who said, ''Why are you driving to the top of Norway? You could drive south in Europe where the same distance would take you to Rome.'' I think that is where *they* wanted to go—we wanted to see most of Norway. There were few bridges and many fjords and much water to cross, therefore, we had the schedule of the ferry crossings and would hurry to arrive on time or slow down and enjoy the sights for a ferry that arrived later. Our lunches were good and we liked sitting on a fallen log near a stream of water watching the pot boil on our stove. Once a wild black animal with a long tail scooted near the water in front of us. What a vision to take from my mind's eye whenever I want.

By this time my minister relative, Osvald, and his wife, Edel, were in Alesund, on the coast. We stopped with them for a few days and their daughter, Sissel, went with us for five days so she could visit a friend. That was a bonus for us because she could translate all the Norwegian into English, plus the fact she was so much fun to be with. After we left her we continued on to the fascinating old city of Trondheim founded by King Olav Tryggvason in A.D. 997. This city was the first capital until

1217 and is the gateway to the center and the north of Norway. The Nidaros Cathedral is most famous and impressive, built on the site of Saint Olav's grave in A.D. 1152 and on a previous church built in A.D. 1075. Norway's kings and queens have been crowned there and blessed there. There are many museums, theaters, universities, and schools to visit. We had to leave before we had seen it all.

Roads were narrow but fine for driving. We had to be careful in the mountains with all the hairpin curves. Often we wondered how they could have been built and maintained. The farther north we drove the longer it stayed light. Finally we got to an area where the light was so beautiful we knew we could not sleep that night. We stopped and asked a man about the Midnight Sun and he told us we were in the best place to see the sun roll across the horizon. Directions were given to us where we would find the perfect spot to see this unforgettable sight. We drove on, found it, and waited for the moment. Yes, the red ball did roll along the horizon, then began going up into the sky, ever so slowly! That daynight was like nothing I have ever seen before or since. When it was over we felt we should find a hotel room for a few hours before beginning the day's journey; however, there was no room because of all the other tourists so we rested a few hours on two sofas in the lobby of a hotel.

We visited Bodo on the coast, then drove farther north to Narvik (where the Nazis had the "scorched-earth" policy during World War II) and farther north to Lyngen. One of our goals was to find Lapps and learn about their kind of life. What a thrill when we finally saw a Lapp couple dressed in their traditional dress with the aurora borealis colors in their headdresses with the points. We even found a small group of them with their tepees nearby. They had a few items for sale: shoes made from animal fur, primitive small dolls, and some trinkets. The women were sitting on the rocks and sewing the fur pieces. How I wished I could have talked to them about their lives as nomads who traveled with their deer across the north lands. Most of them had gone to an island in a lake, and we were told where we could find them. We drove and drove until we came to the end of the road with only small stones on the path. We drove a few feet but were afraid we would puncture a tire so we stopped the VW and walked on to the edge of the lake. We could see the island in the distance so we began shouting, hoping someone would hear us. Finally one woman got into her small boat and standing up paddled from the island. Virginia and I wondered what to do now. What if she refused to take us back after we had been to the island? No one would ever know what had happened to us. Neither of us knew much about these people. We decided we better not get into her boat and visit the summer camp. She was still quite a distance from us when we walked away, back to our car. In retrospect, I definitely would have gone with her; we probably missed out on a precious visit.

Once while eating our lunch in this far north country, there were thousands of tiny black flies—everywhere. Virginia didn't smoke, but she put a lighted cigarette in her mouth and blew smoke around as fast as she could, making the flies leave us alone. We decided we didn't have time to drive way up to North Cape; when we saw the sign for the toll station to enter Finland we did that. When we got south to Rovaniemi we stopped in that town on the Arctic Circle for two days. Interesting, but we found very little English spoken, so we continued south toward Helsinki. Along the way were many "moose crossing" signs, but we never saw a moose; goats on the roofs of wooden unpainted houses eating the grass that was planted there for them; huge black three-legged pots in the yard used for washing clothes; and wooden ladders on the side of most houses. The countryside was beautiful with the forests of stately pines and blue lakes. We finally arrived at the "white city," Helsinki, for several days. There are many, many bookstores in that capital, so we investigated one. What a surprise to find *Chinese Cooking* by two Benedictine sisters—the same ones I had taken the Chinese cooking class with in Tokyo. There the recipes were on cards which we received at each lesson; they finally had the recipes printed in a book. (These two sisters were originally from Minnesota, had been missionaries in China for many years and had to leave when war came, then settled in Tokyo and had classes to make money for their order.) I wanted to shout for happiness when I saw the book. Of course, I couldn't, but when I bought the book, inside me I felt the joy. Travel is the greatest!

Jean Sibelius was probably the greatest Scandinavian composer and lived not far from Helsinki. On Sunday I suggested to Virginia that we try to find his home—but how would we do that? We drove to a petrol station and asked the man where Sibelius lived. He didn't have the slightest notion what we were talking about. I then sang the melody from his famous *Finlandia* (I had played that in high school band in Iowa). Right away he understood what I wanted. At the station were two Finnish men on a motorcycle and they motioned for us to follow them and they would show us the way. We followed until we came to a town. The men were going a different direction but motioned us to go right, which we did.

Every few miles we would stop and try to ask people walking along the road, always having to sing the tune—then they motioned us in the correct direction. We finally found the long lane with the house and buildings at the end. In my mind I just wanted to see where he lived, so we didn't drive up to the house. Sibelius was still alive at that time and if he were home perhaps we could have met him . . . but I didn't want to disturb him. He died a few months after we were there. In retrospect, I wish we had tried to see him or at least left a note at his door thanking him for his beautiful national music.

We crossed by ferry into Sweden and stopped in Stockholm—and went shopping: linens, wooden articles, crystal, hangings which are still used in both our homes. I bought purple colored goblets, water glasses, juice glasses, and an interesting pitcher (my purple period). Virginia had a friend who lived outside Stockholm and spent a wonderful day with her. Then we drove to the Swedish lake district with all the Maypoles, folk arts, and crafts and purchased more items we couldn't live without.

Virginia was an authority on wildflowers, plants, and all greenery. In Denmark we passed a home with a thatched roof and a beautiful flower garden. We stopped so Virginia could ask them (women were having morning tea in the garden) if she could take a picture. The woman who lived there was so thrilled that an American had stopped she went inside her home and brought out a copper coffeepot and gave to Virginia. In return Virginia gave her a pound of coffee we had for gifts in our car. The woman was so happy and pleased to receive it. Yes, experiences such as that one make travel so special.

By now the back seat of our car was piled to the ceiling with our purchases. The first night in Germany we stopped at a country pension where we parked the VW in a long building used as a garage. After dinner I needed to get something from the car, and when I went to it a young teenage boy who worked at the pension was standing by the open door of *my* car. I couldn't believe my eyes. He spoke no English and I didn't say a word but my eyes must have told him he was doing something wrong. I have no idea how he opened the door or what he planned to do—temptation must have been too much for him when he saw the backseat filled with boxes and sacks. I must have arrived just in time because nothing was taken! What a close call.

We got back to Heidelberg safe and sound after a fantastic trip way up to the far north of Scandinavia. A few days were spent getting ready to teach school for the 1957–1958 year, which was my last before going back to the United States.

IV
LONG ISLAND, NEW YORK, AND TRAVELS (1958–1978)

Honor the occasion.

Roosevelt van Williams,
Roslyn social studies teacher

7

Marriage and Teaching in Roslyn

When the ship arrived in New York in June, 1958, Al Golden was waiting at the dock for me. We had known each other for years and had recently begun corresponding again. That was the reason I decided to continue my education at Teachers' College, Columbia University, in New York City, spending a year and a half for my master's degree in music education. My VW had been sent from Bremerhaven and finally arrived—trying to get it through customs was a real hassle. If Al hadn't been there I think I would still be there trying to solve the problem. I did drive to see my family in Iowa and left the car there. One isn't needed in Manhattan, where I would be for three semesters.

After fourteen years of teaching I found working on my master's degree a fabulous experience with excellent teachers, friendships developed with others in the music classes, and opportunities to hear music at its best in Carnegie Hall and the Metropolitan Opera. On weekends Al and I would visit a museum, attend a play, or go sightseeing in and around the city. Since he had lived there for many years, after having moved from Bangor, Maine, we had a good time exploring. He loved music even more than I did and could identify any melody from a symphony, concerto, or any other classical music—and had hundreds of records in his collection. Another collection was autographs. A few were bought but most of them he received after writing to the person. A special friendship was with the publisher of the *New York Times,* Arthur Hays Sulzberger. (I am so sorry I never had the pleasure of meeting him.) Mr. Sulzberger was Al's inspiration and mentor. Al was a copy holder in the printing business and a historian. In March I received an engagement ring. When I went for my piano lesson the teacher saw it and exclaimed, "What is this?" Word soon got around in my classes, and so began a different life for me—someone else to love, to share thoughts and dreams with, and to plan our lives together.

I had to attend classes the summer of 1959 in order to finish the requirements for the M.A. On August 19 Al and I were married. Our attendants were my dear actress friend, M'el Dowd, and Al's brother

Balfour. We had ten days to drive to Bangor, Maine, where we were royally entertained by Al's relatives and his sister, Mimi, before beginning my new teaching position at Roslyn Junior and Senior High Schools on the north shore of Long Island. A new husband, a new environment, a new position, and a new apartment in Bayside, Queens, was my challenge for 1959. I must say everything went well. On October 19 my Grandma Laura passed away, age 92, in Iowa. I learned the sad news when Mom sent a telegram to me. How sorry I was that I could not attend the funeral—with all the ''newness'' in my life it was impossible.

Roslyn was a beautiful town with much history. George Washington had stopped for breakfast when he was in Long Island and on his way to Valley Forge in 1790. That home has been converted into the George Washington Manor. William Cullen Bryant lived at Cedarmere from 1843 to 1878. (At age eighteen he wrote the poem, ''Thanatopsis''. When I was in an American Literature class in college, I had to memorize the last lines: ''So live, that when thy summons comes to join the inumerable throng . . . '' I found that an interesting coincidence.) Bryant is buried in the Roslyn cemetery. In 1943 there was a program celebrating the one hundredth anniversary of his arrival in Roslyn. Christopher Morley, another great writer who also lived in Roslyn, was the principal speaker. Morley, who moved there in the 1920s, wrote, ''I believe Roslyn is one of the loveliest places in America.''

Built in 1895 was the stone clock tower, a paper mill, a nineteenth-century train station, a library over one hundred years old, a savings bank that opened in 1876, a newspaper founded in 1878, the Salem AME Church from the 1860s, and schools dating back to 1863. On the main street are thirty-five buildings saved from the 1800s because of the historic district policy—most of these are homes. Small hills and many trees make the village of Roslyn very special. Added to this scene is Roslyn Park with a pond where Canada geese and ducks live and townspeople often come to feed the birds. Nearby is a white wooden bandstand. The high school where I taught was built in 1925 on land donated by Clarence Mackay. This environment was so quiet and peaceful, from another age. People who lived here were truly interested in a good education for their children. The arts flourished here. I had the privilege to be a part of this for twenty years.

There were three music teachers in the high school. Harold Gilmore taught band and orchestra; Dr. Raphael Grossman and I taught in the choral department. Some years later Ralph Wilkinson, who had arranged music for the *Bell Telephone Hour,* and Anthony Taglino joined Edward Sadowski in the junior high. All elementary schools had chorus and instrumental teachers. Activities in the high school included band, orchestra, and chorus concerts; concerts of larger works, often with guest soloists: Handel's *Judas Maccabaeus,* Vivaldi's *Gloria,* Bloch's Sacred Service, Schubert's Mass; a musical every spring: *Music Man, Camelot, My Fair Lady, The King and I.* (We invited members of the consulate of Thailand from New York City to attend, they did, and when they went back to New York after the performance they sent us a telegram saying how thrilled they were because it is never shown in Thailand.) Roslyn Singers and Madrigal Singers performed often at PTA meetings or other local affairs. Every two years we had a weeklong arts festival with lecturers and performers called "Joy of Discovery" for the high school. Selected students would be chosen for the All-County Chorus, Band and Orchestra for three days of intense rehearsals and a Sunday concert. (In 1963, we were nearly ready to leave school when an announcement came over the loudspeaker telling us that President Kennedy had been assassinated. The music weekend was cancelled; we wept as we watched the events on television.) A few students were chosen through tryouts for the All-State Festival, usually held at the Concord Hotel or in Buffalo. Often I got to go as the chaperon. Each spring approximately forty students from the music department attended the student matinee performance at the Metropolitan Opera, driving by bus into the city. This was truly the highlight of the year's work.

Many of these students went into music making. Danny is a composer; Barbara sings in operas; Ellie is a soprano soloist married to a brilliant conductor in Europe; Michael writes books and in one Author's Note states, "Three teachers of music deserve special mention—Anthony Taglino, LouCelle Golden Fertik . . . this book owes its existence to them"; Andrea has her own choir and conducts a university choir; Neil is a conductor in Europe. The list goes on and on. When I visit with these students they always say it was the "Golden Age of the Arts in Roslyn."

Alaska, Summer 1961

I always had two months off in the summer to attend music workshops or travel. In 1961 Al and I drove our VW to Iowa to see family, then to Minneapolis, where we left the car at a friend's—Vivian, a teacher friend from Heidelberg days. We went by bus from there to Fairbanks, 3500 miles, on the Alaskan Highway for seven days with stopovers at Winnipeg, Saskatoon, Edmonton, Dawson Creek, and Whitehorse. I wanted to see wild animals, listing bear, caribou, elk, deer, moose, in my notebook. We saw nothing for several days, so I made another list of squirrels, rabbits, racoon. Of course, animals did not want to be near that dusty, noisy highway! The night we had to ride without stopping at a motel we did see a moose in a dry creek bed in early morning light. It was an extraordinary bus trip for scenery and people—but not animals.

We saw the usual places—Fairbanks; Anchorage; Columbia Glacier on the boat, *The Gypsy;* Alaska Railroad to Mount McKinley Park; Valdez; Matanuska Valley; but the highlight was a two-day tour to Point Barrow, the northernmost village of North America. We flew by Wien Airlines over the Arctic Circle, over the barren tundra (due to permafrost) and into the land of the Eskimos. The landing field was covered with steel matting because of the moisture. The temperature was 41° on July 19. The Arctic Ocean was almost covered with ice floes—the second day we could see *no* ice. We drove five miles from the airport to the village in a huge homemade bus with balloon tires because there was no road, only gravel. Barrow was the largest Eskimo village in the world with two small tourist hotels, three restaurants, and a few stores. There was no drinking water—blocks of ice were cut from freshwater lakes and stored in sod huts to be melted later. Because of the cold the hotel supplied fur-trimmed parkas, boots, and gloves for our walking tour around Barrow. Houses were painted white with green trim; huskies were staked out far apart so they couldn't fight; fish, seal, and walrus meat was drying on long poles near the houses; oil drums were everywhere. They were used for garbage—litter was everywhere since nothing was thrown away, making an untidy appearance. Because of the cold there were no flies, bacteria, or mosquitoes. On the walking tour we saw food-storage ice cellars where fish, caribou, and seal and whale meat was kept; the schools; a health center; a Presbyterian church, one hundred years old; strips of baleen near the ocean.

Our first meal we each were welcomed with a piece of *maktak* (a small piece of blubber and black whale skin), which tasted like rubber, but we had to eat it since we were guests. The reindeer steak dinner was really delicious. The entertainment was watching the blanket toss and authentic ceremonial dances to the beat of native-made skin drums and chantlike singing. Again, the light was special (Midnight Sun), so Al and

94

I walked to the nearby ocean where we saw a multitude of birds flying and watched some men looking at an Eskimo-type kayak. One of the men was Werner von Braun, the famous scientist. The dogs were howling all night. In retrospect, I should have stayed awake all night instead of sleeping in the "Top of the World" hotel with black curtains on the windows.

The following morning a woman butchered a seal for us, stripped off the meat from the inside of the fur, and stretched it on a board to dry, later making an article of clothing from it. Interesting. That morning it was 35° and sleeting. We were glad to board the plane after this short glimpse into another type of living.

It was Will Rogers and Wiley who made Point Barrow famous when their plane crashed near there in 1935. A monument was finally erected there in 1982, twenty-one years after I was in Barrow. Later, it seemed only natural that I should visit the Will Rogers Museum in Claremore, Oklahoma, on the sixtieth anniversary of his crash and death. There I got a firsthand look and a new respect for this humorist, actor, writer, and the reason for everyone's respect. The eulogy at his funeral in August, 1935, by Dr. Brougher, Sr. at a California Baptist church ended with these words:

> There are many streams but only here and there a great Mississippi;
> There are many trees but only here and there a great Sequoia giant;
> There are many echoes, but only now and then an original voice;
> There are many musicians but only now and then a Mendelssohn or a Mozart;
> There are many politicians but only now and then a commanding statesman;
> There are many people but only now and then an outstanding individual.

Hawaii, Summer 1963

The summer of 1963 Al and I flew to Hawaii for a three-week holiday. We were met by my friend from Teacher's College, Bea Yoshimoto, driven around Honolulu's attractions and finally to our hotel. The next evening we were her guests at a luau, a Hawaiian feast. The buffet tables were spread with tropical foods, fruits, and decorated with their gorgeous flowers: hibiscus, frangipani, bird-of-paradise. With the exquisite leis we had been given, we knew we were in the tropics. During the entertainment it was announced a man would play the "nose flute," and Bea told me to listen carefully because very few could play this instrument. He held it to his nostril, closing the left one with his finger, and blew air from his nose across the open holes in a short bamboo piece. Yes, the melody was lovely from this rather strange instrument. Later I bought one for my collection of instruments, which later broke. Music can come from interesting and unusual materials.

A vivid memory of this trip was receiving a dozen bird-of-paradise blossoms at our hotel from one of the art teachers in Roslyn, Buck Tsui, who came from Hawaii and happened to be there at the same time. It is so good to have friends in faraway places. Part of our holiday was spent at a Coco Palms Resort. Our room had brilliant colors in the bedspread and curtains, but I remember the huge clamshell sink the most. Perhaps because of that clamshell I began my own shell collection as I traveled around the world. What fantastic beauties our earth produces in colors, shapes, smells, sounds, and tastes. I am so fortunate to be able to appreciate them as I travel.

In 1965 my parents flew to New York with my eleven-year-old nephew, Greg, for a visit with us and the opening of the World's Fair's second season. My father enjoyed baseball very much, so we also attended the opening game at the Mets Stadium. One of my former Roslyn students saw me and exclaimed, "I didn't expect to see you at a baseball game." One never knows.

Europe, Summer 1965

That summer Al and I spent July and August in Europe since Al hadn't been there since he was five and I always enjoy revisiting there. Arrangements had been made beforehand for a wonderful tour of Brussels and Bruges (the best chocolate anywhere), Belgium and Amsterdam, Holland. A train trip for the boat across the Channel to England. In London we found a vase filled with red tea roses from our friend Lois (the same one who wouldn't leave Paris without her luggage in 1951), whose husband was stationed in London. She had gotten us tickets for the Sadler Wells Opera, Covent Garden Ballet, and the Rostropovich

96

cello concerto concert at Festival Hall. After the usual sightseeing in London we joined a Cook's motor coach tour of the Scottish Highlands and the English lakes. In Cambridge we spent more hours with Al's cousin, a philosophy professor at Trinity College. A boat took us across the North Sea to Bergen, Norway—sightseeing for three days without rain and a piano concert in Grieg's home, Troldhaugen. A six-day Viking tour of the fjords was so beautiful and was followed by visits with relatives in Oslo: with Pastor Osvald Granborg and his wife Edel and family, and with Bertha in her town of Askim. Stockholm, Sweden was followed by a four-day fairyland tour of Denmark, a small country with much to offer in historical castles, old Viking graves, Hans Christian Andersen's home in Odense, and Copenhagen with Tivoli Park.

We flew to Frankfurt, Germany, and rented a Volkswagen for twelve days. What a treat that was for me to again drive to my former Heidelberg haunts and visit with good friends there. However, Al became ill, and it was necessary to get him to a doctor. I phoned my cousin, James Larson, a Lieutenant Colonel in the Air Force, stationed with his family in Baumholder, asking for his suggestions. He told me to drive there right away. When we arrived he had made arrangements with a nearby hospital and doctors. Al didn't want to stay alone in the hospital since he didn't speak German and asked me to stay with him—which I did, for the two nights he was there. Again, a rather strange first for me. Al had a bleeding ulcer and the staff couldn't have been more caring and helpful—all due to my cousin's friendship with these people. Everywhere we went in Europe had been cold and most places had much rain so it was called the "Green Winter." We then drove our rented car to Luxembourg City, returned it, and went on to Brussels for our charter flight back to New York. It had been a most interesting tour, except for Al's illness.

Another interesting semester teaching music classes in Roslyn High School on Long Island. On Tuesday, November 9, 1965 I was driving from school to Bayside, where Al and I lived, about twelve miles away, when I realized I had forgotten to put away the "coffee money" from the faculty room. I turned around and took care of it, then continued on my way back home. As I was driving across Bell Boulevard and ready to turn left, all the lights around me went out—street lights, traffic lights, house lights—although I could see about eight blocks ahead of me that those houses had lights. By the time I drove across 73rd Avenue, after a few flickers those lights went out. The time was 5:28 P.M. I parked the car, unlocked my apartment door, found Al's flashlight, and got out some candles. When I tried to put on the flashlight again, even *it* didn't work. I put on the portable radio but found very few stations working. I then decided to call my teacher friend Blanche, who lived a couple blocks away—but the phone was dead. Here I was alone in the dark house with two flickering purple candles burning in silver candle holders. It was pitch black outside and the announcer on the radio said for everyone to stay at home and not to drive the car; otherwise, I would have driven to Blanche's home. I had planned to type a music history test for class tomorrow and wash my hair. How could I concentrate on a test at a time like this? Al was on a trip in New Jersey somewhere. How and when would he get home?

The radio announcer said that Boston, Albany, Toronto, and all of New York City were blacked out. I can't help but think that the "enemy," whoever that was, had finally done it. Apparently "they" got to us before the water shortage arrived in 1967. Elevators were stuck between floors; planes couldn't land because there were no lights on the landing fields; subways were stuck in tunnels; television was off; trains were not running because there was no power for signals. Do not use the phone; do not use the car; do not *panic!* That was what the men on the radio said. What a black night. Finally I heard the announcer say it was the power line from Niagara Falls. The Pentagon had just announced that "there is no jeopardy to our defense."

It was cold in the apartment and I couldn't even get warm by putting on the electric blanket on the bed. I just had to sit out the strange evening. Finally I wrapped a large package I needed to send to my Iowa family. After that I looked outside and saw the sky filled with beautiful stars and a large white full moon and I thought about God's creation—but what a way to get to see it.

And so, by candlelight, I sat down at the piano and played Grieg and Beethoven music until it was time to sleep.

What stories we heard the next day. Al had gone to a documentary on Eleanor Roosevelt in a theater almost in New Jersey. When the theater darkened one of the ushers invited him to his nearby home for the night. Al's Aunt Rusha had forgotten the key to her twenty-fifth-floor apartment and the manager and Rusha had to walk all the way up—what a day to forget one's key. Students came to school early because their houses were "electric" and many didn't even have a can opener to open cans of food. That long dark night there were stories of kindnesses and helping hands everywhere . . . people were "lighting" up the darkness. If only that idea of goodwill to all people continued all the days!

A highlight of 1967 was my parents' fiftieth wedding anniversary in February. Al and I flew to Iowa for this most special occasion. Relatives had a dinner at our farm home with decorations of "gold" throughout the house: candles, doilies, flowers, etc. The open house was held Sunday afternoon at our country church, Lake Lutheran, with hundreds in attendance. Albin and Tillie were truly loved by family and friends, having been an uprighteous, Christian, dependable, loving couple.

Europe, Summer 1968

The summer of 1968 we joined a three-week tour of southern Europe. Everyone else on the trip were friends. They soon made us feel like we had known them, too; it turned out to be one of the best holidays we had. When we got back to New York, we flew to Iowa for the rest of the summer. My father was not at the airport to meet us with the others, and Mom said he wasn't feeling well. When we arrived home I went to his bedroom and kissed him, and he told me he didn't feel well. The following day I drove him to see a doctor in Renwick, a nearby small town. What a wonderful visit we had as we drove. He told me about Owl Lake, not a lake anymore, when he was a little boy, about the animals in the area, the games the young men played, his friends. The doctor couldn't do much for him and we drove back home. In a few days an ambulance arrived and took Dad to Clarion Hospital where he remained for over six weeks. The cause of his declining health was heart problems. He was visited daily by family. After Al and I flew back to New York for the new school semester, my mother stayed in Clarion with her brother Joe and his wife, Ruth, so Mom could spend more time with Dad. He passed away on September 10, two days short of his eightieth birthday. Again, Al and I flew to Iowa for the funeral. His memory would always be cherished by his loving family.

8

The Demise of Two Lives

My husband, Al Golden, had a friendship with Arthur Hays Sulzberger, the publisher of the *New York Times,* for thirty years. Al wrote him letters and received many in return. We had talked about making arrangements for me to meet him; somehow, that meeting never took place before he died in December 1968. We attended the memorial service for him at Temple Emanu-El on Fifth Avenue in Manhattan on December 15 at 4:00 P.M., after a two-hour trip from Bayside in a terrible snow and ice storm. We arrived at 3:00 and were seated on the left side near the roped-off section for friends, watching people come in. A tall grey-haired man, David Rockefeller, and his wife; Margaret Truman Daniels and her husband sat in the fourth pew on the right side; Mayor and Mrs. Lindsay sat down with them. At 3:50 there seemed to be an extra bustle of activity with the ushers near the roped-off area. Soon came president-elect Nixon surrounded by four Secret Service men. They all walked to the front at a fast pace. All through the service I could see Mr. Nixon with his black curly hair and long nose. During the service the choir sang three songs: "The Lord is My Shepherd"; the Rabbi read a psalm; the choir sang "In Thee Have I Trusted." The eulogy was given by James Reston, one of the editors of the *Times.* Mr. Sulzberger had written instructions five years before about his funeral and he did *not* want any Mozart. He never wanted Mozart played on the *Times'* radio station either. It was a beautiful eulogy. Mr. Reston talked about "his calendar of kindness and his puckish frivolity." The rabbi then had a prayer and the choir sang, "Hear My Prayer, O Lord"—the service was over.

We waited until others had filed out. Mr. Nixon walked out first and as he went by us he seemed to have rather dark, sparkling, laughing eyes. (*Let's hope he has four good years* was my thought at seeing my very first elected president). He was followed by Governor and Mrs. Rockefeller, Mayor and Mrs. Lindsay, Senator Javits, Theodore White, etc.

By the time we got outside there were no taxis, so we waited in the biting cold and strong wind. Another man and two women were also outside. The man was Robert Moses (recently turned eighty but looking sixty), the one in charge of the World's Fair, Jones Beach, and many bridges. Soon a limousine came for them. Finally a taxi came for us and took us to our car in a parking lot a few miles away.

How lucky Al was to have had such a wonderful friend!

The winter of 1968–1969 in Long Island was cold and more snow than usual covered everything. Al had to take a bus and a subway to get to his job in Manhattan; the weather made it very difficult. He finally got a cold and stayed home for several days. During that time he decided not to take his blood pressure medication (I did not know that at the time). He felt better and again went to work. On Saturday, March 1, he saw the exhibit of Grandma Moses paintings while I went with my friend Blanche to see the opera *Die Walkure* by Wagner. I arrived home about 6 P.M. and a few minutes later Al walked in, sat on a chair for ten minutes—then slumped over. I knew immediately it was a stroke (I don't know why I knew) and phoned 911. They soon arrived and Al was taken to Long Island Hospital; I followed in my car. For three weeks he was in a coma. I visited him each day after my teaching duties. I took his portable phonograph and favorite records thinking they would "awaken" him. Pneumonia developed, and he was given a tracheotamy. I had real hopes he would improve because the last time I saw him he looked so much better. The following morning while I was in my class, a secretary from the office came to the room for me with the message from the hospital that he was worse. Two teachers went with me and when I got to the room he was dead.

When we left the hospital I noticed the American flag was at half-staff and I thought it was that way for Al, who had just passed away. Upon checking later I found out it was for President Dwight D. Eisenhower. With Al's love of history and important people I know he would have been pleased to be "riding on the same train" with a United States president.

My mother and oldest brother, Doc, flew out to be with me for the funeral, as well as my youngest brother, Orin, who was on assignment in New Jersey. Roslyn teacher friends were most supportive during the sad days. Among the flowers was a huge bouquet from the Sulzberger family. After the funeral we flew to Bangor, Maine, for the burial.

It was difficult adjusting to life without one's loving companion and friend, but somehow one reconciles oneself to the fact that the loved one won't walk into the room again. It took me over six months for that reality to set in.

Oberlin, Ohio, Summers 1969 and 1971

The summer of 1969 I received a scholarship to attend the Teachers Performance Institute at Oberlin Conservatory of Music, Oberlin, Ohio. I invited my niece, Melissa Nelson, age twelve, to come with me: practice piano and have lessons, record the concerts, and attend guest lectures. She accepted my invitation, making me so thankful she was with me during those first sad months. One of the choir songs we rehearsed and performed was Motet, Op. 74, No. 1 by Brahms. It began with the words, *"Warum—warum,"* which means "Why—why?" I almost asked the choir conductor, Robert Fountain, if I could be excused from singing that song (I kept thinking of Al and his dying at such a young age of fifty), but somehow I got through the performance.

Another never-to-be-forgotten experience while at Oberlin was the landing on the moon. Several of us had attended a performance of the Cleveland Philharmonic Orchestra at Blossom Center, their outdoor amphitheater. We drove very fast to arrive back at Oberlin in time to see the landing. A huge screen was set up in one building with glass all along the entrance. One woman with us rushed up the steps and ran into the glass, thinking it was open. Blood began dripping down her knee. We were excited and laughed as we went in the door. Another woman already inside then showed us her knee—she had done the same thing. Yes, a few minutes later we saw the fantastic landing!

In 1971 I again received a scholarship to the Teachers Performance Institute at Oberlin. Another dear friend, Joan Cavicci, was also accepted. We had been good friends since getting our master's degrees at Columbia University together. She was an excellent musician and teacher. I again invited Melissa, and she studied piano and attended concerts and other special music events.

I have been forever grateful to Melissa for being with me those two summers. They also helped her musical talents, too. She now has a master's degree in piano and teaches instrumental music in a middle school near her home in Iowa. She is married and has four talented children. (Sam and I chaperoned her daughter, Kelsey, in 1996 for a week at the Beethoven Family Week—she was six years and a budding musician. We will do the same in 1997. What a joy to help young ones learn more about music and making friends.)

V
TRAVELING THE WORLD
(1970–1978)

Take only memories.

> Leave nothing but footprints.
> —Chief Seattle, Suquamish chief

9

Historical Cultural Tour of Southeast Asia, Summer 1970

An eight-week tour of Southeast Asia was sponsored by the Pacificulture Foundation of Pasadena, California, and conducted by Dr. Lennox Tierney, chairman of the art department of Pasadena City College, and his wife, Catherine. He had taught in the same overseas Army High Schools as I—Tokyo, Japan, and Heidelberg, Germany, in the 1950s. I joined the group of approximately twenty-eight for a fabulous tour. Here are some of the highlights.

We left from California and arrived in the Philippines on July 3. In each capital we had the usual city tour, museum tours, visited specialty factories or shops, and the local markets. In each country we flew to a smaller town for a few days. In Manila I had lunch with a former AFS student at Roslyn and had a good visit. We had a day's trip to Pagsanjan Falls driving by car, then a native canoe for the trip up the river, shooting the rapids on the way back. A flight over very mountainous terrain took us to Bagio, a resort high in the mountains and the summer capital. We also saw tribesmen from the Igorot village dance and sing their native music. A long slow walk through the market was most rewarding.

We then flew to East Malaysia, where we visited Kota Kinabalu, Sabah, and Kuching, Sarawak, on the island of Borneo. The highlight of the entire tour was driving 140 miles through lush countryside with many pepper plantations; then we transferred to long canoes propelled by outboard motors for a ride up the Skrang River for a visit to the Sea Dyaks. The whole village lives in "long houses" on stilts where they share the common room in front and private quarters behind. A log had slits in it for steps and no railing—very difficult to climb, but we all managed. We arrived at the beginning of a three-day harvest festival with many Dyaks from other villages arriving. Men took off their weapons, spears, and left them below. The floor of the common long room had matting laid over the floor boards. Everyone was having a good time drinking rice wine from large bowls. Often a man would go to a corner of the common room and vomit over the railing so he could continue drinking. Later there

105

was a procession and each man, woman, and child carried an offering: a rooster, a plate of food, a jug of wine, etc. All were in native dress, and it was beautiful to watch. The men had a red wide band around their middle with a woven belt and a silver buckle holding up a long narrow cloth of white and black. Their legs and feet were bare with many silver large "coins" hanging from wide silver bracelets. Their shoulders and the front of the neck were tattooed, many strands of silver necklaces covered their chest, and wide white bracelets were on each upper arm. Most men had on a white turban with brightly colored feathers sticking out of the top. As the drums were beat and bamboo pipes were played the men danced quietly with hand movements and stamping on the matting. Later, young pigs were butchered; each liver was taken out and put on a leaf, then given to the oldest man of each family so he could tell the future for the family. Some families received good news and some bad news. With the heat and humidity and the strange proceedings we observed, it was almost too much for some of us. We got down the slit-steps and walked to the canoes, where I turned on my tape recorder. One of the Dyaks began dancing again to the music—what a poignant moment. That evening we stayed in the Hoover Hotel in Simangang and ate a delicious Chinese meal in the marketplace. What a Saturday that had been!

The next country was south of the Equator, Indonesia, recently opened again to Americans. Two days were enough in overcrowded hot Djakarta, the capital, where we visited the National Museum and a batik printing factory. We left for Jogjakarta, where we saw the Sultan's palace and an evening performance of a shadow play using puppets moving to a gamelan orchestra. A day was spent at Borobudur, a famous huge Buddhist monument built in A.D. 850—it predates Ankor Wat in Cambodia, which was on our schedule, however, due to war we could not visit it. Borobudur was rediscovered in 1814, and efforts have been made to preserve and restore it. (Later when I began traveling on cruise ships and met young Indonesian men who worked as stewards I would tell them I had been to Borobudur. They were very impressed I had seen this fantastic monument in their country.)

A lifetime dream was to visit Bali, the island of temples, dance and music. Bali was our next stop and the first time I had been to a Hindu area. The markets, the irrigated rice terraces, the temples with the elaborate carvings were interesting but it was the music and dance that made Bali so exotic. We saw the classical dance, the *Legong;* and *Barong,* a story-dance about good and evil; and the *Ketchak,* or monkey dance, which was chanted and danced by 150 men and one woman. It was the most unusual dance and chanting I have heard anywhere. I do hope that twentieth-century civilization comes slowly to this charming spot and it continues to remain "Balinese."

After four days in Bali it was time to visit Singapore, where I became very ill (I think it was from food I ate at the Balinese banquet the night before we left.) I stayed in bed sipping Coca-Cola but finally felt better and went on a harbor tour. I saw enough streets to notice that there was *no* litter anywhere—the cleanest city in Asia.

Kuala Lumpur, the capital of the newly formed Malaysia, was another exotic city with the Moorish-style buildings. While there, I stayed with a former American student from Tokyo High School who was married to Rev. Carl Fisher, president of the Lutheran Church, Malaysia and Singapore. How good it was to be with friends instead of the hotel. Miriam had bought all the "strange" fruit grown there so I could taste them: durian, which smells terrible but tastes like a cheese custard; pomelo, a grapefruit; rambutan or the "red-haired egg"; longans, starfruit, langsat, mangosteens, jack fruit, three kinds of bananas . . . what a thoughtful gesture. I also attended a choir rehearsal at the Chinese church. The Fishers took my roommate, Jean Wood, and me on a tour of Kuala Lumpur to see the new museum, the ultramodern university, the national monument, in this fast-growing city.

A short flight took us to Penang, a tropical island where we had a circle tour of the entire island, spent two hours swimming and sunning on the beaches, visited a snake temple where there were snakes everywhere but the incense made them lethargic, and rode the cable car up 2,200 feet to Penang Peak. If Penang weren't so far away, it would be a great place to retire.

Another flight and we were in Bangkok, Thailand, with all the temples (about a thousand of them): the Marble Temple, the Temple of the Reclining Buddha, the Temple of the Emerald Buddha, the Wat with its one-ton solid gold Buddha, the Temple of Dawn, and the Grand Palace where "Anna met the King of Siam and taught the children." We toured the floating market by boat, visited the museum, and dined in a restaurant designed in the style of a Thai home; the entertainment was Thai classical dances. I did not find too many changes from my previous visit to Bangkok in 1952, but saw much more of Thailand. We flew northwest to Chiang Mai near the border of Burma; then a bus drove us sixty miles north to see the elephants working with teak logs near a river—what an unusual experience. We also visited the Karen tribe where children were smoking pipes and girls had a little bundle of twigs in their pierced ears, adding more twigs to enlarge the holes. A day's drive was most rewarding and I visited a Buddhist school for young boys on the grounds of a large temple. They were learning English words, but we were not allowed to help with the lesson. On Sunday Jean and I attended a beautiful modern Baptist church with a special music service. Back again to Bangkok driving to Ayudhya, the once great, bustling, glittering city which was now only crumbling walls, a few pagodas and statues. We also stopped at Bang Pa In, the king's summer palace.

Our tour group consisted of artists, architects, professors and teachers, and historians—an extraordinary group of people—and two children, ages five and seven. I wondered about them; however, as the tour progressed they seemed to be adjusting to each country, to the terrible heat and humidity (in the bus we would be given frozen cloths to place around our necks to make us feel cooler), and the unusual foods. In fact, these two young ones were so respected by the adults that at the end of the tour a special dinner party was planned for them with each adult giving gifts to the young boy and the five-year-old girl. They were super children!

The last section of our tour was the Orient—China, Korea, and Japan, in that order. I had always wanted to visit China and was very happy to see the red hills of Hong Kong; however, with all the construction they were covered with modern tall buildings. Hills were being leveled, using the dirt to fill up water areas for more land. Hong Kong is a shopper's haven and we all did our share. A day's drive in the New Territories took us to an 800-year-old ancient walled village, Kam Tin, where we walked around and saw people and animals in close proximity; a hill near the border let us peek across the Bamboo Curtain into mainland China; and we visited Repulse Bay and the fishing village of Aberdeen. Then we flew to Taiwan, where we stayed in the Grand Hotel of Taipei. Most of our time was spent in the National Palace Museum, first opened in 1965. This is the repository of the finest relics of Chinese antiquity. The vast collections of scrolls, jade, porcelain, bronze, and lacquerware were brought from the Peiping Palace Museum after WW II. What a fabulous collection and opportunity to get a glimpse of China's past!

After a difficult time getting permission to enter Korea, even though all our papers were in order, we finally got to our hotel in Seoul in the middle of the night. Here again, many new buildings and much construction was visible. A train trip across Korea to Kyongju, the old capital, was filled with green and lush rice fields, the most beautiful agricultural land I had seen. Kyongju had a mixture of old and new. We visited many museums, burial mounds, temples, and shrines. Very early one morning we drove up a winding mountain road to see the rising sun from the East Sea and the Sukkulam Grotto with a great white Buddha statue. Back in Seoul we had a full-day excursion to Panmunjom, the demilitarized zone and site of the armistice talks. I shall never forget seeing a North Korean guard through my binoculars "eyeball to eyeball" as he looked at us through his binoculars! Korea had their twenty-fifth liberation anniversary and everyone was in a festive mood with many flags, balloons, and national costumes. But it was time to move on to our last country—Japan. You can imagine how happy I was to go back after sixteen years.

We spent six hours at Expo 70 in Osaka, where crowds were tremendous and the heat overwhelming; then several days in the classical city, Kyoto. A very dear friend, Kazue Hatano (I had taught him English when teaching), came all the way from Tokyo to see me. He acted as my guide as we saw the Gold Pavilion, Old Imperial Palace, and Heian Shrine. In Nara we saw the deer park with the seventy-one-foot-high bronze Buddha sitting in the Todaiji Temple. How good it was to see Kazue-san again and find out he had gotten his degree and had a good position as an engineer.

Back with the tour group we took the "bullet" train to Atami for a bus to Hakone and an overnight at the Fujiya Hotel (those connected with the armed forces had often stayed at this hotel, including me); however, it rained all night and we couldn't see Mount Fuji. A bus drove us to Kamakura to see the "Diabutsu" or Great Buddha followed by driving on the expressway through Yokohama to "my" Tokyo! It was so good to get back here again. My best Japanese friend, Mary Hotta, took her vacation that week so we could see all my favorite places from '52 to '54. She also invited me to spend time in her lovely Japanese home, an honor not many foreigners receive. Her charming mother had made a kimono and presented it to me. We also visited our flower arranging teacher, Mrs. Tamura, at her home and enjoyed tea and snacks as we talked. (Mrs. Tamura visited me in Long Island after a flower-arranging tour in Europe, a very special woman I consider an honor to know.) I also saw Miss Yanase, a dear friend from teaching days; Margaret Kurtz, who taught at Narimasu with me; and my cousin Jean and Bill Basinger who were working in Tokyo. Members of the tour would often ask me, "Lou, who are you meeting in this country?" A rather nice way to be remembered.

10

Nairobi, Kenya, Summer 1972

I did *not* have a farm at the foot of the Ngong Hills as Isak Dinesen had, but I had been accepted for the American Institute for Foreign Study Summer School at the University of Nairobi, Kenya, conducted at Kenya Science Teachers' College. This was my first trip to East Africa and I looked forward to it with great anticipation. We would have a ten-day safari at the beginning, then attend lectures by professors of the University; there were two four-day optional tours (I signed up immediately). One weekend a friend and I went to Treetops, a world-renowned place to see wildlife.

As we arrived by plane from London we saw Mount Kenya above the clouds, a dark jagged line of peaks. As we descended I saw red barren soil, then green land with a red meandering river.

The director of the institute met us with vans; then we went to the College Inn Hotel for dinner. First was carrot soup, then a cheese mixture in halved green peppers, followed by roast beef, Yorkshire pudding, potatoes, and creamed cauliflower. Dessert was fruit and a cup of tea . . . all served beautifully. My table companions for that first meal were a native from Nairobi, two American girls, and a young black boy from Detroit. He greeted the Kenyan in Swahili and said, "What tribe are you from?" The answer was "Luo, and what tribe are you from?" He answered, "American." The Kenyan said, "Black American?" The young boy said, "No, mixed American. My mother is white, my father is black." The Luo said, "Here in my tribe that is A-OK." The boy said, "You mean it is an honor?" His response was "Yes." I was so happy to have seen these two young boys, from opposite sides of the ocean, get acquainted!

On the plane I had written a letter to my mother and I wanted to post it immediately. I was told to walk outside around the corner to a stamp store. I got the stamp and also saw my first "wildlife" in Africa: a cockroach walking over some of the merchandise at the little shop. Before I had arrived in Africa I had wondered what would be the first creature I would see. Now I had the answer.

Later that evening my roommate and I went to the bar for Coca-Colas. The man who worked there told us he had worked twelve hours that day at forty cents an hour and would soon go home to a place with no running water, no toilet, and would sleep on the floor. What a day this had been and quite enough for the few hours I had been in Nairobi after the long flight from London.

Many adventures occurred on the ten-day safari. We rode in small vans, seven to a van with a top that could be opened so we could stand up to photograph animals. We proceeded across the Athi Plains, the home of the picturesque Masai. Ahead on the road were some small Masai boys herding cattle, which were crossing the road. I leaned forward in the van and took a photo of the scene. One boy began running toward the van with his spear pointed at the front side window. As we drove on, he thrust the spear at the window. Luckily for us the window was rolled up or his spear would have injured someone. Later we found out why he was so angry. Some of his cattle were on one side of the road and some were on the other side. With a photo taken of them, a special ceremony would have to be performed to get the cattle into one large herd again. What a frightening experience! As one travels it is difficult to know all the traditions and taboos of people, but we should try very hard to respect them.

Our first night on safari was spent in Tanzania at the Ngorongoro Crater Lodge on the rim of the crater, 6500 feet below. For dinner we had soup, *talapia,* which is a delicious fish, grilled zebra steak with mashed potatoes, and a green vegetable. Dessert was red bananas in rum; tea was served in another room. There I talked to a young girl and her aunt from Norway. The aunt had been to Africa six times and said, "What is it people who smoke . . . ? Addicted, oh yes, I am addicted to Africa."

I never missed a sunrise while on safari, so Dee and I were outside the lodge at 6:30 A.M., when it was cloudy and dark. We walked to the front of the lodge, and much to our surprise a short distance away was a sleeping Cape buffalo! Did we ever move fast back into the lodge by the window. Soon the buffalo got up, scratched his head, and walked down a path. Close call and a lesson well learned. We listened for the "African symphony" of bird and animal sounds. After breakfast we went by Land Rovers to get down into the crater; a game warden always goes with the five or six Rovers that are part of the same safari. Inside the crater we saw wildebeest, zebras, waterbuck, impalas, lions, hyenas, Cape buffalo, rhino, eland, ostriches, silver-backed jackals, bat-eared fox, flamingo, crowned cranes, fish eagle, Egyptian geese and other birds. What a Garden of Eden! Our group also visited a Masai camp and took photos of the chief with his family.

I was getting acquainted with this crater area, but we had to move on to our next stop, which was Tarangire National Park. This had been a park for only three years; before that it was used for hunting. We stayed in a luxury tented camp built on the edge of an escarpment with a water hole. I really fell in love with this spot, and when I took my shower in the canvas enclosure open to the sky filled with stars and a full moon, I *knew* I was "Ava Gardner"! After dinner in the main lodge we watched elephants at the water hole followed by a generous dusting. The next morning we drove around looking for animals to photograph, but as we drove near they all ran away because they were not used to the motor vehicles. I did add klipspringer, warthogs, hardebeests, mongoose, vervet monkeys, dik-dik, and two pythons to my list as well as the usual ones—zebra, elephant, and buffalo.

We crossed back into Kenya after a few minor border problems and drove to Tsavo National Park after a night in Arusha, the big-little town. In Tsavo West we stayed at the Nguli Lodge, a recently built lodge near a water hole and salt lick, on the edge of Ndarve Escarpment, high up in the Ngulia hills overlooking the Kaluaga Valley game route. Tsavo has huge boulders, lava flows, and is a vast park for huge creatures like elephants, and they seemed to be every place. The vegetation seemed rather scarce, so they often eat the bark of trees, destroying them in the process; perhaps that is how we get plains. Here I added oryx, hippo, lesser kudus, baboons, small lizards, and hornbills to my animal and bird list. At one point a herd of elephants had just crossed the road; our driver, Khimis, stopped the van but kept the engine running. We began taking photos, but a mother elephant felt we were too near her young one. She trumpeted and charged toward our van. No, I never got the photo; I was petrified as our driver drove frantically away.

Meals at all the lodges were delicious, following the same pattern for dinner: soup, fish, entree of meat with vegetables, choice of many desserts and cheeses from the dessert table. Coffee was served in another room with a huge fireplace, or we would watch animals at the water hole. Yes, I always went to the area to see animals. Once when I went to my room I stood on the small narrow balcony to listen to the night sounds. I happened to look to the right, and there was an elephant walking near the building and getting close to where I stood. I made a fast entrance

113

into my room and quickly closed the door. One never knew when the wildness and civilization would nearly collide.

We then drove to Mombasa, chief port on the Indian Ocean for Kenya and Uganda. Fort Jesus was built in 1593, and both the old and the new town were filled with interesting shops and people from many nations. Dee and I met a family from India who had lived there for several generations. They were so kind to us and invited us to meals. One day the mother had an invitation for a party but declined so she could make a special Indian meal for us. From her I got a recipe for tea and a condiment made from carrots; I have made both several times and always remember the visits to these friendly people.

One day we left Mombasa and drove to Gedi, an old thirteenth-century Arab town in ruins; then on to Malindi, a holiday resort one hundred miles north of Mombasa. Some of us rented a glassbottom boat so we could see coral and fish. Because it was too shallow we had to walk out in the water to the boat. No problem getting to the boat, but when we walked back a large wave came and my culottes were soaked. I didn't want to sit with wet clothes for the long bus drive, so I took off my culottes and covered myself with a raincoat as I hung my culottes out the window, letting the breeze dry them. Another one of those strange experiences.

Soon it was time to leave Mombasa and our friends and drive back to Nairobi. The road gently goes "up" from the seacoast to Nairobi, which is 6000 feet. It was rather cool and cloudy after our days on the savanna with red dust, the huge ant hills, the lonely baobab trees, thorn trees, and thatched huts in the country. Never far away were the weaver birds, rollers, bee-eaters, Thomson gazelles and Grant gazelles. Our ten-day safari had been a real success and introduction to our six weeks at the university. Later we had two four-day weekends. One was to Lake Nakuru to see the millions of flamingos, Lake Naivasha (where I met my young lion), and Kisumu on Lake Victoria.

Another strange sight occurred in our hotel in Kisumu. Someone asked for the restroom and was shown where it was. She found it so interesting she suggested we all see it. There was a Western toilet, but it had not been installed correctly. They had put cement around it all the way up to the seat! What a laugh we all got from that installation, a modern convenience they didn't quite know what to do with. (As one travels around the world there are many kinds of "rest stops," but this was the one that has remained at the top of my list!) I enjoyed sitting at

114

the edge of Lake Victoria watching birds fly in the papyrus nearby. Again, I had an introduction to Mr. Ved, a friend of my Aunt Luella and Uncle Gene, who managed a factory in Kisumu, and we had a good visit with delicious Indian food.

The other four-day weekend we drove north of Nairobi to Embu for a performance of thirty drummers dancing in unison and chant-singing in an open area. Just before reaching Meru we crossed the equator, an exciting moment for me. At Isiolo there was a barrier across the road and we crossed with no problem, on to Archer's Post. This area was a desertlike region with the Samburu tribe living here. Several girls were walking near the road with salmon-colored pieces of material wrapped around them and hundreds of strings of beads around their necks. A woven band was around their nearly shaved heads. On the left upper arm each wore a brass wire bracelet, approximately four inches wide. Sandals and narrow ankle bracelets completed their outfits. They were stunning looking girls, about sixteen–eighteen years old; how I wished I could have talked to them and learned more about their life in this part of Kenya. One had a brass wire bracelet to sell and I bought it for my collection; no, it won't fit on my upper arm. These girls had walked right out of the pages of *National Geographic* magazine as so many other people in faraway places had done. How fortunate I was to travel and experience their cultures.

Samburu Lodge on the Uaso Nyiro River was our home here. My cabin was way down at the end of all the cabins. The night before, elephants had uprooted two trees beside my temporary home. After dinner in the main lodge, when I was ready to go to my cabin, a tall native with a long spear escorted me so that I would arrive safely. In this park I added reticulated giraffe, Grey's zebras, and gerenuk. Next our tour group drove around Mount Kenya to the Naro Moro River Lodge where Dee and I decided to spend four hours touring a private game reserve. It was our last chance to see a leopard or cheetah, but they didn't appear. (I finally saw them a couple of years later on another safari in Kenya.)

When we were in Nairobi we did have daily classes. There were several choices, and mine were music, biology, historical Africa, and contemporary Africa with professors from Kenya. Beside the 175 of us in the AIFS program there were other groups using the KSTC (Kenya Science Teachers' College) given by Sweden in 1968 with excellent facilities. Some of those were a Commonwealth group of geography teachers,

115

teachers from Kenya in math, religion, astronomy—many friendships were made among us.

Treetops

A night at Treetops Hotel was a must for me during that summer in 1972 in Kenya. Since it was not included in our schedule, I made my own arrangements for the two-day trip; another student, Joan, joined me.

Early in the morning our bus left Nairobi and drove north about one hundred miles over dusty roads, passing coffee and tea plantations, villages, and markets. Natives, mostly women, carried a variety of items on their heads as they walked together on the road; the men were usually sitting in the shade of a tree talking. After a three-hour drive we arrived at the Outspan Hotel at Nyeri, the entry point for Treetops.

The Outspan Hotel is a luxury country hotel situated in the lush valleys and hills with seventy-five acres of gardens, ground for golf, tennis, horse riding, and fishing. After a tasty lunch and short rest we continued on the final twelve-mile bus trip to Aberdare National Park, where Treetops is located. Each of us was limited to one flight bag supplemented with camera equipment and binoculars.

The bus unloaded in the parking lot about 200 yards from Treetops. Now the real drama began! We were greeted by a uniformed White Hunter with rifle in hand. He gave us a short talk, speaking quietly and periodically looking over his shoulders. Until this moment I had no idea I would have to walk those last 200 yards; what would happen between here and there? As we walked slowly and silently on the path, I noticed shelters built around the trees where we should go if any wild animals approached. There were also ladders on those trees. Lions were not in this area, but there were plenty of elephants, rhino, and buffalo. I looked up and saw another man on the roof acting as a "lookout". Sometimes buffalo circle around behind and these scouts were taking no chances. The White Hunter must be able to kill any animal in our defense, if necessary; however, we got to the steps and climbed up without incident. The steps were pulled up after us.

The hotel was built thirty feet above the ground and supported on thirty straight cedar posts, each forty-four feet long. After the ground level steps was a stairway that led to a landing; another stairway led to the lounge, a small room with a tiny bar in one corner and a long table

116

already set for dinner. We were shown our cubicals with two cots and a window. Now I realized why we were limited in baggage.

I went to the ladies' washroom, a simple room with no curtains on the many windows, but there was glass. When it was first built the windows had no glass, but after baboons got in and took rolls of toilet paper, which unrolled as they climbed out into the trees, the owners decided to install glass. As I was washing my hands, the door opened and another tourist came in and said to me, "Dr. Livingston, I presume?" What a poignant moment!

It was soon teatime, so the guests climbed the stairs to the flat rooftop, where we enjoyed hot tea and scones, beautiful scenery at twilight, and baboons sitting on the railings. If they got too "friendly" the Hostess and White Hunter took long sticks and shooed them away. We had been told to carefully watch our cameras, lens caps, film, etc., which could easily be snatched by a baboon and taken from us—forever.

After tea, each one found a spot on the various levels to watch the water hole and salt lick below. After the sun went down, artificial lights were turned on and we listened carefully, watched in all directions at once, and soaked up the moments. I waited . . . and waited. . . . Little animals came to drink: genet cat, mongoose, hyena, giant forest hogs, Sykes monkeys, warthogs, baboons. One or two animals would slowly approach the water; sometimes a herd arrived to drink . . . buffalo and elephants. My most exciting moment was watching elephants. One stood guard the entire time while the other elephants drank. When some buffalo arrived, the guard elephant caught a young buffalo calf and flung it into the air. The calf did a somersault, landed on his back, got up and hurried to the retreating herd of buffalo, apparently unhurt. After drinking their fill the elephants slowly disappeared into the forest; the guard-elephant never drank one drop!

At 8 o'clock we were called to dinner. Space was small; on the middle of the table was a yard-long food carrier, about eight inches wide. The Hostess, at the head of the table, loaded the serving dishes on it and gave it a push. Each of us helped ourselves as the food went by. The meal was delicious considering we were up in a "treehouse" surrounded by wild animals. One of the courses was called a "savory," which cleanses the palate before the next course—a British custom. This was a new experience high in a clump of Cape chestnut trees. I thought of the other guests who had enjoyed the concern of those in charge of Treetops: Charlie Chaplin, Joan Crawford, Lord and Lady Mountbatten,

Lord and Lady Baden-Powell, the Queen Mother, and countless others who had spent a night there. But the person who made Treetops so famous was Queen Elizabeth. There is a plaque which reads: "In this tree Her Royal Highness the Princess Elizabeth and His Royal Highness the Duke of Edinburgh spent the night of February 5, 1952. While here Princess Elizabeth succeeded to the throne through the death of her father, King George the Sixth."

In such an environment sleep seems unimportant. Knowing it was a once-in-a-lifetime experience, I watched the animals below, far into the night. Even after I went to my cot, I got up many times during the night to see what was below drinking.

Next morning we were served tea. When the all-clear signal was given the steps were lowered. We walked down and across the open area where animals had so recently roamed, to the waiting bus. We drove to the Outspan Hotel, where we enjoyed a hearty breakfast before the return bus trip to Nairobi.

Ever since Treetops opened in the early 1930s a record has been kept of all the animals seen each night. The final count seen on "my' night was 521. How lucky I was to have seen many of that final count: 67 waterbuck, 9 bushbuck, 78 warthogs, 19 rhino, 12 elephants, 268 Cape buffalo, 7 giant forest hogs, 3 mongoose, 2 hyena, 2 genet cats, 15 Sykes monkeys, and baboons everywhere. What a night to remember!

Time flew by. We packed our bags in our dorm rooms on campus, throwing away what we didn't want anymore and leaving some items for certain friends to take after we left. Buses took all 175 of us to the airport, where we sat and waited . . . and waited . . . for our chartered plane to London. Nothing happened, so Dr. Barter, the American dean of students, finally found the correct authority to get an answer. He was told the plane would *not* be coming that day because of problems in Uganda. Planes had been diverted there to take Indians out because of the politics. There was nothing we could do. We returned to the buses with our luggage and went back to our dorm rooms. To our dismay and surprise, people had been in every room and taken anything left there. Every wastepaper container had been gone through and papers were strewn everywhere. What a sight! What a dilemma!

I don't know what happened to the others, but two days later sixteen of the older students, including me, got on a plane in Nairobi bound for Entebbe, Uganda, where many Indians boarded the plane for London. One of these older women sat beside me; I wanted to talk with her but didn't. My heart went out to all those people who were uprooted from their homes and had to begin a new life.

Upon arrival in London I spent Sunday attending two services at Westminister Abbey, listening to the great choral music, a sermon about the Uganda situation, and sitting among my "friends" in Poet's Corner. It all brought me back to Western civilization!

11

Larson-Jotten Ancestry Book, Autumn 1972

During the fall semester teaching in Roslyn in 1972, I invited my mother to come to Long Island to stay with me while we put together the family book of her relatives in America and those who stayed in Norway. During the day she worked on names and dates and in the evening we continued. I very much wanted stories and more information about each person, not just the birth date and death date. Many letters were written to relatives and letters were received with the necessary news. Since two sisters and one brother had arrived in the late 1800s, with the two sisters marrying two brothers, it was not too difficult getting the facts, however, the third brother joined the Merchant Marine and we have not been able to find out about his life even though we continue to check archives. Since Mom had written many letters to relatives in Norway and visited them in her trip to Norway in 1955, she had much information—we included that too. A few letters from long ago were discovered, including the 1851 inoculation certificate for cowpox when Hellick was one and three-quarters years old. Also a letter from the mother Kari written to her two sons, Lauris and Hellick—one side of the sheet was the letter to Lauris and the other side was the letter to Hellick. No date was on the letter, but it was probably 1887 or 1888. The letters are as follows:

> My dear unforgettable son Hellik
> I would like to write you a few lines today but my hand shakes and the tears flow and especially since I see in your letter you are getting married. I was in hope you would come back to Norway but since you are not coming we must pray for each other that we will meet in Heaven. I also want to wish you from my heart A Blessed Marriage and may God watch over us all Amen.
> A few words to you Hellik you must see about Lauritz as good as you can when he is sick. So you are greeted from me and also your wife. As Solomon says, the one that gets a good wife he has a good thing.
> Greetings from your mother

My dear unforgettable son Lauris

You have no idea what my thoughts have been since I heard you were sick. A mother has to worry so much when she can't go see her children. So I want to tell you dear Laurits you must seek and pray to your dear Jesus while you are young. He is always willing to hear our prayers and if you get well don't forget to thank him each time. Read and study God's word each time you have a little spare time. So I will close my letter with hearty greetings to you. You are often in my thoughts and I have shed many tears now in these later years for my children. It is my wish that we all meet in Heaven with our Savior.

Your old mother

[Kari was 63 when these Norwegian letters were written to thirty-seven-year-old Hellik and twenty-three-year-old Lauris. Hellik never went back to Norway for a visit but Lauris went in 1914 and took his daughter Luella, fourteen years old, with him—his mother Kari had died in 1911]

Beside the Hellick and Josephine Larson family of five and descendants, Lewis and Laura Larson family of nine and descendants, the John and Minnie Jotten (the brother who took the name of the farm in Norway) family of five and descendants, we included military service stories; Larson-Jotten family reunions begun in 1927 and continued every two years (in 1990 there were eighty-one American relatives who went to the Stavanger area for a weekend reunion with approximately 200 Norwegian relatives); other relatives who came to live in America; relatives who have visited those in Norway or in America. Part II of the book is the Haaste-Larson family with genealogical charts going back to circa 1270 and the Jaatten-Jakobsen family.

We were almost ready to send the material to the printers when Mom woke up one morning saying she had to call her son, Bob, who now lived in our large family house and tell him to go to a certain place in the attic where he would find large photos of Kari Helleiksdatter, her father's mother, and Jakob Jakobsen Jaatun, her mother's father. Bob found them, sent them to us, and they were included along with many other photos.

What a privilege to work with my mother on our ancestry book: the *Larson-Jotten Family* book, *1972*. (In 1996 I received a phone call from a doctor in California who is related to one of the other relatives who came to America. For years he had been trying to get more information about this book—finally reaching me.) The interest in one's roots and the family tree continues on and on and on. It is another way of traveling beyond the fields.

12

Sabbatical to Study Music and Culture around the World, 1974

Lou Left ... Ruth Right

The sabbatical plans I had given to my school committee were approved and I was granted a six-month leave, at full pay, to study native cultures and music around the world. What a bonus after thirty years of teaching! I immediately phoned a dear friend, Ruth Hanson, from Boone, Iowa, who was a retired music teacher and asked her to join me. She finally said "Yes." Plans were made and in early August we began this world study tour. The year was 1974.

Ruth was in California visiting relatives; I was visiting a friend there too, before our scheduled meeting at the Los Angeles airport for the first leg of our journey. We both knew the departure time of our flight. I got to the airport first and was told the airline and the flight had both been changed and we would leave earlier. My luggage was checked in but Ruth was nowhere to be seen. There were still two more hours before the flight, except with the change there weren't! When she did arrive she later told me, "I was literally dragged out of the car, pushed down a corridor, and thrown into a plane, only to hear, 'You held up the whole flight!'" We arrived at our seats breathless and quickly fastened our seatbelts as the plane immediately taxied to the runway. Ruth looked at me and said, "What was that all about?" I told her our flight to Fiji had been changed and we almost missed the first plane of our six-month world trip. How was I to know that was only the beginning of several close calls?

The young man sitting beside me was from the Gilbert Islands in the Pacific. I didn't want to miss a chance to learn more about the lifestyle there so I asked him, "What does your father do for a living?" He informed me his father didn't work because, "There are fish in the sea and fruit on the trees so he doesn't have to work." I then knew that my study of cultures had already begun. He told me he was taking guitar lessons through the mail. That interested me because I, too, had taken piano lessons through the mail at age seven or eight after my bout with polio. I learned so much about his way of life and realized that this travel-study journey would be even more interesting than I had imagined.

We arrived in Fiji along with Ruth's luggage but mine arrived the following day and was brought to the hotel by the airline. (If I were to recall every day's events, this sabbatical story would never end; only highlights will be included.) Early the next morning we attended a church service a half-hour away from our hotel. As we got out of the taxi we could tell the service was about to begin, not by bells ringing but by the drumming on a slit drum (a large, long log hollowed out). What a beautiful sound as the morning sun peeked over the horizon. The congregational singing was strong and rich in tone, mostly unison. How I wished I had included more time in Fiji for study but we had a deadline to meet with the ISME, International Society of Music Educators Conference, in Perth, Australia, from August 5–12.

Australia

We flew to Sydney (on our return trip there we made five visits to the Sydney Opera House before we really appreciated the building, inside and outside); another flight across Australia took us to the west coast and Perth. We found our hotel, got settled, and looked forward to eight days of concerts, seminars, master classes, and lectures by renowned world musicians and professors from many countries. We were never disappointed in each day's very full schedule.

During the opening ceremony we sat beside a woman, Hazel Potts, from Perth (also studying music) and chatted before the program began. Above us in the balcony, facing the auditorium, were three almost-naked men, Australian Aboriginal musicians who began the ceremony playing a fanfare on three didjeridoos. This is a long hollowed-out piece of wood with no keys or holes. The sound was extremely low and most interesting. What a way to begin a twentieth-century music conference, with sounds from the distant past! Later another group of Aborigines used clapping sticks for rhythm with the didjeridoos. After the official opening speeches by the governor of Western Australia and others, a noted composer from the Soviet Union, Prof. Dmitri Kabalevsky, conducted the Australian Youth Orchestra in "Procession of the Meistersinger" by Wagner. Halfway through the music I realized they were not talking about the musicians in the opera but they chose that composition—and it meant us! *We* were the musicians who had come from all corners of the earth to share these days filled with music. Tears filled my eyes, and I realized how blessed and fortunate I was to be present!

When the ceremonies were finished our new friend, Hazel, insisted we go to lunch with her so we could taste a typical meat pie with tomato sauce. We accepted. The meat pie was delicious as we listened to Hazel tell us about Perth and her family.

When the afternoon session ended she urged us to go home with her for the evening meal. Reluctantly we again accepted her kind invitation. She lived twenty-two miles away and after stopping at a food store we finally arrived at her home and met her husband and three young children. French doors in one room opened to an outside garden. Soon a small animal, a brush-tail opossum, appeared outside the glass doors begging for food—the first wildlife I saw in Australia. After the opossum got some crumbs of bread he departed back into the woods behind the house. What an unexpected moment. . . . After a quick, delectable meal, the husband drove us back to Perth for the evening session, which would include more Aborigines dancing and playing instruments. He drove fast so we would arrive on time. Behind us we heard a police siren—meant for us. We stopped, got a speeding ticket, and arrived at the hall *after* the music began. (Ruth and I each shared the cost of the speeding ticket and gave them the money.) We also learned a lesson that day. Invitations were wonderful to receive, but we could not accept all that came our way or this sabbatical study would not evolve as I had envisioned it.

On August 9, 1974, before going to a music session we stopped at a store to look at opals, the beautiful stone with iridescent play of colors, mined in Australia. As we were strolling on the street we heard two ladies from Perth, dressed in lovely dresses, hats, and gloves, talking to each other. One said, ''We have no bread and no butter but *they* have no president!'' That was how we learned that President Nixon had resigned. The reference to ''no bread and no butter'' meant there was a transport strike in the country and the locals didn't get all the necessary food.

There was also a flood in parts of Australia and a train derailment made us stay in Perth two extra days, making it possible to tour the surrounding area after ISME ended. Headlines of the newspaper said, ''Transport strike—Perth will be in crisis by weekend''; however, by the weekend the strike was settled. We took our baggage to the train terminal where we sat all day outside in the wind and cold—waiting. When the train arrived it was a composite of the Indian Pacific and two trans-Australian trains and approximately one mile in length . . . due to the flood. We climbed aboard, found our seats and stared out the windows trying to see kangaroos. We saw three small gray ones hopping near the tracks. The track bed was rough and the train stopped often during the night to deliver food to settlements. Somehow night slowly disappeared into the next day. In the morning we were served morning tea in our very small compartment, too tiny for both of us so Ruth quickly dressed and left. I came down from the upper berth, dressed, found the dining car, and had breakfast with Ruth: orange juice, compote of fruit, steak with mushroom sauce, toast, and tea. Again we went to the lounge to try to see wildlife. We saw ten kangaroos. An Australian man said we were lucky because, "They hang around the fence for a while and then they carry on." We also saw a few brumbies (wild horses) and some large soaring birds. The Nullarbor plain was treeless with little activity.

We finally arrived forty-five and a half hours later in Adelaide. Because we were late we missed the city tour and immediately had to join our scheduled coach tour to the outback. The redeeming feature was the fact Australia had had so much rain, wildflowers were blooming that white man had not seen for a hundred years. The thirty-three Australians on the tour took it for that reason. The desert was covered with fields of flowers: white paper daisies, wild red hops, lavender Salvation Jane, yellow daisies, lamb's tails, and kangaroo paws. We often stopped to look closely at special flowers such as the Sturt Desert Pea with the black "eyes" in the middle of the bright red bloom, sometimes having tea at the same time. Ruth and I were the only Americans and soon became part of the friendly, hospitable Aussies.

Some days were long, beginning at 6 A.M. and arriving at our hotel or motel built right at a cattle station (ranch) at 7 P.M., but each day offered new sights and sounds. Coober Pedy, one of the richest opal fields in the world, had people living in cavehouses because it was so hot, sometimes 125°. There was even a church underground. We saw how opals were cut, duplet, triplet, or solid, and saw a private opal collection. It was impossible to describe the range of colors—a fiery rainbow caught in a small stone? Perhaps. While there I looked at the sky and saw the Southern Cross constellation for the first time.

Watching for birds I was delighted to see so many in the outback: white cockatoos, galahs, green budgerigars, kites, kestrals, Mulga parrots, topknot pigeons, willy wagtails, magpies, kookaburras, and many others.

126

Any bushes or trees we drove by seemed to have a flock that would fly around, finally settling in another bush. Often we had lunch beside trees with the "billy" boiling in a pail over the camp fire; it was the "Waltzing Matilda" song come to life!

As we were waiting to get off the bus near Ayres Rock, our guide-driver told us there was a little problem here. We should not have any food in our motel rooms and we would be fine and the mice wouldn't bother us. That is what he told us! Our assigned room 23 was at the end of the old block of rooms at the Uluru Hotel. I was in the bathroom when I heard Ruth scream. I yelled, "Ruth, what's the matter?" She said a mouse had just run across the floor. Soon a second mouse ran and I screamed! We placed our cases on the beds, pulled up the spreads (mice don't get on beds, we were told), and left the room for the evening meal. As we were eating, we noticed the carpet around the edge near the walls moving and I realized mice were here, too. Ruth said, "I wonder if they are in the kitchen." I said, "Ruth, don't even think about the kitchen!" We then went back to the room and I began opening my tote bag on top of the spread and mice leaped out, running here and there. It was just awful!

Our evening's entertainment was a slide show, at another hotel, showing the range of colors possible at sunset on Ayres Rock. This phenomenon on the one-and-a-half-mile-long monolith rising out of the plains made a fascinating slide show but we were more concerned with the mice. We had already told our guide about all the mice in our room but we felt he didn't believe us. After the show Ruth and I went back to our room, and at the insistence of another tour member, Tom Deane, the guide also came to see the problem. When Ruth touched her bag, mice jumped out and ran everywhere. That was too much for me and I went outside and wept hysterically. I wouldn't go back to that room for anything! I would rather stand up all night or sleep in the bus, except that was where our bus driver was spending the night (he knew a safe place). Tom and the guide decided we *really* did have a problem so they called the manager, who found us a vacant staff room. The staff couple had left that very day so it had not been cleaned, but we moved in anyway, hoping it was free of mice. We kept the lights on all night, placed the spread on the floor against the door, lay down on the beds with our clothes on, and tried to sleep. I kept my glasses on expecting to find beady eyes staring back at me. None did. Somehow, sleep finally came.

The next morning we heard many stories from other tour members—a small leather purse had been almost "eaten" during the night; other items in other rooms had been chewed on. Because our first room had been in the old section and at the end, mice had gnawed holes in the walls to get inside. Yes, this was a *mouse plague* and was caused by the rains and floods. People at the hotel said, "This is nothing. You ought to be here when the snakes come, followed by the wild cats." All I could think of were the families camping and living in tents nearby! Ayres Rock was one of a kind; so was the mouse plague. . . .

After two terrible nights at Ayres Rock we arrived at Wallara Ranch *and* civilization, with napkins on the table, deodorizer in the bathroom, and a heating pad under the sheet, which had been turned on when we arrived. Ruth and I celebrated by taking hot showers, fixing our nails, wearing our pearls and a different pants suit to dinner. Yes, this was wonderful after our recent experiences. The following day we arrived at Alice Springs with traffic, cars, and many people. Our room at the Territory Hotel had a refrigerator, a toaster, an electric pot for boiling water, coffee, tea, sugar, and cream; a TV, radio with three channels, a bed and a couch with purple and turquoise drapes and carpet. What a paradise after the week in the Australian outback and people forever having problems: too little water, too much water, dust, plagues, supplies not coming through. What a challenge to wake up each day to those unknown adventures. I admire their tenacity.

The outback trip was taken so I could learn more about the Aborigines or indigenous people there. In Alice Springs many were aimlessly wandering about the town or sitting on benches in the park, on the ground, or in the church yard. Many of them do work but when the urge comes upon them, they leave and "walkabout" for an indefinite period. It is hard for them to retain their traditional way of life and they haven't yet become a part of the latter part of the twentieth century. Tradition is very strong and many places are sacred to them. The twentieth century really seems to be destroying them. I asked our driver-guide about these people and he would not discuss them at all. I finally found an anthropologist studying them who told me she saw a girl in a trance/coma/unconscious for several days because a "bone" had been pointed at her. No one knew *who* points the "bone" but it happens. Nurses finally brought her back but later a "feather-hair" moccasin was thrown through her window and she went into the trance again. "Feather-hair" shoes are put on when someone goes out to commit some evil deed—they leave no mark on trail. I was told many other interesting stories. Finally in 1995 I read a book, *Mutant Message,* by Marlo Morgan, and understood better these fascinating people through her adventure with them on a 120-day walkabout. Primitive, native, tribal (whatever term one uses) peoples have much to teach us.

I did collect musical instruments during this study tour and wanted a didjeridoo but was told it would have to fit into a post-bag for mailing. Three times I took one to the Alice Springs post office, but they were too long for the bag; the last one was approximately three feet and I purchased it because it fit. There are typical Aboriginal paintings of black fish with white lines that cross on the outside. The opening one blows through is so large it is almost impossible to make a sound on it; the Aborigines make unusual sounds as they sit on the ground with the end of the didjeridoo touching their bare toes, which is the proper way of playing and the proper length.

Just as one is beginning to learn more about culture, environment, and traditions of a region, it is time to move on for glimpses of another country. Before leaving for our flight to Cairns I bought a newspaper to read as we flew 7000 feet over the desert and rocky hills. Our plane was a Connair DeHaviland Heron with four propellers and had fifteen passengers. I opened the paper and read that Col. Charles Lindbergh had died in Hawaii at age seventy-two. What sad news that was for me. I always thought perhaps our paths would cross and I could shake his hand. Memories came flooding back. A colt was born on our farm in Iowa the same day he made his historic flight across the Atlantic in 1927; we named the colt "Lindy." Later, in 1932, when I was nine, his young son was kidnapped. Someone in our family said that it would be wonderful if we found the child on our front porch. Every morning when I awakened I would rush downstairs to see if the child was there . . . he never was. Years later while living on Long Island, my husband and I drove to Hopewell, New Jersey, and saw the Lindberg home in the woods and the window used for the kidnapping. Now, here I was in a foreign land *flying* as I read about this American aviation hero from Minnesota. Strange. . . .

Papua New Guinea

Cairns, on the Great Barrier Reef, was the takeoff point for Papua New Guinea. (My travel agent in New York had made arrangements for every part of this six-month, sixteen-country, five-continent world tour with hotel and plane reservations, all paid for.) Upon arriving at the Cairns Airport we were told the plane had already gone to Port Moresby, the capital. I couldn't believe what they were telling us! I was so looking forward to learning more about these "Stone Age" people and would *not* cancel this part of my study tour. I talked to authorities and the only way we could catch up with our New Guinea tour was to charter a private plane. So that is what happened, at the cost of another $300. Up in the small craft we flew along the coast looking down at the turquoise-colored waters of the barrier reef, a never-to-be-forgotten sight.

We finally arrived at Port Moresby and read a message in our hotel that said, "Are your valuables under lock and key? Our house-safe is the safest place. . . . Unfortunately we have had cases of theft in suites while guests were sleeping with their entry door unlocked. We must, therefore, request you lock or chain all doors in your suite. Do not allow members of the staff into your room before 7:30 A.M. Should you be suspicious of any staff member entering your room, phone the reception desk immediately." This warning was found only in the hotels in the territorial capital, Port Moresby. The heat and humidity were overpowering but the tropical flowers, especially orchids, were exquisite.

The day after our late arrival we flew with our tour group to the highlands to Goroka where people were more isolated. Most wore traditional dress: women had a waistband with hanging leaves in front and back (when they became soiled, fresh leaves replaced them) and nothing on top: Some wore a loose dress which covered their breasts. Men wore a loincloth, or a penis sheath made from a long gourd, with bead or bone necklaces, feathers, and often paint decorations on their faces. As we drove in our minibus we saw three large opened roasted pigs beside the road; our guide told us it was part of the "bride price," and I thought what a pocketful of memories this day would bring.

Then we saw the young bride walking to the groom's village with women and children from her village with her. She had a somber decorated face with black and red lines, a huge feathered headdress of black, white, and red feathers and long beige feathers streaming out of the top. A fur piece covered her breasts and she wore the band of leaves in front and behind. She was barefoot. On her upper arms were tied long leaves and in the armband money was sticking out. This handsome group posed for several photos, and when I placed some dollar bills in the armband, a loud shout of approval came forth from those with her. A woman then took the money I had just given her and gave it to another woman. (I don't know why she did that and I hoped that the bride would eventually get the money.)

We drove to the boys' village and were told four brides would arrive that day. The sisters of the grooms-to-be were the welcoming committee—one with a hand drum, another had a cane decorated with poinsettias, another had a gun (our guide said he had never seen a gun before as part of the ceremony). On the ground were mats covered with poincianas, poinsettias, and hibiscus, with four posts behind the mats where gifts were hanging, as well as a large slab of meat. They were not quite ready for the brides' arrivals, so we left and drove to Makehuku Village to see the grotesque "Mud Men" perform their ghostly slow dance in a clearing of their village. Fifteen men with grey mud smeared all over their bodies and grey mud masks covering their entire heads slowly walked out from a round house. Not a word was spoken as they silently shuffled their feet and waved leaves back and forth in their hands . . . walking right up to us. Yes, it was spooky and unearthly. Finally they took off the masks and we saw brown-bearded men sweating profusely. Next they shot arrows from bows trying to hit a target, but most arrows missed the mark. They started a fire by pulling string under a round stick near moss; soon there was smoke. Artifacts for sale included combs, boar's tusk necklaces, arrows with three prongs, bamboo mouth harps—all interesting. (I was so excited to see the Mud Men dance that when I put a new film in my camera it didn't wind. The only photos from this unusual event are photos in my mind's eye.)

The next day our six-passenger plane landed at Omakali, the steepest airstrip in New Guinea, set on a gradient of 13.5 percent in very rugged mountains. How thankful we were for our Australian pilot at the controls; nevertheless, the landing was scary. From the plane I took a photo of a native wearing a loincloth on his body, but his face had two long curved boar's tusks through his nose and a large round piece hanging from his septum. From ear to ear was another white bone and a large white necklace was around his neck. On his head was a band with dark spiky feathers—he was a most unusual sight! When I got out of the plane he posed for two more photos. I offered him sweets (wrapped candies) but he wouldn't take them. He asked for one dollar, so I gave it to him. I then walked over to get a better photo of the airstrip and talked to the pilot and a friend on the tour. She wanted her picture with this man and the pilot asked him to pose with her but he would not. I said I had given

131

him a dollar; the pilot was furious and started yelling at the man saying, "Did she give you a dollar?" The old man slowly replied, "She no give money." I couldn't believe my ears! No one had ever lied before, right in front of me. I certainly did not want an incident so I said, "Just forget it."

Then we heard this story. The day before we arrived a native was driving a tractor near the airstrip and another native fell in front of the tractor and was unavoidably killed. The people standing around *axed* the driver of the tractor to death. This is called "payback" even though all these men were from the same tribe. The villagers were expecting police to be on the plane to settle the dispute, however, our plane carried only tourists. Ten minutes was long enough under these circumstances. We took off fast!

Our flight took us to Chimbu, where we boarded a van driving on serpentine roads, the worst roads I have ever been on anywhere in the world, to a village where a pig feast was taking place. We watched the men take the pigs out of the pit where they had been cooked with hot stones and leaves; vegetables were cooked in a huge oil drum. The women take care of the gardens, the children, and the pigs. In fact, if there isn't enough milk from the mother pig, the woman will suckle the baby pig. Pigs are *very important* in their culture. The men used to be the hunters and warriors but there are few animals and infrequent clan wars now—some find work in the towns and cities and many were unemployed.

We then flew in a nineteen-passenger plane to the hot and humid north coast to Madang. Our "Smugglers' Inn" was next to the sea. We visited a village where pottery was made, but my favorite experience here was talking with young teenagers about their education at Tusbab High School. The hours spent with these young men gave us a true insight into their problems, hopes, and dreams. They even showed us a bat hanging from a tree in the schoolyard.

Back up in a small plane flying over mountains, ridges, and rivers to Amboin where we landed on a grassy airstrip and got into a boat for a ten-mile river trip. Once there, we had to climb a steep bank with narrow dirt slots for one's feet. A short ride in the back of a truck (only one and a half miles of road exist here) to Karawari Lodge, built on a high ridge—just like most of the native villages so they can watch for their enemy from this vantage point. The view from our individual thatched roof hut's balcony over the Sepik plains was splendid.

After lunch a motor launch took us to the Kundiman village, where everyone was dressed in few clothes but much paint and many feathers. We watched them chop sago fibers from a palm tree trunk and even tasted the sago flat bread right off hot rocks. As I walked around the village I saw a one-headed drum and told the man I would like to buy it. Word came back to me that the owner of the drum was away from the village hunting for three days. The drum could not be sold without his permission. (Later I bought a model of the drum in Port Moresby.) There were many kinds of carvings for sale and I bought six. When I look at my collection of them on my living room wall, memories of this day spent in a New Guinea village fill my mind.

We then flew to Mount Hagen, the main center of the western highlands; the altitude was 5600 feet. We visited the market and enjoyed the "sing-sing" when people from many villages come together for festival. All were dressed in their fantastic headdress wigs with colored ornamental feathers; their paint decorations as they sang and danced made this the highlight for me. Later we had a terrible rainstorm during the night and a slight earthquake in the morning, but it didn't stop us from driving to a bird sanctuary and wildlife exhibit.

Finally we arrived again in Port Moresby for the last days. There I met a teacher who had studied five years in Australia and the United States. He said, "My people have kept the environment for me; therefore, it was not hard to go back home to my village." He told me so much about his people and the importance of "magic" in their culture; that "shell money" is a bond between a couple and the two families, etc., etc. I would never understand these people, but I was so thankful for the opportunity to visit them and their country. Papua New Guinea received its independence one year after my visit, in 1975, and ready or not, they are now part of the "larger world." I wish them every success as an independent nation!

New Zealand

In Auckland, New Zealand, we visited a friend, Alma Bellman, who had lived in Boone, Iowa, when I was teaching there twenty-four years ago. It was good to see her again as she showed us her lovely city, including lunch at her home. To meet a friend in this pastoral land of green, of grazing sheep, of quiet beauty was a real gift for Ruth and me.

A coach tour then drove us to parts of this North Island. In Rotorua we saw the culture of the Maori village, the museum, and enjoyed a concert of dance and song. One morning a couple of men on our tour went fishing in the lake in front of our hotel and I joined them early in the morning. Yes, we caught enough fish for our breakfast, which the hotel kitchen staff graciously prepared. Yummy! While in Rotorua I had a problem with a tooth. While in the dentist chair he lowered the chair so I was looking at the ceiling—a large picture was up there. Why not have something for a patient to look at during the drilling? Now one gets earphones and beautiful music to keep out the sound. . . .

Another place we saw a live sheep exhibit, which showed us the many breeds of sheep. I found this extremely interesting. My father raised sheep on our Iowa farm; perhaps this brought back "farm memories." We also visited a cave to see the glowworms shining brightly all over the walls and ceilings. No sound could be made or they would stop glowing; a rather strange experience. There was no time to visit the mountainous South Island and I have always regretted that. From Wellington we flew back to Sydney. (When our plane had arrived in Auckland we had to sit in the plane while officials sprayed the entire plane's cabins. It was not pleasant at all. I was so glad when we left New Zealand without that custom.)

Bali

How good to be in Bali again and hear the gamelan orchestra: in the lobby of the hotels, at the traditional dance performances, the *wayang* or shadow plays, almost everywhere. The clang, gentle tones, harsh tones, high pitched ring, played on gong chimes, xylophones, gongs, and drums permeated the island of Bali. I was told there is a gamelan orchestra for every 250 inhabitants. The magic of Oriental music was strongly felt. We happened to be there during a religious festival where processions of women carrying fruit or vegetables on their heads were everywhere. Wherever we traveled during that week we saw stately processions of people going to the temples.

My goal was to visit the Conservatory of Music in Denpasar, where I had the pleasure of meeting the director, Dr. Pandji. He showed me many rooms where students were taking tests on their instruments. I asked many questions about the training program and also found out that each gamelan orchestra is tuned to its own scale. Dr. Pandji gave me two autographed books, one in Balinese notation and one in both Balinese and Western notation for my school's comparative cultural collection. Yes, Bali is the artistic island and I truly hope I can again visit that beautiful paradise in our world.

Singapore

Our travel agent had reluctantly made reservations at Hotel Raffles in Singapore. At my insistance, she finally took my advice; of course, I wanted to stay at the historic hotel, built in 1886, where Somerset Maugham and Rudyard Kipling had once lived for a time. Upon arrival in our suite we found our names printed on the two sets of hotel station- ary! (And she didn't want us to come here.) The entire suite oozed ele- gance from another era, the hotel has since been remodeled and refurbished.

We phoned the brother-in-law of my dear Chinese friend, Mary. She and I met at Columbia University in 1958, after she escaped from China with her son, where we were both students. Dr. Ling invited us to have lunch with him the following day at 1 P.M. His wife already had another luncheon engagement. When we finished with the morning city tour he was waiting for us with his car and driver. We drove to the Phoenix Hotel and took the elevator to the sixth floor to the Dragon Room. On the phone he told us he wanted to take us to a restaurant that served a dumpling filled with soup, a speciality. As we were seated at a table, Chinese waitresses would walk by with carts of food to show Dr. Ling. He decided if we should eat that food or wait for the next cart—sometimes he said "yes," sometimes "no." Beside the steamed dumplings filled with soup and dipped in ginger sauce (they were delicious and most unusual) we had sweet and sour cabbage with peanuts, spare ribs, chicken with mushrooms, and much more. As we were enjoying the tasty morsels he told us about his life—living in China and attending college in 1924 in United States at Cornell and Columbia where he met Helen. However, before they were married she wanted to see China. Apparently she liked it, because they were married in 1927. Recently he worked as a consultant on government projects, especially in agriculture. He had been invited by the prime minister of Tonga to help with problems in their agriculture. He also told us he and Helen would tour Kashmir and Nepal in a few weeks. I must say Ruth and I were happy to have lunch with this handsome Chinese man, who was seventy-seven years young!

After lunch we drove to Helen's Jewelry Shop and met a charming woman dressed in a purple print dress, lavender jade ear rings, and bracelet, and short white hair. Three other women were in the shop who had attended their wedding forty-six years ago (one now lives in Thailand). Helen showed us her shop of exquisite gold, jade, pearl jewelry; another salesgirl took us upstairs to see pottery 4–5000 years old, jade pieces on stands, snuff bottles, silks, batik paintings, furniture, wall hangings. It was like a museum. After Ruth bought a beautiful jade pendant with cutout designs, we said our thank yous and good-byes for those hours we shared with this talented, friendly, and successful couple in Singapore. (Four years before I had visited Singapore but was too ill to appreciate it, which made this visit even more memorable.)

Thailand

Bangkok. What a change since my first trip here in 1952, when I saw open sewers beside the roads and garbage and dead dogs floating in the canals. Four of us had made arrangements with a Thai guide to show us an opium den, arriving through a door with a beaded curtain to keep the insects out, but the children ran in and out. We were shown a wealthy man who lay on a cot smoking his opium pipe—skin and bones . . . what a terrible sight. His wealth had disappeared as had his health. These pictures flooded my mind as we drove to our Siam Intercontinental Hotel. Bangkok was much cleaner but pollution was very bad because of all the cars, buses, trucks, bicycles on the streets. It was also damp, hot, and sticky, so the hotel air conditioning was much appreciated. Again the shops were filled with gold, gems, bangles, necklaces, Thai silk—how could one resist?

A must on this trip was a visit to Jim Thompson's home, made from seven Thai houses put together to make one house. Each room had exquisite Thai furniture—antiques of all kinds. His white cockatoo was still in a large cage, but Mr. Thompson was not around. Why? He was an American "silk king" who built a fortune in beautiful Thai cloth and had several silk shops. One Easter he was visiting friends in the Cameron highlands of Malaysia, had dinner with the friends, and told them he was going for a stroll in the jungle. He was never seen again. He did not take his heart medicine with him, a clue that he meant to be back soon. More than one hundred policemen, soldiers, and civilian volunteers searched throughout the night, but there was no trace of this best-known American millionaire in Southeast Asia. To this day no one knows what happened to him. His Thai home-museum is now open to the public. What a legacy he left—what a sad, unsolved story.

The following morning we were up at 5:50 A.M. to be ready for the *klong* (canal) trip at 7:10 A.M. A bus drove us through not-too-heavy traffic (yet) to a small boat with three Thais: the boat operator, a young boy who helped with docking, and a guide. Some observations and comparisons I made: much less native boat traffic; no dyed material hanging because the company went bankrupt; the same gentleman was greeting everyone as people went by in boats; stones had been placed along the canal's edge so mud and dirt stay in place. We stopped at the Temple of the Dawn and noticed the scaffolding was gone but boys were still glueing broken dishes with designs on the sides of the temple. It somehow looked old and decayed and not as lovely as when I saw it twenty-two years ago. The original broken dishes had come from a shipwreck, but now the boys broke dishes for the repair.

I was in a shop that sold musical instruments when Professor Dansunandana was also there. We talked about instruments, flutes and strings, and decided on a lesson the following day with the mouth organ (*khan*). I was late from a tour but he was waiting. A receptionist told us to go to the mezzanine to play the flutes. He played one and I tried to play the other; they were tuned slightly different. He taught me the scale and we worked on ''Auld Lang Syne.'' Soon a hotel manager came up and said there were many complaints from guests and we should go to the pool area. We did—but there were too many guests at the pool, so we found a bench by the water where pelicans and geese were cavorting. He taught me there for one hour and again Sunday at 10:00 A.M. at the same place. However, it soon began raining so we had to move to the shelter of the hotel. This time he brought a two-string instrument with a carved coconut shell (*saw duang*). If only we could *really* talk about his music and culture, I would learn so much. The king of Thailand gave him his name, and when President Nixon was there, his group performed for him. Yes, I bought the *khan* and the *saw duang* and two *kraus* or flutes from Thailand . . . and have memories of a professor who quietly tried to teach an American how to play them near a hotel pool in Bangkok.

A visit to the Rose Garden auditorium showed visitors what Thailand had to offer: fingernail dance with twenty Thai girls, Thai boxing, Thai wedding, cock fighting, *Karen* dance with boys and girls, sword and long-pole fighting with sparks flying from the blades. Outside we saw two bulls fight, a folk dance on the green, and finally elephants moved teak logs into water and pushed them out.

With the heat and humidity outside and the cool air inside, Ruth developed a cough which the doctor said was bronchitis; my throat was getting sore, too. It was time for a visit to the beauty salon at our hotel, where we had our hair washed and set. The heat from the dryer was what we needed and it felt so good. Also we each had a massage. The masseuse covered our naked bodies with cream, massaging us for one hour. This was followed by a bubble bath in a full tub of warm water. What a treat and just what our bodies required for the next part of our adventure.

India

Our early Thai Airlines flight took us to Calcutta, India. We cleared customs, got rupees for dollars at the bank, and were told to take a taxi to the domestic airport. An old taxi with driver drove and drove—no airport was in sight. We again told him we wanted Air India to Madras. He turned the taxi around and drove back to the domestic terminal. Where was he taking us? Was there a Madras Hotel in Calcutta? Strange!

With three hours to wait before our next flight, we decided to see the city. The tourist information booth gave us a list of places to see, also telling the driver what to show us. Our luggage was placed in "Left Luggage" and we were off, with the driver and a second man in the front seat. My first glimpse of Calcutta: a sign "We demand life sentence for black marketeers and horders"; hundreds of men pulling rickshaws; manure "patties" drying in the sun on the sides of bridges or in the middle of the four-lane roads; a sudden downpour and people scattered to find shelter; Hooghly River had large boats docked at its banks; brick streets with terrible potholes, dirt, mud, and garbage; docile and contented cows walking or lying down anywhere; Howrah bridge crossing at noon with a traffic jam of people pulling loaded carts, rickshaws, trucks, stalled cars with engine trouble or flat tires, people waking, people selling items along the side, etc., etc. . . . . Our taxi kept weaving in and out of lanes to get ahead, the horn constantly blowing, yet no one got hit and somehow the traffic got untangled: the school buses, street cars, public carrier trucks, gas trucks, trishaws, loaded buses with people hanging outside, motorcycles. What an experience for Ruth and me. After stopping at a BP gas station for five liters of petrol, we continued in our old taxi full of rattles and a door handle which fell off, but he was a good driver. Then I heard a bumping sound and knew it was a flat tire. In fifteen minutes the second man with us replaced the tire with another tire with no tread. How long would that last? Along the street another sign read: "Long Live Indira Gandhi"; at a new apartment building was a sign: "To serve the People of Calcutta—It is Your Property, so Help protect It"; "Help Us to Beautify Calcutta."

After this two-and-a-half-hour tour of Calcutta, we paid the driver and tipped the second man, got our luggage and checked it, and sat down with all the others waiting for the same plane. The room was extremely hot even though a few ceiling fans slowly moved. Soon we were called for security check where women went into a small room, one by one, for a body check and hand-baggage check. Again we sat down to wait. An announcement finally said our plane had technical trouble and would be delayed thirty minutes; then forty-five minutes. Talking to those around us we realized we had a little United Nations group—Germany, England, USSR, U.S.A.—all here in Calcutta. While visiting another announcement said, "Plane to Madras is cancelled for today." Ruth and I didn't take that too kindly since we were hot, had had no food since breakfast, were tired, and had too much luggage. Back to the ticket counter to have our tickets returned with an attached ticket for tomorrow's 1 P.M. flight and a voucher for a hotel for the night. This took a couple of hours because we also had to retrieve all our luggage. Finally we got on a bus for the downtown hotels. I sat beside a mechanical engineer who played the Indian flute in a group. He called notes pure (naturals), soft (flat notes), sharp (sharp) notes; I found this conversation very interesting.

The streets were packed with people dressed in white. Our bus horn was constantly blowing as were all the other horns. We moved at a snail's pace, eventually arriving at the terminal, where I refused to get out. Our friend, Christina, went for information but the door was locked on that side. She almost stepped on two babies lying on the ground behind two motorcycles. The next door was open and she was told the bus would take us to our hotel. We were then driven to the Grand Hotel as our voucher stipulated. We walked into a high-ceilinged, huge lobby and were given room 204. The porters took our luggage on their heads up the stairs while we rode in the lift (elevator) with the lift operator. The door to 204 was opened and we couldn't believe our eyes—the suite was fit for a maharaja! There were four rooms plus the bathroom, which had a scale (in all my travels that was a first and the only). Green plants and fresh flowers were on tables, a refrigerator was in the kitchen area; what luxury. So much space for just two people, Ruth and I wished we could invite some of the teaming thousands outside in the streets. Why were we so privileged?

This hotel was one hundred years old and from another era. We walked to another spacious dining room for our first Indian dinner. Here was a dance floor with a nine-piece band: sax, trumpets, drums, piano, and a singer—music throughout the dinner hour. Only a couple of other tables were occupied. After the delicious meal we took the lift up to our room, filled the huge oldfashioned tub with warm water and soaked, one by one, and I could hardly wait my turn. We both felt so relaxed and hoped we could get through the problems tomorrow would bring. When I closed my eyes to sleep I only saw the multitudes of humanity on the streets. This is called "culture shock." My first night in India really made it come to me. Would I ever get used to all the people? I pondered that thought for most of the night. The breakfast next morning of tomato juice, porridge with hot milk, an egg and bacon, toast, and tea made me feel again that "All is right with the world."

The next day the bus never came to take us to the airport; we called a taxi and arrived to begin the whole process over again. We received vouchers for lunch in the cafeteria because our plane was again delayed. At 4 P.M. we finally boarded the plane after being searched and frisked—twenty-six hours late. On board the Indian Airline hostesses passed around a tray of goodies—wrapped candies, a small container with cotton for our ears, and a bowl of *somf* (anise seeds) to chew. We were given a glass of lemonade once we were at cruising speed, an hour later tea with three crackers and three cookies.

Madras, at last. We proceeded into the terminal and immediately heard our names called over the loudspeaker. An Indian man, also on the plane, led us to the area where we should report; the manager of our Madras hotel was there to meet and greet us (he had also been there the previous day). On the way to the hotel he asked us if we wanted the "standard" or "deluxe" room. We said "standard" but once we got there we changed our minds for the "deluxe" at 85 rupees a day ($10.00).

A taxi and driver showed us Madras: museums; South Beach Road with tall buildings and a wide sandy beach at the Bay of Bengal; Fort Saint George, a trading settlement in 1683 by the British East India Company; San Thome Cathedral, where we stepped inside for a moment even though there was a funeral service; coming out a beggar came for *baksheesh* (money) but I had decided I would *not* give money to anyone—a lesson learned at Macao in 1952. Deep in the narrow streets we stopped at a Hindu temple. I opened the car door to see the beautiful carvings better and saw a man walk toward our taxi with a large snake around his shoulders and a small gourd flute in his hand. I quickly closed the door, rolled up the window, and told Ruth to get back in the car. We told the driver it was too late for photos and to drive away. By now the man had covered his snake and shoulders with a beige burlap bag. There never is an end to surprises as one travels, but I wanted nothing to do with snakes! Madras had many beautiful buildings with uncrowded streets even though there were bullock carts, cows, water buffalo, and people everywhere.

Ruth remembered she had received an address of a man in Madras when she was in her nephew's bank in California. She had told the teller she would be in Madras and he said she should phone his father, so she did. He told Ruth, "It is my duty to show you my country." He said he would send his car for us the next day. We were up early for breakfast so we would be ready between 8:30–9:00 A.M. to meet Mr. Govindarajan, a partner in Venus Films. Soon he arrived, dressed in a white suit, so we left with his driver and went to his office. There we met another man, Mr. Chari, and found out they produced one–two pictures a year in Hindi and several in other languages. We also saw trophies they had won for their films. Plans were made for the day with another employee. The driver took us to the largest studio in Asia with ten different locations for shooting. We waited for our permission to enter beside a huge red Packard Super-Eight car which had a seal on the windshield, "Govt. of India." We later learned that the car belonged to the leading hero of Telegu Films. After our permission was granted we watched several scenes being filmed—a desert area with several couples at tables, drinking and dancing (canned music). There were several retakes: lights off, fans on, fans off, and lights on, etc. I had never seen a film in progress before and found all the activity most interesting with makeup people combing hair, putting powder here and there, even bringing glasses of water for the actors.

Next we were driven to another studio with the interior of a huge beautiful home of the 1800s. There was a wide stairway, upstairs corridors, library, living room with all kinds of chairs and couches covered in purple materials. Our guide introduced us to the cameraman, who took us over to the leading lady, Laxim. She was gracious and asked us to sit down so we could talk as we sipped tea. She was planning to visit New Jersey next May, where her uncle lived. I invited her to come to my high school and she said she would be delighted to come. She had been an actress for five years . . . "At first it was a hobby but now it is my profession." Interesting that in this film, *Babu,* she played the part of a teacher. It would take sixty more days to complete. The film was in color and was a talking film so someone would shout, "Silence." During one of the takes I got a coughing spell and could hardly wait for the break so I could cough—what a terrible thing to happen when a guest at a movie set!

We then drove to a recording studio and sat near the man listening and watching the controls and mixer. A large orchestra was in front of us, divided into sections, with the conductor in the middle and the playing and the orchestra was synchronizing the music to the action. Three times they repeated the same music, finally stopping for a break. Each of us had been given an orange Fanta drink as we watched and listened. This was a good time to leave the studio after thank yous and good-byes to those in charge.

The driver drove us to the Indian Airlines office for confirmation of our next flight, then to the State Bank of India to change money—7.98 rupees for each dollar (in 1995 it is approximately thirty-three). Finally we drove to Victoria Technical Institute to see the exquisite articles, especially the carved wooden elephants, and the bicentennial exhibition of Gandhi with batiks, paintings, carvings, pearl inlay in statues, etc. We each bought a wool wall hanging here as a keepsake for this special day in Madras. And what a day it had been! Such hospitality from strangers in this faraway foreign land called India.

The following day a taxi drove us to Kalakshetra, a college of fine arts, at the edge of Madras. (When doing research in preparation for my sabbatical, Dr. Curtis, a professor and authority on Indian music, had told me to be sure to visit this institution.) The previous day, Mr. Chari had made three phone calls before he reached the correct office; exams were being given but an appointment was made for us at 9:30 A.M. Miss Parthi was at the door of the office to welcome us, and we had a short visit. She suggested Janardhanan, a dancer-performer-teacher, guide us.

In one room we saw four girls practicing the *veena* sitting on mats on the floor, all playing the same tune. No teacher was present. Another room had eight girls dressed in saris learning the same folk dance, with the teacher dressed in white sitting on the floor mat beating a stick on a rectangular wooden block for rhythm. A girl beside him had a book with words and they sang the song, stopping and starting many times as the dancers slowly progressed with the steps. All the rooms seemed to have students practicing instruments or dances. She told us the day begins with prayers at 8:30 A.M. under an enormous banyan tree; if it rains they go to the recital hall. Approximately eighty-two students attend classes in the morning. In the afternoon younger children come to practice There were thirty-two teachers and performers. The subjects taught were different kinds of dances (*bharatanatyam, kathakali,* folk dances); vocal music; Indian instruments; English and Sanskrit were compulsory. (I decided it was much like our American Interlochen Arts Academy in Michigan with many buildings on many acres away from people and cities.) Even though the students had a two-week holiday the teacher-performers had to stay and work on a new dance-drama the founder of the school was composing.

The weather was so hot in South India we had to return to our hotel for a rest and toast and tea before we could take a taxi to an Indian concert as Srinivasa Sastry Hall in a suburb of Madras. After going to the wrong hall, we finally found the right one with a library downstairs where many people were reading at tables. High up along the border were many portraits—in the middle was Nehru and to his right was a portrait of John F. Kennedy! How welcome that made us feel! After paying ten rupees each for the concert tickets, we went upstairs and sat in the second row of chairs on the side. First a girl sang a prayer while everyone stood, followed by an introduction and giving the traditional lei of flowers to the speaker and the singer. After a ten-minute speech honoring the late composer, the performers began the concert. The singer was one of the best performers of Karnatic music so the room was filled to capacity. This was my first concert in India, however, I had attended many Indian concerts in New York. An Indian beside me whispered, "All traditional Indian music are prayers to God." As I listened the voice sang, the instrument imitated it, all the while the drone of the *tambura* was heard, along with the *tabla* (drums). To me it sounded like improvisation by a contralto, sometimes singing two tones at once. The music was interesting but so far removed from Western music I doubted I would ever understand the structure of the *raga* or the beats in a *tala,* but the total sound was appealing to me. At this recital one *raga* lasted from 6:30 to 7:50, almost one and one-half hours. It appeared this would be a concert lasting far into the night. We left before it was over.

Sunday we had breakfast in our sitting room and relaxed, but the new Taj Coromandel Hotel beckoned us for the rest of the day. This hotel had been opened only six months so most of the shops were still empty. We sat in the lobby writing in our journals and letters to our family in the beautiful setting of blue-purple-green couches and carpets, wood paneling, and interesting chandeliers, as we listened to Western classical music permeating the room. How good it was to hear Chopin, Beethoven, and Wagner. Later a monsoon storm with rain and wind blew up for over an hour. I was in the bathroom when the electricity went off and had to feel my way along a wall to find the door.

We had an 8 P.M. reservation at the Taj for an Indian dinner—an elegant experience. We were shown our table and we each chose a rose-bud from a tray the waiter brought. Another tray had hot, wet cloths for our hands. Coconut milk from a green coconut was served, but I didn't like the taste. Pappadams (hand-rolled crispy crackers spiced with pepper and aniseed and freshly fried) were served with mutton in a sauce, chicken cooked with capsicum and tomato nan (plain flat bread), mango chutney, tomato cubes-onion-cucumber salad, raita (yogurt with diced cucumbers), and our dessert was gulab jamun (sweet fried pastry balls in rose water and syrup). At the end of the meal a tray was brought with *pan,* a betel leaf stuffed with grated betel nuts, aniseed and cardamom and coconut slivers on top. One chews the entire item, which helps digestion and gives the mouth a fresh "toothpaste" feeling with the taste of clove. *Somf* were aniseeds one chews, followed by another betel mixture, which we did not try. I couldn't believe that I had actually had *pan* and chewed betel leaf and nut! We were fast adjusting to this Indian way of life! The meal was followed by *bharatanatyam* dances by two sisters dressed in rose-colored costumes with jewelry and a diamond cluster on the side of each sister's nose. The feet made a rhythm pattern and loud sounds; the faces expressed emotions, and gestures were many. The dancers were accompanied by two singers, one with cymbals and a flute and drum. What a fantastic evening at the elegant new Taj Coromandel.

Excursions to Mahabalipuram and Kanchipuram were a must in South India, so we joined an all-day coach tour to see the temples and enormous carved monuments from the Pallavas dynasty, which ruled this part of India over one thousand years ago. After walking for some time in the heat we sat down on a veranda and watched. Soon a cow came up six steps, turned left walking on the veranda, turned right and went in a door, the same door people had been going in. Later two more cows did the same thing. Finally the cows came out, walked down the six steps going out to the street and into traffic. What a different kind of a world this was! We had thoroughly enjoyed our visit in South India but we had to leave for the next part of our journey.

When our plane arrived in New Delhi, Dick and Sylvia were waiting at the airport for us, putting beautiful metallic leis around our necks—the same ones they had been given eleven years ago when they arrived as missionaries. Who were Dick and Sylvia? Sylvia had been a student of mine in Heidelberg in the late 1950s, when her stepfather was stationed there in the army. Back in the States in college, she had met Richard Smyth, fallen in love and married (in fact, I sang at their wedding in the States); then they went to India where Dick was the minister of the Centennary Church in New Delhi. They had their own Ambassador car, made in India, and we drove to their lovely brick home next to the church. Our suitcases were taken upstairs to a room with its own bath and balcony. We then had an American meal of tunafish salad, macaroni salad, tomatoes stuffed with cottage cheese, homemade potato chips, olives and pickles, and for dessert bananas in cream. Delicious! It was good to be "American" again with these dear friends.

The next morning I was awakened when the breakfast tray was placed in our room. Soon we left for the airport. Dick and Ruth went together on a direct flight to Kashmir. The pilot was Captain Redy, their friend. Sylvia and I flew ten minutes later on a flight which landed at Amritsar, the holy city of the Sikhs. We kept looking for the Golden Temple but never saw it. Up in the air we saw the Banihal Pass, shaped like a chip in a cup or bowl. Before Boeing planes the fog would keep planes from going through the pass but now one can go in any kind of weather. At last I saw snow on the Himalayan peaks and a dream of mine was coming true. While Sylvia and I were seated in the front row, a stewardess came and asked Sylvia her name. Then she said, "Captain Redy sends greetings." Later the pilot asked Sylvia to visit the cockpit, so she did. When we got to Srinagar our plane landed at the air force airport. Security was everywhere and no photos could be taken. It was good to be met by Ruth and Dick, who had landed forty-five minutes before us. We got a taxi, drove through Srinagar and on to Lake Nagin where we got into a *shikara* (a small boat) and were paddled out to *Sobra,* our houseboat for four nights and five days. I couldn't believe the size of the houseboat and all the furniture. We were soon served lunch: soup with toasted bread, mutton or chicken, potatoes and vegetables, cooked apples or pears in syrup, and tea in the living room. (This meal was typical of all our lunches and dinners.)

Each day morning tea was brought to our rooms at 7:30 A.M. as we watched the sunrise. Breakfast was at 8:30 and consisted of porridge with hot milk, one or two fried eggs, all the toast we wanted with butter and delicious berry jam, coffee or tea. There was always a cracked tea cup for one of us to drink from! I have often thought I wanted to name this part of my memories "The Cracked Cup"; apparently it will only be a story. It was the joke of the trip as we wondered who would get the cracked cup. With all the exquisitely carved wood furniture, vases with flowers, etc., in our houseboat we should have accidently smashed the cup on the floor or thrown it into Lake Nagin—we didn't think of those alternatives. That cup should not have its home on our *Sobra.*

We enjoyed watching the traffic on the lake as the locals went about their work and the men in their small boats came to entice us with their wares: a fruit seller; boat "supermarket"; the confectionary seller had delicious chocolates with nuts, lemon-flavored candies with coconut or nuts, and large macaroons we bought to enjoy with our tea; drugstore products; the arts and crafts made in Srinagar; but most of all we enjoyed the flower boatman with the singing of "good morning" (in descending thirds), "How are you?" and the presentation to each of us of a carnation to make us happy. He then proceeded to fill the seven vases with huge bunches of flowers—marigolds, cosmos, dahlias, cockscomb, daisies. The flowers didn't last too long because each vase was stuffed with so many, or . . . had they been taken from another houseboat and weren't too fresh? I'll never know.

Each day we all enjoyed a *shikara* ride to Dal Lake, to town, or to a mosque, with our boatman sitting down paddling with one paddle, sometimes taking time to light his "hubbly-bubbly" pipe. The ride was slow, quiet, and relaxing as we were gliding through the lotus or other small green plants thickly growing with willow trees holding soil together for small gardens. There were many tall, stately poplars too. When we rode under a bridge I felt I was in a Van Gogh painting. We passed local boats filled with straw, fodder, lotus roots, or people just going about their daily chores. No one waved but all seemed inquisitive and they looked at us as we looked at them. It was the fasting period before "Eid," so they could not eat until after sunset. They were looking forward to the new moon, when the priest saw it, the next day would be "Eid." On Thursday evening we saw the sliver of a moon just above the western horizon, so we knew that Friday would be the "Festival of Eid."

As we sat in our *shikara* we saw the preparations for that special day—plucking the feathers of a goose or duck at the water's edge, washing a sheep in the water, or gathering vegetables from the garden. One girl had a rag dipped in blue paint and was hitting the side of the house with it in preparation for Eid. All seemed busy in a quiet way, sitting on their haunches as they paddled the boat, both men and women. There were shawls and *numda* rugs (light-colored felt with embroidered flower designs) being washed in the lake and then hit against stones at the edge of the water. (In our home in Iowa we had a *numda* rug in the small room upstairs we called a playroom. I always wondered where it came from and where my parents bought it. A little piece of Kashmir got all the way to Three Pine Farm. No wonder I had always wanted to visit Kashmir.)

Dick and Sylvia had been to Kashmir many times before and seemed to know everyone. One day we visited a papier-maché wholesale home of Mr. Sadiq. He and Dick embraced, Muslim style (they shook hands then kissed the right cheek, left cheek, and right cheek again) and visited. At a slow pace we went upstairs where the door was opened to a room filled with tables and shelves loaded with stunning papier-maché articles: taffy boxes, eggs, powder boxes, bangles, frames, boxes of every shape and size, tables, lamps, place mats, etc., etc. I couldn't believe my eyes. He then took us back to a workroom where a man was working with lacquer. We were told that people work in their own homes and alone so there is peace and quiet: "Otherwise they would have coffee breaks, some lunch, some talk." He then had another man bring in a tray with cookies, cups, and a samovar of Kashmir tea. The fragrance of the tea was wonderful . . . cinnamon, ground almonds, cardamon, and green tea. It was fragrant and light and the first exciting cup of tea I had ever had! After tea we discussed purchases. I bought three taffy boxes and a brass-lined dish with cover that had the Shahjahan paisley pattern in orange, pale blue, and gold. I wanted one of each item but the temptation had to be resisted. What a beautiful experience we enjoyed that afternoon in Srinagar.

Another afternoon we drove to a home where embroidery was done on all sorts of items. We proceeded up the stairs and noticed much of the home had been newly decorated with plaster and mud for Eid and soon found ourselves in a room with one bed, mats on the floor to sit on, and hooks were on the wall for clothes. Two older men, brothers, one younger man, two young boys, one young girl, and an older woman were sitting on the bed. The daughter-in-law stood behind the curtain in the doorway because she was not allowed in the same room with her father-in-law. The guide translated the information Dick wanted regarding the size of the pillows and style of embroidery to the two older men, who would do the actual work. Yarn thread of various colors was brought out to see what should be used. The translator, the two older men and one young man kept going over and over the plans as they wrote in a book and signed the page. One young son watched intently for this hour of business but the other son was playing with a toy. We then left the house with a very happy Dick and his pillow covers he had ordered and planned to pick up next time in Srinagar.

We strolled through a courtyard, poked along a narrow winding street where our taxi was waiting. After a traffic jam of tourist taxis, people, and horsedrawn *tongas,* we arrived at a wider street and the courtyard of the Indo-Kashmir Carpet Factory. Inside a guide explained the design on a sheet of paper (the sheet has the instructions for each row of knots); at the loom the instructions were pinned above one man and he read it to the other workers. They sit and tie each knot, having a curved blade in the right hand for snipping the yarn. They did a few knots very slowly so we could see the process. Two hundred and fifty families work at that factory, but only three men were working that day because of Eid. The looms were tapestry looms (another kind is shuttle looms). There were many carpets of various sizes and patterns partially done. We then went upstairs in another building to the display room. All carpets were rolled up, standing along the walls. We sat on a long bench on the opposite side and watched as a salesman elegantly unrolled each Kashmiri work of art. "For a while one enjoys the patterns and designs of each rug—later one talks of prices." The salesman was quite a performer. At one time when we asked about cheaper prices he pointed to his stomach area and said, "If my legs came up to here (chest) I could give it to you." I bought the "Jewel of Kashmir" in browns and gold, three by five feet. It was gorgeous with a large design in the center, the jewel. Ruth also bought a beauty in various shades of blues, also three by five.

Another large tour group were looking at nine-by-twelve rugs. Well, why not.

One morning at our houseboat I watched a nearby landslide where birds were going up and down trees, into holes on the bank, and flying and hopping on the ground. There were no sheep, goats, or cattle in the area, only birds. My birding list that day included: domestic crow, jungle crow, Jackdaw crow, grey tit, chestnut-bellied nuthatch, common iora, white-cheeked bulbul, English sparrow, yellow-headed wagtail, Himalayan pied woodpecker, large pied kingfisher, blue-eared kingfisher, stork-billed kingfisher, white-breasted kingfisher, Palla's fishing eagle, common pariah kite, daubchicks, large pied wagtail, and hoopoes with "zebra stripes" on their wings and a crest that often flared up.

On the fifth day it was time to leave our houseboat, *Sobra,* and fly back to the real world and New Delhi. On the plane in the front rows across from us was Lloyd Nolan and his wife and Mr. and Mrs. Andrews (he wrote the script for the movie *Patton*). Mrs. Andrews told Dick a group from Los Angeles were on their way to Bombay, sister city of L.A., to give money for a high school there. Interesting. Again no photos could be taken, but I enjoyed the Banihal Pass and the snow-covered peaks so near our plane. A lifetime dream had finally been fulfilled. Kashmir was and still is my Shangri-la!

We transferred our luggage from the Smyths' home to the Lodhi Hotel in the same area and found we had a courtyard outside our first-floor room. A tent was set up for a Hindu wedding. We were invited but had to refuse because of previous plans. On Sunday morning we attended church at Centenary with Dick preaching on "Caring for One Another in Society." In the middle of the sermon there were strange musical sounds outside the church, which got louder and louder. Someone inside the church closed all the windows so the sound was muted. I wondered if people were purposely trying to disrupt the service; it was so strange. Later I found out a wedding party had passed by with the groom on a white horse surrounded by a band of drums and horns blaring as they made their way to the bride's home. Again, a first with a lasting memory. After church we met many of the members at a coffee hour.

At 4 P.M. the Smyths' drove us to the home of the baby who was baptised earlier at the service and we enjoyed conversation and tea and delicious snacks: pastries, chocolate petit fours, and *laddoos* (an Indian sweet made of boiled-down milk with butter, sugar, and various flavors made into a small ball with silver paper—yes, one eats the pieces of silver on the *laddoo*). Quickly we returned to the hotel and changed into evening dresses for the Delhi Symphony Concert with compositions by Bizet and Beethoven. I was surprised that musicians from several other cities performed with this orchestra—the British were here for such a long time I would have thought there would be enough instrumentalists in Delhi. What a surprise to find Peggy Jenks from the Woodstock School in Mussoorie playing in the violin section. Imagine knowing someone in the Delhi Symphony! (The world was getting smaller and smaller.) After the concert the Smyths' took us to dinner at 9 P.M. at the elegant Ashoka Hotel, eating in the "Rouge et Noir" room where we enjoyed a delicious fish meal along with entertainment of singing and dancing by artists. What an interesting, full day of activities we had experienced with our good friends, Dick and Sylvia, as host and hostess. It was now time for them to get back to their duties and for Ruth and me to make our own plans.

The following day, Peggy Jenks spent the day with us. (Peggy was the daughter of my best friend, Doris Braithwaite, at Saint Olaf College in Minnesota back in the forties. Peggy had married Peter Jenks, and both were teachers at the Woodstock School in the first range of the Himalayas in Mussoorie. Ruth and I visited the school while in India.) The three of us taxied to the Kathak Kedra Music School and observed a vocal class accompanied by drums and the *tambura* (a four-stringed instrument). The teacher's eyes were closed most of the time as he listened and made corrections. Due to the death of a musician the school was closed. We were lucky to observe one class. Later we had lunch at the Imperial Hotel (recommended by Dr. Curtis) on the outside patio. (During my years in India I often stayed at this hotel in the heart of Delhi; if I stayed elsewhere I would often eat meals here on the terrace surrounded by lawns and gardens. Many times kites, the vulturelike bird, soaring above would swoop down and steal a sandwich or a sweet from one's plate. You had to be watchful!)

Along Janpath near the Imperial Hotel were several shops with Tibetans in charge. We must have spent one and one-half hours in one shop talking to the teenage son until his mother came and explained Tibetan artifacts. One was a singing bell. By rubbing a stick around the rim it made a beautiful ringing sound; it was made from bell metal. A small cymbal made of mixed metals and played with a small black wooden stick with a leather string holding the two pieces together also had an excellent tone. It was over one hundred years old, but she wanted

$22.50 for it; too much for one item from my budget. I tried on a pair of beads—large hunks of turquoise, coral, and amber, again an old piece she would sell for $313. I had to say "No." This woman knew "the lady who always wore a sari and was in charge of Rokeby Hotel in Mussoorie in the summer." That was my friend Sylvia Smyth. This was my very first experience with Tibetans and I have never forgotten the mother and son who introduced me to Tibetan artifacts which Tibetans *had* to sell in order to survive as exiles in India.

In the evening several of us saw the dance-drama, Ramlila Ballet, in three acts, three hours long. The three-platform stage was in an open-air theater with revolving panels for the appropriate background. Beautiful costumes and masks were used for the animals—monkeys, peacocks, deer—and people. As we watched we munched on a box of sweets and rice/nuts; during intermission we had hot tea and an orange drink. A most professional production, which we enjoyed very much.

We went to the beauty salon at the five-star hotel. A man washes the hair and massages the head, neck, down the back, and the upper arms. What a treat that was for me. The massage is always included. Next to me I noticed a girl with reddish colored marks on her hands and fingers and felt sorry for her because it looked at though her hands were burned. In two other chairs I saw other young girls with the same marks on their hands; I asked about it and was told these girls were brides-to-be and beautiful lacelike patterns made with henna were placed on the hands and feet so she would be more beautiful for her bridegroom. Interesting custom. . . .

The newspaper said Dr. Kissinger's entourage would meet Indira Gandhi at Raj Ghat; Ruth and I decided to take a taxi and see them. On the way we saw twenty camels loaded with items from Rajasthan; later we saw an elephant drinking water from a water pump. We finally found the correct gate where we waited with other Indians—no other Caucasians, no women. A jeep arrived, followed by a large black American car with a flag, and Dr. Kissinger and Nancy got out, then Ambassador Moynihan and his wife, Indira Gandhi and other Indians, press and photographers, all went to Gandhi's cremation site. After they left, Ruth and I went to the site and found a class of Indian children having their photo taken with the wreath Dr. Kissinger had laid—green leaves, white flowers with silver threads throughout. Other petals were arranged on the marble slab. It was a quiet, peaceful and well-kept area. From the wall were the following sayings by M. K. Gandhi (Mahatma Gandhi):

The Seven Sins
The Politics without Principle
The Wealth without Work
The Pleasure without Conscience
The Knowledge without Character
The Commerce without Morality
The Science without Humanity
The Worship without Sacrifice

When we got back to the hotel room we looked in the phone book for our American ambassador's number. The phone book read, "Ambassador Extraordinary and Plenipotentiary Dr. Daniel P. Moynihan." Before we left New Delhi we visited the beautiful American embassy and saw the small duck pond in the lobby where the ambassador often fed the ducks.

Every day was filled with activities, such as visits to Sangest Natak Akademi where the music librarian, Mr. Varkey, showed us the collection of musical instruments; concerts; and tours of the many interesting historical buildings in Old and New Delhi. The people were the best part of each day's trips. We saw a Gypsy camp with carts and huge wooden wheels. One woman cranked a small wheel which made air fan the fire so the metal got hot while a man pounded it into a tool. Several women were doing embroidery on colorful pieces of material. All the women were wearing long skirts, ankle bracelets of silver, and bright colored blouses. Every trip there had interesting people and animals to see—we never tired of watching all the outdoor activities.

The Taj Mahal is a *must* for anyone traveling in India, and it was time for our "pilgrimage" to Agra. At the railroad station we had to step over many sleeping bodies to get to the tracks where we waited in our Class A car, assigned seats. Through the window we watched the porters carrying luggage on their heads as well as much activity and scurrying of latecomers. (The train system is excellent in India and is the best way of getting around India.) The countryside was flat and dry, but many birds were on wires and the ground. Soon we had arrived, where we were met by the American Express man who took us to our Clark-Shiraz Hotel with a mango-shaped pool and fountain and a huge brass table and tea pot at the entrance to the dining room. From our third-floor room we could see the dome of the Taj Mahal, a real plus (we thought). After lunch a taxi and guide took us to see the most beautiful building in the world. There were lines of people everywhere because this was the full-moon season. That first view through the archway was breathtaking. We walked by the reflecting pool to the base of the Taj where we had to take off our shoes or put large cloth slippers over them; we did the latter, which made us slip and slide over the shiny marble floors. Inside we saw the lattice work on the marble screen and the two tombs directly under the dome. The guide called two times so we could hear the echo. Then we walked down the narrow, dark, slippery steps to the real tombs—only candlelight and very stuffy. After that we walked outside the Taj and saw the two red sandstone mosques on either side; the four minarets leaning slightly out, so in case an earthquake occurred they would fall out away from the Taj. Every inch was exquisite. Ruth and the guide went to the Fort Agra nearby while I stayed and watched the sunset on the Taj.

Back at the Shiraz Hotel we had dinner in the Moghul Room on the sixth floor to see the dome and the full moon, however, there were too many fires lighted at that time so the air was polluted and we saw nothing. Again our driver came at 9 P.M. to take us to see the Taj by full moon. He had told us to leave our cameras and purse at the hotel because there would be so many people in the courtyard. The moonlight was disappointing and not as bright as we had expected but we stayed an hour to watch this once-in-a-lifetime experience.

The next day as we were eating lunch at our hotel we saw our friends from Singapore, Helen and T. G. Ling. They were on a Women's Club of Singapore tour and had just come from Kashmir and were going to Nepal. It was so good to see these friends again.

Fatehpur Sikri, a ghost city, was twenty-four miles from Agra. Akbar lived there in 1583 for sixteen years, then left this city frozen in time. From our taxi beginning in old Agra we drove through narrow streets and saw varied scenes: a camel train of four; then one camel; then a camel pulling a cart; two herds of water buffalo going to Agra to be slaughtered since there are shoe factories in Agra; many donkeys carrying bricks or stones or anything else; finally two dancing bears, but we didn't stop to watch. In Fatehpur Sikri we saw the Hall of Public Audience, more than 350 feet long; the Pachisi courtyard where Akbar played chess with slave girls as living pieces; the interesting Hall of Private Audience; the Astrologer's Seat, an important cog in the Moghul empire—one duty was to determine what color the Emperor would wear during the day. And so much more in this quiet, huge former capital. No one knows why it became deserted—many think the water supply ran out. After a visit to the marble emporium, where I bought a small box with semiprecious stones, we got our luggage at our hotel and drove to the railroad station for our return trip to Delhi. A Japanese mother and daughter shared our train compartment, so we spent the time learning origami, paper folding. Dick and Sylvia surprised us at the New Delhi train station, taking us to our hotel in their car.

Our next trip was to Mussoorie to visit the Woodstock School. It was five–six hours by taxi. Ajmeri Gate was the place to get the taxi but a huge parade and police would not let us go there. For a while we drove beside the parade seeing bands, dancers, floats, etc., but then our driver took us to Connaught Place to a taxi stand. Eight men talked and we finally arranged a price of 225 rupees; the driver wanted twenty more for a permit to leave Delhi and we said "No." Changing to another taxi we found an older man who spoke very little English; however, he was from Dehra Dun (the town below the hills with Mussoorie above). Perhaps the twenty rupees was a put-up job so we would go with this driver. Who knows?

Sights along the road: At the Yamuna River road there was a procession—a boy with a gong at the head, followed by men carrying a body wrapped in white material with marigold garlands on it (Dick said it is a Hindu ceremony; with wood so expensive the family would probably walk to the river where stones would be attached to it and it would sink in the river); a long narrow bridge where traffic was congested and much washing was spread on the river bank; incessant honking of horns; many brick factories along the way; yarn drying in the sun; trees on both sides of the highway made shade for animals and humans; paved road with a path on either side for slower traffic; finally fields on both sides of the road but no fences anywhere; a very busy town with people, stalls, animals everywhere—we could hardly move in all the humanity. One rest stop was made at Meerut for a cool drink and toilet facilities (such as they were). We passed one town with a huge military base with soldiers marching—many on bicycles in formation.

Finally we saw the foothills in the distance as we drove on a winding road to the plateau of Dehradun. We saw a flour mill, bakery, wood and lumber, a forest college and research center. The horn on our taxi became stuck so we stopped many times to try to fix it. Now the road really began going up with rocks in the center of the road at turns to divide the road. Up, up the narrow, turning, twisting mountain road to Mussoorie.

Signs on the road said: "Drive cautiously—Avoid accident—Reach home alive"; "Live and Let Live." We stopped to pay toll tax: car 2 rupees adult, 1 rupee child, bus 1.50 rupees adult, .75 child. Driver's toll tax was also payable.

Two grey monkeys were on the road with a dog chasing them. At a second checkpoint the collector took half of the ticket. Then we had to "Stop for One-way Traffic." We arrived at the top—finally—and for twenty-five more rupees the driver drove us through Mussoorie to the eastern edge of town to the Woodstock International School. I couldn't believe my eyes when I saw all the hills and ravines everywhere. The altitude is 6500 feet. We found Peggy and her husband Pete, who took us to our "home" while here. The teacher who lived in the house was in Delhi for the week; therefore, he graciously lent us his quarters. Peggy took us there each day after our activities and stayed all night with us. Our meals were taken in the staff dining room with other teachers. So began my visit to this very special school begun by the English in the 1860s. How was I to know then that later on I would spend five years teaching there!

Days were spent attending classes, the assembly each day, tours of the school buildings and getting acquainted with students and teachers. One day I went with Peggy to another private school where she taught some music classes and had lunch with the principal in her quarters. Four o'clock tea in the garden was a relaxing time for staff and chatting while others read their mail that had just arrived.

One day Ruth and I hired a rickshaw, pulled by two men and pushed by two other men, to take us to Happy Valley, a Tibetan settlement four miles or so from Woodstock on the opposite end of Mussoorie. We enjoyed the ride and from our vantage place we saw crowds of people on the road; many had goods spread along the side to sell to those passing by. At a curve in the street we would glimpse the snow-covered distance mountains, and we wondered how the houses could be built on such steep hillsides. Always interesting sights. We finally arrived at the entrance gate to "Happy Valley." The rickshaw men stopped and smoked as they rested. What should we do? We had no idea. Then we heard a voice in the distance say, "May I help you?" That was music to our ears! A Tibetan student was standing on the steps of a building with a sign: "Art Studio given by Norway" (my thoughts told me that if Norway had helped here, we would be all right). Next to the art studio was another building with a sign: "Flour Mill given by Switzerland." The young student came towards us and asked if he could help us. We told him we wanted a tour of the Tibetan settlement and he said he would be our guide. We saw the temple, and a monk brought a long trumpet outside so I could photograph it. We walked on narrow rocky paths that zigged and zagged up and down. He saw it was difficult for me to walk so he offered to carry my pocketbook. When in another country *no one* carries it for me, but I let Tashi take it. In a short time a feeling of good will and honesty had developed. He explained the buildings, the problems, the help given them by many other countries, and showed us the school where one thousand Tibetan children attended, most of them orphans. As we moved about we saw many adult Tibetans twirling their prayer wheels as they walked. Everything was new to me—a culture from the "roof of our world," a small piece of displaced Tibet. A visit to the small gift shop where we saw Tibetan-style pillow covers, striped hand-woven aprons (only married women wear them), handpainted cards, etc. We bought a few small items.

Tashi asked us if we would like to see the art school; of course we would. There were eight or ten teenage boys at tables painting. Tashi explained some of the paintings and showed us some that were for sale. After looking them over I decided to buy the "Wheel of Life" painted by the master teacher-painter. Then Tashi asked if we would like to meet him; of course we would. He opened a door to the next small room, and I saw a sight I will never forget. The master was sitting on a raised area covered by Tibetan rugs. Beside him was a vase with an evergreen branch. On a nearby table were one hundred small brass candleholders which contained flickering lighted candles. One window in the room on his right framed the tops of beautiful trees. The entire scene was one of tranquility, beauty, and peace. Tashi translated and we spoke a few words. The teacher asked him to pass around a bowl of wrapped candies. The meeting was soon over but the memories have lasted for many years. . . .

Before we left Tashi, we exchanged addresses, then roused the men from their rest and rode in our rickshaw back to the Woodstock School, all the while talking about our new friend and the unusual occurrences we had just experienced at the settlement called "Happy Valley." (When I arrived back home in the United States, a letter was waiting from Tashi; he had become my first "Tibetan nephew.") In following letters I asked him if he always acted as a guide to tourists and he wrote that he had

156

never been a guide before he helped Ruth and me. It was one of those experiences that was "meant to be."

Nepal

We had an early evening flight to Kathmandu, Nepal, and got to the airport very early. As we were going through customs the officer looked in my passport and saw three items listed: two cameras and one pair of binoculars. (Someone suggested that these items be written in the passport so duty would not have to be paid.) I had packed one camera in my stored luggage while we would be in Nepal and *now* the officer wanted to see all three items because we were leaving India and going to another country. I told him I could go back to the hotel and get it, but he thought someone at the airport could help the situation so he went to find another man. Time moved along and nothing happened. Finally the officer came back saying, "I *must* have the other camera." By this time our plane was almost ready to leave and I shouted at the man, "I have waited years to visit Nepal and I must go on this flight" . . . to no avail. He wanted to see the other camera or we could not leave. With my blood at the boiling point, very reluctantly I went to Ruth and told her we could not get on the plane. We exchanged our tickets for the morning flight and got a taxi to the hotel where I got my second camera from my suitcase in the storage room. We were too embarrassed to book a room for one night since we had just checked out a few hours before. Instead we got a room at a five-star hotel. (Months later I got a bill from that hotel for a rather large sum for drinks and snacks. I immediately phoned Ruth and asked her if she had had a party that night and hadn't invited me. We both laughed because we knew it was not our bill.) Things do have a way of getting even.

The next morning we were back at the airport with the three items. This time all went well and we boarded the plane for Kathmandu. What a thrill to see the great Himalayan peaks from the air, especially Mount Everest, with very little cloud cover.

Since I had been to "Treetops" in Kenya, I wanted to visit "Tiger Tops" in Nepal. Arrangements had been made to spend a couple of days there at the lodge. After a short plane flight we got in long narrow boats sitting on clumps of grasses while a man rowed. Often water came into the craft and by the time we arrived at the river bank our seats were wet. There was no lodge in sight, only tents. What a surprise that was! We were told the lodge was full and this was the overflow camp. We sat around a campfire where we met other tourists and had snacks and drinks; later our supper. Our guide told us a goat had been tied not too far away and they hoped a tiger would come for it. If that happened a native would run and tell us to come. That finally occurred and everyone went with the guide, including Ruth. I decided not to go because of the rough path through the jungle in the dark so I stayed at the fire with a young native boy talking about the animals in the area. It wasn't long before the others came back, and this is what Ruth told me. The path was rough and she stubbed her toe on a root but managed to continue walking to the blind. Even though we had been told to be quiet and not make a sound, two men from the States had been drinking too much and talked loudly. The tiger had come for the goat, but when it heard the men it went back into the bushes—no one saw the handsome tiger! It is amazing to me how someone can be so careless and spoil an event for others. I was surely glad I had not made the effort to see the tiger and then been disappointed.

Our tent had a zipper that did not work so we could not close the flaps. We slept very little knowing there were rhinos, tigers, and sloth bears nearby; however, the night passed uneventfully and slowly. The next morning we were taken by Jeeps to the lodge, a large wooden building. From a high platform we got on an elephant for a photo tour across the untouched tropical forest to watch for animals, especially the elusive rhino. The only sounds were the swishing as the elephant shuffled through the tall grasses, the various bird calls, and an occasional trumpet from the elephant. The *mahout* (driver) told us the elephant had seen a tiger in the grasses, but we did not. Finally we crossed the Rapti River and the elephant carefully climbed up the river bank to an area with fewer trees. Here we saw two rare Great Indian one-horned rhinos. What a thrill! Once one gets used to the gait of an elephant the ride is most pleasing and relaxing—my favorite kind of transportation. Our second night was spent in the lodge, where we enjoyed a delectable meal, followed by a restful sleep. The next morning elephants took us to the air strip for the short flight back to Kathmandu.

There was a famous Russian man named Boris who owned the "Yak and Yeti" restaurant. I knew I must eat there. (Boris had been in the ballet in Russia, then Monte Carlo, and ended up in Nepal after World War II. He had prepared the banquet for Queen Elizabeth II when there were no roads into the country—everything came in by horses over rocky paths. His book, *Tiger for Breakfast,* is extremely interesting.) We found the old Rana palace and walked into an elaborately decorated hall now converted into a dining room with a large open fireplace in the center of the room, perfect for cool nights. We ordered Ukrainian borscht followed by stroganoff, all delicious. No, I never met Boris that evening but one of his sons was our waiter. A most memorable evening. . . .

Kenya

A trip around the world wouldn't be complete without a photo safari in the national parks of Kenya. Arrangements had been previously made for a seven-day safari. Each day we had an early morning ride to see what the animals were doing, then a drive to the next park followed by a late-afternoon drive, then dinner. At one park, a woman from Norway was in charge of the Keekorok Lodge. She invited us to share her table on the terrace at dinner and we gladly accepted. What an evening of conversation, food, and friendship. As we heard different barks, grunts, and growls she would identify the animal; some sounds were near and some far away. She talked about the problems, the workers, the tourists, and felt she would soon give up the position and go home to Norway. We later saw her in Nairobi at a beauty salon and thanked her again for that special African evening we had shared.

We flew to Victoria Falls for a view of that wonder of the world and a boat ride on the river at dusk. The next morning we phoned our travel agent and asked for a taxi to take us across the bridge to Rhodesia (Zimbabwe) where we would catch our flight for South Africa. We were told that no tourists could cross that bridge—political problems—and we should get a taxi to drive us south to a ferry that would take us across the river. That is what we did and when we got off the ferry we saw a big sign on the river bank: BOTSWANA. We were now in another country! What a surprise. We dragged all our luggage to a bus stop and waited in the hot sun. No, we had not brought any food or water with us (we should have known better). Ruth was not feeling well after taking her weekly malaria pill and lay down on the bench. We waited—and waited—and waited for any kind of transportation to take us to the city airport. Finally a van came that already had four tourists in it. They were not at all pleased to have to share it with two more people and more luggage. Somehow, we all squeezed together and were on our way. Several animals crossed the road including some beautiful oryx. We finally arrived at the airport, none the worse for an unusual and strange day in the middle of Africa in a country we hadn't planned to visit.

When we traveled from city to city and had different hotels we always had a conversation about who was going to sleep in which bed, which towels to use, etc. Finally, a thought came to me and I said to Ruth, "I've got the answer to our problem: Lou—left, Ruth—right." We discussed the plan and decided it was a good one. I took the towels on the left side and the left side of the sink; Ruth took those on the right. The same applied to the beds. Now when we came into a new room we needed to have no conversation about room arrangements. Why hadn't we thought of that at the beginning of the trip? At least we still had several weeks left to put the new plan into action.

South Africa

This was a new country for me; therefore, we were happy to have an introduction from our good friend Me'l Dowd, now an actress, to Clarence Wilson, a Canadian living in Johannesburg. We phoned him and told him we were going to see *Meropa*—The Drums of Africa: A Musical Legend—on December 18. (Clarence was the producer of this show and had designed the scenery and costumes.) He told us where the stage door was and to come backstage after the performance. We arrived early at His Majesty's Theater and enjoyed the Barbara Tyrrell paintings in the foyer. (Barbara had traveled around primitive areas of Southern Africa and painted details of dress and behavior. Her works are of great historical value. I bought her book, *Tribal Peoples of Southern Africa.*) We bought two records of the show, one for Me'l and one for my collection.

Before the curtain went up, the drums were softly beating and the costumes with all the beads would rattle. As we looked around us we noticed the audience was composed of only whites—a real shock to us. The musical was so alive, so energetic, and powerful and the music was excellent. The actors were the singers and dancers and I wondered how they could keep up the energy level.

Afterwards we went backstage and met Clarence, Louis Burke (another producer), Victor Ntoni (the black composer of the music), and the girl who played the part of the "outcast." The stage seemed so much smaller than it appeared from the audience. We were invited to join them and drove to "Pot Luck," an elegant, cozy cafe where we had coffee, walnuts dipped in crystalized honey, cakes, etc. Others at the table were a dancer from Germany, a makeup artist in films, and a photographer. Around the room were several bouquets of flowers, huge arrangements; I was amazed at the size! Stimulating conversation included the apartheid question. We were driven back to our hotel, where very little sleep came after all the events of the evening.

The hotel desk had a slip of paper from the post office saying there was a package for me and I would have to appear in person to receive it. Ruth and I found the post office, which had different lanes with signs above—whites, blacks, colored, Indians. We went to the white lane, presented the slip, and received the package sent by my good friend and fellow teacher in Roslyn, Roosevelt Van Williams. It contained a Christmas poem signed by many other teacher friends and solid perfume in a gold lion's head case. I wondered what they would have done had the post office known that black hands had wrapped and sent this Christmas gift.

We left on a tour along the coast of South Africa that included Swaziland, Durban, Umtata (a small town but memorable because the heater on the roof rumbled and boiled loudly all night. We were afraid we might be scalded during the night and no one would ever know what happened to us). On to Port Elizabeth, and Cape Town where we saw the Cape of Good Hope and the swirling waters that had sunk many ships. At a port on New Year's Eve at midnight all the whistles and horns of the ships are sounded for one big celebration of sound! The tour was interesting and included beautiful flower gardens, native dances and witch doctors, and historical sites.

Back to Jo'burg we again phoned Clarence (he had asked us to phone him when we returned) and he invited us to lunch on Sunday. After seeing the Bantu Gold Mine Dancers, we took a taxi driven by an Afrikaan who had been driving forty-five years and would not follow Clarence's directions. He was really bullheaded. After a radio call to his office we finally found it. Clarence, in a long kaftan, was standing at his gate beside his large Great Dane. Since we were so late in arriving we went right to his open veranda surrounded by fig trees and a small pool with a fountain with birds drinking from it. The centerpiece on the table was a Agapanthas lily in a crystal vase. Our luncheon: grapefruit drink, a molded fish mixture (delicious), marinated mushrooms, tomato and lettuce salad, brown bread, strawberries in pink gelatin mould, and jasmine tea. After lunch he showed us each room of his lovely home. He is an artist and two painted ostrich eggshells stood on glass stands on a coffee table; a painting of rats eating mealie from an overturned sack with the peace sign (banned in South Africa), all on gold leaf, symbolizing South Africa and gold. In his studio he showed us a new painting for Victor. I assumed it would be a portrait of him and was totally surprised to find a large painting divided into nine sections, like a window with shelves—basket of figs, cow's skull, basket of fruit, bars of a jail, mandolin, etc. Another wall had a cracked ostrich egg painting with large writing: "South Africa, April, 1974." Another painting showed many black faces looking out with a sign above: "Blacks Only." After tea he drove us to our hotel. What a memorable occasion this had been.

Clarence had invited us to see *Meropa* from backstage, later phoning us to say we could not come that night because it was a performance for "blacks only," but we should come another night. That was the very first time blacks had been allowed into His Majesty's Theater; slowly progress was being made. What a treat to see this musical drawn from traditional tribal folklore from the wings of the stage. A three and a half-year-old boy, son of one of the performers, danced backstage exactly as the dancers on stage did. What will he be when he grows up after seeing the show night after night? What a darling little fellow. When the "outcast" girl was caught by the witch doctor, she rushed offstage where a man was positioned to catch her and hold her until she got her composure again. Rain was made by peas dropping onto a skin drum head near a mike. One dancer couldn't dance for a few days because his leg hurt, but he did most of the steps backstage anyway. All was fascinating.

When it was finished a black photographer took photos of the entire cast, then various scenes. He also took photos of Victor as the witch doctor talking with Ruth and me and a photo of Ruth and Victor shaking hands, saying good-bye. A black reporter had written that at the performance for blacks on Monday evening at the "white" theater, the audience had been mixed. Mr. Burke, the organizer, had spent the day telling the cultural minister that was *not* true; he told him the reporter would have to retract the statement in the newspaper. He also told the cast that if people should ask anyone in the cast, they should not talk about it but refer it to Louis, Clarence, or others in charge. Clarence said that black reporters were trying to stir up trouble. It must be terrible to keep hitting one's head against a wall all the time. Clarence thought it may be time to let someone else open more doors. He already had done much to help rid South Africa of apartheid.

Again we went to the Pot Luck for coffee and cakes. This time I asked to see a passbook and a woman brought one of the young men's passes so we could see it. Each month the signatures of the employer must be in it, a photo of the person with his or her name plus the name of the tribe. It must be carried by the person at all times and if it is not the person is in real trouble. What a shock to actually see a passbook I had heard so much about. We talked and talked about all the problems, what should be done, etc. No one seemed to have the answer or know what was best for all.

I had seen *Wait a Minim!* in the 1960s on Broadway in New York. This was a musical entertainment of songs and instruments from South Africa and included two brothers, Paul and Andrew Tracey, along with others. They are sons of Dr. Hugh Tracey, the world's foremost authority on African music, who also founded the African Music Society. I had attended several lectures by Dr. Tracey on Long Island. I knew if I ever got to South Africa I would have to visit them. Now was my chance. They lived in the Transvaal near Jo'burg. One day Ruth and I took a train to their town and taxied to the building. Andrew met us and invited us into a room with instruments everywhere: thumb pianos; the kalimba, a kind of thumb piano designed by Dr. Tracey and usable in Western music; drums, bells, rattles, marimbas, etc. They also had collected songs and instrument sounds for records and they published journals. This is what I purchased. Records: Uganda Music, Reeds—Mbira, African Music Society's Choice, Music of Africa, Music of Roadside, Mine Dances Parts I and II, Guitar, Musical Instruments—Strings, Xylophone, Musical Instrument—Drums, Flutes and Horns, Zulu Songs of Princess Constance Magogo, and African Stories. Books: *African Dances, The Lion on the Path, Ngoma,* and *Chopi Musicians.* I ordered eighteen volumes of their *Journal of the African Music Society.* I bought a large *mbira* or thumb piano with twenty-two keys. Andrew told me it was a rare instrument and if I wasn't going to learn to play it, he didn't want to sell it to me. (All these purchases arrived three months after I arrived back in Long Island.) This had been one of my most musical days of all the sabbatical and one I shall never forget.

Back in Jo'burg we attended a medieval banqueting evening at the President Hotel. Papier-maché stones looked like a stone wall outside the heavy wooden door with many hanging banners. We all assembled here and a page, in a loud voice, announced the parties by saying, "Master Jones and party—keeper of the king's treasury," or "Master Keith,

163

Lady Diana's gatekeeper and party,'' etc. Some of the introductions were hilarious. Each party went in and were seated to the accompaniment of three people in costumes playing recorders. The six waiters and waitresses were also in medieval costumes. Ruth and I went in last because the master of ceremonies knew we were interested in the music, so we were seated near the musicians. The M.C. read a poem telling about proper behavior in medieval times, such as hitting the table instead of clapping.

There were three long wooden tables with benches on either side, a head table, and a few small tables at the side. We were each given a white terrycloth bib tied around the neck instead of a napkin. Lighted candles were on the tables and several large bowls with water and a few flower petals floating; another bowl had sand (ashtray). Bowls were placed at our end as well as a steaming kettle of soup. The waiter ladled the soup and the bowl was passed by guests down to the end of the table. All the food was served in that fashion. The soup was a heavy barley soup. A loaf of brown bread with a hunting knife completed the first course. One could choose white or red wine, and the tall silver goblet was kept full for the entire meal. After soup, the performers were introduced and played recorder trios. Course two: swordfish with mint—no forks. Recorders played two numbers as the waiters and waitresses danced typical dances of the period. Course three: chicken browned in honey, lettuce and tomato salad—no forks. More music and poems were performed. Course four: vanilla pudding with burnt-sugar topping. Miriam sang with a guitar while two others played recorders. Then we all went to the lounge for coffee while the music continued. About twenty of us stayed much longer to hear Miriam sing folk songs with guitar. This had been another interesting evening in a most unusual setting.

It was soon time to leave this part of the world. Clarence offered to drive us to Jan Smuts Airport. He gave us each a small Benin brass bell and one to give to Me'l. We gave him a bag of pecans in the shell we had bought on our tour. He was certainly one of the most interesting people I had met, and we especially thank Me'l for sharing her marvelous friend with us!

We flew to Luanda, Angola, for a quick stopover before landing in Rio de Janeiro, Brazil, where we spent three days doing the usual sightseeing. I best remember the days tour to a German village near Rio where we had a delicious German meal. I was sure I was back in Heidelberg,

Germany, instead of Brazil. Finally, it was a flight back to New York and home.

We had been gone for six months, traveled around the world, learned about cultures and traditions, met interesting people, and heard so many kinds of music sung and played on unusual instruments—the bullroarer of Australia where women are not even suppose to say the word; the cacoons of South Africa that are filled with pebbles then tied together and worn on the upper legs of dancers; the *rkan-dung* or short trumpet made from a human tibia bone and ornamented with coral and turquoise from the Tibetans. Yes, this sabbatical had taught me that there are many ways to express oneself through sound and song. Dr. Menon, president of the National Center for the Performing Arts in Bombay, India, said in his speech at the ISME Conference in Perth: "The upright piano in an English-type school should cease to be the symbol of music education in Asian and African countries. Music like all the arts, is created wherever we are!" It is only in recent decades that non-Western music is finally being recognized—not as "exotic music" or "primitive music" but as "ethnic music." I surely appreciated the opportunity to spend time with various tribes and peoples as they expressed themselves in their own ways. To paraphrase what Marco Polo said on his death bed: "I haven't told half of what I saw or heard. . . ."

13

Istanbul, Turkey, Winter 1976

A science teacher from Roslyn, Bertha Pataky, and I joined a two-week tour to Istanbul during our winter holiday in 1976. It sounded good to me even though I knew nothing about this part of our world. I read that in A.D. 330 it was Constantinople and the capital of the Roman Empire. After many wars the Turks conquered it in 1453 and a new era began, now the capital of the Ottoman Empire, for 470 years, until 1923. The main religion was Islam, and it is the only city in the world that stretches on two continents. There would be much to see and so much to learn.

We flew to Istanbul and drove by bus to our hotel on the Bosphorus. On the way we saw crowded streets, narrow and often winding roads, many old buildings but many new tall office and hotel structures. Street vendors seemed to be selling anything and everything; men had large trays of bread on their heads or on pushcarts. From our hotel we could watch the ships from many different countries (if only we knew the flags); we even saw a Soviet submarine. We were sure authorities were keeping track of the ships going up and down this important waterway.

The city was filled with mosques, palaces, Turkish baths, and fountains. Powerful Suleyman the Magnificent had been in power for forty-six years in the sixteenth century and over three hundred masterpieces of architecture occurred. We visited the Suleymaniye Mosque, the most important Ottoman building in the city. It stands on one of the seven hills and consists of an outer courtyard, an inner one, and the prayer room with the dome. One has to see the mosque to realize how large it is. Another great building is Haghia Sophia, a church whose legend goes back to A.D. 325, a building with fires and collapses and finally in 563 Justinian dedicated the church again. Minarets were added by the Turks after their conquest. It is presently a domed basilica museum with magnificent mosaics of Jesus, Empress Zoe, Constantine IX, and others.

Another "gem" in this fabulous city is the Topkapi Palace built in 1467 by Sultan Mehmet II, now a museum. It is an extensive building complex of courts, mosques, fountains, and pavilions with displays in every room—10,700 pieces of Chinese and Japanese porcelain, arms, silver, embroidery, Imperial wardrobe, miniature paintings and much more. I enjoyed seeing the unique and rare pieces of jewelry once owned by the sultans. All items were "decorated" or "bejeweled" with emeralds, rubies, turquoise, pearls, coral, brilliants, enamel, jade, whatever. Gold bejeweled swords and daggers, jeweled turbans, Spoonmaker's diamond, the seventh biggest, 86 carats, mounted in silver, surrounded by forty-nine brilliants; a diamond-decorated dessert service (I have seen that item in my mind's eye many times since 1976); a golden music box with a golden elephant motif. One must have walking shoes for a tour through this palace to see items used by the sultan, his harem, and court—and how they lived. A one-of-a-kind place to visit.

In the old city one sees many crumbling walls. Aqueducts were needed to get water into the cisterns in this often besieged city; remains are still visible. (In 1993 when Sam and I were in Istanbul we ate a delicious typical meal in a restaurant, formerly a cistern.)

One should never miss the bazaars of the East. Istanbul has two of those—the Spice Bazaar and the Grand Bazaar or covered bazaar with over 5000 shops. It is a giant labyrinth of narrow passages. Watch where you go or you will soon be lost. Bert and I enjoyed our "looking tour" and finally stopped at a jewelry shop. The salesman asked if would like tea and we said "Yes." He sent a young boy for the tea, who came back with two small glasses, approximately three inches tall and one and one-half inches wide; each had two gold stripes around the glass and a wide gold band around the top. I remember warming my hands as I held the tea glass. It felt so comforting and tasted so delicious in the rather dark, damp, huge space with shops piled with copper, brass, gold, silver, rugs, leather. Name it and it was there somewhere! We each decided to buy a bluish turquoise ring with a large center stone surrounded by sixteen smaller turquoise. Each stone was so perfect, we couldn't believe they were authentic stones, we don't want to have them appraised for fear we will find out they are . . . something else. The memories of shopping in exotic places are unforgettable.

(Again, in 1993, I wanted to visit the Grand Bazaar to buy brass pepper grinders. The bus stopped several blocks away from the entrance so I had to walk, finally resting in front of a carpet shop. A young blond man came out, asking if he could help me, and we talked. I asked him where he was from and he said Istanbul, but added that his grandmother was from Norway, had come to this city, stayed here, married, and now the grandson was in charge of the store. What a coincidence that was.

Both of us were surprised at our common ancestry. Yes, I found the grinders, purchased several plus a brass tray, and carried the heavy packages all the way back where the bus was parked.)

The long Galata Bridge takes one to the modern European city with fewer tourist sights, but there are interesting places to visit. One can take a boat trip along the Bosphorus to see the many palaces and castles on the European side and on the way back one sees the Asiatic shore of the Bosphorus.

We did have a bus tour into Turkey, stopping at Bursa and other towns. I always enjoy seeing people in their own environment in native clothes going about their daily activities with donkeys and horses pulling carts or wagons, older women caring for the small children, the workers in the fields, everyone quietly doing his or her task.

Another story Bert and I often laugh about happened at our hotel dining room. We had ordered fish for the entree and when the waiter brought it he asked us if he could cut it for us. We said yes, thinking he would fillet it and give us each a piece. Instead he cut the fish in half and gave the top to Bert and I got the tail section. Strange, but a long-time memory.

In 1976 United States had the bicentennial year of the founding of our country with special coins minted to honor the occasion. I decided it would be nice to take a number of the coins and give them to people I met in Turkey. After I arrived there and realized how many centuries old their civilization really was, I felt embarrased. Perhaps the children kept them in their coin collection and remembered when an American lady, very proud of her heritage, visited their magnificent city and culture, talked, and asked them questions.

When I get homesick for Istanbul I reach for my Turkish tea glass, make tea, warming my fingers around the glass, and think of the interesting people I have met while visiting Istanbul. The turquoise ring may not be authentic but I *know* the gold-trimmed small tea glass is. . . .

VI
IN THE SHADOW OF THE BEST

My heart is warm with the friends I meet and better friends I'll not be knowing.

—Edna St. Vincent Millay

My family home in winter at Three Pine Farm, Eagle Grove, Iowa.

My parents, Tillie and Albin Nelson, with Doc, Lou, Orin, Carol, and Bob, 1959.

In a Japanese kimono when I taught in Japan.

My first husband, Al Golden, and me at the northernmost village of North America.

Ruth Hanson and me in a *shikara-boat* on Lake Nagin in Kashmir, India.

With a Masai family in front of their home, Kenya, Africa.

A Sea Dyak dancing at his longhouse in Borneo.

My teacher, Professor Dansunandana, playing a Khan (mouth organ) and me, playing the Saw Duang (two strings) in Bangkok, Thailand.

A New Guinea tribesman in paint and feathers.

The entrance to Woodstock International School in the hill station of Mussoorie, India.

My niece Melissa Nelson with students at Woodstock School.

Yeshi Dolma, Tibetan friend who walked five miles to visit me
each month at Woodstock School.

Ladakhi woman we visited
in Leh, Ladakh.

At the beautiful and famous Taj Mahal in Agra, India.

Thupten and Tashi, Tibetan friends (brothers), in Katmandu, Nepal.

"Auntie" Lou with Tibetan children at the Pokhara settlement in Nepal.

The Rohtang Pass in northern India.

My husband, Sam, and me on the Great Wall of China in 1985.

14

Special Music Moments, Special People

Every year singers from many communities in Iowa would gather in Fort Dodge, Iowa to perform Handel's *Messiah.* On December 7, 1941, I was singing in the performance, on that fateful day. We had heard the news about Pearl Harbor and during any lull in the singing there was a buzz of conversation! "Did you hear about the bombing?"; "What have you heard?" etc., etc. It was a performance I will never forget. Eleven years later I was teaching in Japan and sang in the chorus of the *Messiah,* only this time there were many Japanese singing along with the Americans. It seemed rather strange! Fifty years after that December 7th day, while living in Miami I joined the "singalong" chorus at the University of Miami to perform in the *Messiah.* Others observed that awful "fiftieth anniversary of the bombing of Pearl Harbor" in other ways; I chose to observe it the same way I had experienced it in 1941—by singing God's praises. "And the Glory of the Lord. . . ."

* * *

The summer of 1945 was spent at Interlochen Music Camp in northern Michigan, a wonderful place to learn more about music and make friends with musicians from other states and countries. Our university choir practiced the *Requiem* by Fauré, among other compositions. When World War II ended in August 1945 our choir performed this stirring work to honor this tragic event, which had finally come to a close. It was a very moving performance; afterwards I walked to the nearby lake, alone, and dissolved into tears thinking of the lives lost, the destruction, the maimed, and their loved ones.

* * *

While teaching in the army school for dependents' children in Heidelberg, Germany, I joined the Bach Verein: perhaps three or four were Americans, the rest Germans. At the first rehearsal, vocal warmups began. I opened my mouth and sang the exercise on "ah." The next thing

I felt was a slight punch on my right arm from my friend, Eva; she whispered "hum." Did I ever feel foolish! After that I was very mindful and listened and watched others before I sang any exercise.

* * *

A three-day trip to Berlin by train from Heidelberg with a friend, Margaret, was taken in the early 1950s. We traveled at night and couldn't see any of the land; there were blackout curtains on the windows, but I often peeked during the night. We toured the main places in West Berlin and finally decided to go to East Berlin. We felt we should leave our passports in our hotel but as we talked more about our excursion to this area we decided we *must* have passports, so we went back to our hotel to get them. (That was a very smart idea and should have been included in our original thinking.)

Opera performances are always included in any of my travels. In Berlin, the opera was Verdi's *Nabucco* (I had never heard of it nor is it listed in most opera books) and I decided to attend even though I did not know the story nor would I be able to read the program notes in German. The opera tells the story of Nebuchadnezzar from the Old Testament. One beautiful chorus, "Va, Pensiero" or "Chorus of the Hebrew Slaves" is sung by the Jews in their Babylonian captivity, lamenting the loss of their homeland. On stage the huge chorus was in sackcloth and chains singing this powerful lament. Never having heard the chorus before, I deeply felt the emotion it portrayed. After the song ended, the audience burst into tremendous applause and would not stop until the entire chorus was repeated. To the audience it was their way of expressing their own feelings at living in a divided city and not free to travel as they wished. It was not a Babylonian captivity but rather a Berlin captivity. I have never had a more poignant or emotional moment in opera.

* * *

One December holiday while teaching in Germany, a friend and I went to Italy to visit Rome and Naples. In Naples I attended the San Carlo Opera House performance and heard a fantastic soprano for the first time. The next day I went to a record shop to see if they had ever heard of her, or if she had recorded any records. After telling the clerk how much I had enjoyed her voice and her singing I told him her name, *Renata Tebaldi.* How he laughed; he showed me dozens of albums she

184

had recorded. And all the time I thought *I had discovered* this glorious soprano voice. Live and learn!

*   *   *

Since I enjoy Wagner's music so much I attended the Bayreuth Festival in Germany twice. In the summer of 1955 I heard *Parsifal* and in 1957 I heard *Die Meistersinger* with all the pomp, the robes, and flags. There is nothing quite like the dignified theme of the Mastersingers. The operas presented there were excellent . . . but so was the audience. Everyone must be in formal attire and it was thrilling to see the Begum Aga Khan (a Parisian beauty) dressed in a emerald chiffon gown with long matching emerald earrings. Also, for a moment I talked with **Wieland Wagner,** the grandson of Richard Wagner.

Seventeen years later when I attended the ISME (International Society of Music Educators) conference in Perth, Australia, the Youth Orchestra of Australia conducted by Dmitri Kabalevsky played the ''Procession of the Meistersingers'' by Wagner. I finally realized why this composition was chosen! We, the musicians who had come to the conference, were being honored. Another poignant moment in music.

*   *   *

One of England's great twentieth century composer was **Benjamin Britten.** On May 26, 1955 several of us who were teaching at the dependents' school had tickets to see the opera *The Turn of the Screw* by Britten, and conducted by him, at Schwetzingen, west of Heidelberg. On the grounds were beautiful stately trees, flowering bushes, and gardens surrounding a small theater. On the grounds was also a small cafe with tables outside. In springtime one of the specialties in Spargel und Schenken (asparagus and ham); that is what we ordered and enjoyed in this beautiful setting. I happened to look over at the next table and there was Benjamin Britten and the famous tenor Peter Pears, who sang the lead role that evening. How I wanted to talk with them; but I didn't, knowing they would soon be involved in the evening's performance. Schwetzingen is a very wellknown place for music. As a very young boy, Mozart had played there in the theater, too.

*   *   *

The Mannheim Opera had been destroyed during World War II. My friend Eva and I were fortunate to get tickets for the opening of the new opera house on January 19, 1955, where we saw *Der Freischutz* by Weber. Because of the new opera house and their excellent opera company, I often went to this town west of Heidelberg to see operas. I also had some voice lessons from one of the fine opera singers there, Herr Grimm.

* * *

Un Ballo in Maschera, or *A Masked Ball,* by Verdi holds special memories for me. On April 6, 1968, I had a ticket for the matinee at the Metropolitan Opera in New York City. Before the performance began Rudolph Bing, the general manager, asked everyone to stand in silence because of the assassination of Martin Luther King. Again on May 22, 1991, I watched the same opera on TV's Great Performances from the Metropolitan''; the next day I heard about the assassination of Rajive Gandhi in South India. What a coincidence! What a waste of lives of great men!

* * *

When I was growing up in Iowa, on Saturday afternoon I always listened to the opera from the Met in New York sponsored by Texaco. Opera was an interesting art form and I enjoyed listening as I ironed or did other chores on Saturday. My father, who really loved music (he played the fiddle, ocarina or ''sweet potato,'' sang, yodeled, and whistled, and played the Jew's harp) would hear these strange sounds (to his ears) and would say, ''What do you want to listen to that stuff for?'' I don't remember how I answered him but I was so grateful he never turned off the radio . . . and I continued to listen.

* * *

One teacher in our school in Heidelberg remembers me as the teacher with an extra ticket. Yes, since I was going to the box office for my ticket I could just as well get several more tickets for staff or students. The most I got was one hundred tickets for the Vienna Choir Boys concert. Later, as I ran into former students, often they tell me they went to their first opera with me, and thanked me. Opera has all the best—orchestra, dance, singing, acting, scenery, costumes. . . . Why not take advantage of this beautiful art form?

186

* * *

Vienna seems to me to be the music city of Europe. In 1949 I finally visited Austria for the first time of many later visits. It was then a four-power city with England, France, the U.S., and Russia each having a section. My goal was to visit Composer's Corner in Central Cemetery. Alone, I got on a street car and found it. I asked the cemetery guard where many of my favorite composers were buried and he told me. I walked until I found the resting place of Beethoven, Schubert, Brahms, and many, many more. Whenever I am in Vienna, Composer's Corner is always one of my stops.

* * *

While living in Bayside in the 1960s, New York City tore down an area and built a new Opera House, a State Theater, and Philharmonic Hall, together called Lincoln Center. Al and I attended the gala premiere of the New York State Theater and the champagne reception and dance on February 22, 1966. The opera for the opening night performance and North American Premiere was *Don Rodrigo* by Ginastera. What a significant, rare, and unforgettable evening we enjoyed along with other opera devotees.

On April 12, 1966, the last performance at the old Metropolitan Opera was given. I stood outside from 5:00 to 8:30 P.M. to watch former opera singers enter for the last time. Among others was Gladys Swarthout (as a teenager I tried so hard to part my hair in the middle with waves on either side to look like her), Marjorie Lawrence, Marian Anderson, Richard Crooks (the first opera singer in recital I heard while in high school at the state music contest in Iowa City, Iowa). I was in a crowd of opera lovers from Ohio, Chicago, Pennsylvania, etc., who recognized singers and called out their names. They would smile and look pleased at the attention. It was a thrilling ''outside'' evening for me.

Again, on September 16, 1966, Al and I stood outside the *new* Opera House for four hours to watch the audience enter for the first time. It was good to live near Manhattan.

* * *

At a Carnegie Hall concert I left a few minutes before the end. As I was walking to my car, I recognized **Marian Anderson,** coming toward

187

me. I stopped her, shook her hand, telling her how her concerts had inspired me as a young contralto (hearing her while in high school in Des Moines) and how much I enjoyed her rendition of the spirituals. She was gracious as we spoke; I was so grateful I could thank her in person. The famous conductor Arthur Toscanini said, "A voice like hers is heard only once in a hundred years."

* * *

While teaching at Roslyn I was asked to be the director of the youth choir at Salem AME Church near the high school. What a wonderful experience this was for three years—working with the talented and dedicated young members of the church. We rehearsed on Saturday and sang at the Sunday service. I have never forgotten the love and music they shared with me . . . and the helpfulness of the adults. The farewell program with original songs, poems, speeches, and afterwards a dinner where I received a plaque that states:

Presented to
Mrs. LouCelle Golden
In appreciation for her deep concern and
participation in advancing the musical
talents of the church.
Salem A.M.E. Church
Roslyn, NY
June 25, 1978

* * *

Igor Stravinsky, probably the most famous twentieth-century composer, passed away in New York City on April 6, 1971. The *New York Times* stated that his body was taken to Frank E. Campbell Funeral Home at Madison Avenue and 81st Street. Knowing it would be impossible to attend his funeral I wanted to pay my respects. As soon as my classes finished in Roslyn, I drove to Manhattan, found the funeral home, parked and walked inside. As I got into the elevator the operator said, "Are you family or friend?" I answered, "Friend." In the room was a flower-covered closed casket, bouquets of flowers everywhere, and five other people. As I sat in the silent room I thought about his life—Russia, France, and United States; his music—*The Rite of Spring* (*Le Sacre du*

Printemps) which created a riot in 1913 in Paris at the first performance, and his influence on music. Before I left I wrote in the visitor's book words from his *Symphony of Psalms,* because I had recently been a member of a choir which sang that inspiring music: "Alleluia, Laudate Dominum." His funeral was the following day; burial was in the Russian portion of the island—San Michele Cemetery in Venice, Italy.

* * *

Even though I was involved with music very seldom did I see or meet the really great musicians and composers. My aim was to hear them lecture or at least "see" them. I was in G. Schirmer music store in Manhattan and recognized an elderly gentleman examining books. I went to the music books, found one written by him, took it over and asked if he would autograph it. As he wrote his name, **Aaron Copland,** I told him how much my students at Roslyn enjoyed his music. It was good to spend a few minutes with him.

* * *

The summer of 1967 I was accepted at Meadow Brook School of Music at Oakland University, Rochester, Michigan. The music director of the choral and orchestra institutes was **Robert Shaw.** For years I had wanted to study with Robert Shaw, who was the greatest choral director in United States. For the first two weeks I audited the Early Music Institute "New York Pro Musica" classes—John White, music director. I was a member of the Meadow Brook Chorus, which rehearsed and performed Haydn's *Lord Nelson Mass*; Stravinsky's *Oedipus Rex*; Beethoven's Ninth Symphony; the final concert was Bach's *Passion According to St. John.* Guest soloists came from New York and performed with the youth chorus, the Meadow Brook Chorus and the orchestra at a beautiful church. Many parents came to hear and see their son or daughter perform—and wanted "proof" by taking pictures with flashbulbs. Halfway through this difficult religious music, Mr. Shaw turned to the audience, saying, "These are not animals in a zoo to be photographed. I swear unto you if another flash goes off the performance will be stopped immediately." Then he stomped out of the room. Complete stunned silence followed! After an intermission, the *Passion* continued. The audience was quiet as they listened to this masterpiece by Bach. One does not "fool around" when the greatest choral conductor has worked so hard to have every word, every dynamic marking, every harmony, and nuance perfect. What a lifelong lesson we learned that day.

* * *

Oakland University was located twenty-five miles north of Detroit. There was much tension in Detroit that summer of 1967. In fact the problems exploded with fires burning building after building in the inner city. That same night the Meadow Brook Orchestra gave a concert at the school performing Stravinsky's *Rite of Spring*—the same composition which had caused a riot in 1913 in Paris. One had nothing to do with the other, in this case, but it seemed an interesting coincidence.

* * *

Rudolf Serkin, one of the world's great pianists, established the Marlboro Music Festival in Vermont. One summer I attended some concerts there and met Mr. Serkin, telling him I had studied piano at Interlochen Music Camp in 1945 with his Swiss friend, Felix Witzinger. He seemed pleased to hear that news: I was pleased I could tell him.

* * *

A master cellist, **Pablo Casals,** conducted his own composition, *El Pesebre,* dedicated to those who struggle for the cause of peace and democracy, in New York. I attended because I wanted to see this great man, who had left his country, Spain, when Franco came into power and vowed never to go back to his homeland until Franco left. He went into self-imposed exile in France. Later he lived in retirement in Puerto Rico, where he began each day by playing a Bach work on the piano: "A benediction on the house," he said.

His oratorio, *El Pesebre,* became his mission for peace as he conducted it in major cities in the Western world. When he discussed his mission in 1962 he said, "As a man, my first obligation is toward the welfare of my fellow men. I will endeavor to meet that obligation through music, the means which God has given me, since it transcends language, politics and national boundaries." What an unforgettable evening of music conducted by the great musician, who was in his nineties. I was truly "In the shadow of the best."

190

* * *

Another twentieth-century composer was **John Cage,** who lectured in Miami. I wouldn't miss his talk because I wanted to hear from himself about a composition, *4′33″*. I had bought the piece—not a note on it. He said, "Music does not have to consist 'of tones and notes but can be anything that takes place during a fixed duration." That piece meant the pianist sat in front of the open keyboard for four minutes and thirty-three seconds of silence marked only by whatever environmental sounds occurred. Interesting . . . but music?

* * *

Whenever I am in a foreign country I always try to find "composers' haunts." In London in 1951 I went to the church where Handel had played the organ and wanted to see the organ in the loft. The caretaker would *not* let me go upstairs to see it. Why? Because some visitors had taken pieces of the wood of the organ as a memento; now no visitor was allowed. I pleaded, I told him I was an American music teacher, and nothing helped.

One can go to Vienna and be shown all the homes where great composers lived—Mozart, Beethoven (he moved often), and many others. I always enjoy that "composers' tour."

* * *

During the ISME (International Society of Music Educators) Conference at Interlochen Music Camp in Michigan in 1966 I had the privilege of shaking hands and talking with **Zoltan Kodaly.** He was one of the world's leading composers of choral music and in the forefront of Hungary's prominance in researching folk music during the time of the Communist occupation. Fourteen years later, I was in Hungary. My friend, Anita and I found the bus in Budapest that would take us to Kekskemet, Kodaly's birthplace, where the Kodaly Institute was located. The bus ride was approximately two hours. Along the way we saw churches, the House of Science and Technic (formerly a synogogue), and the city hall with a large square in front, and we drove to the center of Kekskemet. There was a statue of Kodaly facing a group of singers on a white background—the first time I had seen a famous musician with his face looking at the choir. It was beautiful. A short distance away was

191

the Kodaly Institute, newly whitewashed building with a ramp and on the entrance glass doors was a notice: "No Visitors." That was not going to stop me. With my ISME button on my lapel (we had just attended the ISME Conference in Warsaw, Poland), I opened the doors and walked to the information window. The registrar of the institute came and I explained who we were and what we wanted. By now two French girls had joined us. The woman in charge was so kind and warm and said she was happy to see anyone from ISME, and conducted our tour. The corridor was spotless with heavy brown chairs interspersed between huge plants against the white wall. One modern tapestry was hanging from a wall. The lecture room was free, so we were escorted inside. Again specially designed chairs, white walls, and fifteen flags of the countries of the forty-one students who were now at the institute were in the back. She explained the small exhibit of pictures—one had a wooden xylophone of only seven–eight bars. Kodaly always said the bars should only be made of wood. We then went to the courtyard, where a tree was planted in the middle and white basket-woven chairs were around round white tables. Here we asked questions about Kodaly, the institute and the research. What an opportunity to study at that institute; I was happy to visit and spend a few hours there.

When Kodaly died in 1967, his widow sent me the black-rimmed card from Hungary which stated: "Accept my profound gratitude for your words of sympathy on the death of my beloved husband" and her signature. It came in a black-rimmed envelope. I was very touched by her thoughtfulness.

* * *

The great negro bass-baritone, **Paul Robeson,** passed away on January 25, 1976, in Philadelphia. An article in the *New York Times* stated his funeral would be in New York City. The hours of the viewing at the Harlem Funeral Home were also given. Since I had never heard him sing in person, I felt I must pay my respects. After a day of teaching, I drove alone to Harlem and found 141st Street. The room was filled with friends and family as I walked up to the open coffin to pay homage to this very controversial man, whom I believe was trying to help the cause of his own race. In his hand was a beautiful flower.

January 27th was the funeral at the A.M.E. Zion Church in Harlem at 8:00 P.M. My teacher friend from school, Roosevelt Van Williams, and

I drove to the church, arriving a couple hours before the service began. We knew the sanctuary would be filled and we wanted to be part of the congregation. Recorded songs by Paul Robeson were played until the service began: the spirituals, "Ol' Man River," etc. What a concert. And what a collection of black people and white people who had come to finally accept his courage and the many injustices done to him during his lifetime—friends, foes, press, strangers, musicians, everyone seemed to be there. His closed casket was draped in black with a covering of red roses and was placed at the foot of the pulpit. During the service, several people spoke, and the large choir sang several songs. The words of his son, the last speaker, were eloquent and he thanked the "great and gentle warrior" who was his father. As the coffin was carried out of the church into the cold rain, strains of "Deep River" were heard throughout.

I am sorry I never heard him sing during his life but grateful I could be part of the end of his life.

* * *

The first performance of a live orchestra was the Minneapolis Symphony when I was attending St. Olaf College. The conductor was the world famous **Dmitri Mitropoulos.** I was thrilled with the orchestra sound. When living in Long Island, we had a subscription to the New York Philharmonic with **Leonard Bernstein** as conductor. What a mountaintop experience!

* * *

In 1943 the *Trapp Family Singers* gave a concert at Saint Olaf College, where I was a student. I sat in the fifth row and was intrigued by their long braids, their Austrian traditional costumes worn by these sisters and brothers and their mother, Maria. They had recently arrived in the United States after they had escaped from the Nazis. They were not well known. The folk songs and madrigals were beautifully sung by this family. Later I bought records of their songs. Once on a bus trip through Spain in 1955 their record was on the loudspeaker for most of the day and it made the trip even better. In 1958, when I came back to the States after working in Germany, I wanted to attend a session on recorders (the small wooden instrument with eight finger holes) at their mountain lodge in Stowe, Vermont. How disappointed I was when we drove there to find out that those lessons were no longer given by the members of the Trapp family.

On January 7, 1976, **Maria von Trapp** spoke at the Saint Olaf Alumni Dinner in New York City; I knew I would be there. As I was visiting with other alumni, we noticed Maria come into the room. She had grey hair, wore a scarf over her hair; her dress was the dirndl-type, wine colored with a dark blue vest. The white puffed sleeves had lace around the edge as well as the neck. She wore two strands of pearls and a medal on a long gold chain; she had a gold band on her right hand. She then posed with some people in front of the fireplace as we watched. During dessert and coffee the speeches began and finally Baroness von Trapp was introduced. Part of the introduction said she skis every day in Vermont, and she corrected it to "almost" every day. A young photographer was there and sat down on a chair in the front. She said, "Please take the pictures," which he did. Then she said, "Now will you go someplace else." She read off the charities that would benefit from the Saint Olaf choir concert in Lincoln Center a few days later (she was the patroness of that concert) and said her favorite charity was refugees and exiles. Since she and her family had been refugees she knows what it is like. "Whole peoples are being moved now with the latest ones the Vietnamese people. Even Jesus and his family were exiles when they were told one night to move to Egypt because someone was trying to kill them." The next part of her talk was about music and the twenty or so years the Trapp Family Singers had brought music to people everywhere. "In the audience would be 500 or 5000 individuals with hearts, with brains, with their own problems. Something happens in a concert which welds them together until there are not 5000 people anymore but one heart and one body. People will be better people after they come towards loving, a state of mind, a state of the soul. We are allowed to do this to our fellow human beings. The lines I like best from the *Sound of Music* are:

> A bell is no bell until you ring it
> A song is no song till you sing it
> And love in your heart isn't put there to stay
> Love isn't love till you give it away."

She received a standing ovation from those present and much applause.

For me, it was wonderful to see and hear this strong woman. As she was ready to leave, I took my pen and card and asked her if she would give me her autograph so I could give it to my niece, who had just performed as one of the children, Marta, in the local school production of *The Sound of Music.* As she started writing her name I told her my niece's name was "Jennie," hoping she would write that, but there were so many other people waiting to talk with her she just wrote her name. How lucky Jennie was to receive it.

The Trapp Family Singers proved what music making is capable of doing. Even though the songs used in the musical were composed for the occasion, it touched the lives of millions around the world. It was the folk songs and madrigals, the authentic music the family sang that touched me.

* * *

On September 22, 1960, my husband Al and I arrived at 3:30 P.M. to have a short visit with **Grandma Moses,** having made the arrangements by phone a few days before our drive to Eagle Bridge, New York. Mrs. Forest Moses answered the knock on the door and asked if we were Mr. and Mrs. Golden. She invited us into the living room and told us Grandma had just awakened from a nap and we would have to wait a short time. We sat down and looked around the room. On the walls were a portrait of Grandma, four pictures she had painted, a picture of "Ike" with greetings for her one-hundredth birthday on September 7, a bust of Albert Schweitzer on the large old-fashioned piano (top down), along with many other items. We commented about the piano to Mrs. Moses and she said it didn't work but Grandma had brought it from Virginia and kept it for sentimental reasons. She also told us about the IBM exhibit of Grandma's paintings through October. While she went to get Grandma another white-haired lady came from another room and introduced herself as a daughter-in-law.

Then *the* moment arrived and a tiny, very stooped lady came through the dining room with the help of Mrs. Moses. Grandma wore a figured dark dress with a soft pink crocheted sweater. She had a velvet ribbon around her neck with a pin decorating the ribbon. She wore heavy stockings and black shoes. Her bright sparkling eyes twinkled behind her glasses. She sat on the davenport as Mrs. F. said, "Grandma can sit down and then the guests can introduce themselves." I shook her hand, which was so velvety soft and told her what an honor it was to meet her, and Al introduced himself. I then sat down in an armchair right beside Grandma, on her left side. Al had bought her book at the gift shop in Eagle Bridge, hoping she would sign it. Grandma saw the book and started talking about the "queer way it got written," so I asked, "How's that?"

She proceeded to explain. She didn't dot the "*i*'s or cross the "*t*'s", but Mrs. Forest said, in a very soft voice, "She is a little mixed up about it" and asked Al if he wanted it autographed. He said, "Yes, here is a ballpoint pen," but Mrs. F. went out and brought back a bottle of ink and a dip pen and said, "Grandma likes hers." Quite a discussion followed regarding the page to sign. I suggested a certain page but Grandma said, "If you are Scotch, you can tear that page out and use the book again." Mrs. F. softly said, "But there aren't many Scotch left anymore," and Grandma pointed to herself. So I told her I was of Norwegian ancestry and we felt the same way. Grandma said, "The Scotch are thrifty, not stingy, but thrifty." Then she signed the page: "22 Sept. 1960 Grandma Moses," taking her at least five minutes.

Grandma started talking about paintings, telling us she had painted a picture of Gettysburg. "Mr. Eisenhower has Angus's cows and there was a little empty place so I put in a Holstein. You know, he never paid me for it, nor thanked me. He sent me a card from Europe and I think it was to get my vote; I think he knew then he'd be president. I liked Harry. I have boyfriends all over the world." She then asked Al how much he paid for the book, and he said $5.00. Mrs. F. said, "One gets so little from books, only eleven cents for each copy sold." Al asked Grandma how her 1913 Overland was doing and she answered, "Oh, that's away in the woods; it's dead." Mrs. F. was curious and asked Al where he found out about the Overland.

Grandma didn't like the picture on the front of *Life*'s September 9 issue. She took the magazine and pointed to her neck and said, "Just look at that neck!" She told us how the photographer was on his knees, almost under the piano. Al asked her if I could take a flash picture and Mrs. F. said yes, so I had to walk to the car to get the camera. While I was gone Al told her that he liked her philosophy of keeping busy and thinking something funny. Before I took the photo Mrs. F. pulled down the venetian blind behind Grandma . . . who said she was not dressed up for the picture, but I told her that the photo was for the two of us as a memento of our visit. I asked her if she saw spots after the flash and she answered, "Not when I don't look at the flash." Mrs. F. said Grandma was used to flash pictures.

When arrangements were made, Mrs. F. had told us to stay only ten minutes because Grandma tired easily. I told Grandma we were leaving now and she said, "I feel all right." As I shook her delicate hand she said, "I hope we meet again, even if it's on the moon . . . and it might be." Mrs. F. thanked us for cooperating as she led us to the door. I looked back at Grandma and she was busy fluffing the pillows where she was sitting. We had been with this "primitive" painter, a late starter, for twenty minutes. The atmosphere had been most pleasant and friendly. Now that we were leaving the daughters-in-law could continue sorting and counting Grandma's birthday mail from two huge sacks. Grandma truly did have friends all around the world!

* * *

When I moved to Long Island I needed more nature but didn't know where the wildlife sanctuaries were; therefore, I joined the Audubon Society and found there were many nearby. Jones Beach had a good area where one drove on the narrow dirt path with bushes and small trees everywhere. I could stop anywhere, observing the variety of birds. Often after teaching all day I would drive there for a relaxing "birding" hour to be soothed and have my senses put in tune again. Another sanctuary was near the airport but one had to walk through it. Attending the monthly evening Audubon meetings was interesting, informative, as members shared their unusual-birds-sighted lists, etc.

The National Audubon Meeting was held once a year in Manhattan with a banquet in a hotel, a speaker, guests, and members from many states. Once **Roger Tory Peterson,** the famous American ornithologist who has written and illustrated many bird books, was the speaker. What an honor to hear this renowned authority talk about his world "birding" experiences: "In a world that seems so very puzzling is it any wonder birds have such appeal? Birds are, perhaps, the most eloquent expression of reality." Because of his excellent illustrated bird books he has helped generations of people enjoy nature by using their eyes, their ears—listening and looking and identifying these free tenants of the sky and land. He certainly has made a "birder" out of me.

* * *

Richard Leakey, the anthropologist from Kenya, Africa, was the lecturer one evening at Town Hall in Manhattan in the 1970s; I invited my nephew, Jim, to attend with me. His lecture was most informative—for me it brought back memories from my visits in Kenya.

His parents, Louis and Mary Leakey, were famous English anthropologists who spent a lifetime excavating and studying prehistoric sites in the Rift Valley. In Olduvai Gorge in 1959 they discovered the skull and tools of a Stone Age man. At the site of this discovery a monument was erected. When I was studying in Nairobi the film *The Dawn of Man* about Dr. Leakey and Olduvai Gorge, made by *National Geographic,* was shown. I wanted to see Olduvai for myself; I got there in 1974.

Our van drove as close as possible to the site; it had rained the previous day. When we stepped out of the vehicle onto the wet, tan, claylike soil, immediately clumps of clay stuck to our shoes, making them look like snowshoes. We tried to walk down the slope, but the clay was so slippery I fell on my seat and slid right to the monument. What a way to get there! I wondered how many other tourists had arrived at the monument the way I had. After the lecture I wanted to tell Richard my tale but the opportunity didn't occur.

* * *

My good friend from teaching days in Heidelberg, Germany, Ann Brookins, asked me to go with her when she interviewed **Ralph J. Bunche,** Under-Secretary at the United Nations. I gladly accepted her invitation in 1963. When we got to the correct building we had to sign papers at various security stations before we finally entered the room where Ann could interview Mr. Bunche. She was interested in writing his biography; there were many questions and answers. What a pleasure to be in the presence of such a great human being! I have never forgotten the moments with him at the United Nations.

* * *

Margaret Mead, anthropologist and curator of ethnology at the American Museum of Natural History in New York, had studied people in the Pacific Islands in 1929 and revisited them in 1953. These primitive people were uninfluenced by the twentieth century in her earlier study. She wrote books about her studies; I read most of them. I wanted to hear her lecture. The opportunity arrived when she spoke at Great Neck High

School, not far from Roslyn, where I taught. I arrived at the school at 5:30 P.M.; the lecture began at 7:30. So many people came, the auditorium filled. Others were placed in another room with a loudspeaker system. It was good I had gone early.

She arrived on stage with a long staff in her hands; the first time I had seen a person using one. I was already impressed. Her lecture was one of a kind—extraordinary.

Because of her, I chose primitive peoples and their music for my sabbatical study around the world.

VII
LIVING IN INDIA (1978–1982)

The journey of a thousand miles begins with one step.
—Lao Tzu, Chinese Philosopher (570–490 B.C.)

15

Teaching at the Woodstock School, 1978–1982

It had been four and one-half months since I was notified of my acceptance as a music teacher at the Woodstock International School in Mussoorie, India; at last, I was flying from New York via London, Frankfurt,
Iran, to New Delhi. The days had been filled with packing, buying, sorting, packing, cleaning, and more packing. My seventeen-year-old nephew,
David, had spent two weeks with me attending the end-of-the-year activities at Roslyn High School, where I was ending my twenty years as a
choral music teacher. The last musical had been dedicated to me, saying:
"This production is dedicated to LouCelle Golden upon her retirement
from the Roslyn Public Schools. We will always remember how much
music she gave us and salute her as Our Fair Lady." What a lovely
gesture! David had helped me so much with boxes and clearing out the
music room, carrying the footlocker and five duffle bags into the building
at the airport for early departure to India. I could never thank him enough
for all his help. We had driven to Iowa for a short visit with my family.
I gave my Dodge Dart Swinger to another nephew, Mark, for use at
college. Soon I flew back to New York, making final arrangements with
my good friend Anita, who would take care of my apartment and business
while I was gone. These thoughts and many more soared through my
mind as I relaxed, looking forward to my new way of life for three
years in the foothills of the Himalayas flying at 31,000 feet over the
Atlantic Ocean.

While waiting to use the restroom I talked with an Indian woman
also waiting. She was from Delhi and had been teaching math at a school
in Nova Scotia; her new job was in New York. I was teaching in New
York, now going to India to teach. What a coincidence! We became
instant friends, talking most of the way to India. She was on her way to
meet several men her family had chosen for her to meet; she was excited
by the thought that perhaps she would get married. We exchanged addresses and hoped to see each other in India.

For part of the trip my seat companion was from Teheran, Iran,
with the usual headcovering. She had a beautiful smile and wrinkled her

nose when she smiled. Immediately she offered me some candy, telling me about her married son in London. Later she sprayed perfume from a new purchase on her blouse and that was nice. There were four seats available together so I lay down to sleep; I was so tired.

Our Pan-Am flight arrived in Delhi at 1:30 A.M. Customs took an hour, waiting for luggage and health clearance, writing down the number of my typewriter, my cameras and telephoto lens, etc. When I was finished, Dan Lind, the head of the music department, welcomed me to India and took me to the YMCA, where I would spend two nights. After three hours of sleep I was up at 7 A.M. wanting to take a shower after the long flight. There was no washcloth or towel. I had not included them in my hand luggage so I used a sponge and a tiny piece of soap; already it was extremely hot and humid. I heard sounds outside so I went on the terrace and saw many Indians washing clothes by hitting them on hard slabs, which must wear out the material quickly. They did it in rhythm in many tanks of water. Yes, it was the local "laundromat." I knew I had arrived in interesting India.

After breakfast I was introduced to Mr. and Mrs. Silver from New Zealand, also new teachers. Much was made of the fact our names were "Silver and Golden"; there were also Muttons and Beans already teaching at Woodstock. The Silvers and I got a taxi and drove to customs for unaccompanied baggage, signing many papers. Then we drove to another "godown" (storage area) where we had to open all of it. My seven pieces were opened: five duffle bags, one saxophone I was taking to the school, and one footlocker. Because I had sent it so early in June and didn't arrive until a month later, I had to pay outrageous storage fees. With the help of a supervisor the amount was cut in half. After three hours there, coolies carried it all out to a taxi along with Mr. Silver's wooden box and cases; we were loaded. Back to the YMCA for lunch. I took the Silvers' sixteen-year-old daughter and a new Chinese student to the Tibetan bazaar and found Chagga's shop. I had met her in 1974 and asked her if she had gotten the photo I sent of her and her son. She answered, "I have it framed." I bought Anna a small silver ring and Lob a stone for a chain as welcome presents. Then the three of us stopped at the Imperial Hotel for Coca-Colas before going back to the Y. I had rested for a couple of hours when there was a knock on my door. It was my good friend, Richard Smyth, a minister in New Delhi. We talked about his wife, Sylvia (a former student of mine from Heidelberg teaching days), their furlough in Italy and the U.S., his church, etc. It was so good going back to India where friends were. I always think the *second* time to a foreign country is better than the first time!

After a ten-hour sleep that night a rap on the door told me I must hurry. Anna said the taxi was waiting for our long five-hour trip to Mussoorie. After a very quick breakfast we loaded the taxi. I sat in front with the Sikh driver, my typewriter, tote bag, small suitcase. The four Silvers were in the backseat with a long Maori spear in a yellow case. All the luggage was on the top and in the trunk. There wasn't an empty inch anywhere! We didn't mind because we watched out the windows and saw carts pulled by small horses, cattle, goats, buffalo herds, bicycles, motorcycles, cars honking horns to pass, people walking, working in the fields, villages and towns with various activities. Finally we stopped at Deer Park for restroom facilities and a cheese sandwich and Limca for lunch. Then the beginning of the hills and the busy commercial town of Dehra Dun, after which came the long, narrow, winding room up to Mussoorie—potholes, and rocks, which our driver removed.

At last, we arrived at the gate of Woodstock School and were met by staff who helped us find our new homes. Mine was right there in the quad area with classrooms nearby. Coolies carried my luggage to my room on the second floor where I would spend not three years but five, because I extended my contract. Thus began my new life teaching music at an international school with students from forty countries. Yes, it was like a "United Nations" and I was so pleased to be a part of it.

New teachers were told to take it easy the first few days because of the altitude of 6500 feet. I did have meetings of the music staff, was shown the classrooms, the schedules, met other staff, many invitations for meals, and a potluck dinner for all the staff. Classes began and I found out I had students from the following countries in various classes: England, Sweden, Norway, India, Iran, Thailand, Bhutan, Canada, Pakistan, Tibet, Switzerland, Kuwait, Malaysia, New Zealand, Australia, Uganda, Korea, Kenya, Laos, Jordan, Lebanon, Afghanistan, Scotland, Ireland, the U.S., and several Westerners living in Nepal because their parents worked elsewhere. What a fabulous assortment of students. There were seven music teachers. Two were Indians who taught instrumental music and Indian music and dance. All grades had music classes; elementary choir made up of grades five and six; required music in seventh and eighth grades; senior choir; two bands, one orchestra; private lessons on all instruments and piano. One building contained only practice rooms, with a music secretary assigning the rooms and helping students. The

English started this music tradition way back when the school was first established in the 1860s. Yes, the "hills were alive with the sound of music."

The bazaar of Mussoorie was approximately one mile from school; students and staff walked there on Saturdays for shopping, browsing, or a restaurant meal. Three Jeeps and two motorcycles were owned by the school or staff. I would usually get a ride in a Jeep to the rickshaw stand, where I changed to "my" blue-painted rickshaw pulled by two men; if there were two of us, two more men would push. The men waited for me, puffing on beedies, while I looked in a cloth stall, or a Kashmir shop filled with the carved wooden objects and embroidered shawls, or a food store. Leona, a teacher friend from school, and I would have our lunch at the Kwality restaurant, sitting near a window that overlooked the street with such a variety of people walking below. This became my favorite spot for people-watching. After our lunch we got into the rickshaw for the long ride back to school. Along the way we saw men carrying heavy loads on their backs navigating steep steps; hill women in their long traditional dresses and arms covered with bracelets, gold rings in their noses; Tibetan women in long skirts with the colorful striped aprons selling sweaters along the streets; and children in various school uniforms (there were approximately twenty private schools in Mussoorie). The shops and stalls were so varied—a man sitting on the floor in front of his sewing machine busy making a Punjabi outfit; next might be a spice or grain shop with large sacks open showing the contents; perhaps a cloth shop or a sweet shop where we would watch as he put batter in a cloth bag and squeezed it out into designs in hot oil, then taking it out for a coating of a sweet honey mixture. I *never* tired of the sights, sounds, and smells of that hill station with the winding narrow road through the bazaar! When looking north the snow-covered peaks were seen; looking south was the beautiful Doon Valley with green fields and forests.

Monsoon rains fell almost every day in the summer and with them—no electricity. With the first flash of lightning, electricity was affected. One time it rained for twenty-seven hours straight, without letup. Umbrellas were a *must* there. When the season ended and a sunny, cloudless day appeared, the headmaster of the school announced to all, "It is a Fair-Weather Day with no school." Everyone spent the day outside hiking, visiting friends, or walking to the bazaar. It truly was a meaningful day in sunshine and fresh air.

Another special day was "Independence Day," August 15. At 9 A.M. all students gathered in the quad courtyard for Indian flag raising, speeches about the 1947 Independence Day, poetry in Hindi and English by students—closing with the singing of the national anthem accompanied by the harmonium and a string instrument. All students received their bag lunches and left for a day's outing in town or in the hills. Because Leona had worked in India for nearly thirty years, she had many friends and invited me to visit several with her. The first Independence Day we walked up the steep hill above school to the home of the Buchanan sisters, where the four of us sat on their veranda overlooking the snows and hills far away. We were at 7000 feet and saw the huge *Lammergeiers* with wing span of nine feet soaring above the valley. Edith and Ruth's mother had been a missionary in India (originally from Canada), so they had grown up in India. One had become a teacher in Delhi; the other was a doctor who had begun a school there. They told the story that when one had worked in a village for several years, one of the village men always spent his night guarding the house so no danger would come to her (it was not requested; he did it on his own). We shared our bag lunches with them and they shared coffee.

Now they were retired and close to eighty years old. The older one had rheumatoid arthritis, walking with a cane with difficulty. Edith loved flowers, birds, all of nature, and knew all their names. She always furnished the flowers for the altar of the hillside church. The sun became too hot, so we all went in the house where there were shelves and more shelves filled with books, various Indian collectibles, comfortable chairs, and scattered rugs. One room had a fireplace, which would be needed at that altitude. Ruth soon went to her bedroom saying, "Now it is time to rest and that means no talking. . . . Tea will be at 3 o'clock." However, we left before that time. Leona had given them homemade pickles and yak cheese from Nepal; I gave them macaroon cookies. Edith went to another room for a small folder of Nepalese paper with gold blockprint. On the bottom it said, "Sanchi Stupa 2, 2nd Century B.C., Jan. 27/67, EB." (Edith must have had it printed in Nepal.) Inside was a portion of a poem:

> Musicians, painters, poets, man
> Who made the world more lovely then. . .
> Men, from whose handiwork we see
> Horizons in Eternity
>   —from "In Glad Thanksgiving" by John Masefield

It was so sweet of her to give that precious gift to me because I was a "musician." Leona thought I should get a "dandy" (a canvas chair carried by two men) to take me back down the steep hill. Edith sent her servant for one; however, he came back saying there was none available (I gave him a rupee for his trip). I had a feeling I would have to walk down, which I did. Before arriving at school, the heavens opened and the rain came down in torrents. We were soaked to our skin by the time we arrived at the quad. After drying myself, resting under my electric blanket, I felt fine.

The evening celebration of Independence Day was an Indian buffet meal. Students had painted steps and the floor in certain areas with Indian designs. Butter lamps were placed here and there in the designs. On the tables were candles in cut-out clay lanterns. After the meal everyone went to Parker Hall for entertainment by the students—Indian dances and songs; the staff danced a peasant dance; the sweepers ended the program with a circle dance picking up sticks, which they struck together in rhythm, making loud cracking sounds. What an interesting day August 17 had been.

We had many special days. Another was Servant's Day, when the staff and students did the work of the servants; all their work of cleaning, cooking, and serving them the noon meal. (I helped with the cleaning of the sacks of rice, taking out stones or bits of leaves; sometimes it was preparing vegetables.) On that day the servants played games and had other activities. The students served them their meal on a large banana leaf while they sat on the floor in a classroom. Servant's Day made for good relations between those who taught, those who learned, and those who worked at Woodstock.

Since the school was a boarding school there seemed to be work for the staff at all hours. No one minded in that unusual international Christian school. After school hours were the sports activities; teachers had study hall duties in the evening; on Saturday staff often chaperoned hiking groups for the day or the weekend on the many available treks. With no television the environment was healthy for character building, global interests, and living among students with other cultures, customs, and religions. The cooperation and organization of the school made this a "heaven on earth" in my thinking.

Because I planned to be there for several years I made many purchases so my large room would look "Indian": small Kashmir *numda*

rugs, curtains of Indian fabric for the windows, lamps and Indian collecta-
bles scattered on small carved Kashmir tables. It was such fun making
my room into "my home." I also had a large storage-bathroom with a
sink, toilet, and tin tub, which was usually full of water for emergency
use when the electricity was off. I had to buy wood for my small black
potbelly stove; wood was stored in that room behind a cupboard for my
supplies, electric skillet, etc. About 5 P.M. my sweeper would bring a
four-gallon can of hot water with a padded cover. If it was cold, at the
same time he would light my stove. (Usually no classrooms had heat, only
the rays of the sun.) Because of this, the semester ended on December 10
with students going to their own countries until the middle of February;
in the summer there was a three-week break between semesters. The
system worked very well.

I bought a sitar and made arrangements for lessons from the father
of our Indian folk song and dance teacher. I planned to practice after
school and take a lesson each week. It turned out that plan didn't work.
Because I was right across from the dorms for the young girls, with the
seventh and eighth-grade girls up a flight of stairs, some of them came
to my room to play games such as Yatzee, spelling games, etc. It seemed
that I was needed to help them with their loneliness and adjustment to
boarding school—that was much more important than learning an Indian
instrument. One evening when the faculty had open hours for students
three girls in seventh grade came and confided in me that they were
homesick; they felt as though no one liked them. One had lived in Afghanistan and had home tutoring, then moved to Bangladesh (her father
was an engineer); Kamala was from Canada and thought I talked like
her grandmother in Ohio so she planned to call me "Nanny"; Supriya,
also from Canada of East Indian heritage, was so homesick she cried and
cried. I was afraid she wouldn't stay to the end of the semester. She was
so sweet I did hope she would adjust. Once she told me, "Did you tell the
month goodbye?" I never forgot that statement; now I try to remember to
tell each month good-bye! She did adjust and stayed. Near the door of
my room I placed a "nature table" with interesting stones, a beautiful
butterfly (I called it a cathedral butterfly because of all the colors), shells
I found in Sri Lanka and South India, etc. Often there was a rap on my
door and two girls would bring a feather or rock they wanted to put on
the nature table. I hoped they would appreciate beauty in the small objects
with them. I would never know if their interest continued.

Happy Valley, the Tibetan settlement, was about five miles from Woodstock on the other side of Mussoorie. I already had met Tashi in 1974 at the art studio there. Now his sister, Yeshi Dolma, was a student at the tailoring school there. She often walked that distance once a month when students could leave on Sunday. Usually a friend was with her bringing delicious *momos* (steamed dough with a meat filling) as part of our snack after we talked. I helped her with words in English and we played other teaching games like Yatzee. Before they left we had tea and snacks. We became good friends—I learned so much about her life and she learned about the American way of living. Each month I looked forward to her visit at school. When Happy Valley had a three- or five-day "picnic" I was invited to see special activities by the students from several Tibetan schools participating from various parts of India.

I became friends with Dolma, a Tibetan woman who was a nurse's aide at Woodstock. She also invited me to attend functions at Happy Valley. I would never forget the movie I saw with her one evening outside in the courtyard surrounded by all the Tibetans living at that settlement. The Dalai Lama's brother and other Tibetans in exile had permission to go to Tibet and make a movie of anyone or anyplace in Tibet. This was the first film Tibetans had seen after they escaped in 1959. When they recognized a place or person in the film they quietly clicked their tongues as they saw the ragged clothes, the destruction, or a familiar sight. It was a traumatic experience for all the Tibetans; it was a real eye-opener for me!

16

Bus Tour Around India, Winter 1978–1979

Melissa, my niece, graduated from the University of Iowa with a degree in music; I wrote her asking if she would like to join me for a six-week bus tour all around the outer edge of India. She replied that she would be happy to accept my invitation. Since she had not traveled out of United States I was concerned about her safe arrival in faraway India. I wrote her saying, "You can memorize a complete Beethoven Sonata, I am sure you can get from Iowa to New Delhi without any problem." December 29, 1978, I arrived at the Delhi airport for her Pan-Am 1:30 A.M. flight, only to be told it was late and would arrive at 4:15 A.M. The wait was long—what a relief to see Melissa come through the customs area clearing her three bags and trombone! A quick hug and kiss and we were off to Viswa Yuvek Kendra, a youth hostel, passing several camel carts along the road. We talked and laughed and were so happy to be together again for an adventure around India. She brought me Hershey bars, granola bars, and other goodies I missed; I gave her an Indian Punjabi outfit for the trip. We did some exploring of Delhi, took extra luggage to Mrs. Rugh's for storage, and ate meals at my favorite restaurants. I wanted Lissa's two days in Delhi to impress her. New Year's eve several other staff members met us for our Chinese meal, going to an ice cream shop for dessert.

January 2 the bus with two drivers from Dehra Dun arrived for tour members at our hostel at 7 A.M. Luggage was loaded on top of the bus with a tarp over it. Almost at every corner the driver would stop for directions to the road leading us out of Delhi. It made me wonder if we would ever complete the tour. Finally, we got to the country with villages, bullock carts, goats, seven-eight camels, three dancing bears, ten Sauris cranes, one elephant, and twenty-two peacocks, all the first day. At all stops I told Lissa, "Don't drink the water." And again I told her until I was sure she got the message; we drank boiled Hindustani tea at stalls using our own tea cups.

Mathura, a holy city, was our first overnight at an international guest house next to the temple and birthplace of Krishna. Loudspeakers beamed music day and night, making it almost impossible to rest. Parents of two students lived in Mathura and made arrangements for a tour of the museum, filled with objects from before the Maurya dynasty from 325 to 184 B.C., and from foreign conquerors such as the Parthians and the Greeks. We then had a tour of his insecticide plant having tea with spices, sandwiches, carrot halva, a rice mixture, fruit. As we enjoyed the food he told about his family leaving Delhi (persecution) 350 years ago and hiding in a temple in Mathura. What a story! Later, after our evening meal at Kwality we drove ten kilometers to Brindavan and visited four different temples. Back to our guest house for a night of chants, calls, noise, bird songs; it was too much for my sensitive ears.

Every day was filled with travel and sightseeing. Dick, a teacher at Woodstock, was the leader and made all arrangements for the twenty-five or thirty tour members; all cooperated and for the most part there were very few problems, mainly with the bus drivers, who did *not* know the route or what was expected of them. Many times they got out of the bus and sat down beside it saying, "We will not continue." Somehow, they did complete the entire trip—but with many mistakes. Once they drove under the wrong cement arch, which ripped the tarp and many suitcases on the top of the bus. Another time they hit a pig, a terrible violation. When we went by train from Madras to Calcutta, leaving much luggage on the bus, which they would drive, they were told not to pick up anyone, but when we boarded again in Calcutta there were small bits of grain on the floor *and* Melissa's suitcase was gone. In Goa they parked the bus, not on the concrete slab but *beside* it in the sand. Dick had to spend our three days in this seaside area trying to get help. After various attempts, the bus got on the solid foundation. That winter tour sponsored by the school had always used train transportation; using the bus was an experiment—most of the time it was great with a few huge exceptions.

A brief summary of the tour by bus took us down the west coast to the tip and up the east coast traveling by train, boat, elephant, horse carriage, rickshaw, and bicycle rickshaw. After Delhi and Mathura, the other places of interest were Bharatpur Bird Sanctuary, where we saw millions of birds; Fatepur Sikri, the ghost town built about 1570; Agra, with the Taj Mahal; Jaipur, the pink city in Rajasthan; Bundi, where we stayed in the guest house of the Maharaja on a lake; Ajanta and Ellora cave temples carved out of rock from 2 B.C. to A.D. 7—certainly "wonders of the world"; Bombay for a few days then to Goa by ship; Bangalore and dinner at the home of an Indian music friend, Christine; afterwards the three of us attended a concert by a string quartet from the University of Iowa—what a coincidence. When the beautiful Western music, including Barber's "Adagio for Strings" (my favorite piece), was over Melissa introduced herself to them as a recent graduate from the same university. The first violinist took off his garland of white flowers interspersed with six red roses and tassels of marigolds he had just been given and placed it around Melissa's neck. What a poignant moment and thrill for her! I was pleased Christine shared that experience with us.

Next came Mysore with an interesting museum; Mudumalai wildlife sanctuary where we rode elephants at dawn with bird calls, the quiet padding of the elephants, and the swishing of grasses as they were torn off by his trunk—for two hours he could just as well be eating. With the tall grass it was difficult to see animals but we did see spotted deer, one jungle cat, two black bears, langur monkeys, sambhar, elephants, and bonnet monkeys as we slowly swayed in the howdah on the lumbering elephant . . . the first of many other rides during my time in India. Then we drove to Ootycamund, the Queen Hill Station in South India; Cochin, a large port in Kerala with history from the first century to now and a beautiful synagogue built in 1568 with handpainted willow pattern floor tiles from China and exquisite chandeliers. On to Kovalum where we stayed right on the beach with the highlight—seeing the performance of the *kathakali,* a classical dance form with lavish costumes and exotic masks, on the rooftop of a five-star hotel with stars shining brightly above, after which our entire group had a buffet dinner there.

Then down to Cape Cormorin, where three waters meet: the Bay of Bengal, the Arabian Sea and the Indian Ocean, and people watch the sunset and sunrise on those waters; Madurai, an old town of temples; to Kodaikanal, the sister school of Woodstock in the south where we all stayed with staff and enjoyed their hospitality, a tour of the school with special programs; Pondidcherry, a former French enclave but now known for the work of Sri Aurobindo, seeing weaving, medicine making, paper making, and the art museum. We drove to Auroville, a new concept of life in a "perfect environment"; to Madras, where we took the train to Calcutta lasting a day and a night with students on the tour taking turns watching all the luggage; Calcutta, where we took Victorian Carriages of former days to our YMCA.

We visited Tagore's home (now a museum), spent one beautiful day in the country at the home of an Indian doctor whose son had graduated from Woodstock; we didn't get to see the work of Mother Teresa, which was a disappointment; to Maithon to see a dam patterned after our TVA: Bodhgaya came next and is the place where Buddhism was born twenty-five centuries ago. Pilgrims were there from many countries and I found it to be a photographer's paradise . . . mainly those from Bhutan and Ladakh living in tents behind the Tibetan tent where we ate our meals because it was a restaurant—what an interesting place. Varanasi, or Benares as most call it, with a boat trip at dawn on the Ganges River to watch the religious pilgrims do their rituals. Some of us shopped for silk saris. To Lucknow for a luncheon at the home of a student's family; on to Delhi and home to Mussoorie. We had an overview of India, the traditions, customs, dress, making friends with those on the bus and those we met along the way. (No, Melissa was never given any compensation for the loss of her suitcase and many irreplaceable items; I felt so angry about her loss but happy we had not gotten ill on the adventure around India.)

Melissa stayed on as a volunteer music teacher for the next semester, teaching piano, private trombone lessons, accompanying choirs, and conducting groups. Imagine having your first teaching position in faraway India; she did a great job and was loved by all, with many staff saying, "She is a breath of fresh air."

Near the end of the semester there were a series of very unusual events. One Saturday night she was one of the chaperones at the dance at Parker Hall when someone rushed in saying a bus had fallen off the road and gone down the *khud* (hill) with the injured passengers taken to the hospital. People were needed to help them and perhaps even give blood. Lissa, along with others, rushed to the hospital almost half a mile away to see how they could help. Later when she came back she stopped in my room, telling me the news about the accident.

The following Saturday night we had the faculty banquet in the quad courtyard, always a lovely affair. When the cooks closed down the kitchen they put all the ashes from the stoves in the usual spot away from the school; however, there were still some live coals, which gathered momentum, spreading into a fire. Girls in the dorm saw the blaze and began getting basins, pails, large cans together, filling them with water and walking out on the roof to throw it on the fire below. They woke Lissa, who helped with the project. By the time word spread to staff houses below on the hillside and men came to help the fire was almost out. It could have been a real disaster. No one could believe that two weekends in a row there had been an emergency; everyone said, "What could possibly happen next weekend?"

The next Saturday night about 4 A.M. I felt the bed shake and the floor move—an earthquake (I had experienced many while teaching in Japan). I knew Melissa had never been in one but I didn't dare walk down the long hall to her room for fear of more serious movement; I stayed where I was. Next morning when I saw her I asked her how she slept and she answered, "Fine." She had *not* felt her first earthquake! We knew bad things happened in threes and we had had our three strange events; we didn't need to worry anymore.

During her semester she wrote a poem about the trip around India. Here it is:

Ode to the Winter Tour

This is the story of the bus tour and places that we've been.
So many tea shops, so many towns, do you think we'll get
there again?
We started off in Delhi one day; nearly thirty were in our group,
But the Muttons we left in Jaipur where Greg caught malaria
instead of the croup.
"Never fear," said Dick, our fearless guide, so we continued on
our way,
Loaded down with pills and iodine though it doesn't hurt to pray.
So then we were Tim, Beth, John, Hugh, Mike, Lark, Kiran, and
Auntie Lou
The Kernaghans, Hagues, Robert Silver, and Anita, not one but
two,
Berenice, Becky, Melissa, Ken and don't forget little Jenny
And bus drivers dear, though they bickered not one time but
many.
With grace, skill and ease the drivers maneuvered through
crowds, mountain roads,
Let me boast that now that we're safely at journey's end,
What's a pig, a tarp, and a post?
Well, southbound we traveled, saw palaces, birds, and the Taj
Through caves we wandered and tea shops we plundered
Used fields, didn't complain, very good sports.
Bombay at last and we all gave a smile as civilization is now at
our feet
Ashokas and Taj's and beaches, shopping sprees on every street.
There the Silvers joined our happy group with Mr. and Mrs.
and Anna

By this time we'd consumed ten times our weight in biscuits,
    oranges, and banana.
The boat ride to Goa was a pleasant change; the beach when we
    got there was great,
The bus got stuck in the sand; when we left, Anita, of course,
    was late.
Through Mysore, Bangalore, Mudamali we rode and there in the
    jungle pitched our tent.
And Dick had to pay when he heard Doris say:
"Look, there goes another wild elephant!"
Through Ooty in mountains and back to the coast; the Roberts
    had now joined the pack.
And traveling each day, Dick Wechter would say: "Gents front
    and ladies in back."
From the southernmost tip of India we went up to Kodaikanal.
How nice were the homes, the lake, school, and dance,
Fernandes, they say, fed us well.
Through Pondicherry, Madras, and Cal by train; we stood guard
    at night in the aisle,
We took buggies, once there; people stopped to stare; I agree, we
    made quite a sight.
Dick was right when he said, "Calcutta was best," once we
    invaded New Market place
The things there to buy, clothes piled to the sky.
When the bus left, there wasn't free space.
Now the journey will soon see its end,
It's time to give credit where credit is due
To Dick Wechter, tour director and friend
A hundred-man task force he's been.
Waker-upper, lodge-getter, food-finder,
Through thick and thin, it's always been him,
Ne'er a man with such patience, nor kinder.
We thank you, Dick Wechter, for fond memories
In the future we'll even shed a tear
When we think of your voice and hear Sammy rejoice
When you say, "Boys in front, ladies, rear!"
                                            Melissa Nelson
                                            Spring 1979
                                            Mussoorie, India

Each year there was an "activity week" the end of October when
students from grades 6–12 did a special project—a weeklong trek, a class-
related venture in Delhi, Bombay, or a village to help build a school, or

216

learn more about the culture in another part of India. Grades 1–5 had special events but closer to the home base of Mussoorie. I was one of four chaperones, using a chartered bus, to the Kulu Valley, driving for two days with our first night's stop at Chandigarh, a completely planned city and the capital of the Punjab state. The next day we were driving over narrow mountain roads, in the gorge for twenty-five miles caused by the Beas River. We stayed at the far end of the valley at Manali and found a beautiful valley with well-kept rice terraces, wooden buildings, and a thousand-year-old wooden pagodalike temple. People were dressed in another traditional garb with women wearing beautiful silver jewelry. One day our bus drove up the Rohtang Pass at 13,500 feet. Students spent time playing in the snow, collecting rocks, walking, and one boy even took a dip in a pond, which was very cold. Because of the wind we all ate our picnic lunch inside the bus; it seemed like a banquet! On a free day another chaperone and I hired a taxi (we asked the other couple to go with us but they declined) and visited Naggar where we saw an old castle believed to be over 1400 years old. We also visited the former home, now a museum, of the Russian artist Nicholas Roerich, and enjoyed his paintings. (I was very pleased to visit Roerich's home because he had been the collaborator with Igor Stravinsky in *Le Sacre du Printemps,* first presented in May 1913 in Paris.)

When Joan and I arrived back at our hotel we were told that Derry and John had gone walking around Manali; Derry looked over the edge to see a waterwheel below, the ground gave way, and she fell forty feet. Her husband got a taxi to the small hospital where she stayed until we left. Joan and I immediately went to see her and found her in extreme pain. No Xray was available, so she was on pain pills only, not knowing what was fractured. John told us that when she fell he was sure he would not see her alive again. Students were so helpful on the return bus trip, carrying her from her four seats, where she lay as we traveled, into the motel when we arrived. When we got to Mussoorie the Xray in the hospital showed a broken pelvic bone. What a brave woman she was on that long bus ride through the mountains and valleys!

Anytime we had a three-day weekend I planned a trip back into the hills. A notice was placed on the bulletin board telling the dates, where we would go, and to sign up if interested. The car was always filled with other staff. Diana, the music secretary, who had been at Woodstock many years, was a trekker and knew the best places to travel. Whoever went planned the food supplies needed for the short holiday. We usually left

217

around 6 A.M., filling the car's trunk and roof with our sleeping bags and food. Diana, Leona, Barb, Anne and I were going to the inner Garhwal Hills via Chamba, Uttarkashi, to Gangotri, a distance of 300 kilometers. The weather in late April was warm and clear. Not everyone had had breakfast so we stopped at a tea stall, then drove through the deodar forest with coolness and peace.

As we drove farther north there were many Gujjars, nomadic people, who graze their cows, goats, and buffaloes in the upper Himalayas during the summer—walking along the road or pitching tents under a clump of trees; some children gathered sticks of wood and some went to the small stream dipping their bowls and drinking. One child walked into the water washing the dust off his legs, then dipped his bowl into the water and drank. A pied kingfisher sat on a rock flicking his tail when excited. How I wished I could have stopped and spent a day or two with these people to learn about their lifestyle. It is always hurry, hurry, hurry.

After a quick rest stop at Uttar Kashi, a bustling busy town, where we had a cold drink and used the facilities at the Traveler's Lodge, we all felt better as we continued along the narrow, winding road beside the Bhagrati River rushing by. We went through a small village, Bhatwari, and on to Ganganani where there were many buses standing. It turned out that was the end of the road; we had planned to go sixty more kilometers to Gangotri but because of a landslide in that area in August, 1978, the village of Ganganani had been destroyed as well as the bridge and road. Diana got out of the car and mingled with the army people, border patrol, coolies, and mules. She found out there was a forest bungalow up a rocky unfinished road—perhaps we could stay there. She picked out six coolies to carry all our gear up to the bungalow.

I knew it would take me forever to walk the path so arrangements were made for me to sit in *kundi* or basket on the back of a coolie. One sits back to back with a cut-out in front for one's feet, which are placed on a narrow thin board; a twine strap holds one in the basket, so I wouldn't fall out. (These *kundis* are used for women pilgrims who need to get over the hills and the landslide area; I really didn't fit well in it but I did get to the bungalow without any problems). All of the coolies were from Nepal. There was a green lawn around the bungalow—anemone bushes with white flowers and purple iris were growing on either side of the veranda steps. Diana had been told we could use the veranda but when she talked to the *chowkidar* he said the doctor was away for the weekend and we could use his room. There were three beds and an attached bathroom. Our gear was put there and food supplies went in the "go-down." We washed, and ate our delicious food of potato salad, meat loaf, raw kolrabi and carrots, dill and sweet pickles, with brownies for dessert. What a feast for the stomach and for our eyes with two snow-capped peaks, the rushing river far below with the steep mountainsides.

Diana and I slept on the wooden veranda floor, on our foam mats and in our sleeping bags, but the wind was blowing so strongly everything was rattling around us. Some pieces of plaster fell down and I was glad I wasn't in that spot. Sleep never comes easily the first night outside on the ground. Many times I put on my glasses to see what was looking at me but there were only shadows of trees, the posts holding the barbed wire around the yard. After much wiggling, twisting, and turning in the sleeping bag I finally fell asleep.

The next day after breakfast, the other four went hiking farther on while I stayed at the bungalow and enjoyed the peace and serenity alone as I meditated and read. I also wrote the following:

The Himalayas are majestic, rugged, beautiful, and cruel. My view of them at the moment is from 6500 feet at a forest bungalow overlooking the Bhagrati River far below, as it courses over huge boulders; the source is about thirty-five miles away at Gangotri, where we planned to go. The landslide destroyed the entire road, the bazaar of Ganganani which disappeared in the slide. As I look across at the other side I only see bits of the paved road, and the remnants of the pilings of the bridge. A new road is being built on the opposite side of the river and up much higher. On the top of the mountain I see a few spots of snow, then the barren rockside which was a landslide and formed a lake below. Thinking of the *kundi* ride yesterday, I realized how uncomfortable it was as I felt every movement of the coolie's body as he labored up the steep, zigzag path holding the strap over his head with both hands. When we finally reached the bungalow he was covered with sweat and coughed continuously. When we leave I suppose I will use the same transportation.

And that was what happened. We enjoyed the rest of our visit in the Garhwal Himalaya, sometimes called, "the abode of the gods, and of eternal snows" and arrived safely back at Mussoorie.

Another three-day weekend we hired a car with driver and went to Corbett National Park in the hills east of Mussoorie, taking eight to ten hours to get there. Permits were necessary, and we would stay in the double-storyed forest rest house in the middle of the park; again we would take our own food supplies. Early morning we would ride on an elephant through the grasses looking for animals—wild elephants, sambhar, tigers, Himalayan black bear, hog deer, etc. I was looking for tigers; to see one in the wild was my greatest wish . . . but I never saw one in India! One time, if I had been out five minutes sooner, a tiger was lurking very near our rest house, but it was gone when I arrived. Once when there were two cars of friends in the park we were on the road following one another. A man on a motorcycle went by the car I was in and motioned to his right; however, none of us knew what he meant. The first car finally arrived at the spot and there was a tiger lying at the edge of the forest, so the driver honked the horn to tell us a tiger was there. Of course, by the time our car arrived, the tiger had gotten up and walked back into the forest. Why didn't that Indian driver blink his car lights instead of honking! There went my best chance of seeing an Indian tiger. In spite of that, the rides on the back of an elephant hold very unusual memories.

I was fortunate to be able to attend the NE/SA (Near East/South Asia) Teachers' Conference in Delhi, the first one held in India. Six hundred delegates from private schools were there from many countries: Jordan, Dubai, Egypt, Greece, Saudi Arabia, Pakistan, Nepal, Syria, Dhahran, Sri Lanka, and India. We all met each day at the American Embassy School near the embassy. The first morning Robert Goheen, U.S. Ambassador to India, gave a welcome speech on the "Spirit of Learning," which was followed by other keynote speakers. Lunches were at the school under two *shamianas* (tents), and choices were varied. One noon I sat across from a music teacher from Pakistan, who said, "I am also the acting principal because our principal was in Iran that weekend of trouble and was told to go to the Embassy, the safest place—that was the 'hostage takeover' in November 4, 1979." What a shock to hear that news from someone sitting across from me.

Most of the twenty-five present from Woodstock stayed at the Viswa-Yuvek-Kendra, a youth hostel, all on the third floor; however, a large group of Russians came so we had to move to the second floor so they could all be together. The next morning we needed breakfast at 7 A.M. before the 8 A.M. session began. We were told by the staff we would have to wait until after the Russians had eaten—that was too late for us. Since I had bought a member's card we went to the American Embassy restaurant where we had a good American breakfast. (I always tried to

220

remember the Japanese saying, "Bend with the bamboo" when plans had to be changed.)

Each day was filled with talks, looking over new resource materials, making new friends, and doing a few errands (I had to get a new passport). One evening the entertainment was the Light and Sound Show at the Red Fort; I had seen that so I did not attend. Instead some of us again went to the American Embassy restaurant for steak, salad (one didn't eat them in Indian restaurants), Cokes, and ice cream chocolate sundaes. Then home to our youth hostel—to the room with three beds but meant for two, a noisy ceiling fan, and a huge dead cockroach on our bathroom floor.

The final evening an Indian *mela* or fair was held on the grounds of the Ashoka Hotel. Garlands of marigolds were wound around the railing of the stairway that led to the grounds. At the entrance was a decorated elephant standing quietly while a group of Rajasthani women sang a welcome. Everywhere there was activity—a potter making pots, a magician, a fortune teller, two trained monkeys, acrobats, a dancing bear, two stages for folk dancing with instrumental accompaniments. The buffet tables were numerous and spread throughout the grounds with ice-sculpture birds as centerpieces. Such a variety of Indian foods—curries, birianis, chutneys, raita, dhal, chappatia, pappars, parathas, on and on. Dessert tables had ice cream, fruit salad, puddings, fruit, sweets, laddoos, gulab jamun, etc. Later from a coffee table we enjoyed demitasse coffee, as the fireworks began above us—pinwheels, rockets, four-color fire balloons that sailed off over Delhi. Finally there was dancing for those who wanted to stay longer. What a fantastic conclusion to an educational event. The only other affair I could compare it to was the Lars Christiansen weekend in Norway in 1948 on his whaling factory ship in drydock and the evening spent in his home. I also thought about my dear friend Van Williams, a teacher at Roslyn, and how much he would have enjoyed this splendid evening!

One day when teaching at Woodstock, I had to do some typing in my own room midmorning. I left the door open as I rapidly typed. Out of my left eye I thought I saw something at the door and thought it was Diana's big dog, Botoo, so I said, "Botoo, get out." The shape did not move so I turned my head to face the door and saw a huge male rhesus monkey sitting there. I yelled "Get out." Diana was passing by in the quad and said, "What's the matter, Lou?" I told her a rhesus monkey was at the door and she said, "Be very careful." I then stood up and began moving toward the doorway; the monkey saw that and he slowly wobbled out, climbing a water pipe up to the roof. Yes, I was scared for a few moments but also felt it was quite an experience to be teaching in a part of the world where such an incident was possible. One always had to close windows in the rooms and not hang clothes to dry on a line outside. If you did the article of clothing would not be there. Melissa lost her bathing suit that way! Langur monkeys were around too and sometimes got in rooms.

The Indian friend I met on the flight to Delhi came to visit me at Woodstock; she told me about the men her family had chosen for her to meet and selected one she thought was a possibility. She wanted me to meet him and give her some advice. We arranged for the meeting next time I was in Delhi in a few weeks. When I got to my Delhi hotel I phoned her and arrangements were made. She arrived by taxi at 6:45 P.M. and we drove to her brother's home for dinner and the evening. The two children, ages ten and twelve, were very excited about my coming and had been practicing their English all day. The six-year-old girl was sweet but knew no English yet. Every time I spoke to one of the boys, he would stand up to answer me; all three were very well behaved. I was introduced to her tall, handsome friend, who seemed very nice. We had a tasty Indian meal: mutton curry, rice, pureed spinach, eggplant with ginger and tomatoes, chappatis, and a pudding with orange slices and tea. Only the two guests had china plates; the others used the traditional metal plates and a spoon. The children ate in another room. After dinner I told them my lion story, which they enjoyed. The adults visited and we had a friendly time together, as though I had known them forever. Soon it was time to depart, so she and her friend took me to my hotel in a taxi. She told me her friend would like to talk to me alone, so we went to the hotel lobby. He told me how much he loved her, why she should marry him, but he was eight years younger than she was with interests in poetry, English literature, and geography. Her interest was mathematics. I liked him very much but didn't want either of them to be influenced by my opinion. Was he *really* interested in her or was it because he wanted to leave India! I certainly hoped he was sincere—they would have to make their own decisions.

Several months later I received the wedding invitation and knew I would be in Delhi for the occasion. I even got a new Indian outfit for the affair. When I got to Delhi I phoned my friend, telling her I had arrived. She then said, "I am not going to marry him; I just can't see myself walking around the fire seven times (part of the ceremony) with him. I have cancelled the wedding!'' I have no idea what happened; I was so shocked it took me quite some time to register what she had told me. After that we went our separate ways. So much for knowing personally about arranged marriages in India!

I found India to be such an interesting country in which to work and live. Wherever I found myself there was something new to see; such a variety of peoples and customs; and an excellent teaching situation with hardworking students and dedicated staff. I felt I could stay there forever, especially when a hill woman would come to my room after school once a week to give me a massage. She would see the fire was burning in the potbelly stove, place the sleeping bag on the floor beside it, put a sheet over it, and massage my body. It was so relaxing and comfortable—the hour always went too quickly. She wasn't a trained masseuse but a village woman who had many skills—how I appreciated her massaging ability.

Three years passed quickly for me in this extraordinary teaching situation; I was asked to extend my contract, which I did . . . for two more years. One winter vacation I did fly back to Iowa because my mother had gone into a nursing home and the contents of her house would be auctioned off. I felt I *must* be there—to help sort, to help keep those momentoes that meant something special to her children and grandchildren, and to visit with her in the nursing home. Clearing out the house was a huge task and I was so happy I could help, along with my sister Carol and daughter Jean, and other family members. It was the beginning of the end of an era—living on a beautiful farm in Iowa. After two months I returned to teaching in India.

Teaching days were filled with classes, lessons, recitals after school, rehearsals, tests and report cards, meetings, and all the activities connected with a boarding school. During the semester breaks I planned trips around India and the nearby countries. Each excursion began with one step . . . and went on and on.

17

Tibetans in Exile, 1978

Tashi, my Tibetan friend from Happy Valley in 1974, invited me to spend a week with him and his family in a Tibetan settlement in southern India. I accepted. However, before going to the settlement I wanted them to enjoy a few days in my kind of environment. I flew from Delhi to Bangalore and took a bus to Mysore, suggesting they meet me at the former summer palace, now a guest house, on a hill near Mysore on a certain date. I arrived by taxi at Hotel Rajendravilas Imperial on Chamundi Hill before they did. When I checked in I told the desk clerk I was expecting Tibetan friends and please let me know when they arrived.

I rested awhile in the huge "more than a double" bed with mosquito netting over the top, had lunch, and finally sat on the terrace to enjoy the view, the birds, and sunshine. After 4 P.M. a hotelkeeper came to me and said, "Your guests have arrived." With beating heart I walked down the beautiful staircase with mirrors on both sides, turned and continued to the bottom where "my" Tibetan family stood. Upon meeting, the mother placed the traditional white scarf of welcome around my neck. It took me by surprise and felt it was a special gesture. Then Tashi introduced me to his brother, Thupten, and his mother. They were carrying backpacks and a bedding roll (they didn't know if they had to furnish their own bedding, usually the case in India). They later told me when they got off the bus and saw "what a grand hotel it was, we hired a coolie to carry it for us."

Our two rooms were side by side with a sitting room in front of them. Each room was spacious and had a large bed with a soft mattress, and each had a large bathroom. After seeing the boy's room, I ordered tea in the sitting room and we chatted. The mother knew no English; Tashi was shy about using his few English words; Thupten did all the talking in excellent English (he was a college student studying science). We had so much to chatter about now that we were all together. After dinner, I gave them the presents I had brought for them from U.S.: a wristwatch for the mother (she probably would give that to her daughter at tailoring school); a watch for Tashi and a book on Japanese painting;

a pair of jeans and a jacket for Thupten. They seemed pleased with their gifts.

The mother and I shared a room. She went to bed before me. I did not want to awaken her so I undressed in the bathroom and left my clothes on the windowsill. There were many mosquitoes and during the night I received many bites; I didn't sleep too well. Next morning she was up long before I was. When I went into the bathroom, what should I find but my clothes, all washed, hanging from the curtain rods, the shower, etc. I had expected to wear the culottes and blouse and hose that day. Apparently she thought I left them there for her to wash! Now I wondered what other surprises would be waiting for me. When I saw Thupten at breakfast I told him to thank his mother for washing my clothes. The boys had not slept well either because the bed was too soft, so they informed me, "We had to try it one time but the floor is better."

We walked to the bus stop where a bus took us near the Maharaja's palace where we had a tour—700 rooms with paintings, marble floors, teak wood from Burma carved into doors, semiprecious stones inlaid in china, etched glass, three huge silver engraved doors, crystal chandeliers—what a building. After the tour we went by *tonga* (horse-drawn cart) to a restaurant; then ten miles by taxi to the Brindavan Gardens and later to see a large dam. When we drove by the river our driver stopped at a fisherman and bought four large fish. We had tea at a hotel sitting on the terrace facing beautiful flowers; we stayed until after the illumination finished. As we drove back near a temple a cow came to eat the flowers and fruit meant to be sold to pilgrims; the seller picked up a coconut and whacked it over the cow's head. The cow quickly left. And I thought all cows were sacred.

When we arrived back at our hotel we were told that Indira Gandhi, the prime minister, had been jailed. What a shock that was for us. The following day we found out that Mysore had a bus strike and everything was closed; Bangalore had strikes, buses were burned and trains wrecked. We had no choice but to stay at our hotel all day. The next day we were planning to take a bus to their settlement. How would we get there? Stores and banks were open the following day but no buses were running. The hotel got us a taxi, and after much talking he said he would drive us to Kollegal settlement for 400 rupees (that was a lot of money but we had no other choice). We stopped in Mysore, where they went food shopping and I changed traveler's checks after going to four banks. Another unexpected turn of events.

After many hours we arrived at Dhonden Ling Tibetan Settlement near Kollegal. This was a rather new settlement in an area that had been covered by forests and a few Indian villages. There were still wild elephants and wild pigs in the Nilgiri hills. Bulldozers had taken down the trees and the MYKADA agency had built houses with funds from Holland and other European countries. Each house had an area around it for vegetable and flower gardens, with fruit trees of banana and papaya, a shade tree or two, a cow shed, a grass storage area, all fenced in with bamboo and stones. The land around the villages was planted with corn in August and harvested in December, depending upon the rainfall. While the corn was growing someone stayed in the fields on high platforms in the trees to chase away the wild pigs by shouting and beating on a tin pan. Once a wild elephant was eating in the field; a night watchman tried to chase it away and was trampled to death. Each family had a section of the big field and took care of it. At harvest the corn was brought to the area of the house where a part of the soil was made hard by using water and beating the soil with a heavy wooden plank with one end pulled up by a rope and dropped by pressing with a foot. After the soil had dried a paste of cow dung and water was applied and the ground became very hard. The settlement had four threshing machines and one, pulled by a tractor, came to the hard area and ground the corn. The same family had a different part of the land each year by drawing a paper from a bag supervised by the chief of the settlement with one member of each family present.

A few years before I had sent some money to Tashi to help in the family's farming. He had bought a cow and thirteen chickens; however, the chickens died. I was pleased to see the cow and calf were thriving. There was a dairy farm nearby with two bulls and eighteen cows. A poultry shed stood beside but it was empty because all the hens had gotten sick and died (I often heard about the difficulty of raising poultry in India). I enjoyed hearing all the sounds: the tinkling of cow and goat bells, bird songs, the barking of dogs and meowing of cats. It was good to be in a country atmosphere again.

The house had one room with three couches against three walls covered with Tibetan carpets (used as beds at night), a table in the middle of the room, and a cupboard with the sacred articles on it. The kitchen was a separate small building where Tashi and his mother prepared the meals while Thupten told me about the settlement and took me on tours by Jeep to visit the carpet factory, the flour mill, a consumer store, the

226

school, the building on top of a hill where the Dalai Lama stays when he visits the settlement. We heard seven monks chanting very low with one monk beginning and the others joining in—like a tone cluster. Tashi had painted the beautiful sign above the building for the Dalai Lama's recent visit. We visited the home of an instrument maker and he told me about the material Tibetan instruments are made from. I ordered a smaller horn called a *kan-thung* and saw the long instrument *dun-chen,* and the medium-size oboelike horn *gayling,* etc. He then invited us for tea—and small biscuits and individually wrapped candies, and the typical Tibetan sweets. We discussed the Indian situation with Mrs. Gandhi in jail and the angry outburst in Bangalore; and of course, the Tibetan situation. Before leaving I took a photo of this interesting man with his small son on his tricycle.

We then went to the machine area and saw the four threshing machines for shelling of corn, the fifteen tractors (only one was a Ford), and a few wagons, all part of the cooperative society. Our young guide told us other settlements were much more progressive. I thought this settlement was doing very well from all the variety of activities I had seen. It was time to go back to our home in "N" village; Thupten invited the driver for tea and cookies . . . and for his pay, which was seventy-five *paise* a kilometer. We had gone twenty-two kilometers, so I gave him seventeen rupees and an extra ten rupees for all his help. He very reluctantly accepted the extra rupees.

Tashi and his mother prepared delicious meals. Meals each day were: breakfast—boiled eggs or omelet, *khura* (Tibetan round pancake) or chappati, and papaya or other fruit. Lunch was tomato and radish salad or a vegetable salad of cooked spinach with cooked chilies served cold; and *momos* (ground meat in a dough, steamed) or *hrukchoikee* (meat in dough cooked in bone broth). Dinner we would have a thick soup of vegetables, meat, small pieces of cooked wheat flour shaped like a bean; a salad of radishes and carrots or tomato; chappatis; or green beans and small round beef balls; dessert was sometimes khir (rice cooked with milk, and pieces of coconut and walnuts). Tashi knew I liked lemonade, so he made that for me with boiled water. We always had tea with our meals. I was told there should be special dishes for an auspicious time. Some of the food was always placed in small bowls on their special altar before we began to eat. Water was placed in other bowls there by the mother.

227

While I was with them there was a special festival day with lighted candles and prayers recited. There were eighty-five candles in front of the house, on two windowsills, on the wall and the bamboo gate. What a beautiful sight and a substitute for my Christmas Eve tree with lights. We all stayed outside until the candles burned down and we were in darkness. Tashi then got the gift he had painted for me—a thanka with the painting of the "King of the East" holding a musical instrument. Brocade from Varanasi surrounded the painting with two strips of red cloth coming down from the top to the bottom of the painting. Yellow thin material was at the top, used to cover the entire item if one wanted it covered. The wooden rod on the bottom of the thanka had ends made of Japanese silver. Tashi told me that in a temple there are four of these king's thankas (the four directions), but for a private home, one was acceptable. What an unusual, interesting, cherished gift from my first "Tibetan nephew!"

Often, Tibetans would come to the house and ask Thupten to write letters or other messages for them. He was in college and knew how to do it correctly; I was very impressed. The mother made *chang,* a traditional Tibetan fermented drink, and others came to buy it. One day Tashi put the *chang* in a tall wooden cup, decorated it with three kernels of white corn, and inserted a bamboo straw for me to enjoy. When the liquid was drunk and just the brown "seeds" were left, Tashi poured in more water. A unique drink. One early morning as I looked out the closed window through the mosquito netting over my couch, I heard strange sounds. There was Tashi with a friend digging the dirt near a tree. I asked him what he was doing and he answered, "You wanted to take a proper bath today, not just a 'cat's wash' in the shed, so we are digging up planks to put on the shed floor." (They planned to use those planks to improve the kitchen; if they weren't used right away, they were taken from them.) I couldn't believe all the trouble these kind friends were going through to make my visit comfortable!

Any time of day or night I heard the sounds of shouting and beating on the tin to scare away wild pigs from the fields. I also heard the chanting of prayers in the nearby house, punctuated with drums or instruments. When I heard the monks praying in the temple Thupten said it was because of encephalitis—they wanted the outbreak to stay away from the Tibetans. Each evening before the mother went to bed she sang her prayers. A light was always burning in front of the painting with five metal bowls with water—it is necessary for life. The closeness of nature and people here surely made me think of my childhood summer days spent at Grandma Larson's helping her feed the chickens and goslings, and other chores. One afternoon here I helped them take the dried corn off the cob, sitting on the ground near their small corn field. What a memorable afternoon . . . helping my Tibetan family, in South India, but reminiscent of Iowa fields.

Soon it was time to leave my extended family. Goodbyes were difficult for me (they always have been), but Thupten insisted on going with me on the bus to Mysore, which took six hours. He helped me get the bus reservation for Bangalore and then he left to go back to the settlement, where he studied for his upcoming university exams. How blessed I was to have such a caring and loving Tibetan family.

Dharamsala, the Government in Exile

I spent two activity weeks at Dharamsala as a chaperon for Woodstock students. The Tibetan Government in Exile is located there in the mountains. It was a sixteen-hour bus trip from Dehra Dun, beginning in the afternoon and traveling all night. In Dharamsala Tibetans met us with one Jeep for luggage and helped us to our hotel. All arrangements had been made beforehand. We were to study five areas: government, education, health care, religion, and music/drama/art. We had been told we could not have an audience with His Holiness the Dalai Lama because he was out-of-station. Special lectures were given and we toured various facilities. In the library we saw Tibetan books brought out of Tibet. Most were wrapped in cloth; some were 350 years old or older. There was a Tibetan typewriter made by Remington years ago. In the hallway was a brass plate on the wall with the names of groups who had given money for the building:

Library of Tibetan Works and Archives

This library is dedicated to the timeless cultural links between Tibet and India. The construction of the building is financed by the following: H.H. XIV Dalai Lama, Government of India, World Council of Churches, Swiss Aid to Tibetans, Tibetan Road Workers, Tibetan Society of America, Care, Division of World Services of the United Church of Christ, American Mongolians, and Mr. Lowell Thomas. It was built in 1972.

In the museum were many treasures but also torn books vandalized by the Red Guards that had been found in the razed ruins of a monastery in South Tibet. (Over five hundred monasteries had been destroyed.) We visited TCV, Tibetan Children's Village, where the motto is "Others Before Self"; the homes where children live in family groups with house parents; the baby home where our Woodstock students played with them, picked them up and hugged them, carried and laughed with the sweet fat children, two or three years of age. (Norway had just given this baby home.) We walked up a long zigzag path to the top of a hill where the Institute of Performing Arts was located and were shown costumes, masks, their facilities; during tea we met many of the artists and their director, Mr. Norbu.

All of our students agreed that the visit to the Tibetan Medical Center was the most interesting. After the tour of the center, which included the making of pills, we had an interview with the doctor, Dr. Tenzing Choedrak, the chief doctor in Tibet before 1959. He had been imprisoned for seventeen years by the Chinese and had recently been released. He very recently patiently answered the questions of our students through a translator, Mrs. Samten. Her husband, Lobsang Samten, was the director of the center. He was also the brother of the Dalai Lama, and had been on the first official Tibetan delegation to Tibet in 1979. He stood right beside me and uttered these words, "The only Tibetan culture that is left is *outside Tibet;* all has been destroyed there." What a sad commentary!

How fortunate I was to have chaperoned students to Dharamsala two times and learned firsthand what these religious, quiet, peaceful people have gone through before they left in 1959 when the Chinese took over. Man's inhumanity to man seems to go on and on. Will people ever learn to "Love Your Neighbor as Yourself"?

Jigme and Rinchen Dolma Taring

On March 9, 1988, we were invited to afternoon tea at the Taring House, the home of Jigme and Rinchen Dolma Taring at Rajpur, near Dehra Dun, India. Sam and I arrived by taxi and were met at the gate by Mrs. Taring, showing us into the living room. There were couches along the three walls with a table in the middle of the room. It also was the third birthday of their great-granddaughter. Approximately twenty family members were present as well as an English couple (he had been a tea taster in Darjeeling years ago and had imported tea to the United States). One by one the relatives gave the little girl, sitting quietly with her aunt, presents, touching their foreheads as they embraced her. Later Mrs. Taring and the aunt helped open each present. What a family moment they shared with us.

I had questions prepared to ask Mrs. Taring but decided not to spoil the happy atmosphere; we talked of many other things. One of her concerns was about a grandson who needed a scholarship in Seattle. "He speaks Tibetan, English, and Chinese and could be a great help to His Holiness the Dalai Lama in the cause of Tibet." As we visited we enjoyed fish sandwiches, cream-filled pastries, other pastries, and a decorated chocolate birthday cake with delicious tea.

The Taring story should be understood. Kasur Jigme Taring was born in south Tibet in 1908, the eldest son of a Sikkimese prince. Rinchen Dolma was from the famous Tsarong family. They both studied in Darjeeling when young; therefore, they learned English. They later married, doing valuable work in Tibet. Then the Chinese came into Lhasa, Tibet, in 1959, and 100,000 Tibetans fled with the Dalai Lama. Mrs. Taring escaped by one route; her husband fled by another route. After several months, they finally found each other and spent their years in exile in Happy Valley, a Tibetan settlement in Mussoorie. He was appointed principal of the first Tibetan school in India; she was the director of the Tibetan Homes Foundation, established in 1962. In her autobiography, *Daughter of Tibet*, she states that they had no news of their children left in Tibet until twenty years later! In 1979 they heard their grandson speaking on the radio from Lhasa, and found out *all* were alive and well. Several came from Tibet in 1985 "when the Chinese were more lenient." Mrs. Taring told us they had a very difficult time in Tibet. I noticed the youngest daughter looked scared, worried, and inwardly upset. Most of them were illiterate in the Tibetan language and religion, so she had been teaching them. Perhaps you now realize why this party was so very special for the entire Taring family!

Before leaving I gave her a gift and letter from my Tibetan friends in Kathmandu, and a photo and letter from our Miami Tibetan family (she had helped him get a job at the American Embassy in Delhi when he had escaped from Tibet and he was forever grateful). We had brought them a large tin of candies. Both of them walked with us outside their home and he showed us his work . . . the stone paths and the beautiful flower gardens. Several Taring family members have homes around the compound. There were two sets of four generations. We said our good-byes and "Tashi Delek" and were on our way after a warm and friendly visit.

Jigme and Rihchen Dolma Taring have been an inspiration to hundreds and hundreds of young Tibetans in exile; they are loved by all Tibetans and others who have been fortunate to meet them.

(By the way, when the news-broadcaster and writer, Lowell Thomas, and his son went by horseback to Lhasa, Tibet, in 1947 it was Mrs. Taring who acted as their interpreter! She knew English because of her schooling in Darjeeling as a young girl.)

The following day was Tibet National Day, March 10. Sam and I arrived early for the day of talks followed by a protest march from the park to the town of Dehra Dun. Mrs. Taring was the main speaker and after her speech, we were introduced and asked to come to the front; a path immediately opened for us to walk through. (By this time I was the Regional Director of the U.S.–Tibet Committee in Miami.) She then read a prepared speech in English, especially for us. She placed the traditional white scarf around my neck and we again had tea. She told us to tell our Miami Tibetan friends, "we are keeping well in our old age." More good-byes with the Tarings and others presents—all thanking me for my work as Regional Director in Miami.

On October 9, 1990, I received an invitation to a Taring grandson's wedding on 26th October, 1990. Inside was printed in red ink:

Mr. and Mrs. J. Taring request the pleasure of your company to grace the auspicious occasion of the wedding of our grandson . . . etc.

On the right side of the card the same message was written in gold ink in Tibetan. The program for the day's events was printed on the back of the card:

7:00 A.M.   Arrival of bride to Taring House
7:00 A.M.   to 8:30 A.M.   Family traditional ceremony
11:00 A.M.   Greeting scarf from wellwishers
1:50 P.M.   Lunch
4:00 P.M.   Tea
6:00 P.M.   Dinner
9:00 P.M.   Thanksgiving scarf to all
            Tashi Delek

How I wanted to accept this unusual invitation from my notable Tibetan friends; there were too many thousands of miles between Miami, Florida, and Rajpur, India. I had to mail my congratulations and best wishes to the young couple and include my regrets to Jigme and Rinchen Dolma Taring.

Every Christmas season I receive greetings from Mrs. Taring but I was sorry to learn that Jigme Taring passed away in June, 1991, at the age of 83.

Tibetans in Nepal

Sam and I visited my Tibetan family, Tashi, Thupten, and mother in Kathmandu, Nepal, in 1988. I met the wives and children for the first time; also another brother. Dolma, the sister, was also present (she was at the tailoring school when I was teaching in Mussoorie). What a wonderful reunion we had right after the Tibetan New Year at their home. They had left the farm in South India and Tashi was now an art teacher and owned a carpet company; Thupten was a teacher in a Tibetan school there; later he became the headmaster of the school. Again we were served delicious food for this auspicious occasion, later we entertained them at a Tibetan restaurant. They made arrangements for us to drive with a driver to the Nepal/Tibet border the following day with the young brother acting as our guide. First, the driver had to purchase a road permit. I soon lost count of the many police checkpoints where we had to stop and show the permit. They even had us open the trunk to see what was in it. It was an exhausting but interesting day in a part of Nepal I had not seen before: friendly children and curious adults, narrow roads with many hairpin curves, views of the great Himalayan mountain range and a peak of Mount Everest before it was again shrouded in clouds. (During our stay at the Kathmandu Guest House we saw many trekkers and rafters; what stories they told us.)

We took a bus to Pokhara and on the way we saw many wedding processions along the road. First came three men playing long trumpets, then men playing curved horns and drums. The groom was always carried in a chair on the shoulders of two men while another man held a parasol over him, more men and boys followed him. The bride was dressed in red and gold with downcast eyes, walking and followed by women and girls, but the instruments were flutes. Softer music was played instead of the shrill music for the groom's procession. We enjoyed watching this Nepalese tradition.

In Pokhara our friends John and Jane Stout (he was an engineer working on a water project in the hills there) had made reservations for us at a hotel owned by Tibetans. There were many of their paintings on doors, in the lobby and dining rooms. In our roombox we found an invitation to be the special guests at a Tibetan dinner hosted by John and Jane. What a lovely surprise that was. Jane taught English to many of the Tibetan children; later we toured the school where we saw English letters printed on small rocks (there aren't always books to go around); we also met some of the young monks. We also toured other facilities of the settlement—the carpet factory, the furniture-making, and the very small children on a terrace, all sitting on potty chairs.

The evening for the party arrived with about twenty-five or so Tibetan men and women present. We were introduced to each one by our hosts, then sat at long tables in the dining room. I gave a short speech about my work on the U.S.–Tibet Committee in Miami—human rights, making others aware of the Tibetan plight, especially out elected officials, etc. They seemed pleased with what they heard. The man in charge of the settlement spoke, as did a few others. After the delicious meal of Tibetan food, one by one each person came to me and put the traditional scarf around my neck. I truly felt I was actually in Tibet with these precious people—not with people who were in exile. It was an unforgettable evening!

Regional Director of the U.S.–Tibet Committee

When I retired and moved to Miami in 1983, I continued to help Tibetans as the Regional Director in Miami. I was especially interested in human rights. Each year around the Tibet National Day, March 10, we had a Tibetan exhibit of artifacts, books, paintings (most were painted by my "nephew" Tashi) and a program with talks, slides or videos about the problems Tibetans face in exile. Through newspaper articles, letters to elected officials, the March 10th day importance, I hoped others would better understand the plight of these very special people, whom I came to know and love because of having the opportunity to teach at the Woodstock School in Mussoorie, India.

18

Houseboat Holiday in Kashmir, Summer 1979

After eleven months of teaching at Woodstock, I had planned a summer holiday on a houseboat called *Boojum* on Lake Nagin in Kashmir, but first I was a chaperon taking two students on a six-hour taxi ride from Mussoorie to Delhi, where the temperature was 109 degrees. I took the students to their destinations and arrived at my hotel exhausted and hot. The air-conditioned room was all I needed for a good sleep in anticipation of the flight the next day.

A taxi got me to the airport and the driver took my duffle bag and gray suitcase to the counter where baggage tags were placed on each with the destination "Amritsar." My ticket said Srinagar, so I had them changed. I sat down in the lounge and waited and waited. Finally the announcement said our plane would leave at 4 P.M. instead of 12:40. All of us waiting got coupons for a buffet in the upstairs restaurant. A young man carried my small bag upstairs so I sat with him, his wife and two small children. They were from the Pakistan-India Partitioned area so he said, "I have no homeland." They were now living in Kuwait, where he was the Max Factor sales representative for U.K. products. He even gave me two lipstick testers; I was grateful because my lipsticks were almost used up. After eating, we walked downstairs only to find out that no flight was going to Srinagar, only Amritsar. We all had to go to the clerk to have our tickets changed, receive a voucher for hotel and food for that night in Delhi. Most seemed agitated with the delay; we all arrived safely at Qutab Hotel near Nehru University, as guests of Indian Airlines. My room had air-conditioning, so I fell asleep almost at once. Later I found out the toilet didn't flush properly, the tube-light only blinked in the bathroom, only a trickle of water came from the faucet in the tub (after an hour there was enough to cover the bottom of the tub). Dinner was at 8 P.M. and the decor was such a mixed bag in the dining room . . . I couldn't figure it out. One room was Paul Revere, the dining room was the Williamsburg Room, etc. New England–type rocking chairs were on the New England–type rug with an Indian brass-topped table in the center of the room. When the waiter came I asked him about it and he told me this had been the AID Club but was turned over to the Indian government in 1973 by the American ambassador, Patrick Moynahan. There were units for sixty families, a swimming pool, bowling alley downstairs, and a club-dining-bar area. Now I understood the "mixed bag."

I ordered Steak "Nicosia" (buffalo meat), French fries, carrots-peas, and several sweet cool lime drinks. At my table were a young German student, an Indian journalist from Madras, a professional photographer, and a stamp collector-seller. In the middle of the meal the lights went out with a "thud." The waiters had to hunt for candles, so it must not happen too often. There was live music: a piano, drums, and electric guitar which got progressively louder as the evening wore on. The lights had come on during the meal. I was escorted to my room by the German and one of the Indians. What an exhausting and frustrating day this had been!

The next morning just as I was leaving my room for breakfast the electricity stopped again, so the air-conditioning and lights went out. (I felt so sorry for all the people who must work in hot hotels all day. It was called "power shedding" but the electricity board had said there would not be anymore of that; already it had happened several times. The workers just plodded along doing their work without complaining. This was summer in Delhi and it was 109° outside.)

A taxi to the airport, the same routine of waiting in the airline's long line with all the others. First in line was a young couple from Massachusetts on a Pan-Am trip around the world. He had been ill most of the night and looked it! They were disappointed with India and felt Latin America and Brazil were better to travel in. She majored in developing countries, Third World countries, and "yet when one comes eye-to-eye with the real thing it becomes disgusting and one can only criticize . . . the pages of books don't quite come alive as it really is," she said. Finally the clerks came, checked tickets; the rumor was we would fly directly to Srinagar and not go via Amritsar. Well, why not? Yesterday the plane went only to Amritsar. The security check with a guard going through my purse and small carry-on bag; a small private room where a woman guard felt all over me, including investigating the collapsable cane I had. She pulled so hard to take it apart, I was hoping the elastic wouldn't break; it didn't. Another wait and delay . . . finally I was flying to Kashmir for the second time. The sky was filled with clouds so I could not see the land or Banihal Pass but did have a peek of the snow-covered mountains before landing at the Srinagar airport.

It was quite a walk from the plane to the building and as I moved a man came toward me and said, ''Mrs. Golden?'' He also had an envelope with my name. His face was familiar and he told me he had been our guide to the carpet factory in 1974. This man was Sultan Ota, owner of the houseboat, *Boojum,* where I would spend three weeks. We went inside the building for custom formalities, got the luggage, and went to an old rattletrap of a taxi. It wouldn't start so Mr. Ota tried cranking it; no luck. Another man joined him and they pushed the car. It started and we were on our way to Nagin Lake, going through the busy town of Srinagar with *tongas,* people everywhere, bazaars, bridges over canals. Finally we turned into Nageen Club where we came to a halt. *Boojum* was moored on the banks of the lake near the clubhouse. We walked on a narrow path, went over a narrow board to the deck of the houseboat. There it was, my home for several weeks. As we were riding there, Mr. Ota told me he had been to the post office to see if there was a telegram; he had tried to phone my friend, ''Mr. Dr. Smyth'' in Delhi but couldn't get through; he had prepared lunch for me on the previous day. I was so sorry there was so much confusion about my delayed arrival. Things like this were so disconcerting; I hope I was forgiven . . . even though it wasn't my fault.

The *Boojum* looked just like the *Sobra* of 1974. If it weren't for the location on the opposite side of the lake I would think it was the same houseboat. Mr. Ota introduced me to his brother; apparently these two men and a servant do all the work on this boat. The bags were taken inside but I stayed in the open area near the entrance to enjoy the scenery as I sipped a cool soft drink. The boat wallahs (men selling items from their boats) seem to know when a new tourist arrived, and my arrival was no different. They came along the side of *Boojum* asking me to ''just look'': papier mache, furs, carved wood, shawls, silver jewelry, food, fruit, flowers, etc. There seemed to be a never-ending line of wallahs trying to sell their wares. I couldn't resist the flowers and got a bouquet for five rupees, after which he gave me four carnations as his gift to me. Then he wanted a contract to deliver flowers every second day; no way! I let the wallah selling silver bring two small trunks on the ''porch'' and he showed me silver bangles and necklaces. First he showed me the type of necklace I had already bought in South India at Kodaikanal . . . I had been told villagers in Kashmir wore them. Now that I am here in Kashmir, I am told, ''No, that is not Kashmiri, but Tibetan.'' I *know* it is not Tibetan. I looked at the old village jewelry which he carefully unwrapped:

a huge ring the village girl gets when she becomes engaged; a necklace with three pointed silver pieces hanging down—one a toothpick, one an ear-picker, one a fingernail cleaner (practical as well as beautiful); village women's earrings on a silver chain which is placed over their hair and tucked with a pin—over this goes the scarf—one size fits all. What a wonderful way to look at treasures, even though he had called it "my box of junk." I bought some small items so I wouldn't have to look anymore. What a joke that was! Sitting on the porch I could enjoy all the scenery and views, the boats and birds. In the distance I could barely see the mountains with snow; it was cloudy, hazy, and looked like rain.

Finally at 7 P.M. I was called for dinner. I was the only one at the huge table and I truly felt like a queen (not for a day but for three weeks). Only the servant and me. What a life! My niece, Melissa, who had spent six months with me at Woodstock teaching music, had planned to spend a week with me here but she was called back to Iowa because her mother, Irma, was ill. My good friend, Sally Sutton, a physician, was supposed to come to Kashmir from Iowa but she had to write a booklet on muscle energy. It looked as if I, the "Queen went to the party alone"—my friends had backed out. If I waited for people to do things with, I would probably still be in my home state. Life is much too short to spend it waiting for others. Here I was alone in the Vale of Kashmir with all the beautiful nature, artistic Kashmiris, and the peace and quiet of the household. All these thoughts went through my head as I enjoyed my first dinner on *Boojum*: soup and a slice of bread, roast chicken, French fries, creamed cauliflower, baked tomato, and the dessert was stewed apricots, all delicious.

After dinner the two brothers and I went to the living room to get better acquainted. I told them about my experiences in India and they told me about Kashmir. Moghul emperors had visited Kashmir since 1587 seeking refuge in this idyllic vale where they had laid out many fantastic gardens. Kashmir never became a "hill station" because no European could own land or build here. That was the reason for the houseboats, where they could come and enjoy this bit of heaven. Now tourists continued to use them. Yes, here too the lights went off! I went to my room. Mr. Ota brought a lamp but it soon went out. My trusty flashlight came out of my bag and I unpacked a few items. Finally the lights came on. I turned on the faucets in the bright blue tub, had my bath, read from my newly purchased book for this trip, *Far Pavilions* by M. M. Kaye, about India. How happy I was to have earplugs because the cookhouse where they all lived and worked was right near my bedroom windows. In spite of the noise I soon fell asleep.

I had ordered breakfast for 9 A.M. the next morning so I could sleep late. When I finally awakened the canopy on the sun roof was up and in place, the cloth shading the windows was down, and a slight breeze was blowing as I ate my toast, eggs, and tea. Later I wrote in my journal, watched, listened, and relaxed. Lunch at 1 P.M. arrived with lamb chops, mashed potatoes, gravy, boiled cabbage, stewed cherries. The weather seemed very warm in the afternoon so I decided to read on the porch. All of a sudden the curtains parted and a young man said, "Good afternoon, madam. I have some wood carvings I'd like to show you." I had not heard a sound of his arrival. These Kashmiris are something else.

After siesta and tea, boat wallahs came by with copper, huge brass plates, vases, more furs, and more wood carvings. I said, "No." One wallah answered me, "Looking is free." Yes, if it only was! I remembered what Dick Smyth and his wife, Sylvia, my friends from Delhi, said in 1974 when they and my friend, Ruth, and I were on *Sobra* together: "If you are interested, look; if you are not interested, don't look." Of course, I want to purchase an example or two of their exquisite arts and crafts, and just looking is such fun.

I had asked Mr. Ota if it were possible to have a massage here. While I was enjoying my tea I was informed he had come. After finishing the tea I went to the entrance and met Mr. Abdu Gani: Barber, Hairdresser, Massage . . . all words painted on his black tin box he carried with him. A thin mattress was placed on the rug in my bedroom, two sheets were placed over it; a pillow was taken from my bed and placed under the sheet for my head. Never having had a Kashmiri massage before I didn't quite know what to remove. I lay down but just pulling up my yellow blouse wasn't going to work well, so I unbuttoned it and took it off leaving only the chemise. When he got to my legs he suggested my culottes come off, which left only my underpants. He coated his hands with Kashmiri almond oil and rubbed it on my body, an excellent massage of kneading, rubbing to stimulate my skin and muscles, and lasted one and a half hours. When he had finished I asked him what I owed him and he answered, "What you please." I hate answers like that and said again, "What do you charge?" He said, "Twenty-five rupees." In Delhi I had paid forty, so I thought it was a fair price. I had many more relaxing massages from Mr. Gani during my stay on *Boojum*.

240

Dinner was delicious as usual and for dessert they served French toast with honey. That was a new one for me. A massage always makes me tired so our conversation was short about Kashmir. I was off to my room and sleep.

During the day I had checked every room of this houseboat, 106 feet long and 16 feet wide. It looked something like this. Steps from the water led up to the entrance or porch where there was a ledge to sit on with small cushions. Green linoleum with pink roses covered the floor and ten panels of curtains kept out the sun (blue with red, yellow, pink, and orange flowers) making seven different floral designs on the porch. One step up led me into the living room. On either side of the entrance was a window seat with cushions, a cozy place to curl up and read. A long Kashmiri carpet in green and darker colors in the center design lay at the entrance. A large square carpet covered the rest of the floor; it had a green background with designs and a bright blue border with more designs. The furniture was along three sides of the walls. I counted three large overstuffed chairs, five tables, some with lamps and one with a radio. A large beautifully carved table was placed in the middle of the room. There was a desk and chair, a carved chest of drawers with a long mirror in a gold frame above it, and a book case. I also counted fifteen ash trays, six vases (for the flowers the boat wallahs wanted me to buy), six different patterns in the carpets and seven small lights on the walls near the ceiling. Most of the light came from the four large windows, which had lace panels between the drapes, the same drapery material covered the chairs and two couches.

A door led to the dining room, which had a red-figured carpet with a large dining table in the middle of the room. Along one side was a sideboard, a Kelvinator refrigerator, a built-in corner cupboard for dishes, and six chairs placed along two walls when they were not used for dining. From a hallway one could go up the stairs to the roof; under the stairs was a pantry and nearby tin trunks were piled. From the same hall one entered the bedrooms. Mine had two beds with a Kashmiri carved three-drawer chest between. There was a built-in cupboard, a dressing table and chair, a table with a fan standing on it, another carved table near the center of the room, a comfortable red chair and a covered straw basket nearby. The carpet was navy blue with red designs; eight different patterns were in my bedroom. A door led into the bathroom with the same green linoleum with pink flowers as on the front porch, a bright blue bathtub, a sink, and a toilet. This houseboat was certainly well-furnished and had bright colors and designs.

Kashmir was having a very hot spell of weather. I spent time trying to keep cool and found two favorite spots for reading and relaxing. One was on the porch sitting on the cushioned benches and the other was on the roof where I got an excellent view of the lake, the boats, the birds, and people on the shore. I asked to have my 7 P.M. dinner on the roof and enjoyed the antics of two Eurasian kingfishers on a wire. How I would love to sleep there when there was a full moon. After my meal the servant came up and took the cloth covers from the umbrella table and the curtains and canopy. He told me he had spent one month going to and staying in Ladakh as a guide for tourists from Singapore. He said Leh was dirty and there was nothing to do but visit monasteries. As we talked I could tell he wanted to close up the roof, so I reluctantly went down to my bedroom and read *Far Pavilions* until I became sleepy. The fan was on all night, so it was cooler, and as I began to doze off I wondered what was going on in other parts of India and the rest of the world. Perhaps this isolation was getting to me after all.

The next day I rented a *shikara,* a gaily decorated boat with curtains on the side where the passenger sits. A man paddles the boat around the lake or whatever area you want to visit; usually he has a hookah (waterpipe) by his seat. I rented the *shikara* for a week and paid thirty rupees a day whether I used it or not. The first day we left soon after 8 A.M. for birdwatching, hopefully. He paddled through the lotus pads, the bulrushes, in canals, and back areas eventually arriving in front of a new mosque, saying, "It is as busy as Mecca." Later a flock of 200 or so geese flew overhead, honking loudly. Then home to *Boojum* for lunch and a short siesta. I again went in the *shikara* and saw swallows, kingfishers, and the large trees which were the rookeries for rooks. Yes, there are birds named rooks; it was not just the card game I played as a child. Another delicious dinner on the roof: lamb roast, cabbage, mashed potatoes, caramel custard and iced tea. I prefer the fresh or stewed fruit of mango, cherries, or apricots for dessert. I watched the sky and pink clouds above the mountains in the east, then silver-lined clouds to the west and finally the pearl-gray sky. Stars appeared one by one; I should have sat there all night watching God's creation. "Stars are the pin-pricks of heaven."

The following day I received a telegram from my friend from the Woodstock School, Leona (she spent a total of thirty-one years working in India, her home country was Canada), saying she was arriving June 28. Mr. Ota received one from Singapore saying people could not come, "Daughter very ill." If it isn't illness, it is the airlines. What problems for the houseboat owners! A taxi took me into Srinagar so I could go to the post office and the bank to exchange traveler's checks for cash. I also bought a pound of fudge—white, lemon, and chocolate—and shared it with the Ota family when I got home. Three German guests had arrived to share my *Boojum*. After lunch I tried to rest on the roof, on the bed, near a fan but it was too warm everywhere. Even a couple of cold soft drinks did not help. I later found out it was over 100° that day.

At 5:30 Mr. Ota and I took a taxi to the tourist bus stop-station to wait for the Jammu-Kashmir bus. On the bus should be Leona, thirteen other Woodstock students, and two staff chaperons, Barb and George. There must have been thirty or more buses with Indians, Ladakhis, a few Westerners with possessions in tin trunks, suitcases, duffle bags, large bundles tied up in one huge piece of cloth, straw baskets, etc. There were many police and soldiers watching people and questioning some younger boys; salesmen trying to convince the tourists to come to their houseboats; and coolies taking luggage down from the top of the buses. Tourists gathered their possessions in a pile where part of their family waited, often for several hours. Two old Indians with long gray beards, a younger son, two small children, an older wife and a younger beautiful one in turquoise-colored Punjabi garb gathered their items, which filled one cart pulled by hand. They all walked out of the courtyard into the darkening evening.

It was a very noisy three hours of watching and waiting, but so interesting. About 8:45 P.M. a young man with a pink folder sat beside me and said he was waiting for a group "from Woodstock School." I said I was too. What a surprise for both of us. He told me that Mrs. Lehman was already on his houseboat and she expected her husband to be with this group. I had already seen two couples from Woodstock who had taken the all night train to Jammu, then flown to Srinagar. Eventually I saw two brothers I recognized on top of a bus throwing luggage down; a cluster of familiar faces stood nearby. At last, they had arrived. Mr. Ota and I found Leona, her luggage, and a coolie to carry it to the taxi. Before leaving I told George the name of our houseboat and we expected all of them to lunch on Monday; he said, "Fine."

It took us an hour to get home because all the local buses were filled with tourists visiting the mosque. But when we got there dinner was waiting for us—roast chicken and all the trimmings with watermelon for dessert. It was good to get caught up on all the "gossip" from school and news of the outside world. She also brought letters to me—one from Melissa saying she got home to Iowa OK; her mother looked so ill; she had prepared a *pukka* (real) Indian meal for her family and was getting used to the same routine in "flat Iowa." She had thoroughly enjoyed her six months in India and thanked me for letting her have the experiences. I was sorry she couldn't enjoy the Kashmir houseboat holiday but knew it was best for her to help care for her ill mother.

Leona and I left for church after our breakfast of boiled eggs, I had toast and she had Indian chappatis, and coffee. We told the taxi driver to take us to the Church of England church, which was now called All Saints Church of North India. He finally came to a halt outside a wall where several lepers and beggars were standing near the gate (the poor, the lepers, the beggars always stand near a church on Sunday). We walked toward the church but realized there was only a brick/cement shell and a wooden belfrey with a bell. We then saw that the church building was burned! This was a result of the May 7, 1979, mob of students, in the middle of the day, who burned the Srinagar Club, the church and some other buildings after Bhutto was hanged in Pakistan. I did remember reading about it but had no idea I would ever be here. Where would the service be now? In warm climates like this one does not really need a building to worship—we found the carpets laid out on the ground under a huge chenar (plane tree); a small table covered with a white cloth had two bouquets of flowers . . . the altar. Nearby was a pump organ played by a woman. A few benches and chairs were near but most people sat down on the ground covered with the carpets. Soon two ministers walked to the altar dressed in long white robes with gold stoles. One was an Englishman in charge of a private school in Srinagar; the other was a Ladakhi who spoke his part of the service in Hindustani, a mixture of Urdu and Hindi. The Scriptures and prayer were in English. There must have been eighty or ninety people sitting on the carpets, all without shoes except me. After the sermon and offering there was communion, using one silver cup. Everyone stood as we went to the altar to receive this special blessing. How beautiful to have a service outside with birds flying and singing around us. In retrospect, this was the only time I have been part of a service beside a burned-out church. I hope I never see another church in that condition.

After visiting with some parents of Woodstock students and inviting them to tea at our *Boojum,* Leona and I found a scooter which took us to the Oberoi Palace Hotel on a hill overlooking Dal Lake. This Palace Hotel was built in 1854 as a maharaja's palace; since 1956 it had been a hotel. On the huge lawn were four fountains, many *chenar* trees, and flower beds. We ordered espresso coffee as we enjoyed the view and quiet. It took some time to find a taxi and get back to Boojum for lunch. That day we had mutton curry, saffron rice, curds, and stewed cherries. Since Leona arrived we always had a chutney or curds as part of our meal; she told them it was always served and they complied with her wishes. Mr. Ota showed us small packets of saffron, approximately ten grams and cost 25 rupees each. Kashmir is one of the few places where saffron is grown, and I hoped I would see it growing.

Our guests arrived for tea, a mother and three daughters, they seemed very impressed with Boojum and all the furnishings. We had tea on the roof and were served cheese bits on crax, Kashmiri sweet bread with raisins spread with butter and honey, ginger cookies, and fresh cherries. The girls had soft drinks called "Thumbs Up" and the adults were served tea. Kashmiri tea has cardamom and cinnamon in it, the most delicious tea I have had anywhere in the world. The girls ate like they hadn't eaten for days and we were delighted they enjoyed the repast. The sky darkened with an approaching storm, so they felt they should leave before the downpour. The wind began to blow, clouds were almost black, and the rains came to break the weeklong hot spell. I watched the raindrops on the lake from the porch but it began to rain so hard all windows had to be closed; water still came in the cracks. The wallah in the small *shikara* beside *Boojum* really got tossed around by the waves, but after an hour the storm abated and we could enjoy a short ride in the *shikara.*

By this time there were also three German staying at *Boojum,* and we all had dinner together, after which we played caroms at the dining room table. (I wonder what happened to our checker carom board we used when I was growing up! I have such happy memories of winter snowstorms on the farm and playing caroms with family members.) We played three games, but the father and son won them all. The weather was now cool and a good night for sleeping—no fans needed, after an unforgettable and interesting day.

Monday arrived with a cool morning and the promise of a good day for the "party on our houseboat." Of course, the flower man was waiting in his boat, as was the confectionary man. (I wonder how they knew about our party?) I bought pink and lavender asters, a few bright-colored zinnas, some large daisies and some rather wilted pinks. Yesterday the German couple bought two large bouquets of glads and tiny, thin, long lilacs—six bouquets for our party. From the wallah selling sweets I bought two dozen butter cookies and almond cookies for dessert. We had the food ordered and prepared which would be served to our guests; we were all dressed in our Punjabi outfits and awaited for guests' arrival. At 12:15 the two *shikaras* arrived with thirteen students and two chaperons. They came up the steps, put their swimming gear on the porch, and walked into the living room for visiting. How good it was to see these friends from school.

Soon, Mr. Ota came and asked me to check the roof where our lunch would be served. Two tables were set under the tent canopy with a vase of daisies and zinnas on each table. Plates, glasses, and silverware were at one end of the buffet table. There was a huge platter of white rice; several bowls of mutton curry; cauliflower with spices; peas and potato curry; salad of beets-onions-tomato. I approved and the students were asked to come to the roof to lunch. I had ordered two soft drinks for each student and in their bottles were "pipes" (straws) but the "big men drink from glasses," the servant said. For dessert a large brass tray contained mangoes, apricots, and cherries; another plate had the almond and butter cookies. Some of the students sat on lounge chairs, some sat on cushions on the floor. Most of them saved one drink and a cookie until after the swimming. One of the girls gave me several strands of water-lily stems; she had already draped them over the porch railing with lily leaves here and there. It was so sweet of her to leave this beauty on *Boojum.*

Before the party was over I had each one write their name, age, and countries they had lived in. It was interesting because of the variety: Serena 10, Olinda, 8, Nigel 12, Kevin 13 (from the same family and had lived in Tanzania, India, and Kuwait); Roksana 12 (she wrote her countries in her own language and I can't read or remember what they were); MiKyong 10 (Korea and Iran); Fouad 14, Bardia 14, Shahram 15 (all from Iran but not related); Hansoo 13 (Korea, India, Vietnam, Iran); Kim 14 (Korea, Iran, India); Alan 8 (Iran and India) Faigh 13 (Iran and India); Barbara, a chaperon from England; George from North Ireland, the other chaperon. With only a month-long summer break in our school schedule, it was impossible for some students to go back to their homes for such a short length of time, so this trip was planned for those wanting to visit

Kashmir; these teachers volunteered to be their chaperons. I was so happy I could share my *Boojum* with them and treat them to lunch in Kashmir.

After lunch the storm clouds gathered and they decided they should not go swimming and left before the rain came down in torrents. This day had been a real bonus for a teacher in an international setting.

There were several all-day trips from Srinagar. "Gulmarg with altitude of 8500 feet is known for golf and a seven-mile-long circular road which affords a magnificent view of the entire Kashmir Valley," our guidebook said so beautifully. This was the day to have a driver and car take us to Gulmarg. We began at 7:30 A.M. on a cloudy-bright day after last night's rainstorm, hoping the sun would shine later. As we drove along the two-lane road we saw rice paddies, a wild duck game reserve for shooting ducks in the winter; poplars lined the road on both sides; later apple orchards were in abundance; farther on the road was lined with willows planted in a ditch near a stream of water. There were several lumber mills with stacks of cut wood: I counted forty-two men riding small horses (larger than ponies) and in one corral were approximately 125 horses. Many tourists rent horses at this point and ride the trail to Gulmarg. We stopped at a "view point" and saw a glacier and a river. Nearby a woman was carrying wood on her head. She had two beautiful silver earrings, so I asked if I could take a photo of her. The answer was "yes," however, our driver asked me to give her some rupees and translated to us what she had said, "I have no husband." Leona and I both said, "We have no husbands either."

We arrived at Gulmarg, breathing cool fresh air as we walked along the street with a few shops and food stalls, then took a muddy path to the Tourist Hotel. We sat near an open window so we could watch the pony boys and men helping the tourists get ready for their ride. Tourists had to put rubber overshoes over their shoes and put on a fur-lined cap and overcoat. One man seemed to be in charge and used a whip to move the ponies back so the correct one could be in line for the rider. The men all seemed to be pushing, shoving, talking, arguing; the ponies were sometimes too close to each other and the front one would raise his hind legs and kick the pony behind. So much activity made it difficult for us to concentrate on our tea and macaroons. Afterwards we looked at the shops in the hotel and used the "ladies' room"—a hole in the ground and two places in cement for our feet; this was not unusual in this part of the world and we were both very familiar with it.

247

As we came out of the hotel we saw a crowd watching some amateur performers. Nearby were two men with bright-colored turbans and strange-looking knapsacks. They had oils and medicines in their bags as well as a small black book. They showed us pages and pages of words in English—one kind of ointment would stop hair from falling out, another would give couples better love-making, another better eyesight or brain power. No, I did not want any of their wares. (I should have gotten the one which helped hair from falling out. After a permanent in a salon in Delhi, every time I brushed my hair, many strands would come out. The permanent didn't take, either. Was baldness next?)

For more rupees our driver took us around the hotels in Gulmarg. The bungalows were quite far apart from each other; an international golf course was being built as well as several army roads, which we were not allowed to drive on. Sheep were grazing on a green meadow. We found a quiet spot for our picnic, in attendance were two crows and several solid-colored yellow, white and black butterflies. Later we drove down the mountain road to the builtup platform with a tea stall where we enjoyed the mountain view, the rushing river and valley below, and our cup of tea.

Back in Srinagar the Shalimar Gardens had a light and sound show called "The Romance of the Moghuls, 1526–1707." The Hindi show was from 8–9 and English 9–10 P.M. We had to wait until the first show was over and when they came out, what a throng there was. There were not quite so many for the 9 o'clock show, so we walked down the lighted path of the garden to the wooden platform with chairs. Since we had purchased 7.50-rupee seats we were ushered to the second row from the back near the aisle. The ushers were still talking when the show began and more people came in. We moved way over to an empty section on the other side. An usher followed us and told us they were 7.50-rupee seats. We then had to produce our tickets again and were finally left in peace to enjoy the show, which told the history of the area with words, the sound of horses' hooves, chopping of wood, sighing; and stories of Nur Jahan and his love; the beauty of the Vale of Kashmir; laughter of the women in the flower garden for the festival of flowers, his death and his son coming. It ended with a story of the "Nargis and the Bee" which said the flower gardens are for everyone, everyone, e v e r y o n e. After that show we *really* appreciated this bit of paradise.

Another day we had the privilege of entertaining another couple teaching at Woodstock, Danny and Gerilee Lacy and their three-month-old son, Kip, who slept the entire time. It was so good to hear all the stories of this energetic couple, traveling in Asia with such a small baby. Mutton curry and curds were served with chappatis for that meal and we had the usual dessert, stewed apricots. (Food was served that was raised and found in the area; still there was quite a variety.)

Leona and I decided to photograph carpet weaving, visit a copper shop, and a furniture shop. At least that was the plan. Every shop was filled with beautiful objects and there was never enough time to wander through them in Srinagar—never enough "day" for each visit. First we stopped at the Indian Airlines to check our plane tickets, then a bank to exchange traveler's checks for cash, to a chemist shop for Leona, and a newspaper shop for a paper to see what had happened in the world—a taxi strike in Karachi; Philip Cousteau was killed in a plane crash; Elizabeth Taylor's husband, Michael Wilding, had died; and "No one should die as the result of Space Lab falling" which meant that the metal should fall between July 8–18 in *India*. I bet people in this part of the world appreciated reading that! Our errands were finished after mailing letters at the post office.

Now came the "Kashmiri" part of the day. We drove to the Oriental Carpet Factory and saw the design room, with numbers being placed on papers from the original design. Then to the weaving room, where various-size boys and young men were weaving, some as young as eight years. They sat crosslegged on raised planks off the cement floor, several working on a carpet. Then the carpet was taken to the clipping room, where the top of the carpet is clipped. The next step was to wash it with various type of tools and brushes used for soaping and rinsing and drying. The final step was the show room, a very long room where several salesmen were unrolling carpets for the prospective customers. We too sat down to look at three-by-five-foot rugs; many had colors or designs we did not like. I was looking for a small one to purchase for my friend, Anita Schwarz, in New York, who was taking care of all my affairs there while I was teaching in India. Finally, I spotted one in beige and browns called "Kashmir Garden." It was so beautiful and I knew she would enjoy it in her home. (In 1974 I had bought one for me called "Jewel of Kashmir," which it truly is.) By the time purchase arrangements were made and we went to another shop for a chain-stitch rug Leona wanted, there was not time for the copper and furniture shop. Probably it was just as well for our pocketbooks. I am often reminded of a cartoon I saw many years ago when Dagwood, carrying an armful of purchases, said to Blondie, "So this is what women would rather have than money." How true!

That evening we had dinner on the roof where we enjoyed a full moon making the sky bright as day. The lake and houseboats were lovely in the reflection; the cool breeze made it a perfect spot to spend hours. The clubhouse near us had a party and a small boat crossing the lake had singing and fireworks with rockets coloring the sky before falling into the lake. It was the kind of night one should stay awake to look at and listen to. Not many nights like that have I experienced—one in Point Barrow, Alaska, with the Midnight Sun and Eskimo dogs yelping and birds flying; the night in Norway when I saw the sun roll along the horizon continuing the twenty-four-hour day; another full moon on the Nile River while I was enjoying a ride on a *felucca* (a fast sailing ship). And now this perfect night on a houseboat in Kashmir. Tomorrow was another day and we had to be ready for whatever it would bring; we left our cozy rooftop spot and went into our stuffy bedrooms. It is almost criminal to have to get under a roof when one could be under the sky, stars, and moon. . . .

The next morning we ordered delicious French toast with Kashmiri honey and fresh cherries, a good change from eggs and toast. We decided to drive to Pahlgam, sixty miles east of Srinagar. Knowing that saffron was grown in Kashmir, I told our driver to show us a field of saffron. On the way we saw a huge army cantonment; school students all dressed up, going on a picnic; Silk Worm Seed Control Board offices and small mulberry trees; large groves of almond trees; the ruins of a temple from A.D. 855 with many stalls where walnuts, cashews, raisins, almonds, and candies were sold; green rice paddies; three *sadhus* (holy men) walking toward us on the road, no shoes; cricket bats for sale near several factories for sports goods with drying wood piled up high; overhead fighter planes went whizzing by; a trout fish farm; and huts blending in with the earth. Finally we stopped at a bare field and our driver pointed toward it and said, "Saffron." What a surprise that was! At this time of year the saffron fields are dormant; however, he did go into the field and got an old flower and three bulbs and gave them to me. Saffron is the dried stigma of the purple-flowered crocus and is used to flavor and color foods. (I did take the bulbs back to Woodstock, put them in a dresser drawer and months later when I looked at the bulbs, they had sprouted.)

We came to a rushing river which came down from the mountain snows, drove on the valley road up into Pahlgam. There was one wide main street with hotels, huts, tents scattered here and there, and many different peoples: Kashmiris from the hills, Rajastani women dressed in colorful skirts and tops and men wearing brilliant colored turbans, *sadhus* with only a loincloth and an orange mark on the forehead, children enjoying picnics. One man was carried in a "dandy" for several miles; it was too difficult for him to walk on his pilgrimage. We stopped at the Pahlgam Club, operated by the government tourist office, found the dining room, and inquired if we could order a trout lunch. We had seen men fishing in the cold rushing stream and thought the trout would be delicious. A man answered, "No, you can not get trout in Pahlgam. It costs twenty rupees a day for a license for six fish." (If this were another place in the world, I knew there would be special trout dinners!) We drove to the edge of the rushing stream under the shade of a tree and spread our picnic hamper contents: cold chicken, egg salad sandwiches; salad of cabbage, carrots, tomatoes, cucumbers; and cherries for dessert. Leona had brought coffee in her thermos. No, it wasn't trout but a delicious substitute high in the hills of Kashmir.

There were many photo opportunities on our trip back to Srinagar—a *sadhu* (a Hindu mendicant ascetic) arranging flowers on a brass tray; a woman cleaning pots near some water; a Kashmiri woman from the hills wearing traditional heavy jewelry around her neck and a wide silver bracelet with some plastic ones on one arm . . . a bright colored scarf covered her hair, which was braided in tiny braids; and nomads with their cattle and a few horses grazing on the green hills. The main road was wide and smooth because it was an army road; we often drove on narrow side roads with piles of sand on either side. Often when we tried to pass a bus we had to drive behind it and got those terrible black fumes from the exhaust, making it almost impossible to breathe. That was the way it was with most Indian and Jammu–Kashmir buses. About 4P.M. we noticed women had taken food to their husbands working in the fields. They then sat by the side of the road, resting and drinking tea. They appeared so relaxed and comfortable it reminded me of harvest time on the farm when we took lemonade in a big gallon jug, sandwiches, and cookies to the men working in the field. As a youngster I felt I was helping and contributing to the family work. (When I travel I never know when a scene will jog a memory of growing up.) By now we had descended into the valley where it was very warm and we would soon be home where a warm bath would remove the dust of the day, followed by Kashmiri tea with cardamon and cinnamon and a slice of white raisin bread covered with honey to refresh us.

Before our trip to Ladakh we had errands—our final visit to "Suffering Moses" shop and say goodbye to this elegant man, Mr. Moses, and buy a few more papier-maché items. I had one more massage from Mr. Gani and even wrote a short recommendation in his little black book. A couple more lazy *shikara* rides through the lotus as we watched the ever-present variety of birds. It was time to leave the Vale of Kashmir, where we had been so isolated from the rest of the world. It was like no other place I had visited. What a memorable holiday this had been!

When Sam and I were in India and Nepal in the spring of 1988 we had made arrangements to spend a week on *Boojum;* however, snow and land slides prevented the plane from flying there—that part of the trip was cancelled.

19

Ladakh, Summer 1979

July 11, finally arrived for our Ladakhi adventure. Up at 6 A.M. we dressed, finished packing, had breakfast, got our "lunch foods" from our houseboat staff, and taxied (a sign on the dashboard said, "Do Not Sleep On Frunt Seat") to the J and K tourist bus area. We were the second people on the bus in seats 5 and 6. Others arrived—well-dressed Indians (they travel in their best clothes), a couple from Long Island working as anthropologists in Lahore, Pakistan, and many "hippy-type" younger persons from several countries—our traveling companions for two days. Finally the bus was loaded, also the roof, with a strange assortment of baggage. We drove to a fuel depot and got 114 liters of diesel. One woman said, "No wonder it takes two days to get to Leh, one day to get out of Srinagar!" How true. The bus stopped again so the driver could talk to a friend, and again near a mosque to pick up another driver and several sacks of stuff. At last we were on our way.

What did I know about Ladakh? It is called "Little Tibet"; it is one of the most elevated regions in the world with high plains and deep valleys; it is in eastern Kashmir and Jammu, the northernmost part of the Indian subcontinent; the western Himalayan Ladakh range and the Karakoram Range were part of it; the climate was cold and dry; Leh had been a very important town on the trade route years ago; the whole of Ladakh was sparsely populated; the country was rocky, harsh, dry, strange; and Ladakh meant "the land of high mountain passes." All these thoughts were going through my head as we were driving on a narrow winding road. First there were green rice paddies which changed to rocks and stones everywhere. Midmorning we stopped at Kangan, a small town nestled in the hills where pines trees grew. When we moved on again I saw a narrow footpath with a footbridge over the rushing river. One could hardly call it a road with a narrow strip of tarmac in the middle of the twisting highway; the only road from Srinagar to Leh, 160 miles. One could fly, but we had been told to take the two-day bus trip, an unforgettable experience driving up the Kashmir Valley to the mountains of Ladakh. Soon we were beside a glacier, our bus had climbed that much. Farther

253

on were many horses grazing where nomads had found grass for their animals. The brightly colored clothes shone brilliant in the sunshine.

We stopped for a break, so Leona and I ate our cold-chicken lunch as we sat on the bus. We then used the "facilities" there—bushes behind the building. There was one other small shed, which was occupied. Someone yelled, "Are you sure someone is in there?" From within came the answer, "Yes, there is, and I am constipated and I can't believe it."

On the other side of a bridge was a large sign saying "Welcome to Ladakh." Now our adventure really began! An army convoy of thirty-four trucks had stopped on the road because some trucks weren't working. After some time, we began moving again on the narrow rough road with no railing and a river far below. Again the convoy stopped because of mechanical problems. (This country was of strategic importance with borders of Tibet and China and the other side was Pakistan; therefore, the army was there.) Signs along the road read, "Look for Rolling Boulders"; "Do Not Change Gear"; "Leh—333 kilometers"; "Srinagar to Leh—434 kilometers"; "Be cautious, be slow and a long way you go." We drove on and again saw a huge glacier far below us. Another sign read "Rough road—Drive slow" and far below we saw a smashed truck in a stream. That wasn't a very comforting sight! Finally the road cut right through a wide snowfield. Later we saw a hillside covered with sheep grazing on the green grasses. Most of the time there was so much white chalky dust on the road our entire bus was enveloped and the windows had to be closed. By now our convoy had approximately one hundred vehicles, perhaps more—private taxis, jeeps, buses, and army trucks. No wonder there was so much dust with four hours driving on stones and rocks; finally we got back on tarmac. We saw a few mud huts near each other and a small religious building in the middle of the settlement.

The journey went on and on—more mountains, more boulders, more rocks, switchbacks down to the rushing river, then hairpin turns back up ochre cliffs. Finally at 5:30 P.M. we arrived at Drass, the coldest spot in Asia, we were told. This was a check-point so we filled out tourist registration forms, gave our passports to our bus driver, who took them into a tent for checking. We never got out of the bus—no toilet building and no bushes. (One never realizes the importance of good kidneys until trips such as this one.)

Two and one-half hours later, at 8 P.M., our bus arrived at the stop for the night, Kargil. Many men holding signs advertising their hotels were waiting for our bus. Leona and I chose Hotel Green Land because his sign said, "Sanitary Fitting." He led us to his hotel, going up the outside steps to the second floor. Inside were two beds, clean, and an attached bathroom. We ordered our food—scrambled eggs, toast and tea. When supper arrived the eggs had been mixed with milk and sugar and tasted more like bread pudding. Why should eggs, scrambled, in Kargil, Ladakh, taste just like eggs scrambled in Eagle Grove, Iowa? We quickly ate them in spite of the different taste. We had found the water faucet and toilet in spite of no electricity, went to bed exhausted from the treacherous but interesting journey, and were lulled to sleep by men singing nearby.

The following morning we were up at 4:15 A.M. (our bus left at 5). We had no matches to light two candles, so we used our flashlights. They brought breakfast: two eggs each, toast, apricot jam, and coffee. We quickly signed the register, paid eighty rupees, ate fast, walked to the bus and were off while it was still dark. Kargil is the second largest town in Ladakh and is Muslim; too bad we couldn't spend some time there. We did have a beautiful bonus for leaving so early—the full moon was shining brightly on the snows followed by the never-to-be-forgotten sunrise! A sign beside the road read, "Be careful today—tomorrow will be too late." Hairpin curves were in abundance, hundreds of them, in this strange rockfilled moonscape land of ochre and reddish-brown windswept emptiness.

After a couple of hours on the road we began to see prayer flags flying from houses, mud bricks drying, wild rosebushes everywhere, a statue of Buddha carved on a tall boulder, and a green valley with very little water in the river. The mountains had changed from jagged peaks to smoother rounded humps. No animals were in sight, very few birds, and the grass was sparse at the tiny village where we stopped to pick up two Ladakhi men and one woman. Namikala was at an altitude of 12,200 feet. The woman wore a black headpiece, a long brown wool skirt, and a top coat. She wore a turquoise necklace with two small coral beads between each turquoise and a silver pendant covered with turquoise. She had earrings of the same stones and coral bangles. (Women there always wear their collection of jewelry whether working or traveling.) Later I saw a woman with a hoe working in the field wearing the traditional headpiece, a perak, which covers the top of the head and goes down the middle of the back. This material is covered with turquoise stones. What an exquisite piece of jewelry!

At another rest stop we took photos of the village, walked down a path where we found a secluded spot while two donkeys waited to go down the same path where we were. Oh my! These outside "facilities" are something. Back on the bus we couldn't move until an army convoy of thirty–forty trucks drove past us. Soon we stopped to let a second convoy go by. At one point there were barriers across the road indicating one-way traffic. The highest point on this part of the trip was 14,000 feet, where snow peaks glistened from the strong sunlight. From there we had more switchbacks, driving slowly. Our Ladakhi woman had been ill most of the time and kept her head out the window, silently retching. I felt so sorry for her.

After all the emptiness and lack of humans we arrived at Lamyuru, nestled in a valley. We stopped. The area was filled with lamas in their wine-colored robes. They all waved to us on the bus going to Leh. I talked to one lama and he told me there were 200 lamas at that monastery. An older woman wanted to go with us but we had no room for her. As we continued our trip there was the same barrenness in the land and more frightening hairpin curves. We stopped for lunch at Khaltsi, a small village, and ate at the Moonlight Hotel, where we were served two glasses of sweetened tea, rice, vegetables, and dhal. A young boy showed what he was selling, plant fossils in a small slab of stone. Of course, I bought one for my "show-and-tell" collection.

As we began our ascent from the very hot gorge to Leh, thirty-five kilometers away, another sign said, "Safety Ever—Accident Never"; another said, "Be alert lest you meet with an accident." Now the valley was wide and rather flat with a good road. As we got closer to Leh we drove by the army contonment and the air strip with barbed wire fence around. Leh was nestled against a hill and looked smaller than I expected. Snowcapped mountains could be seen in the distance. The bus went to the middle of Leh, stopping in front of the tourist center. We all clapped to show our appreciation to our drivers for our safe arrival.

Unloading the bus began with bags tossed down from the roof, including our duffle bag. Leona stayed with the luggage while I went into the center to check on a hotel. The office sent a coolie to carry our heavy duffle bag to the Yak-Tail Hotel. Our room was in the older section, on the second floor; to get there we walked through a courtyard where there was a week-old calf and a coop with chickens. In the room we found the beds so close together we could barely get between them; at least we didn't have to use our sleeping bags. We had tea in the garden—a delicious welcome to Leh. Leona went to rest while I walked with the young native guide, helping the same thirteen students we had entertained on our houseboat to their guest house. Six of them had been in a Jeep and an army truck hit the side. Luckily, only two heads got bumped. Were they ever lucky. They showed me the rooms—the dining room had cabbage and onions in one corner; the room was dark and smelled stale. The bathroom had the usual hole in the floor; one bedroom had a musty scent. It was so good to see them and hear their adventures from Srinagar to Leh. Finally one of the students from Iran escorted me back to my hotel. What a pleasant surprise to find friends in this faraway land!

We had our supper at the Dreamland Restaurant, only two rooms. We waited one and a half hours for a table and our soup. With it we ate a piece of buttered toast from our Kargil breakfast. (One never throws anything away while traveling, especially in Asia.) Back to our Yak-Tail room, a quick wash in cold water and to bed in Leh, altitude 11,500 feet.

Friday the 13th. It felt so good to leisurely dress before having breakfast in the garden. A room was available in the new section on the second floor, so we moved our things. We had a view of snow peaks, rice paddies in terraces with huge stones around each field, a running stream nearby and a new building where two girls carried baskets of dirt up a ladder dumping the dirt on wood shavings on the flat roof so plants could grow. The girls seemed happy, talking and laughing as they worked.

At last, it was time to explore the town. The bazaar was the best area to see people and produce. Tibetans were selling antiques with merchandise spread on the ground on cloths. There were tea cups, prayer wheels, spoons, turquoise, coral, yak-bone necklaces with silver and coral, rugs, round chunks of stuff that looked like amber but one woman from Darjeeling said it was plastic. Unusual items were in many shops. Ladakhi women were selling turnips; another woman had a few unshelled peas in a pan under a tree, the only vegetables for sale I saw at a market when wandering in the narrow streets.

Ladakhi women were dressed in beautiful traditional clothes: long trousers, a blouse and over that a long coat with slits up the side. Usually clothes were brown or black; the coats had a bright green or turquoise lining. A tall velvet or corduroy hat with embroidery was worn on the head over their long braided hair with one or two braids hanging down the back. (Such elegant hats for this strange, rocky, stark environment).

Often over their back was slung a longhaired white goat fur hide or a red embroidered shawl. Beautiful turquoise, coral, silver necklaces and long earrings of seed pearls completed the outfit. Ladakhi men usually wore a long wool or cotton coat and pants and many wore homemade Tibetanlike woolen shoes (some women also wore them). Men often wore the same kind of hat as the women.

A beautiful Ladakhi woman was near us and we asked if we could take her photo. She wore a deep green velvet traditional coat and hat . . . but she was shy. A Buddhist lama talked to her—then she posed for us. I told her I would send the photo to her (which I did). Leona and I sauntered along with her walking beside us. When I sat on a step she took my arm and tried to pull me up. Leona asked a shopkeeper to ask her what she wanted. Word came back to us, "She wants you to come to her home for tea." Leona turned to me and said, "Lou, what do we do?" I answered her, "We accept." So off the three of us went—down the main street to the end, a turn left, another left into a narrow street with shops on either side.

Finally we came to a gateway and walked into a small courtyard of houses. She then went to the second-floor, climbing a ladder attached to a platform without any kind of a railing, pulled aside a curtain, unlocked a door and went in. She motioned for us to come up the ladder. We were so flabbergasted by the sight of the ladder, but if an invitation of hospitality is accepted, one carries on. (It was Friday the 13th.) I climbed up first, looked inside and saw a dirt floor, uneven, a small broom, some food and garbage near the door. She motioned us to sit on a rug on one side of the room on the floor. A low table was in front of us. She removed a jar with dried weeds and placed a small tea cup without handles in front of each of us and poured hot buttered-salty tea from a thermos into mine. Leona asked for black tea but she had none so her cup remained empty. I slowly sipped and found it wasn't as strong as the Tibetan tea I had had at my friend Tashi's home. Then she showed us eggs she wanted to fix for us, special barley flour in a tin for *tsampa,* or she would send to a hotel for *momos* (a small steamed dumpling with meat inside), but we said, "No." She showed us almonds in a tin but we again said, "No." As she put more kerosene in the stove and got the fire going to make more tea, we noticed the many shelves on the walls with a variety of containers, cooking utensils and teacups. Behind us was the one window covered with bars.

Leona tried to talk to her using words in various Indian languages but communication was almost impossible. Two young girls came in and she gave them cup after cup of tea. An older woman arrived and sat by the door but was given no tea. Later a man came and tried to help with the stove; he left after a few minutes. Who were those people? Did they come to see us? Were they part of her family? Who was our hostess? Then I remembered I had some individually wrapped hard candies in my purse so I passed them around. We sat there enjoying our sweets and looking at one another.

By this time, thirty or forty minutes had passed and our legs were going to sleep from sitting on the floor. We slowly got up, thanked her for her hospitality, and stood by the door. Yokal, her name, went down the ladder first by sitting on each rung, then to the next . . . so we did likewise. More photos were taken of this friendly woman in green with exquisite jewelry of strands of seed pearls, turquoise and coral. She walked with us to the main street where we again said good-bye and waved to each other. What an unexpected gift—a visit in the home of a Ladakhi woman in a very faraway country. (Years later when I think of my trip to Ladakh, this experience comes to me—it is indelibly imprinted in my mind.)

We slowly went to our hotel and ate some of the food we had brought with us: apple juice, crackers with cheese or peanut butter, dill pickles, and ginger cookies. We were thankful we had brought it all the way from Srinagar.

In the bazaar I noticed people were trading all kinds of items: Bic pens, clothes, etc. I saw a small Tibetan silver pendant with turquoise and coral but the shopkeeper wanted 500 rupees; I asked him if he would trade it for my sleeping bag. He said he would come and look at it. He came and looked and I told him I wanted 400 rupees but he said, "No." Then I said my last price was 350 rupees. He thought about it and agreed that I give him the sleeping bag and 100 rupees. In return I got the beautiful old Tibetan pendant. Since this was the first time I had ever bartered I wondered who won or who got cheated. These people have been traders for centuries, so I am sure he lost nothing. But me? Well, I'm not sure. . . .

A Jeep-taxi driver took us to see the Moravian Church, founded in 1855, but it was closed. Our guidebook said we should visit the Christian cemetery near the army base, so we did but saw few tombstones and did not find names and descriptions of early travelers. I saw one small lizard

259

scurrying in the sparse grasses. We then saw the Kider House, a Ladakhi home where a family lived, open to tourists. A woman took us up steps, through a small storage room into the kitchen room with benches along two walls with tables in front where guests ate. Shelves were loaded with copper, brass and tin pots, coffeepots, chang pots; plates and cooking utensils—all bright and shiny. A large black stove had two pieces of coral imbedded in the front as decoration. Charcoal was placed in the middle of the stove to heat four burners on top used for cooking rice, vegetables, tea, and heating water. Hanging on two center posts were many kinds of jewelry, including the large turquoise—covered headpiece or *perak*. She let me hold this heavy item with approximately 400 bluish-green stones arranged in rows. When we left we thanked her for showing us the home and gave her a few rupees.

We had dinner at the Dreamland Hotel Restaurant again in the company of an English couple and six Belgians who arranged their own travel each summer by buying a truck and driving. They were a most interesting group of teachers and mechanics who had many unusual stories to relate.

Night at a high altitude is never-to-be-forgotten. The sky was brilliant with stars—no pollution. I had never seen so many stars before and should have stayed awake to watch all night but I knew the next day would offer unusual activities. After gazing upwards in the cool night breezes for a last long moment, it was time to sleep.

Next morning our Jeep-taxi arrived at 8 A.M. to spend the day exploring monasteries. As usual we stopped at a filling station for petrol first, then went about ten miles out from Leh to visit Shey, way up on the rocks. The path was too rocky so we turned around and got in the Jeep. We drove farther on in a green valley with many "mani walls" (stones heaped together by people passing, many had writing on the stones), always flat on top. We also saw stupas, crumbling, as part of the wall. Often our Jeep had to drive in ditches and through waterholes. I kept looking for yaks and finally saw a *dzo* (female yak) walking along the road with a bell in the bottom of each ear. Thickshey was the next monastery perched on the side of a rock. From a distance it looked like a small version of the Potala in Lhasa. The Jeep driver drove to the beginning of the rocky path and stone steps. The entrance fee was ten rupees each; then we climbed up very steep smooth steps to the prayer hall with rugs on the floor for four rows of monks. In the room were two huge drums, two conch shells inlaid with turquoise, and two long trumpets. After looking at the wall paintings it was time to leave. The driver helped me down the steps back to the jeep where Leona and I drank apple juice before the next monastery, some distance away.

Hemis Gompa is the oldest and wealthiest monastery in the area. Our Jeep drove closer to it than the buses—a good thing we hired the Jeep. Our young Ladakhi driver again helped me over numerous stones and rocks: high stone walls were on either side of the path. At last the courtyard! It had been a rough trek for me but I had read so much about monasteries in remote lands I wanted to see this one for sure. There were old and faded paintings on the walls around the courtyard, three tall poles with prayer flags flying in the breeze, then up a few more steps to the prayer hall with a huge seated Buddha draped with traditional white scarves; other items were on the altar. The room was so dark one could hardly see the wall paintings or the cubbyholes in the walls where books were kept. Rugs were on the floor but no musical instruments were in sight. We soon left going down the same entrance steps to a courtyard with many trees and chairs and tables under large umbrellas, an outdoor cafe. I ordered fried rice and hot tea but the rice had very few vegetables and was not very tasty; however, sitting in the chairs was relaxing. After an hour it was back to the Jeep and the trip back to Leh. He drove rather fast—no curtains or doors on the Jeep—the wind blew hard and it was cold. We finally stopped at the Tibetan Refugee Center with a few items in the showroom. In Leh we halted at the Ladakhi Handicraft Center and saw young people making sweaters on knitting machines. The items for sale were embroidered cushions (I bought two), masks, thankas (paintings), and carpets.

Back in Leh we placed our order for a 6 P.M. dinner but we had to wait even longer for the mutton curry with a couple pieces of fat mutton, too tough to eat. Leh had two meatless days, Friday and Monday, but I think the other days could also be called ''meatless.'' After eating, we sat on our veranda and watched the clouds, the snow peaks, and the setting sun in many colors, but the cold wind was still blowing so we didn't remain long. In our room we only had three candles in small juice cans; not enough light for reading or writing so we had to go to bed, but the dogs barking at each other was too loud for sleep, even through earplugs. I also knew this was the last night in Leh. We had spent five days in this place called ''Little Tibet'' and tomorrow we would leave this unusual and strange environment. I hoped I would someday come back for more exploring.

We were up at 6:30 to finish packing our possessions in one duffle bag and four small hand carrying bags; breakfast in the garden and a Jeep-taxi ride to the tourist office. At 8:30 the bus arrived to take everyone to the airport. An older Ladakhi man carried our heavy duffle bag into the building but would not take a tip for his kind act. We waited outside the Quonset hut, during that time a group of tourists rudely pushed their way in front of us. Finally the door opened; a soldier with a gun let a few people at a time into the room. A man behind a desk checked our tickets again; another man weighed the duffle bag and yelled out the weight to the ticket man. The customs checkpoint was at the far end and had me unlock the duffle bag for checking. We again stood in a line, went through another door where a soldier stood with a gun, gave our passports and ticket to the man who wrote down the numbers; then we had to write all of it in a book, go into a small room where a Tibetan woman wrote down my name, passport number, checked my purse and small hand bags, then through a door, down two steps and got our boarding pass stamped, found chairs, sat and waited. Who should I find beside me but "Mrs. Anthropology" we had met on the way to Leh. She had twisted her knee the first day in Leh and was limping using a stick as a crutch. Their first day they had gone to a monastery and were invited by a Buddhist priest to attend a cremation service and had permission to photograph the entire ceremony—others from other countries were not given permission. She was such a vivacious, kind woman; she reminded me so much of Aunt Margaret, especially the way she talked.

The plane finally arrived and again we all lined up before we went out the door where there were more soldiers with guns. We walked along the rocky long path to the Indian Airlines plane, went up the steps, were told to take any seat. At 11 A.M. we began to taxi down the bumpy runway. I have *never* been jostled so much in any plane and I wondered if we would be able to get aloft knowing that the air is so thin at this altitude. Somehow we made it and soon found ourselves right beside the peaks of the mountains, at first scary, but then we relaxed and enjoyed the magnificent views, including Num Kun Peak at 23,400 feet. All too soon, just twenty-five minutes of flying, we landed at the Srinagar airport. It had taken us two very long extremely interesting days on the bus to Leh and now we were back again in twenty-five minutes. I wouldn't have missed any part of this adventure and wished we had spent more time in Ladakh. Perhaps another time. . . .

20

Birthday Trip in the Himalayan Foothills, March 22, 1980

When I found out my birthday was on a Saturday four of us hired a car and driver for the day for a trip to Chamba, Rishikeshk, and Dehra Dun. Ever since I came to the hills in India, I had wanted to visit Rishikesh, where the Beatles had studied with a guru.

I awakened at 5 A.M. and got the water boiling for coffee, dressed, had one boiled egg and a piece of French toast left over from the previous breakfast. With peanut butter on it the taste was quite good as I drank my coffee. I took my belongings for the day downstairs and listened to sounds. At 5:45 it was just beginning to get light and I heard the footsteps of a man jogging on the road below, many bird songs, the prayers from the mosque a mile away, and I watched the *chowkidar* (watchman) walk around the quad area turning off the lights. Chelsea slowly came up the steps after her long walk up the hill from her home; Ruth arrived from the quad area; the taxi honked its way around the curves on the mountain road until it arrived beside us. Leona came with her large box of goodies. We packed our water jugs, picnic boxes and bags in the trunk, arranged ourselves in the car, and were ready for our trip at 6:15 A.M.

Nature was laden with "birthday presents" for me that day: birds were singing, flying, and crossing the road and even though we couldn't identify most, they were much enjoyed. The scenery was spectacular with the terraced green fields on the hillsides; the fruit trees were blooming —the entire scene looked like a painting. The rhododendron trees, thirty or forty feet tall, were loaded with the red puffy ball-like flowers and looking like Christmas trees. I felt each one was presenting themselves to me. The best present from nature were the snow peaks of the Himalayas. They were so clear one could even see snow blowing off the peaks, rather like clouds. As we rounded one curve the view was only white peaks—what a gift.

We turned south at Chamba, a big-little village with steep terraces all the way to the bottom of the valley. At a waterfall we stopped for a coffee break. As we continued on we passed the maharaja's castle up on top of the village of Norendranagar, where he had spent most of his time; now the beautiful buildings were government offices. Then the road descended to the plains, the Ganges River, and Riskikesh.

Before entering Rishikesh, we came to a check point and saw a man wipe another man's arm, then put a needle in the arm. I told the others, "Get out your health cards and show them the cholera shot." Yes, we were stopped, the man came over, saw the cards and let us go on. I was so glad I had told our Indian music secretary we were going on this trip and she told me to take the health cards or we'd have to get the shot. (Anytime a town gets ready for a *mela,* a religious festival, they don't want people getting sick so everyone gets a cholera shot. The next *mela* was here in two–three weeks.)

As we drove along the Ganges, steps were going from the street to the river from temples and other buildings across the river. We parked the car and walked on the narrow footbridge high above the river to the far side. We looked into the Hanuman Temple where the monkey god had a scarf over his shoulders and at noon a priest pulled a brightly checked "quilt" in front so he couldn't be seen. Leona and I sat on a bench to watch the people while the other friends walked on down to another temple. It was so hot down here on the plains, I almost felt ill. We noticed many soldiers standing around, other people with change to sell so one could give to the beggars and temples and to many dressed in orange-colored *lungis* (a wide piece of material one wore around the waist falling to the ankles) who were begging beside the main road. We then walked back across the bridge, up the steps, got in our car and asked the driver to take us to a place where we could enjoy a quiet picnic. Leona had been here before and she suggested an ashram, so Mr. Singh drove up the road, through the gate, past many buildings to the end which was a dining hall with people in front. We asked if we could eat in the shade of the building but the man suggested we take our food and eat in their dining hall. We got the boxes from the trunk, went inside, saw that we had to take off our shoes before we could walk upstairs, where we would have to sit on the floor on carpets. Finally one said we could use a small room near the entrance; there were two benches and a wooden table, and we decided that was the better choice. What a picnic in a "godown" (storage room) of an ashram! We had potato salad, smoked clams, Danish salami, brown bread, cheese, dill pickles, oranges, bananas, *and* a birthday cake Leona had made for my birthday! As we ate we noticed at the far end was a wooden bed, some pictures of deities, some water vessels, an alarm clock in a screened wooden cupboard, so perhaps it was not a godown but someone's room. There was also a very large screened cupboard with many apples and bananas. When we finished eating we wanted to tour the ashram; however, there was no one around to help us. From 1–3:30 was quiet time and no one was visible. Also, we wanted to give a donation for letting us eat there but we couldn't find the place to leave the money. When we were by the river, Ruth had talked to a girl from Austria who was spending two months here and she had said there was a library, a press, someone was saying prayers for twenty-four hours every day, but we just happened to be in the wrong part of the ashram. Signs on the walls of the dining hall said, "Be silent"; "Shut off the water tap"; "Shut off the fan when you leave your room."

We packed our things and drove down the main road to see Rishikesh—a touristy town for religious pilgrims. A rather long drive to Dehra Dun where we saw many goats and sheep being taken up to the hills for grazing for the summer months. There were several herd-dogs and shepherds moving them along. On some of the large rams sacks were strapped on both sides of their back. One shepherd was carrying around his neck a newborn lamb. Yes, another picture right out of *National Geographic* magazine.

In Dehra Dun we each had errands after our espresso coffee at the President Hotel. I had to get back my passport from the travel office so I could get a new one at Eastertime in Delhi. Dehra Dun was our "big" city, a busy commercial town, and from there we began our climb up the winding road to Mussoorie, 6500 feet up. What a perfect day it had been with nature and friends—a beautiful way to celebrate my fifty-seventh birthday in India!

Before retiring for the night, I was reading the brochures on Rishikesh. This is what one said: "Prohibition: Rishikesh is a prohibited area for liquor and non-vegetarian food." And we had smoked salami and smoked clams right *in* the ashram. I do hope all was well there after we left. . . .

21

Music Conference in Poland, Summer 1980

The fourteenth ISME (International Society of Music Educators) Conference was held in Warsaw, Poland, July 6–12. My music teacher friend, Anita Schwarz, from Roslyn, planned to meet me there. She would fly from New York to Warsaw; I would fly from New Delhi to Warsaw. We hoped the flights, reservations, and tours would not be too complicated and we were not going on a "wild-goose chase" from different parts of the world. The destination was behind the Iron Curtain—we needed visas, we needed reservations for the conference; so many questions about my permission to leave India and return in a month; therefore I would also need police registration papers for clearance. All went well and it was two very happy friends who met at the Warsaw airport . . . a small miracle.

An opera was performed the evening before the conference began; we didn't want to miss it. It was difficult finding a taxi to take us to the opera house from our hotel but after much searching we got one. During intermission we met other Polish ISME members and were so surprised when the Polish men kissed our hands when we were introduced. How elegant! When the performance was over everyone immediately left; we couldn't because there were no taxis. We looked and looked in the dark but to no avail. After some time a man who spoke very little English offered to take us to our hotel in his car; we accepted. As we drove he told us he was a salesman from East Germany, Dresden, on business in Warsaw. He liked music very much and had attended a performance in the other concert hall in the same building. He couldn't have been more gracious; if he wouldn't have helped us, I don't think we would have gotten to our hotel our first night in Warsaw. A real miracle. . . .

Breakfast was included with our hotel reservation, so Anita and I went to the buffet. What a buffet—cold cuts, cheeses, breads, black currant juice, strawberries in a glass sprinkled with powdered sugar, sweet rolls, scrambled eggs and ham, coffee. Since I was coming from a private school in India where we often had cereal, toast, eggs, and coffee for breakfast, this was a real feast! (When we told others about our breakfast buffet, they said this was not typical in most places because Poland was going through very difficult times.)

266

Many sessions were held in the huge Congress Hall built by the Soviet Union in the middle of Warsaw. I attended the meetings related to choral music, folk songs, and choirs . . . Czech choir; Hungarian choirs; Boys' Choir from Tbilisi, USSR; Bretan Bagpipes; Brigham Young Choir; Polish choirs and others performed. For the final session all choirs performed separately, then joined together on stage and along the sides of the auditorium for a number, "Viva Musica," composed especially for the XIV Conference. The flag was given by four Polish students to the British group, where the next ISME conference would be held in 1982. It was a most moving ceremony at the end of a very successful music conference.

A tour of Warsaw included the palace of Paderewski, Saint John's Cathedral, Town Square, Madame Curie's home, the statues of Chopin and Copernicus, and the Jewish ghetto where 400,000 Jews were placed in 1941—later the whole area was burned and now it was an open grassy park with a black commemorative marble monument. Of course, we went to Chopin's birthplace, Zelazowa Wola, near Warsaw, and attended a piano concert by a fantastic young Polish performer. Both of us were thrilled to be there. I also remembered my visit to his room in Majorca where he spent a wet miserable winter with George Sand in the 1840s and saw his piano and a few other belongings. Now I was making my second Chopin pilgrimage.

After the conference we had reservations on a four-day ISME bus tour of southern Poland. En route to our lunch break our guide told us the history of Poland, beginning in 966. He told us the religious holidays were state holidays, most unique in a socialist country, and so many more facts. Food tells one so much about a country—what is grown, what is eaten. For lunch we had black current juice with strawberries and currents in the bottom of the glass, mushroom noodle soup, minced hamburger (tough), boiled potatoes, tomato/onion salad, apple roll (similar to a jelly roll), and hot tea. For dinner at our overnight stop at Lublin at 8 P.M.: vodka, boiled eggs with yellow caviar, steak, *gryka* (whole wheat kernels rather like wild rice), lettuce salad with eggs/dressing; dessert was Jello with peaches with a whipped cream design, and strong coffee.

Bus trips are the best way to see what people are doing and what is growing on the land. A market in a small village had horse-drawn carts carrying vegetables, milk cans, and flowers. One large white pig was in a crate beside the road. There was a blacksmith shop with a man shoeing a horse and a stork nest on a roof of a house protecting the family from disease and fire. Red poppies and blue cornflowers were growing in the grain fields making a colorful scene. The poppy seeds were used on the delicious Polish cakes and breads. We saw one blue house along the way and were told that in the thirteenth-century it meant a girl lived there who wanted to get married. We stopped at a seventeenth-century cathedral and were told there would be an organ recital on a 300-year-old organ, repaired only three times. As we waited for the organist we looked at the altars, the frescoes, the gilded pulpit but still no recital. Our guide went to a nearby farm and found him picking strawberries. The bus group of music educators loved that story! We finally had our organ recital.

Lunch stop arrived and we had one of the best meals on the trip—current juice, orange and mineral water, a whole trout each, vegetable soup. The third course was pork chops, tiny French fried potatoes, cucumber/tomato salad—but no dessert or tea. After lunch we toured the famous seventeenth-century Potocki Palace at Lancut and saw the collections of paintings, sculptures, china, antique furniture; the tapestries had been taken to Switzerland days before the liberation. We then went into the huge ballroom and heard a cello and piano recital, after which the doors were opened into a large dining room. On a very long oblong table covered with a mirror were 125 filled wine glasses along the edge of the table, one for each of us. What an elegant surprise—many toasts were given. Then we went across the park to the stables to see fifty-three carriages. The entrance room had heads of fifty or so stuffed animals on the walls—giraffe, deer, bison, moose, lion, rhino horn. The thought came to me that when night came and the doors were closed to everyone, I hoped the animals had a party and did a jig, had a bark and a howl!

On the edge of Krakow was a pediatrics hospital built with American money. Presidents Ford, Nixon, and Carter had all visited this place bringing more gifts. Krakow, built in the 800s, was one of the oldest cities in Poland. We stopped at the cathedral and saw the burial places of Poland's kings; also the throne chair Pope Paul had used the previous year on his visit. A walk across the stony courtyard to a museum of tapestries, 132 of them. They were beautiful, but walking on stones, cobblestones, and all the steps surely took care of my weak left ankle.

One day Anita and I spent the day exploring Krakow while the others drove some distance to the underground salt mine. We visited Saint Mary's church, small shops with Polish folk arts, saw a movie being made in the large square—actors were dressed in heavy oldfashioned clothes.

Next stop was Czenstochows to visit the Shrine of the Black Madonna, a painting that was extremely old. The shrine was filled with people, even standing in the aisles—mass was said every half-hour. We went into the treasury room and saw cases of coral, turquoise, silver, and one tiny rosary made from bread—in a concentration camp. Back to the courtyard, where there were many horse-drawn carts decorated with leaves . . . a scene right out of the Middle Ages.

Some of my impressions of Poland: Polish men seemed to be smoking all the time everywhere; in Warsaw, men whispered in one's ear as we walked on the street, "Change money?" (they want American money so they can travel out of their country); we had much rain, cold, and wind; small farms had one or two Holsteins in the farmyard; religion and music seemed to be alive and well; Krakow was the most beautiful city in Poland; I was often surprised at the elegance of customs and the people. I surely do wish them well in their country's adventures after their freedom is received. Our trip behind the Iron Curtain had been very interesting and informative.

A flight took us to Budapest, Hungary, for a short visit. During the evening meal at Restaurant Hungarica, a Gypsy orchestra played—the leader played violin with others playing violin, cello, string bass, cembolum, and clarinet. What heart and soul in the songs! For a moment it was too much for me as I remembered the Gypsy orchestra I heard in 1956 in Heidelberg just before the Hungarian uprising. Later I met some of the sixty Hungarians who came to the Heidelberg German-American Woman's Club Christmas party and I invited four of them to dinner the following night; I also invited a few of my friends, too. What an evening of conversation that was. I was so pleased I could offer my guests special mints in the shape of trees, stars, etc. As they were passed around, one Hungarian said, "You mean they have to have red stars here too?" What a letdown that was for me. The next day I bought a German-English dictionary for one who had requested it. Now, I was in their city . . . and I wondered what happened to those sixty who had fled twenty-four years before.

Anita and I spent a day at the Puszta National Park (a state farm), to see a horse show. When we arrived in midmorning we were given apricot brandy and a slice of bread with one piece of sausage on one part and a slice of onion on the other half. Later we had bean soup with a few pieces of carrots, turnip, and meat; boiled potatoes with pork slice with cut-up pieces of pickle and ham; dessert was a lemon bar, delicious. The horse show was outstanding—the rider had the horse lie down and cracked a whip over the horse; a huge round ball was kicked with hind feet first and followed by front feet; five horses galloped while a rider stood up and straddled two horses; each horse had a bell tinkling and the man yelled loudly as he rode by the bleachers. (That was the highlight of the entire show.) The one- , two- , and three-year-olds stampeded past us; one got lose and two black dogs turned it back. The people who wanted to ride horses got to do that after lunch. As part of the program, Gypsies were suppose to dance and play instruments for us, but they had a wedding the day before and were now sleeping. Because we only got one-half of the day's program, a German engineer working in Saudi Arabia stood up and objected, but it didn't help.

Soon we got on the bus for the long drive back to Budapest. We had gone only a few kilometers when we heard a terrible scraping sound in the wheels of the bus. We stopped and found it was oil from the brakes. Very slowly we drove to a bus repair center. Some of us sat on the hot bus but many got out and climbed into a farmer's horsedrawn wagon to the next town where there was a restaurant; some walked. A local bus finally came and the rest of us rode to town where we spent the next two hours waiting and talking until a different bus came to take us the rest of the way. Our guide told us, ''I enjoy being a guide but I feel ashamed when the program does not work out and I want to stop.''

One day our taxi took us to the Liszt Ference Academy to see the building. At the entrance up above on a ledge was a statue of Liszt; the foyer had carved marble pillars and was beautiful. I just *had* to see the place that had produced so many world-known musicians, named for the great Hungarian composer, Liszt. Of course, we had a tour of the cities Buda and Pest. All too soon it was time for the last part of our trip, Vienna. Upon arrival we realized we were *free* again, and not in an Iron-Curtain country.

A former student of mine, Marjorie Wade, was studying in Vienna, so she reserved a room for us at Goldenes Einhorn, a 200-year-old hotel, but no food was served, not even breakfast. Directions for buses and cafes were given us but all eating places were closed, so we stopped at a fruit market and bought rolls, salami, and other cold cuts, tomatoes, strawberries, peaches, cheese, apple juice, yogurt, nuts and pretzels. The hotel gave us two soup bowls and two soup spoons and a pitcher of hot water for Sanka each morning. The next morning we pretended we were natives and created a tasty "Golden-Schwarz" breakfast. Others followed each day; yes, improvise when traveling.

What an elegant city—such style, colors, shop windows filled with goodies, flowers and parks abound (one would never see a scrap of paper on the street). It truly is the Queen City of the World! The Opera House is the center of the city and buses and trolleys always stop there. My many visits to Vienna always impress me. It is also a musician's city. A music tour showed us where composers had lived: Gluck, Vivaldi, Mozart, Haydn, Beethoven, Schubert, Wolf, Brahms, Schumann, Strauss, Lehar, etc. We also went to Composers' Corner in Central Cemetery twenty square kilometers; it's huge) and saw the monuments and tombstones on their graves. (When Vienna was a divided city after World War II, in the 1950s I had taken the tram by myself and found Composers' Corner—my pilgrimage to my music friends.)

Marjorie, a student of mine in Heidelberg for two years, now had her Ph.D. in medieval German and taught at the University of California. One evening we met at a Keller and enjoyed hearing her experiences in Vienna where she was taking zither lessons. The entertainment was zither music—she knew the performer so we also talked to him. She seemed to know all the makers of the instrument, the teachers, and players. What a special evening that was. Another evening she invited us to her apartment—she played the zither for us and we ate *gugelhup* or pound cake with raisins she had baked. It was such a pleasure getting reacquainted with this charming young lady.

We visited the Hapsburg private apartments, the Stadtpark, and listened to Strauss waltzes played by the orchestra as we sipped lemonade; Schonnbrunn Palace and Saint Stephen's Cathedral, so many interesting sights.

The last Saturday morning I went to the supermarket (stores closed at noon) and bought salamis, cheeses, and candy to take back to India; I hoped it wouldn't spoil or melt before I got there. Back in our room packing, a Polish woman we had met at our hotel came into our room to say good-bye. She saw a pair of brown shoes I had thrown away in the wastebasket, took them out and said, "Leather?" I said, "Yes." She tried one on and it fit. She was so grateful, she kissed me on both cheeks and wished us well. It was our last night on European soil.

The next day Anita flew to New York and I flew back to New Delhi, India, for another semester of teaching at the Woodstock School. What a wonderful three weeks Anita and I had in Poland, Hungary, and Austria.

22

Kuwait, Winter 1980

A very talented tenth-grade student at the Woodstock School came to me for her piano lesson on September 24, 1980. I asked her how she was and she said, "Fine . . . but not really. I am from Iran and all my friends are there and fighting is going on between Iraq and Iran. The airport was bombed at Teheran yesterday and then Iran bombed Baghdad." I then told her I was going to Kuwait on December 8–10 as a member of the Middle States Evaluation team and hoped I could also travel to Baghdad, a place I had always wanted to visit. "With the trouble there, I know I can't fulfill my childhood dream of Baghdad and only hope I will get to Kuwait," I said.

Yes, I did have an all-expense-paid trip from New Delhi, India, to Kuwait as part of the team to evaluate the Kuwait American School, a three-day activity. There were nineteen of us, all chosen from American-type schools in the area: Lucy from Thessalonica, Lynne from Damascus, Tony from Karachi, Paul from Saudi Arabia, Robert from Abu Dhabi, Frank from South India, also one from Islamabad, from Cairo, from Dubai, and others for the elementary team. The two administrators to head the team flew over from Delaware and Pennsylvania. Each team member was assigned subjects. I was chairman of the Music and Art, worked on the Student Activities report, and helped with the Industrial Arts report. The days were very busy—observing classes, reading reports, talking to students and teachers, and finally writing our own reports. I was up at 6 A.M. and finally got to bed around midnight; however, the experience was most interesting and I thoroughly enjoyed the evaluation process.

Talks given by the administrators and the school's teachers were the introduction to the country and the school. I especially remember one speech telling when "sweet-water" was finally discovered years ago (sweet-water is drinkable water). Many topics in the speeches made us aware of an American-type school, but in another culture. The administrator often mentioned "keeping a low profile." We all agreed that the school building was too small for 1000 students—an elementary wing, a high school wing, an outdoor stage in the courtyard, three portable buildings on either side, and a new "bubble" over the pool and courts. (There was no space to expand so they were stuck with the present plant.) Girls were not allowed to go outside the school walls. There was also a dress code. All programs and sports events had to be approved first by the Kuwait Ministry of Education. (Perhaps some things didn't get done because they didn't even ask for permission.)

At any Middle States Evaluation, the first evening includes a dinner by the host school so everyone can become better acquainted. This time the dinner was at the home of the secretary of the school board; she was Lebanese and her husband owned an airline, among other things. What a home and what a buffet! Two servants came to each of us to take the order for any kind of drink, soft or otherwise. There were bowls of various types of nuts here and there—almonds, cashews, hazelnuts, pistachios, what a variety. Having spent one and a half years in India, I thoroughly enjoyed these delicious fresh nuts. On the buffet table there must have been at least fifteen different items; later we went back for dessert—cakes, Arab sweets, fruit, cheeses, and Turkish or Arab coffee. I chose to eat outside on the veranda with other teachers but probably should have eaten inside where members of the school board and other men in long white robes and traditional headdress ate and talked.

We were only in four large rooms of the house. The first room had a large black trunk with a ship's wheel and huge sea shells. Another brass table was covered with various types of copper coffee pots. The next room was a living room with many Persian carpets, couches, lamps, and brass tables with a collection on each. Two tables had antique silver bracelets from the Bedouins; one onyx bowl was filled with various size eggs made from gem stones. One wall had wooden paneling decorated with antique silver jewelry. The next room had a huge desk, a television, and a beautiful carpet hanging on the wall; several also were hanging on walls in other rooms. The dining room had twelve chairs scattered around, a long table and on another table was an embossed large coffeepot. Over the sideboard was the biggest round copper tray I had ever seen! What a gorgeous home, delicious food, and gracious host and hostess. A most memorable evening.

The committee was housed in the Hala House (hotel). Most of us had a suite of rooms; there were three of us in my suite. Upon arrival each person found three gifts—a bottle opener with Hala House stamped on it; a bottle of Eau de Toilette "Flamme" from Paris; and a passport case, black leather with gold print "Kuwait—Hala House" and the telephone number. The case had a place for tickets, disembarkation cards, passport, traveler's cheques, cards, and certificates. (I carry this case whenever I go to a country where a passport is needed.) Hala House was very well run and a perfect setting for the necessary small and large meetings our committee needed in the evenings. The help-yourself breakfasts were delicious.

One night the window in our kitchenette was left slightly open, and the next morning the floor, counter, stove, and table were covered with a layer of very fine sand. A most memorable picture in my mind's memories. Sand . . . sand . . . sand. Years ago I had heard this story of an Arab in New York. As he left the hotel he tried to take the faucets with him. Why? Because out of the faucets came water. Now, some decades after that joke they have truly put "faucets" in the desert with both hot and cold water. I had wanted to see a real desert in Kuwait; I didn't have to go anyplace because the desert came right into my own room!

After our final oral reports and written comments were finished, four of us went to the bazaar or souk to have a look, and we found it was fabulous. There were gold shops with huge gold chains, too large for most of us to wear, gold bracelets of all shapes and sizes; carpet shops with old and new ones and pillows made out of carpet pieces; a hardware area; a shop with only Bedouin items; material and tailor shops (the women were covered from head to toe); money changers; fruit and vegetables displayed beautifully in stalls; but my favorite stalls sold a variety of nuts, shelled and unshelled. One could spend days wandering around taking in the sounds, sights, and smells. We then went to the Kuwait Towers for dinner. One of the towers revolves, and we spent time there getting a good view of the city. We ate in another tower and laughed at the English spelling on the menu—"coooocked" and "lamp" for lamb were two examples. Our meal was fish and vegetables and cost approximately $16 each.

An Indian couple from South India worked in Kuwait and sent their four children to the Woodstock School in India. I taught all of them in music classes or private piano lessons. (When I left Woodstock for good I gave my metronome to one of the girls because she was doing so well on cello). Before I had gone to Kuwait, the parents invited me to stay with them for a few days after my work; I accepted their kind invitation. What warm hospitality and friendship I received from them in their quiet, soft manner. During my stay, the children were to fly from India to

Kuwait for their Christmas holiday. An all-day sandstorm delayed their flight. The parents made phone calls but no one knew where their children were. After many hours of difficult waiting, the children finally arrived into the arms of very relieved parents.

Each day the parents went to work early, so the four children and I ate breakfast together. All the food on the table had to be imported: eggs from Lebanon, onions and peppers from India, cheese from Austria and Germany, marmalade from Australia, honey from England, milk from Denmark and Holland, cornflakes from the U.S., butter from Denmark, and chocolate mints from Denmark. Many friends came to see the children and me during these days. One woman brought a cake that said, "Welcome Home," another brought wine with cinnamon, etc.—all friends from India. There didn't seem to be much mixing of peoples or opportunities for such—few restaurants or tea shops. Mr. S., my host, said this was done on purpose to keep the groups from various countries separated.

I was driven around the city to see the sights. The most lasting impression was money, money, money! There was lots of it in Kuwait and they spent it on all the twentieth-century items, including the longest cars one could see. I even saw a car with wipers on the headlights—in a country which has very little rain. Perhaps they were used during sand storms. The biggest Rolls Royce agency in the world was in Kuwait. Anything can be purchased there—Kleenex, Dr. Scholl's foot pads, medicines, chocolates, tinned goods, perfumes—supplies came in from all countries.

The architecture was most interesting and many shapes were used in the windows and buildings. This should be a paradise for designers, builders, and architects. Many tall buildings were going up as they pulled down the souks or bazaars and the old Arabian houses of clay and bricks. Soon it will all be changed to new. It would be sad if none of the old is left.

One afternoon we drove along the street and came to an open gate in a wall. Inside was a courtyard with one object—a wooden platform, a tall pole with a rope noose hanging from it. What a jolt that was for me. Apparently it helps keep the people in line and less crime. We then drove to the sheep market, where I saw Bedouin tents; birds in cages for sale; carpets rolled and stacked high; a shed with old Bedouin items such as carpets, woven bags, copper pots and trays; and finally a large area with sheep for sale. There was also plenty of twentieth-century plastic, steel, modern chairs, and other furniture with people loading their cars with the modern pieces.

I ate my meals with my friends, which included two large meals each day. Each included several dishes—chicken, fish, or steak and vegetables and a curry. The dessert was served in lovely crystal bowls. We never ate dinner in the evening until 10:30 to 11:00—the usual time for Indians from India to eat.

The day I was driven to the airport, Mr. S. told me that all stop-and-go lights are blinking-red, beginning about 11 P.M., so everyone must stop at these blinking lights. It is a good way to have people arrive at their homes before they begin to blink and a good way to catch anyone that needs to be caught. There was a steady rain as we drove, but no problem developed and the plane left on time. I was sorry to leave this interesting country. The World Bank called it the richest country, per capita, in the whole world.

I had learned so much about Kuwait, about an American school in a very different culture, and had met interesting teachers who were ''gypsies'' like me, teaching in distant places. Most of all, I had enjoyed the hospitality of a very special family from India working in Kuwait.

* * *

January 14, 1991. It is very difficult for me to believe that, as of tomorrow, January 15, the United Nations has said that war with Iraq could commence. Kuwait was invaded by Iraq on August 2, 1990. I heard that news on August 3 when we were with our relatives, Trygve and Sissel Eriksen, in their home in Gjedrum, Norway. For five and a half months Saddam Hussein and President Bush have been at odds—the troop buildup in Saudi Arabia desert is tremendous—in hopes that Hussein would pull out of Kuwait. He has not budged. I am so fearful of a world holocaust. War is never the answer and this one seems so wrong. Shall we go to war? Shall we have peace? For months we have been bombarded with this on television. I watched most of two days as Congress members gave speeches about going to war or continuing to use the sanctions only against Iraq. Those who said there should *not* be war made such sense—but what if Hussein *is* another ''Hitler''?

Our hearts are saddened by this turn of events in the world; our eyes are wet with tears; our silent prayers are forever on our lips: ''Let there be peace on earth and let it begin with me. . . .''

276

January 16, 1991. I was watching the world news on TV in our Miami, Florida, living room. Tom Brokaw showed photos of the Gulf area with Tom Aspell, a newsman reporting from Baghdad. All of a sudden at 6:47 P.M., our time, the reporter announced that he saw a light in the sky and heard the first bomb drop on Baghdad. Yes, I too saw what he saw and heard what he heard right in my own house halfway around the world. For three hours I listened and watched as *it began.* The next day most programs on TV were about the war news. The second night I watched TV for four hours—Baghdad, Saudi Arabia, and finally saw the Scud missile over Tel Aviv. Yes, right here in my own home in Miami!

The freeing of Kuwait, eleven years after I had visited there, continued day and night with bombing by the U.S./Allied aircraft. Will peace ever be given a real chance by *all people?* Will this be the war to end all wars? Will good finally triumph over evil? Will we ever learn?

A Christmas card with a short note finally arrived from my Indian family in January. The note said: "Owen and I are with the girls in Cyprus. Nigel is with the Indian Red Cross in Kuwait and Kevin is working for the Far Pavilian Restaurant in Orlando, FL. December, 1990."

I was so thankful they got out of Kuwait alive and well, I bought flowers for the altar at Bay Shore Lutheran Church on January 13, 1991. The note in the bulletin said, "The altar flowers today are given by Lou Fertik in thankfulness for the recent news that friends from India who were working in Kuwait are now safe in Cyprus. We thank the Lord for His guidance and blessing."

23

Pakistan and Sri Lanka, Winter 1980

When I finished my work and visit in Kuwait in 1980 I planned to meet Leona in Sri Lanka (formerly known as Ceylon) on a certain date. I had to fly to Karachi, Pakistan, first in order to catch a flight there. My flight came into Karachi in the middle of the night; when I told Tony Horton, the head of the Karachi American School, at our evaluation meeting, he said he would meet me or send someone for me and I could stay at his home. When I arrived, there he was waiting to take me home. The following morning I met his wife, Nana, and daughter and had a tour of their beautiful home filled with objects from all the countries where they had taught. After breakfast I had a tour of the school, and called the airport to find out when my plane left for Sri Lanka, only to be told it had already gone. I said, "When does the next plane fly there?" I expected him to say in a few hours; instead he said three days from now. What a shock that was!

The Hortons didn't mind at all and invited me to stay with them. Such hospitality. I found out Tony was from the East but had graduated from an Iowa college; his wife was from Cherokee, Iowa. It must have been meant to be, more Iowa hospitality in a faraway country. Because of them I had a tour of Karachi, Nana and I attended the opening exhibit of photographs of the Moenjodaro excavation at Goethe House one evening; another couple took me to the Christmas program; and I went shopping at a bazaar where I purchased a lovely vest and an embroidered wedding belt worn by a groom in the Kutch area (with the help of Nana, an authority on native items). The last evening I attended the Christmas program by the school students. Again, Tony had to take me to the airport in the middle of the night for the flight to Sri Lanka. I was so grateful for their concern and hospitality . . . and friendship.

I found Leona at our small hotel at Negomba, a picturesque resort town on the coast where we explored the batik factory, saw an old Dutch church and Dutch canal where boats used to carry cinnamon, an aquarium containing fish from all over the world, and to the tourist section with one hotel and shop after another. Our bullock-cart transportation two hours at a time for two days worked well; certainly a new mode of travel for us. I began to get red spots on my arms and wondered if they were from the cart or the bed. One day I counted forty-one; next time I counted sixty. At least they didn't itch. The last time I counted 110. Were they mosquitoes, sand fleas, or bedbugs? I never found out.

A taxi drove us for two hours to Colombo, the capital city where we had reservations at a private home where they rented out rooms. Mr. and Mrs. D'Silva were interesting and helpful. It was a busy household and we learned so much about ordinary life in Sri Lanka, instead of the "tourist thing." She had kindergarten classes at the home, taught private English lessons, and often went to church—a lovely hostess. He was a retired civil engineer (hydroelectronics) but still very busy. They were Burghers (descendents from the Dutch). We ate breakfast at the home and other meals at restaurants or hotels; however, they did invite us to a Christmas night supper with the family. At each place was a paper crazy hat and a "Christmas cracker" (when one pulls at each end there is a loud pop). We each got a prize—I received a plastic kangaroo and Leona received a small top that would spin. What a dinner—turkey, dressing, cold meats, mashed potatoes, vegetable salad, cabbage, and garlic bread. Dessert was a moist delicious plum pudding with brandy poured over the top. Inside the cake were hidden a coin, a thimble, and a button, each with their own significance. In my portion I found the coin, which meant that 1981 would be a good year for me. Here the greeting was "Happy Christmas" instead of "Merry," but it seemed to me that some of the New Year's customs were mixed up with Christmas. We gave the D'Silvas a large tin of Kjelson butter cookies; we were each given a scarf made in Japan.

We were also included in a family weekend eighty miles outside of Colombo at their daughter's home; her husband was the manager of a large tea plantation. That was another memorable two days of chatting, eating, and relaxing. Outside my bedroom window were many bushes; suddenly they were filled with small brown birds flying frantically here and there—they were more like a swarm of bees than birds. As suddenly as they arrived they all left. It was the beginning of the wildlife we had come to see in Sri Lanka.

After some days in Colombo, where we spent time in gem shops—garnets seemed to be everywhere, even tiny pieces were in rocks on any path. Garnets were cut in many shapes for necklaces, so I purchased several. Batik shops seemed to be everywhere, too.

One evening we attended the concert by the Colombo Symphony Orchestra at the Empire Ballroom at Mount Lavinia Hotel. I was very impressed with the Mozart Violin Concerto No. 3 played by a twenty-one-year-old soloist and the Grieg Piano Concerto played by a seventeen-year-old girl. During intermission waiters with trays of fruit punch in goblets served all the audience, after which an a capella men's choir sang Christmas music. It seemed to me that music making in Sri Lanka was very much alive and well!

There had been a Third World country conference in Sri Lanka in 1976, so hotels were hurriedly built; tourism continued to increase with Germans at the top of the list followed by the French and Swedes. Everyone talking to us would say, "You are from Germany?" I finally started saying, "No, from the United States of America—there are other countries besides Germany."

We went by train to Kandy for several days and found much to see and do. The Kandy Dancers with masks and costumes performed interesting dances to the accompaniment of instruments. We visited the "Tooth Temple" with much chanting and drum beating; we saw many elephants with decorations parading down the street, etc. We wanted a week-long trip by car and driver and finally made arrangements with a Sri Lankan driver. When he arrived at our hotel he told us he was taking his German girlfriend because the passenger seat in front would be empty. Leona said, "And she will help pay for the trip?" His answer was "No." Leona told him that we would not permit anyone else to go with us (we had hired him as *our* guide and driver and we knew he wouldn't pay much attention to us if she were there). He had to change his plans, which he did. From then on, the trip went well.

Sri Lanka is a beautiful country with gentle hills and valleys covered by tea plantations, spice gardens, teak trees with large clusters of beige flowers on top (they belong to the government and no one can cut them down). Everywhere we looked we saw many different shades of green. Two nights we stayed on two different tea plantations learning so much about that industry. One tea estate had 550 acres and employed 800 people. Early one morning when I awakened I found a pot of tea: a perfect place for that good custom when one is just waking up. We drove farther north to Sigiriya, a rock fortress built on top of this large rock. It was difficult climbing the narrow path but we did get to the area where the frescoes of the "Lovely Maidens" were painted right on the rock.

What a panoramic view from the summit. Driving farther on we came to Polonnaruwa, a well-preserved ruin of the ancient splendor of Sri Lanka.

Our goal was to spend time in national parks. The first was Yala on the east coast. Arrangements were made for several drives through the park, which seemed to be filled with wildlife: jungle fowl, spotted deer herds, two leopards along the road, a herd of wild boar, two buffaloes chasing one another, langur monkeys, jackals, many crocodiles, and elephants (Sri Lanka has many elephants for work and processions), and so much more. After two days here we went to a bird sanctuary called Wirawila for a couple more days of birding: painted storks, Indian rollers, green bee-eaters, blue-tailed bee-eater, whiskered tern, sacred ibis, marsh sandpipers, pheasant tailed jacana, purple sunbirds, many flamingoes, a flock of hundreds of painted storks, another flock of white pelicans, plovers, Caspian tern, twenty-five grey herons, hoopoos, etc., etc. It went on and on. We were also fortunate to have a guide who knew his birds! What a paradise for wildlife.

Our trip continued along the southern coastline with white beaches, beautiful trees, and people going about their daily chores. There were many coconut plantations, and many men fishing for prawns standing on poles stuck in the ocean. Matara, the southern most town and the end of the railway from Colombo, had a picturesque fort. Galle was built in 1755 and a seaside resort; we visited the old Dutch church with an old graveyard where Dutch families were buried. After several more small coastal towns we arrived back in Colombo. We kept asking where Arthur C. Clarke (he writes about space and our universe) lived; we never found out. It was soon time to leave this beautiful small country we remember best as Ceylon.

In 1996 when I was on a trip around the world by plane and cruise ship, we were suppose to stop in Sri Lanka for a day; however, the State Department said our cruise ship could *not* stop because of terrorists. What a sad turn of events—it made my trip fifteen years ago that much more precious!

24

Darjeeling, Summer 1981

The summer of 1981 the monsoon arrived in Delhi on June 29. Rain came down in torrents all night. The following morning my Indian friend, Maya, and I asked for a taxi at our hotel to take us to the railroad station for our trip to Darjeeling. We were told the streets were flooded (more rain had fallen in one night than in thirty-five years). They ordered a scooter instead; we loaded our luggage and off we went in the water—a scary ride. When we got to the station I gave the driver ten rupees extra and he said, "This is excess." We smiled and motioned for him to keep it. Amid much activity we found a coolie to carry Maya's back pack, my suitcase, and a tote bag, while she carried another tote bag and I had the water bottles. Up the stairs and over to track 5; we found places to sit while we waited for the Assam Mail train. Maya found the reservation chart on a wall, found the "bogie," and we went into our compartment for two. How lucky we were to have it.

We looked out the window as we traveled and saw water everywhere—in the fields, in the ditches, surrounding the villages. How sad India looked that day! One bus was completely covered with water. When we went by railroad stations people were everywhere sitting and waiting. There was nothing else they could do. I wondered how many disasters there would be before the water subsided. Monsoons were a blessing for all, but they could be a distructive force too.

There were two berths in the compartment so I climbed up to the top berth for some sleep; however, the train jerked so much it was difficult to rest. When night came, we locked all the windows and the door and turned on the two fans but the electricity was so low they barely circulated the air. The night was so hot at 4:30 A.M. I climbed down and sat by the window watching India pass by. At dawn, Indians were squatting in the fields, or ditches, or by bushes, or the train tracks, each alone and each with a small pot of water. They neatly covered themselves and all one saw was a crouching person. After two hours or so we arrived at Barauni and had to change trains. Maya went to the ticket booth while I stood by the luggage. Finally, the conductor of our last train got the seat reservations for us. On the new train there were two cars with only soldiers. We were in the next car in seats 45 and 46.

This compartment was already filled to overflowing. We had to walk on knapsacks and bedrolls on the floor of the passageway, and many illegal Indians boarding from the back door were pushing and shoving us. We finally got to the compartment, and Maya sat in the window seat with me next to her. They were all men dressed in civilian clothes but were in the army. Maya soon whispered to me to be careful because they looked like *goondas* or troublemakers. We settled down for a ten-hour train ride, never leaving our seats because we wouldn't have been able to get through the crowded corridor. Lucky for us we didn't have to use the bathroom during that time. There should have been four on each side for a total of eight. I often counted as many as thirteen, fifteen, or even seventeen. This was an Indian train for the public, without cars with compartments for two, and I was part of it.

Finally the train came to a halt out in the country where there had been lots of trouble and we saw men outside the window running carrying sacks and cardboard cartons and realized they were smugglers. Someone on the train had pulled the chain to stop the train; the smugglers got on the train and we were off again toward Siliguri. That was to be our destination and we talked softly about how we would do it. Already some women and children stood in the compartment doorway to take our seats when we left. We gathered our belongings. Two nice men from our compartment told us they would carry our luggage out. I went into the crowded aisle first, clutching my brown purse under my left shoulder with the two straps over the shoulder. One water bottle was in my left hand and my collapsible cane in my right. I was afraid the cane would get caught in all the bedrolls underfoot. The left side of the aisle was packed with people trying to get out and others trying to get in. It seemed to take forever to move an inch. I was yelling, "Move, I have to get off another—memsahib is coming." Maya was also screaming in Hindi. A man to my left said, "Go home, lady." We were almost at the exit and a blind man with others was trying to board. I finally stepped off the track onto the platform and Maya came to me and said, "Is this your black notebook?" I said, "Yes, where did you get it?" "A man back on the train gave it to me." It seemed strange to me because I knew I had put it in my purse before leaving but we had to get our luggage from the two kind men who had found us a coolie, so the three of us went up the steps to cross the tracks, then down into the station. At last we were in Siliguri, a trade-route town with much legal and illegal activity. Maya did not want a taxi and preferred to take a bicycle rickshaw. There were many rickshaw wallahs who were almost fighting each other to get our business. Maya picked out a young, healthy-looking fellow to take us to the Tourist Lodge. The two of us, the rucksack, gray suitcase, and two tote bags got aboard and off we went in the twilight. The lodge was not too far away, for which we were glad; I am sure he was, too. They had a double room on the ground floor for us. The boy there soon brought us four cold sodas since we were hot, sweaty, and very tired after a long, hard day of travel.

Then . . . I looked into my purse and discovered my cosmetic bag was missing. I couldn't believe it! How did someone's hand get into my purse to take that small bag and the small notebook as I was trying to get out of the train? The next question was, "Whose hand was it? Was it one of the men from our crowded compartment or a stranger? I'll never know. I am sure they were after my billfold and money. What did they get? A new lipstick I had bought in Kuwait; two partly used lipsticks; one spray travel perfume bottle; one silver Cross pen; one Swiss Army knife I had purchased at the PX before leaving Germany; one gold toothpick in a case given to me by my late husband for Christmas; a fingernail scissors; one nail file; the key to my gray suitcase and all the keys for my room at Woodstock (cupboards, school music cabinets). The total cost was close to $100. What a way to begin a new month and summer holiday!

The heavy rain continued all night in Siliguri. After breakfast—two boiled eggs, toast, and coffee (we each saved a boiled egg for lunch)—we took a scooter to the railroad station to purchase our return tickets for July 21. The train was already sold out for July 20th. Back at the Tourist Lodge we got our luggage and went to the bus stand, in a drizzle. Our large bags were placed on top of the bus under a tarp while we sat in the front seats for a four-hour bus drive to Darjeeling. My original plan was to board the "toy train" for the fifty-two-mile journey from Siliguri to Darjeeling, but it took eight hours and we had already been on a long train ride, so we changed plans. The route was so scenic with the road crossing the narrow gauge tracks often, long ferns hung down along the steep banks, tall trees—cryptomeria, a type of evergreen—bamboo, waterfalls, and villages. The bus stopped wherever one wanted to get off or on. We ate our picnic lunch on the bus: boiled eggs, crax, cookies, and packages of raisins my sister had sent from Minnesota weeks before. Halfway up, at Kurseong where the train tracks were in the middle of the street with shops very close on both sides, the bus stopped and we had tea. At one stop several police boarded with a man who had a strange-looking bracelet on his right wrist. As he passed my seat I realized he was in handcuffs. A motley group seemed to be on the bus but we arrived safely in Darjeeling . . . at the stop where hotels were available. A Jeep took us to the New Elgin Hotel, where our room had glass windows on one side, making it bright. The fireplace was blocked up but still had the brass bucket for wood. On my bed was a wool blanket and a thick comforter, both needed since we were at 8000 feet. Finally, I am at the Queen-of-the-Hill-Station . . . Darjeeling. A downpour of rain developed so we ate our dinner at the hotel, a Western meal of soup, vegetable cutlet, fish pie (delicious), and bananas for dessert.

The rain was still coming down in torrents but after breakfast we put on boots, an umbrella over us, and explored the mall, went to the top of the ridge, and found a shop recommended by my principal at Woodstock who had also been principal of a private school there for many years. The son of the owner showed us "museum Tibetan pieces"—long, three-inch turquoise and silver earrings, silver boxes once owned by a lama, a silver and ivory stick used by a lama for healing, necklaces, etc. What a wonderful hour of "just looking." As we were ready to leave we gave him greetings from Beulah and Bill Jones; he was pleased and said he knew them well. Our lunch was at Glenary's, one of the best places to eat in Darjeeling. Rain continued so we walked back to our hotel to rest and read.

Saturday, July 4. It was still raining but we found a driver in a Land Rover for exploring. First, out of town to visit Mount Herman School and a music teacher friend who guided us through the music rooms, the main building, the dorms for 800 students, etc. After having been a teacher for thirty-seven years I decided that "A school is a school is a school!" Next we drove to the Mountaineering Institute Museum, where we saw photographs of climbers and their climbs, charts, letters of permission to the Dalai Lama to climb in Tibet, high-altitude equipment such as tents, shoes, gloves, food, and the boots of one climber whose toes had been frostbitten and fell off. A dead eagle someone had found at 26,000 feet. It was all so interesting. Over the door of the auditorium were these words:

Climb if you will, but remember that courage and strength are naught without prudence, and that a momentary negligence may destroy the happiness of a lifetime. Do nothing in haste; look well to each step, and from the beginning think what may be the end.

A high altitude zoo was near the museum, so Maya and I walked up a ramp into a building. When we asked if this was the zoo, the man said, "No, it is a psychological research center." Then he turned to me and asked, "What happened to your leg?" I answered, "I had polio." We saw cages with some birds, two Himalayan bears, two Siberian tigers, some leopards, but we couldn't find the yak or red pandas. I wished they were all free, not in cages but in their own free environment.

After a very busy day by the time it was evening I realized it was our Independence Day and I had not celebrated in any way. Before I went to sleep I said the words to myself of the "Star Spangled Banner," and pondered the meaning of each phrase.

Every morning bed-tea was brought to our room, a wonderful custom left over from the time of the English. Some days we had breakfast in our room, too. With so much rain we now had water dripping from our ceiling into our tub . . . it was still raining. We ate our lunch in the room: instant soup, cheese, bread and cookies. We had had crackers but a couple of nights before, I got up to go to the bathroom and opened a dresser drawer—a mouse jumped out and our crackers were gone. After that each night we put a spread at the bottom of the door. I didn't want a repeat of my "mouse plague" in Australia in 1974!

By afternoon the sun was shining and we walked to markets and bazaars to see the interesting people. There were Tibetans, Bhutias, Nepalese, Lepchas (probably the original natives in Darjeeling), all in their traditional dress, many with large necklaces, nose rings, all in vivid colors. When I think back on my days in this special hill station I see the handsome and beautiful faces of the diversified population. No wonder many of the paintings for sale were portraits. Other paintings were of the king of the mountains there, Kanchenjunga, the third highest peak in the world after Mount Everest and K2. We finally saw the snow-covered peak in all its glory; then the clouds covered it as if to say, "Only a peek today." I kept looking for birds there but saw very few—tree sparrows, yellow-browed tits, and Eurasian black birds. Once we watched a flying squirrel eating wood pulp on a tree. He was large with a bushy tail hanging down as he clutched the tree; then he sailed to another tree for more food. Another first for me. (The natives call it a flying cat or flying fox.)

Each day we learned more about our hotel and were surprised to learn that originally it was a guest house of the maharaja of Cooch Bihar and the present Indian owners had bought it in 1962. They had added a new wing with all the glass windows. The older section was dark with English-type pictures on the walls and brocade on the chairs. All the lampshades were red, making the rooms even darker. Once I tried the piano but found it very out of tune. Many repairs and construction was going on everywhere (that was probably how the mouse got in our room). One morning as we waited for breakfast, we saw the daughter-in-law greet her father-in-law by kneeling down and touching his foot, a sign of respect. He then kissed her on the forehead and whispered a few words.

One evening we ate dinner at the Sinclair's Hotel, in the Pink Room, where a five-piece band called "Rhythm" was playing—two electric guitars, an electric organ, one trap set, and a huge man played two large bongos. Maya paid for our meals and when the change came she was given a few rupees and some *stamps*—four tigers on 15-*paisa* stamps and one family planning stamp on a ten-paisa stamp. I never imagined one would get change in stamps!

Before we began this holiday I had spent two days in Delhi going from the regional foreign registration office to the foreigners' division of the Ministry of Home Affairs, filling out papers for permits. (One man behind a desk said, "When I finish this cigarette, I'll go to the other office to see where you can get a permit." When he finally left, I looked at the contents of the small windowless room—one calendar of tribal pictures, one motorcycle helmet, one desk, eleven chairs, one steel cabinet with keys hanging down in the lock. He came back and told me I should come back in eight days but I said I leave tomorrow. I received a pass to go to another office; that man told me to go to the Darjeeling office on July 7 or 8 and my permit for Sikkim would be waiting for me.) Now Maya and I were at the foreign registration office asking for a seven-day extension for Darjeeling with two days in Kalimpong. After a long wait I received those two permits, but there was *no permit for Sikkim.* I really wanted to see that country; Maya was going there to visit her brother, who was stationed there in the army. These areas were on the north border and restricted. Few foreigners were permitted.

By 9 A.M. the next day we had checked out of our hotel and were on our way to Kalimpong, about thirty-two miles east of Darjeeling and lower in altitude. It used to be the starting point for the trade route to Lhasa, Tibet. Just as we left Darjeeling, the beautiful Kanchenjunga peaks appeared. The taxi took us down the narrow road past one tea plantation after another with various shades of green. We crossed the Teesta Bridge, opened in March of 1981, followed by the checkpoint where I had to show my permission to Kalimpong for two days (forty-eight hours); Maya was Indian so they asked her nothing. All too soon we had arrived at the West Bengal Tourist Lodge, formerly the home of Mr. and Mrs. Morgan. The best way to describe this lodge is to quote from the newspaper clipping on the wall in the living room. The title was "Up in Cloud-Cuckoo-Land."

Beyond Gouripur House (where Tagore lived and wrote poems and in 1938 he broadcast a poem "Janmadin" via telephone link-up with Calcutta radio station) is the government-run stately home of Mrs. Morgan, the widow of a jute magnate. She was from the wealthy Wethersall family who owned indigo plantations and when indigo married jute the grand house was built to commemorate the alliance. With its wild stone walls, leaded windows, immaculate lawns trimmed with flowerbeds, and its sweeping driveway. Singamari looks for all the world like an English country manor transposed to these distant hills by a wave of the wand of an indulgent, if somewhat whimsical, conjurer. The house was built in 1932. Mr. Morgan died in 1959 and Mrs. Morgan in 1961. They had one bearer, one cook, and fourteen gardeners. One son was the last Governor-General of Kenya.

This was our home for our two-day stay!

Kalimpong was known for good schools and cultural institutions. Many Tibetans and Bhutias did their trading in the markets and bazaars; we wanted to see as much as we could in the short time allotted us. First our driver took us to the Graham School with mist so thick we could hardly see anything. Two teachers told us the school had 800 students from kindergarten to grade 11. We also saw the rehearsal for the kindergarten–grade 2 program. All the children were neatly dressed and looked healthy. Then we drove to the Kalimpong Arts and Crafts Center where we saw many Tibetan women dressed in the long wool dress with a striped apron. We bought a few cosmetic bags. By now it was raining hard so the driver drove us back to our "mansion" where we had tea in the lounge and heard croaking frogs everywhere. We finally got our food, fish curry, for our evening meal. It was the day of the funeral of the father of a servant who had worked at the home for many decades; he had died at ninety-eight years. Most servants had gone to the funeral, so we were lucky to get any food.

The next day we drove to the Tibetan monastery where I saw three young monks, ages fifteen, sixteen, and seventeen, who had white stones; using mortar and pestle they ground it into tiny pieces. We stood at the door of the main temple and heard about two dozen young monks chanting their lessons, all aloud, all at different speeds. I wondered how they could learn that way. Four other older monks were making a sand mandala, a graphic symbol of the universe, using colored powders from stones. What an interesting room! We drove to the Swiss Welfare Dairy but it was closed; also to the central sericulture station (mulberry and silk worms); and the orchid nursery. . . . Only one orchid was blooming.

Back at our lodge we enjoyed the sunshine as we sat on the veranda looking at the lawn, the flowers and trees, two ponds with goldfish, cats and dogs, and many birds. Mr. Mukhia, the Nepalese manager for many years, gave us a guided tour of the six bedrooms with baths upstairs, and downstairs we saw the office, dining room, and living room. Our bedroom was also on that floor. He told us Mrs. Morgan ate four times a day with a different tablecloth and arrangement of flowers each meal. There were three acres of flowers and fourteen gardeners during her years there. Again we sat on the veranda and saw the snow peaks right in front of us. I might have known that this exquisite home would have a perfect view of Kanchenjunga! I counted nine peaks but soon a gray cloud gently passed in front of them as if to say, "That is all you will see today."

One other couple, Mr. and Mrs. Roy from Calcutta, were the only other couple at the lodge. After dinner we listened to many ghost stories about buildings and people in "Cal" (Calcutta). They really were spooky. Soon, Maya and I went to our room for the night. I was all tucked in ready for sleep when she called from her bed, "Lou, do you see the light by the curtain?" I put on my glasses and there was a firefly going merrily on his way near the ceiling. After the ghost stories it was too much. Since we were "Up in Cloud-Cuckoo-Land" we decided it must be Tinkerbelle!

As we left the following morning, our driver stopped to pick up his friend, who slid into the driver's seat. I was surprised and said, "No, we have hired this other man to be our driver." They then exchanged places.

We stopped at the checkpoint to show the guard I was leaving after forty-eight hours, crossed the Teesta Bridge, the men repaired the broken fan belt, and we were back in Darjeeling in two and a half hours. I was so glad I had visited Kalimpong.

25

Bhutan, Summer 1981

Our Darjeeling trip was over. Maya left by bus for Sikkim to visit her brother in the army and his family. I left by taxi for the nearby Bagdogra airport where the rest of the tour group for Bhutan would assemble. I waited three hours before the tour director appeared and the Calcutta plane arrived bringing more for the tour. The seven of us each had a double seat in the brand new Toyota van. We drove through green countryside with forests and rice paddies, through the small town of Dam Dim, until we arrived at the Indian border town. At the border guards' station we had to leave our passports (yes, our passports) because our visas had not come through yet. (I had spent almost two years trying to get permission to enter Bhutan—I couldn't believe it!) We did get permission to drive on through the brightly painted arch-gate into our first Bhutanese town of Phuntsholing, driving on a winding road to a hotel, Kharbandi. Young men working at the hotel were at the entrance welcoming us dressed in their traditional striped woven coats with white cuffs, plaid kneelength socks and various kinds of shoes or boots. They seemed so polite as they carried luggage to our rooms, which were at the end of a corridor and down many steps. Our room smelled mouldy and mildewy, probably because it was so humid and hot. Everywhere we looked we saw plaids—curtains, the material on overstuffed chairs, the young men's clothes. It looked much more like Scotland than how I thought Bhutan would look.

Soon after we arrived we were served tea and biscuits (cookies). Later we went upstairs to a large room with no air-conditioning for dinner, which consisted of rice, chicken, mutton, au gratin potatoes, pork, vegetables, cucumber-onion-cheese salad, and whipped Jell-O on top of plain Jell-O for dessert. For drinks we were offered brandy, apple wine (a slightly fermented drink), apple juice, and Limca or Thumbs Up (sodas). Our first meal in faraway Bhutan was delicious.

I surely did hope our visas would arrive because I had two students in my Woodstock classes from the royal family in Bhutan and had sent a letter home with the girl saying when I would be in Thimphu, the capital. Bhutan was a buffer country between India and China. Only recently had tourists been allowed into this small, mountainous country. The king was His Majesty Jigme Singye Wangchuck, in his twenties. Because of the isolation for many centuries, Bhutan had remained untouched—that was why I desperately wanted to visit this "Land of the Peaceful Dragon."

Next morning breakfast was at 8 A.M.—apple juice, eggs fixed any way we wanted them, pork and beans, French fries, a slice of meat (like Spam) fried, toast, jams, and coffee. Quite a morning meal! Then we sat around waiting for our guide to come for our town tour. My roommate, Gloria, and I went outside the hotel to a flower garden where we saw such a variety of butterflies—black and white spots sitting on zinnas; brown ones edged with white; some were brown, orange and white; white ones had wings tipped with orange; and large black butterflies with iridescent bluish-purple wings. What a magnificent feast for our eyes! When it began to rain we had to retreat into the hotel.

Finally our van with the driver and guide arrived and told us the visas had *not* arrived—we couldn't leave until they did. We all got into the van and drove back to Phuntsholing, where I got some cold and cough medicine at a new store called a supermarket. Some went to the post office for three-dimensional stamps and stamps in relief of famous paintings only Bhutan produced; others went to the bank for Bhutanese coins. Rain soon fell again so our van took us back to our hotel where rain continued for two more hours. Yes, it was monsoon time here in this country, too, in the heart of the Himalayas. We waited, rested, had lunch and finally at 1:15 word came our visas had arrived and we could continue—we were one-half day late. (For weeks they had known we were going on this tour; what could have happened, or was it always like this? We never did receive an explanation.) Our guide told us only one hundred tours had been in Bhutan in 1980—not many. I felt very honored and privileged to begin the tour in such a remote land.

It was a six-hour trip to Paro Valley, hoping to arrive at 8 P.M. The rain had stopped but clouds and mist blocked out everything but the green plants and trees along the two-lane road. Everywhere seemed so clean, almost sterile, with few people around. We stopped for tea in a rustic building where we were suppose to have lunch. Darkness fell before we arrived in Paro Valley at Olathang Hotel with individual small cottages for two. Gloria and I had number 7 so a man carried our luggage and showed us the way. When we got inside I had never seen such beautiful, unusual rooms! The carpet was a gold color, the curtains were wine with gold stripe trimmed in cobalt blue; the walls were light yellow with many paintings of the auspicious signs associated with Buddhism—the banner of victory, parasol, conch shell, fishes, lucky net, lotus flower, and wheel of law, all in bright colors. The ceiling had blue-gray painted beams with rust-red between each one. A couch had painted panels with a wooden painted chest in front and a stool on each side. Small painted tables were in each corner of the living room. A curtain separated it from the dressing room and the bathroom. The veranda also had painted designs, overlooking a pine forest; we could hear the sounds of the rushing river beyond. It seems the Bhutanese cannot live without colour, and nearly every house was painted with religious symbols such as the dragon. Our cottage was surely a home, "out of this world." How I wished I could spend many months writing or reading in such a peaceful and beautiful atmosphere. In Mr. Mehra's book on Bhutan he states: "Bhutan will always have a magnetic appeal for people all over the world who want to escape from too much 'civilization' and come closer to nature and a kindly culture. One could steep oneself in the leisureliness of the place and try to know oneself for a change."

Dinner was served in the main dining rom at 8:30 and was similar to the first one; however, for dessert there was a large caramel pudding on a tray. Written in whipped cream were the words, "Welcome and Happy Stay." A lovely touch. Above the table was a gas lamp and a tall silver candlestick holding three candles. (The lights had gone out at 7:30 instead of 10 as the card in our room had stated.) On the table were salt-and-pepper shakers and cutlery made of heavy silver, probably used for the recent coronation.

Because it was dark, a man showed us our way back to our cottage. How helpful everyone seemed in this unspoiled country. No one had his hand out for *bakssheesh*; in fact, tipping was not allowed in Bhutan. We each slept under two blankets—one from India and one from China. Why not treat the two large countries on either side of this small country as equals? Because we were at a higher altitude the air was fresh and a really good night's sleep was the result.

Next morning when I awoke it was still dark but I wanted to peak out of each of our five windows that had drawn curtains. When I went from one to another I stumbled on Gloria's shoes and fell down with a crash that awakened her. I wasn't hurt. We then opened the door for a view from our veranda and watched the sunrise, but no mountains or

293

exotic birds, only sparrows. Again we marvelled at the beauty of our "home" and the environs.

Breakfast was in the main building at 8 A.M., and we were served cornflakes from a large silver bowl with lid, and a silver ladle; pineapple juice, toast, scrambled eggs, but I didn't like their flavor so didn't eat mine; ham and French fries, and tea. We left by van at 9 for a tour of Paro Valley—green with rice paddies, hills were not too steep, and the painted houses of farmers. Next was a stop at a fortress with a steep climb up so I stayed in our van and watched natives sitting on a long, low cement wall—women and children with a few men all dressed shabbily and clothes seemed rather dirty, but all the women wore the silver brooch, the *koma,* with turquoise stones. They just stared at me as I photographed them. Gloria gave the children balloons and plastic bracelets.

A short drive took us to a monastery which had an old section built in A.D. 608. We looked into the area in front of the altar where we saw a depression in the wooden floor where monks had stood and prayed and bent down in the two footmarks. Also on the floor were many pieces of coral and turquoise left by pilgrims, now imbedded in the wood. At the newer section a monk with a book was chanting. At the end of each line his voice dropped in volume so almost no sound was heard. He used one breath for each line. This was the temple where the Queen Mother went for approximately three months a year praying for the late king, who died in 1972. We also saw the white wall surrounding the royal palace where the royal family stayed while in Paro Valley.

After lunch the others in our tour crossed a bridge and walked up a steep hill to a monastery, or *dzong,* then continued up to the National Museum. I was sorry to miss the museum but the walk would have been too much for me. I could tell I was getting a cold. Resting in our colorful cottage would be the antidote. After a good sleep I sat on the veranda listening and looking for birds. Finally I saw a male and female scarlet minavet on a green pine branch. What a bonus! Soon a young girl came by, herding four cows. She stopped and watched me. Then a young man arrived wearing a wool cap which had a pin with the King's picture. He also stopped and stared. I took separate photos of them and gave each one an orange creme cookie; they then departed. If only I could have talked with them and found out more about their lives.

The following day was the tour to the Taktsang Monastery (Tiger's Nest) perched along on the side of a high cliff. The others went on ponies up the wooded hill, walking partway to the monastery. They also had to walk down because the steepness didn't permit them to ride the ponies. It would have been a thrilling adventure but Gloria and I decided to stay below. First we stopped at a Bhutanese farmhouse. Inside on the ground floor we saw grain and animals. We climbed a narrow stairs to the first floor (our second floor) and were shown their family chapel, which included two elephant tusks. The other large room had a wooden floor, bare except for a pile of bedding in a corner. We walked into the smoky kitchen where several pots of food were cooking with a woman sitting on the floor beside the stove. On shelves were many shiny pots and pans, and a butter-tea churn was hanging from a hook on the wall. In the hall was a log with narrow slit steps, very steep, taking us to the flat roof where wheat and straw were stored; birds and the wind took their share of the crops. What a privilege to actually enter an ordinary Bhutanese home.

We stopped at a woodcarving shop; however, no one was working because they were helping with the field work. In the show room I did purchase a round wooden flat fifteen inch disk with carved and painted auspicious Buddhist symbols, which reminded me of the decorations in our cottage. After that we visited a demonstration school where we talked to several staff while children peeked around the curtains to watch us. We also visited a class with all the youngsters sitting on the floor. Beautiful art work was on the walls. That was the only school we were in while in Bhutan.

Our lunch was at our hotel, where Gloria and I talked with a charming man from Switzerland. He was a technical assistant in Nepal and Bhutan installing wood stoves that heated water as well as cooked food (it sounded just like the stove I grew up with in Iowa). The stoves now used by Bhutanese gave off smoke in the room, which caused many health problems.

In the middle of the afternoon the rest of our party arrived and most of us boarded our van. Because of all the rain the old section of the road was impassable, so the Swiss man drove his Land Rover to the van, where we boarded this vehicle, almost tipping over and getting stuck in the clay muck. A second Jeep got to the new road construction where it ran out of gas, so the Swiss driver backed his Land Rover all the way back to the Jeep, where two of our tour and their luggage transferred. After some time we were all in the van and on the new road. It had been "Switzerland to the rescue."

The road from Paro to Thimphu was winding, with thick forests on the hillsides. We saw few people and arrived at our Motithang Hotel, out of the town, in late afternoon. There was construction at this hotel, too—the connection between the two buildings was slabs of stone covered by rugs. I went to the front desk and asked if there was a message for me—there was none. I wondered if Namdon, my student, had given her mother my letter.

At 8 P.M. we all gathered in the dining room for a buffet, much like the other meals: soup, rice, a mutton dish, chicken, pork with vegetables, vegetable dish, potatoes, a salad of onion and tomato slices with a piece of lime. No dish had juice to use over the rice. Each of us had to pay for any drinks of apple juice or Limca as soon as it was ordered, which interrupted our meal. While I was eating the receptionist came to me saying I had a phone call. When I answered the phone it was Namdon's mother, who wanted to know my plans for the next day. I said I was busy in the morning but free in the afternoon; however, she told me she would check with the tour director. I was pleased that Namdon had arrived home from school in India and had given my letter to her mother.

After dinner I phoned Mr. R. D. Singh, the principal of the Central School in Thimphu. Mr. Singh was a friend of our Indian music teacher at Woodstock, Ajit Singh, who had suggested I phone him. R. D. was out but I talked with his wife, who said he would phone me back. Then I phoned Dr. Pinnanger, from England, a friend of another Woodstock teacher; however, we couldn't get through to her home or hospital, both far from Thimphu. It seemed of our tour group I was the only one with any connections in Bhutan; lucky for me.

The next morning the mask and folk Bhutanese cultural dances were performed in a grassy area in front of our hotel. Our members sat in comfortable chairs while the Bhutanese children and others sat on the steps and the ground behind us. Many types of instruments were used—drums, long trumpets, cymbals, harmonium, etc. Costumes were exquisite in brilliant colors, often with animal masks such as stag with long horns or yak masks. Six girls and six boys performed several folk dances playing instruments and singing as they danced. What a beautiful performance—I was sorry to see it end!

Our group was going to town, so we waited inside the bus. A gray Corolla came to the hotel and I saw Namdon sitting in the backseat. I left the bus went to her and gave her a big hug and we talked. She said we would have a tour of the town, have something at the Swiss Bakery, then drive to her mother's home at 11 A.M. I accepted her invitation and we drove off. We were talking about this and that when she finally asked me, "Was that a tiger or a lion that bit you?" It took me a second to realize what she was talking about. I told her, "No, I wouldn't be alive if it was one of those. I had polio as a child." And she said, "Oh." Apparently it had been discussed at her home.

Our first stop was the handicrafts emporium. It was locked, so the driver went upstairs and soon lights were on and the store opened. I saw silver-gold boxes, *komas* (silver and gold brooches used at the shoulder to hold the woven material together for the women's dresses), thankas (religious paintings), calendars, stationery, woven materials, belts with designs used at the waist on traditional dresses, small bags, silver-gold pendants, woven placemats, and more. It was difficult to decide but I bought several items to remind me of Bhutan when I got home. The driver took the packages from the clerk; I never touched them. After all, I was riding in a car belonging to the royal family! We stopped at the Swiss Bakery for a glass of apple juice each. Namdon told me her mother had given her money for it; she counted the change when we got back in the car and said, "My mother will want the change back." She seemed very concerned that we were still in town at 11:00 when we should have been at her home but added that 11:30 would be all right too.

We drove back up the hill past the home of the sister of the king with a special fence around the property. Next to it was Namdon's home. We drove through the gate, down the drive, and parked. I could see many steps leading up to the lawn and the house; this way no one saw the cars below the home and no view was blocked. As we stopped Namdon said to me, "You better comb your hair," and I answered, "Oh, did the wind blow it?" After combing it I asked her if that was better and she answered, "Yes." I climbed the many steps with Namdon, walked on the sidewalk, and saw her mother was coming to meet us. We shook hands as she said, "Please come in." As I walked in I heard Namdon tell her mother, "No, it wasn't a tiger or a lion, it was polio." I was taken into the living room and introduced to her husband and her brother-in-law, who was the consular in the Royal Bhutanese Embassy in New Delhi, having arrived the previous day. Later his wife came into the room and asked the same question he had already asked: "How can we get our daughter into the Woodstock School?" I told them the correct channels to follow. The next year she was admitted.

Namdon's mother announced that we would have special Bhutanese tea and sweet rice. They soon arrived in exquisite bowls and cups. The tea was the hot butter-salted tea; the heaping bowl of sweetened rice had golden raisins and tiny strands of saffron—served at all social occasions. We were chatting about Namdon and school, her three brothers. (One was also at Woodstock. In one of my classes another boy pointed to him and said in a loud voice, "Do you know he is a prince?" I answered softly, "Yes, I know.") The three and a half-year-old handsome boy came to the couch and sat down so I placed my arm around him and he nestled close to me. The husband went to another room and brought back the one and a half-year-old boy. I asked to take the pictures of the children—the boy beside me left to find his shoes. We walked outside to a perfect spot for the photo. I commented about the beautiful home and the sister told me it was her sister's third home as we went back to the living room for more visiting.

Namdon's mother had very long loose black hair and wore lots of makeup. She wore the traditional dress in pink with a black brocade jacket. Her long fingernails were painted pink to match her dress. On her feet were high-heeled strapless shoes. Her sister also wore the traditional dress with brocade jacket and red strapless shoes. She offered me a cigarette, but I told her I didn't smoke. She lighted hers and continued to talk about her three sisters. I looked around the room and saw a wall with windows showing the valley below. Another wall had shelves with many antique bowls, Chinese cloisonné vases, books, and other treasures. In front of each couch or chair was a carved painted chest with silver ashtrays or jade trees. On the floor was a large carpet with the Tibetan dragon design, mainly blue. Near the wall with the shelves was a smaller carpet with many colors, an ornate design. It was a beautiful setting as we enjoyed interesting conversation.

Namdon's mother asked me what I wanted to do in the afternoon—eat uptown or go back to the hotel. I answered, "Whatever you decide would be fine with me." The two sisters discussed the situation and decided that the hotel had the best food in town. After lunch they would send a car and driver for a tour of Thimphu and environs. Namdon couldn't go with me because she helped the kindergarten students at school in the afternoon. When I left she told me that she and Namdon could come to the hotel the next evening to tell me good-bye. I shook hands with everyone and thanked them for the pleasant visit. Namdon and I got into the Corolla for the drive back to my hotel.

After lunch the driver arrived for the tour. I asked him if he knew Namdon's mother and he answered, "Yes, everyone knows her, but she doesn't know me." I said, "How do you know her?" "Everyone knows her because she is a member of the Royal Family." When the driver's sister joined us for the tour I asked her what "H.R.H." in front of her mother's name stood for and she answered, "Her Royal Highness." I also asked then what her husband's work was. They told me she was a princess and he didn't have to work . . . he was her husband. Later when I looked in a phone book I saw this on the first page:

His Majesty's Garden Palace [phone number]
His Majesty in Dzong
H.R.H. Royal Grandmother
    Queen Mother Palace
H.R.H. N. Wangchuck
H.R.H. Ashi Sonam Choden Wangchuck
H.R.H. Ashi Pema Lhaden Wangchuck
    etc. etc.

I never saw Namdon and her mother again in Bhutan. They did come to the hotel the following night but I was still at a drama performance and couldn't see them. They left two packages. One had two *komas,* the silver-gold brooch worn on traditional dresses; the other had three lengths of woven gold/rust/green material. What a lovely gesture. I would never forget my visit with these hospitable and friendly members of the royal family of Bhutan!

During the afternoon tour of Thimphu, with descriptions by the driver, at a 7600-foot altitude, I saw the Tashichhodzong, Bhutan's administrative and religious center on the banks of the Wang Chu River, climbed many steps to see numerous rooms recently built according to ancient traditions using no plans and no nails. Originally it was built in 1641 but fires and earthquakes had destroyed most; the new construction began in 1961 with over one hundred spacious rooms for departments, ministries, and an assembly room. The floors were bare wood and very smooth under my shoeless feet. Many thankas covered the walls. Everywhere there were boy monks talking and playing. In one room older monks chanted while some played instruments. This monastery was the largest one in Bhutan and was the summer headquarters for 2000 monks. In winter they went to a warmer area at the Punakha Dzong, the ancient capital of Bhutan. I walked in a courtyard and saw a monk throwing seeds to the pigeons and roosters with rose beds and blooming roses nearby. By now it was raining and the driver and I hurried to the car. Inside he told me he would drive me to Dechencholing, the Queen Mother's Royal Palace, approximately four kilometers out of Thimphu. The drive was scenic beside a swift-flowing river. We saw several white walls around various palaces. We drove over a narrow bridge past a primary school to the courtyard of the palace where we saw a tower gate with guards with guns standing at attention.

(I knew one of the ways one could go to Bhutan was by an invitation from the Queen Mother. The other way was to go on a paid tour like mine.) It was time to drive back to Thimphu. Again the driver drove me to the basketball court where the young king often played basketball in the afternoon. The day I was there to see him, he was not playing . . . perhaps because of the rain.

When I got to the hotel I phoned R. D. Singh and he told me about a drama performance for the Bhutanese public in a school auditorium. He invited our group for the following evening and I accepted for them. I told my friends about the invitation—they began to call me "our social secretary" . . . rather a nice compliment.

We left early the next day for Punaka, the winter and ancient capital. The road was narrow, winding, and hilly driving to the highest pass, 10,218 feet, where we should have been able to see mountains—again, we only saw clouds. (I never saw a mountain in Bhutan; wrong season.) In the Punaka Valley there were many horses/ponies and people with sacks of vegetables at the market. When we arrived near the *dzong* we got out of the van, walked on a stony path, crossed a shaking narrow walk-bridge over the rushing Mo Chu River—almost too much for me. At the far end of the bridge was a rough cement ramp; with Dean's help I made it. Inside the gate were trees with bright yellow blossoms and monks and older Bhutanese sitting around fingering their prayer beads. Up twenty-five more cement steps, then wooden steps from 1637 with a railing just above the steps, not much help. Most of the monks were at Thimphu, but we saw four young boys studying their lessons with a teacher nearby. Gloria gave them some school stickers, which they stuck on their scripture pages—I wondered how much they memorized that day. Another monk checked on red and green chilies drying in the sun. This was the fifth *dzong* we had visited, so we didn't stay long. Our lunch was in a nearby park with many flowers and trees, where we sat on concrete benches beside a concrete table under a colorful painted roof. The restrooms near the river had Western toilets, sinks, and towels. After lunch we again drove through the high Dochula Pass and saw only clouds, no mountains.

Back at our hotel we had tea and left at 5 P.M. for the drama performance. At the school auditorium we were royally welcomed and escorted to the front-row couches with low tables in front. Next to us was a professor and his wife from California, who were guests of the Queen Mother because one of the Bhutanese princesses had lived with them during her year's visit to United States. In fact, the drama was produced by her as a thank-you for the excellent response to the leprosy drive—eight performances were given for the public. When Mr. Singh had invited us to a drama performance at his school auditorium, I thought it would be a school play. Instead it was a historical drama about Bhutan with gorgeous costumes, jewelry, scenery, staging, music—it revealed so much about traditional Bhutan. Our English-speaking escort told us the story as it progressed. What a magnificent evening we experienced!

The auditorium was filled to overflowing with people sitting on the windowsills and standing because all the chairs were occupied. Many women had young children and babies with them, which surprised me—then I realized the mothers were breast-feeding them. The little ones needed to be there for the three-hour production. When the drama was over the cast bowed individually and as a group. Everyone stood and sang their national anthem, then quickly dispersed.

A young student ran to Mr. Singh's home, and soon he arrived in his jeep to take us to his home. His wife was charming, as were the two young sons, who attended school in Dehra Dun, near where I was teaching. We had drinks and Indian snacks and learned that R.D. had been Principal for four years, had a staff of twenty-one for 380 students, and most students were first-generation students. Recently many came of their own free will instead of someone going to the villages to persuade them to attend school. He also told us we should have been at their home the previous evening because the Bhutanese man who had invited Shirley MacLaine to Bhutan was there; he was sure we would have enjoyed meeting him. Yes, I was very sorry to have missed him. The Singh's home had a view over Thimphu with the twinkling lights all around. After thankyous and good-byes, Mr. Singh drove us back to our hotel. What an enjoyable evening; *however,* I was late for the good-byes of Namdon and her mother. I wrote them a note thanking them again and telling them how sorry I was not at the hotel when they came. The hotel staff would deliver the note the following day.

Before we left Thimphu the next day, we stopped at the one petrol station with all of the colorful decorations of auspicious symbols; we stopped at a huge market where we walked around and took photos of produce and people. We saw one native carrying a large red Macy's bag—it certainly was out of place—and it made us all chuckle. We also stopped to watch an archery contest, the most popular sport in Bhutan. The men were dressed in their traditional outfit with the white cuffs showing.

After driving all day we arrived back in Phuntsholing for our last night of our trip. When we went through customs our luggage was checked and we signed a form that said, among other things: "His Majesty's Government of Bhutan prohibits the export of the following goods. . . . 1) antiques, 2) musk, 3) bear biles." No, we didn't have any of them. That list confirmed we had been to an unusual and exotic country.

26

Bharatpur Bird Sanctuary, Winter 1981

Ever since I lived on Long Island and found so much cement in New York City, saw the crowds of people, and only private beaches were along the ocean, I had to find a way to get back to nature, so I joined the Audubon Society and through them found many bird sanctuaries near the airports, at Jones Beach, and elsewhere. Birds became the focus for me, and trying to identify them. I spent many hours enjoying this hobby.

Years later, in India I was going to spend a whole week at Bharatpur (sometimes called Keoladeo Ghana) by myself. A friend had planned to go with me but at the last minute she had to cancel; no way would I cancel. The train ride from Delhi took several hours and I got off at the nearest station to the sanctuary. There was still three miles to the actual place, so I engaged a *tonga* (horse-drawn cart) to this birder's paradise. I had reservations at the Forest Lodge right in the reserve. (This was the same lodge where Prince Charles had stayed not long before.)

Why was this place so special? Two hundred years ago or so the area was a semi-arid region and during the monsoon the depression would fill with water. Ducks and other waterfowl were attracted but the water soon dried up. That was when the Maharaja of Bharatpur took over. Since the land was under the migratory flyway of thousands of waterfowl from Central and Northern Asia, he had water diverted from a nearby irrigation canal into the area, and soon the birds came and stayed much longer. In a few years there were bushes, grasses, trees, fish in the lakes, attracting the birds from October to March, when the migratory birds began their flight back to their breeding grounds 3–5000 miles away. The Maharaja built two lodges for friends, for the "shoot" they enjoyed. The lakes were created around 1900, the sanctuary in 1956, the shooting stopped in 1964, and it became a national park in 1981. People came from all over the world to these wetlands in Rajasthan. Some I met were: a young biologist from Switzerland; a young man from England; four Swedish men majoring in biology who had just finished a twenty-one-day trek around Annapurna in Nepal; another Swedish man looking only for warblers (now that was someone who knew his birds); the German ambassador to India; an Indian film star, Sunil Dutt, and his entourage; and a girl from Zimbabwe, traveling alone all over the world—much braver than I and with great stories to tell. We had lunch together and spent one afternoon birding, she riding a bike and I on a bicycle-rickshaw. Those in charge of the Forest Lodge couldn't have been more friendly or helpful. Tea-time every day I was included in the group that joined the assistant manager. When I left the last day he treated me to the Sunday buffet, sent someone to the train depot to buy my ticket back to Delhi, and made arrangements for a Jeep to take me to the train station. I have very fond memories of caring people there as well as the abundance of bird and animal life. No wonder I had "my pond" where I sat for an hour every day in order to see the types of quiet activities that occurred.

I sat quietly on the ground near the small pond with bushes and trees around the edge, not far from the lodge. Some of my observations: a white-breasted kingfisher with his rich chocolate brown head, turquoise-blue back and tail feathers perched on a bare branch above the water, then flew down into the pond to catch a tiny fish; three pairs of rose-ringed parakeets were at the water's edge drinking—at the appearance of an Indian tree pie with a long tail, they all flew away; a yellowheaded wagtail had been flitting to and fro for most of the time; in a nearby tree I spied a tailor bird with its rust colored crown (I was shown the sewing skills of this bird making a nest when I was in Sri Lanka); a sandpiper pecks away and is still nameless as it was last year; a huge nilgai (gray large antelope) crossed the road, looked at me, then ran through some water into the thick underbrush; an Indian roller with its many shades of blue wings landed on a branch for a short visit; many birds were getting settled on the trees, as I was settled on the ground, when a buffalo walked near the pond and then went up the road—not knowing what he would do, I decided it was time to move on—the disturbance had caused the birds to leave also. I would be back again tomorrow to see more activity at "my pond."

Each day I had a bicycle-rickshaw man come to drive me around the numerous paths. He stopped pedaling whenever I asked him to and even helped identify birds and waterfowl. In the water were teal, widgeon, Brahminy ducks, greylag geese, cormorants, pelicans, and many others; in the grassy expanse would be open-billed storks, Siberian cranes, sarus cranes doing their dancing display, Pallas' fishing eagles were sitting in trees waiting for their opportunity; in wooded areas were bee-eaters, Indian rollers, painted storks (2–3000 spend several months there); in the grass were hoopoe (a fawn-colored bird with black and white zebra markings on the back, wings, tail and crest) with a curved beak always pecking in the ground for food; the red-wattled lapwing—the "policeman" of the birds with its distress cry; any branch over the water had kingfishers (pied, small blue, or whitebreasted) waiting to dive for food. Sounds came along with all the birds—screeching, squawks, rattles, whistles, warbles, quacks, caws, trills and tweets, and that indescribable loud harsh scream of the peacocks.

I sometimes rented a boat and the operator would take me to different parts of the lake, but I saw very few new waterfowl, however, I did find many exquisite feathers floating on top of the water. I picked them out of the water and saved them for my feather collection.

One afternoon one of my students from the Woodstock School came with her father (he was working in Delhi) and an Indian ornithologist. I was invited to join them as they drove around the sanctuary for several hours. How lucky I was to be on this trip—over fifty birds were identified. I already had identified forty, so that left only 310 more—the total was 400 different birds in Ghana. I needed to work at this hobby! We also saw a python pit with one python curled up right beside the road. Oh, my. . . .

One morning when the weather was beautiful I had breakfast on the terrace. As I was watching and listening and eating, three adult wild boar with four young walked very near the terrace. Later nilgai came and chewed on some grasses. Animals didn't often come that close to the lodge; I was lucky. Later the German ambassador came out to finish his tea. We began talking and I told him I had taught in Heidelberg, Germany, and taken German lessons but had gotten stuck on the "*der, das,* and *die.*" We both laughed at the story—and he left. Just as I was ready to go on my morning bird walk, he came out holding a box and said, "Since you were in Heidelberg, perhaps you remember these German Christmas cookies," and offered me several (heart-shaped chocolate with chocolate frosting). Of course, I remembered the Christmas cookies and could even "smell" them in the German bakery. I thanked him and left for my walk. Memories of those special days in Germany filled my head and tears filled my eyes. A most unexpected poignant moment. . . .

I would go back to Bharatpur, this paradise for birds, anytime. I long to sit beside "my pond" and see what activity goes on there today. Truly this place is a piece of heaven on earth.

* * *

In Delhi I had the pleasure of shaking hands with India's greatest ornithologist, Mr. Salim Ali, an elegant man but frail from age. (He has written many books on birds from various states in India—some written with the American ornithologist S. Dillon Ripley.) Mr. Ripley lectured on Indian birds and environment and I was fortunate to be in Delhi and attend his informative lecture. The added bonus was seeing Mr. Ali and shaking his hand.

27

Rajasthan, Winter 1982

My Japanese friend, Mary Hotta, visited me in India for three weeks during December–January 1981–1982. Since my favorite Indian city was Jaipur we spent several days there at the Hotel Bissau, where I always stayed when in this walled city. The intimate Hotel Bissau was a small palace belonging to the Duke of Bissau and was still run by his family. The hotel was very charming, both the main house and the newer wing. Guests enjoyed the book-lined library, a family portrait gallery going back many generations, and a small armory of antique weapons. I often sat in the garden enjoying afternoon tea and watching the peacocks fly from tree to roof and identifying the variety of song birds. I felt so at home here and Mrs. Singh even told me, "You are part of the family."

New Year's Eve, 1981. Mary and I attended the gala party at the Rambagh Palace, one of the Maharaja of Jaipur's residences set in a beautiful garden. Now it was a luxury hotel with tennis and squash courts, golf course, and covered swimming pool and exquisite refurbished rooms. The public rooms, the lounges, dining room, Polo Bar with polo photos, were definitely in palatial style. (In 1974, Ruth and I spent one night here; I often ate in the dining room.) There is no hotel anywhere in the world that is as elegant! What a lovely thought to spend New Year's Eve here with my dear friend. We arrived at 8:30 and were escorted to table 16, very near the outdoor stage. One large table was between our table and the stage. Soon a maitre d' came over and asked us if everything was all right. I answered, "Yes, it is fine and we hope the people at the table in front of us don't arrive." He answered, "You will enjoy them very much," and left. The buffet was to begin at 9:30 but it didn't. At 10:00 Mary and I walked to the buffet tables to look at the decorations and food: shaped-margarine eagle and horse (perhaps a polo pony since the Maharaja Jai Singh was a polo player who died in 1970 playing polo), tunafish salad shaped like a fish in the mouth of a ''pretend'' crocodile; mixed salad in tomatoes; one large section of bread sticks, rolls, and a variety of breads—also an oven for making nan (Indian bread); other ovens with charcoal fire for keeping food hot with some set out among the guests tables. One table had only desserts—a huge cake with the words HAPPY NEW YEAR, plum pudding with whipped cream, Indian sweets of all kinds. Another had fruits—bananas, apples, tangerines and oranges. The entree table had large platters of cold slice chicken, beef, salads, cooked vegetables, rice, curries, and many other dishes. People finally came and chose their foods.

By 10:30 the people at the table in front of us had arrived. We recognized the nephew from Mrs. Singh's introduction to us, also another man from the Hotel Bissau. A most attractive smiling man sat facing us with three other men. One woman sat directly ahead of us with her back to us. She wore a yellow scarf over her head as part of the yellow sari with red trim and red shawl. The attractive man was most attentive to her and to the young girl sitting across the table from him. It was only the next morning at our hotel when I saw a photo of the same couple in the living room and realized they were the present Maharaja and Maharani of Jaipur! How I chuckled to myself when I remembered I had said, "I hope they don't come." Foolish Lou. Another one of those unexpected moments. . . .

New Year's Day, 1982. Mary and I took a scooter to a gem factory and shop which were both in Mr. Khan's home. We sat on soft mats on the floor. He was nicely dressed, good-looking, and well-mannered, and he told us much about his life as we looked at trays of stones: garnets, amethysts, black opals, topaz, etc.; rings, necklaces, bracelets in silver or gold set with various gem stones. He had eight sons and three daughters; had had three wives but two of them had died. This was an extended family with three brothers and all their families living together. He could count up to fifty! All I could think of was having to cook for all those people every day. Of course, there are servants for all the daily work. Yes, Mary and I learned so much that day about the jewelry business and a Jaipur family, on this, the first day of the New Year.

That same afternoon at our hotel we sat in the living room before the evening meal and found an Indian couple with their year-old son preparing a makeshift stage for a puppet show for a German group. We watched as they placed two *charpoys* (string cots) on end with curtain material between them for the stage. A few puppets were hung for decorations. Then the man tuned the drum, which was played by the woman as the little boy crawled among the puppets and walked along the end of the cot peeking around to see the puppets in action. The father came from behind and sat him near the wall, where he began crying. The mother pulled him over near her as she continued beating the drum and singing the story! It was such a human, natural moment and unexpected minute of the show. The father moved the puppets by strings so cleverly that the figures fought, danced, one man was on an elephant and another on a camel, and one was almost thrown off. Two lighted torches were held by a man on an animal doing somersaults; the snake charmer had two snakes. There was no continuous story, just individual scenes. The man often used a whistle for emphasis or a jingling sound when the puppets danced. At the end he showed us how to move the puppets and had some of the audience try to move them, very difficult. He also sold puppets; of course I wanted to help these wandering entertainers so I bought a puppet or two.

Through a travel agent we got reservations to spend one night at Jogi Mahal, inside Ranthambhore Game Sanctuary, 400 kilometers from Jaipur. The driver and car arrived for our two-day excursion and we drove through green farmlands with camels pulling carts loaded with a variety of merchandise. Women working in the fields or on the roads were dressed in their bright blue full skirts and red or yellow tops and the flowing cloth covered their heads. Silver bracelets were on their ankles and all wore arm bracelets. One time we saw a huge flock of goats and sheep, perhaps a thousand—I had never seen so many in one flock before. Two pillars along the road stated ''Newab of Tonk,'' a minor kingdom. Red peppers were drying everywhere—as far as the eye could see, even over on the hills. It was quite a sight. Later we saw camels loaded with beds and household items, and women walking beside them had boxes on their heads filled with pots and pans. Their arms were covered with ivory (or bone) bracelets from the wrists to the shoulders. The group was moving from one area to another and I was thrilled that I had a glimpse of their life.

Our driver was so knowledgeable and he told us about each small state—Tonk, Uniara, the forts built on high rocky barren hills, and the palaces. This certainly had been a most interesting trip off the beaten track. We stopped at Madhapur to ask where the Jogi Mahal was and were told it was eight–ten kilometers from the town. When we finally arrived we were told they had not received any reservations for us—our agent in Jaipur had told us we *did* have reservations. What to do. The manager told us to wait a half-hour while he checked, so we sat on the terrace overlooking the lake, a most beautiful spot in the sanctuary. A few crocodiles were basking in the sun, wild boar were wallowing near the edge of the water, and birds were singing everywhere. We waited and waited. Finally someone brought a plate of sandwiches, two bananas, and hot tea (our lunch at 3:30 P.M.). We still didn't know if we had a room but were invited to join the twilight drive in a Jeep. The Indian driver was young, another man was quite fat and had a brace on one leg (polio), another Indian couple and Mary and I got in the jeep.

Ranthambhore had once been a hunting preserve of the Maharajas of Jaipur but was now a national park and one of the eleven Project Tiger reserves. The terrain was varied with hills, deep gorges, rivers, savannah grasslands, which afforded an ideal habitat for many kinds of wildlife such as tigers, leopards, sambhar, cheetal, nilgai, wild boar, and sloth bear. The Jeep meandered in the dry deciduous forest, then a rather flat section with sparse vegetation, and beside rocky ravines. It seemed so dry to me, even the water holes were dried up. We did see the deer (cheetal, sambhar, and nilgai), wild boar, grouse or quail, many peacocks and peahens, and some saw two sloth bears but I couldn't spot them. If we looked up above us we could see high on the cliffs the broken fort walls where animals often rested and relaxed. We kept on driving down a narrow rocky path with branches and boulders everywhere, finally coming to a dead end . . . huge rocks everywhere. Three of us got out of the Jeep and watched as the Jeep bounced, jerked, sputtered while the driver turned it around. He drove up to the top of this rocky path while the three of us had to follow—walking. And this was real tiger country, too! We didn't see one but I wonder if the "silent predator" didn't see us?!? It added enough suspense for the entire two days.

Arriving back at Jogi Mahal we were told there *was* a room for us. I am sure it was because of Bittu Saghal and his wife, Madhu, from Bombay. He had just begun a new ecology nature magazine called *Sanctuary* and was spending time in this sanctuary doing research. Madhu was a genuine hostess. There two darling daughters, Miel, ten, and Tara, seven, were with them. We were so thankful for the room we immediately went into this small marble building built years ago as a lodge for the maharaja. There were four bedrooms and baths, no electric lights, so we were given a lantern. We spent the evening in the grass-thatch-reed–enclosed hut with logs burning in the center, for light and heat. About 10 P.M. we finally had dinner in the dark, in front of the burning fire. We were served rice, dhal, chappaties, gram (red beans), cauliflower and for dessert one of the most exotic desserts I have ever seen—burnt sugar (probably gur) in tiny strands made into the shape of a basket. Inside was vanilla pudding with banana slices. There was even a handle for the basket made from the tiny strands of gur . . . served in a small round bowl. Surprises, always surprises when one travels! We sat around the fire as one family while the other men asked Bittu questions about tigers, wildlife, nature, ecology, etc. Mary and I helped entertain the girls and we all drew pictures of birds and animals and people's faces.

Just before retiring for the evening we were told that a tigress with two cubs had killed a large 700-pound buffalo calf the night before but had not eaten it. The men had found the kill, which had been carried quite a ways, and they had covered it with branches so the vultures wouldn't eat it. At 6 P.M. the branches had been removed by the men because the vultures were not active then. The men expected the tigress to come and eat that night. A tracker would be halfway between the kill and the lodge and if he heard any animal warning sounds of the tigress coming to the kill, we would be awakened and drive to see her with the aid of the spotlight on the Jeep. Mary and I went to our "marble room" with hope in our hearts that tonight just might be the night we would see a real tiger in the wild. Several times during the night I awakened and remembered that we still had not been called. . . . Once 4 A.M. came we knew there was no chance.

At 6:10 A.M. Mary awakened me and we got dressed by the light of the lantern that had burned all night. At 6:30 we were at the Jeep ready for our morning drive. Since the tracker had heard a few sounds at night, all the men were sure the tiger was still at the kill. There was such an element of quiet excitement and anticipation as we waited for everyone to get to the Jeep. A tray of tea had been placed on the hood of the Jeep and it tasted so good as dawn gradually lightened the sky. The two Jeeps left about five minutes apart. When we got to the area where the kill had been, the occupants of the Jeep that arrived first told us they had not seen the tigress because the kill had been dragged away. The tracker and two drivers then walked down the *nulla* (rocky ravine) and saw the tall grasses had been broken as she dragged the kill. . . . Then they found the remains in a little pond of water. She couldn't move it farther because it got stuck in some rocks. She had eaten sometime during the night. So again, the tigress won and ate in peace and quiet with no spotlight or camera flashes to disturb the dark jungle. I was sorry not to see her but I thought, *Bravo for the secretive tigress!*

As we drove back we saw very few animals—a few sambhar standing still staring at our Jeep as we passed and some langurs jumping from branch to branch, occasionally howling. Breakfast was served outside on our marble terrace. We had toast, scrambled eggs, and a fruit salad of cubed papaya, bananas, apples, and tangerines. We sat in wicker chairs and listened to the sounds, mainly peacocks and jungle babblers (noisy birds). Beside us was a huge banyan tree mentioned in Akbar's time, so it was at least 600 years old. If trees could talk wouldn't that one have fantastic tales to relate. . . .

Midmorning our driver came for us. How sad to have to tell our new friends good-bye. I gave 100 rupees to the manager for our two Jeep drives. When we said good-bye to Mr. Saghal and two daughters, he gave back the 100 rupees, saying the businessman from Bombay had paid for the jeeps for five days and wouldn't take our money. What a kind gesture! We did pay for the entry fee into the sanctuary, the camera fee, our room and food, but not the Jeep drives. This was India. . . . (In 1996 I was invited to the wedding of one of the daughters in January; however, we wouldn't be in Bombay until March. I was sorry I could not attend.)

We drove several hours through the countryside with the usual scene of camels, goats, sheep, and people. A fort appeared on the top of a hill, and Mary said she would like to see the thickness of the palace-fort walls at Uniara. Our driver said, ''Yes, we could do that.'' We drove through narrow streets with shops on either side. At the end we turned into the fort, went through several gates until we were at the palace. Our driver got permission for us to go inside and up the narrow winding stairs with servants' sandals lying here and there. Mary asked if we had to take off our shoes and he said, ''We are not servants; only servants do that.'' Upstairs in a large room were many stuffed chairs where people waited for an audience with the Maharaja of Uniara. He soon came and greeted us. He was a tall thin man with a huge mustache and wore a brown suit. He explained the paintings to us; some frescoes showed forts and palaces in ''my kingdom''; also a huge carved elephant out of one piece of rock was shown us through an open window (later we drove closer for a good look). He suggested we go upstairs to the third floor to see more frescoes. By this time his daughter had arrived, and she suggested we see the women's section. Then she said the family was going on a ''shoot'' (wild boar), in a few days camping out in tents for several days. We still had many miles before we got to Jaipur, so we said our good-byes and left. Another unexpected bonus—but in India one never knows.

Later, we found out our driver's father was the Maharaja of Ethawa, a minor kingdom near Jaipur. No wonder we met the Maharaja of Uniara. No wonder we had learned so much about the area from this knowledgeable "driver" who really was the Prince of Ethawa.

We arrived back in Jaipur tired and exhausted and decided to eat our meal at the Hotel Bissau. We went into the dining room and asked the waiter if we could eat there at the large handsome wooden table. He said, "No." He escorted us into a small room with small tables. We were told that evening the Maharaja and Maharani of Jaipur were coming. Soon dear Mrs. Singh came in fussing with tablecloths and plates. She came over to us and invited us to meet the maharaja. What a surprise that was! I told her we were tired after our two-day safari to the game sanctuary. She said he was coming at 8 P.M. for drinks and snacks and that, "You are like a member of the family." (What a compliment that was!) After eating, Mary and I went to our room, talked about the invitation and decided we really were too tired for this most auspicious occasion; we told Mrs. Singh that we had to decline. If only we could accept all life offers on a silver platter. . . .

*   *   *

Another visit to Jaipur I was alone. I hired a driver and car to take me to a different wildlife sanctuary. The Hotel Bissau gave me a cooler with food and cold drinks for this all-day trip. When we got there we saw the usual wildlife, but nothing special. Near twilight a calf was tied where it was hoped a tiger would come. We waited and waited but nothing happened. By now it was dark. Before we left the park the driver told me, "We will lock all the doors and I am going to drive very fast because there are *decoits* (thieves) in the area." That was certainly a shock for my ears! Thank heavens all went well during the drive and we saw no one on the road. Upon arriving at the hotel, I went into my room and he carried the cooler. I paid him and he left. Later, on top of the cooler, I saw a mouse. I swear he said to me, "You wanted to see wild animals, well, here I am!" He then escaped under the door.

*   *   *

I have a dear friend, Vija Vetra—we call each other "Gypsy sisters"—who has specialized in dances of many world countries, including India. She visited me while on a dance tour in India. Of course, we went

313

to Jaipur. Another friend from school, Leona, was also with us. What a glorious time we had staying at the Hotel Bissau and visiting the sights, including the Amber Palace, seven miles from Jaipur. A taxi takes one there; high on the hill is the old capital, now deserted. It was built in the seventeenth century so the Moghul influence is seen everywhere. Amber was the nucleus of Rajput history. Instead of walking up the steep hill to the palace, most ride an elephant, a lovely way to slowly get to the top. Once as we were going up, another elephant with passengers was coming down—as they met us they said, "Bon Voyage." What an unusual greeting, high on an elephant.

Many elephants are needed for the tourists . . . and they have many. While my dear friends, Vija Vetra, and Leona Cressman and I were in Jaipur, Mrs. Singh invited us to a very important Rajput wedding reception, and we accepted. How surprised we were, at the bride's family home, to see the arrival of the bridegroom on an elephant! Why not? Elephants were available. What a memorable entrance!

28

Pony Trek in Nepal, Winter 1982

January weather in Nepal is good, without rain, so in 1982 I spent four weeks there visiting my Tibetan friends in Kathmandu, learning more about the culture of the Nepalese, and planning a trek. Since there was no way I could walk it as most other trekkers do, I knew I would have to ride a pony. There were two other staff from my school in Katmandu at the same time who were willing to go with me. I also invited my "Tibetan nephew," Tashi, to join us. The four of us took the bus to Pokhara, a five-or-six-hour bus ride up and over hilly, not very good roads. We found a small hotel there near a lake. We found the Pony Trek Company and made arrangements for four ponies for four days with guides. We then bought snacks, fruit, and candy for our trek and had a good night's sleep in preparation for our big trek!

A taxi drove us to the edge of Pokhara, where our four horse-ponies soon arrived. I was given Raja, and we got along fine. The other ponies had no names; by the third day each were named from their characteristics. Fred called his Lazy Baby; Aru, a secretary in our school, named hers Dopey; Tashi named his Tashi. We had a Sherpa guide and I had made arrangements for him to lead my horse (I was sure I would fall off since I had not ridden a pony before). We had a Gurka porter to carry our sleeping bags and small cases in a large basket on his back; a strap around his head helped with the weight. A few words of advice were given to us novices: to bend forward when going uphill and lean backwards when going downhill. Now we were ready and with great fear in my head and heart our adventure began. A river was to our right; later we went on a road near a Tibetan settlement, then through small villages where dogs or cows would come and look at us. There were always children and women watching us. We came to a broad valley with harvested rice fields. All seemed to be going well until I looked back and saw Aru on the ground. Her pony had shied away from something and thrown her off. We all went to her and found she had a badly sprained elbow but she wanted to continue. . . . by walking. My guide then led her pony and I was on my own. (I still feared that I would fall off so during that break I gave Fred the name and address of my oldest brother in Iowa in case anything happened to me.) We slowly continued on this level area and met traders from Dolpo and Mustang coming to Pokhara. Tashi could speak to them in Tibetan, so I could ask them questions and take photos. Tashi turned out to be such a great help to me. At a village with a stream running through it, we stopped for lunch. To get to the cafe we walked across a wooden plank. Many trekkers were coming from their 8- , 17- , or 24-day trek in the high mountains. Usually there were fifteen trekkers, often from Australia, with forty porters and cooks to carry their gear. I had often read about these expeditions but this time, *I was there seeing it with my own eyes!*

After lunch we mounted our ponies and ambled to the end of the valley. In front of me all I could see were slate-slab steps that went up and up. On this steep climb I hung on for dear life and hoped I would not fall off as we continued up the steps, about 2000 feet! We finally reached the top ridge, where there was a level path. In Nepal, porters carry heavy loads everywhere so there are stone walls built where they can lean their loads and rest. Usually there is a tree or two for shade at the wall of rocks. That was how I got on my pony. There was no way I could put my foot in the stirrup and pull myself up. Instead I climbed on the wall and would sit down on the pony. Sometimes the path was so narrow that rocks jutted out, almost crushing my leg as I went by. That happened because the Sherpa leading my pony just walked on and didn't guide Raja. Several times the rocks bruised my leg, bringing tears to my eyes. At the next rest stop when Tashi came to me I rolled up my pant leg and showed him and the Sherpa what was happening as blood oozed from the cuts. Tashi told the guide to be more careful. From then on all went well.

Our first night was spent at Naudanda in a new small hotel with a fantastic view of the snow-covered peaks of Annapurna. The rooms were clean, it was not too cold, and we ate food they prepared—Tibetan bread, rice, dhal—with our snacks (chocolate bars, sunflower seeds, raisins, nuts, cheese, and crackers), and hot tea. It seemed like a banquet after the strange and exhausting first day. I thought my seat and spine would ache but it was from the hips to the knees which were sore. We all slept well.

The next morning we packed our gear, had a good breakfast with the mountain view around us, and were off for Chandraket. The path was rocky; a few slate slabs were in place to go up or down, but in some locations it was almost straight down with boulders and rocks every-whichway. I had to get off Raja and walk down with Tashi's help. It amazed me that natives walked up and down these trails as though there were no problem. On all paths were small rocks and dust—I had to look down instead of watching the beauty of the mountains or villages, plants, and trees. No wonder it is called a *"trek."*

We finally arrived at Lumle, a village stretched along the road. We stopped at Lumle Lodge for lunch, where we were shown a small dining area with a window cut out of the wall overlooking a valley. *That* was what I call a "picture window." The kitchen was beside us, and we could watch the mother and son cook the food over the clay stove on the floor. When one of us ordered meat, the mother took it from the beams in the ceiling. Tashi could talk to them as he helped with the food preparations, adding to the friendliness. After the meal and a short rest we were on our way again. Three hours later we arrived at Chandraket, a very small village at the end of the road. (One can continue on by going down a steep path to a river far below, then walk up to continue to the *real* mountain country.) The Infinity Lodge was right at the corner with the wind blowing strong and cold, but we decided to stay there anyway. A woman led us up a narrow stairs to a large dormitory with ten single cots. It didn't look too clean and there were used blankets on the beds. Aru and I didn't want to sleep in such a place. We asked for a room for two. We then went through a dark tiny room with baskets of little potatoes, onions, and other vegetables into another small room. A large board was covered with a straw mat with one part having a mattress of straw and a blanket; the other part had books. One was *The Story of Physics.* There was a small kerosene lamp. We could tell this room be-longed to someone, perhaps a trekker who had gone on a trek, we thought. One wall had wide boards with one-inch cracks between each board—there were seven or eight of these large cracks. In the middle of the wall was a window of wood that one opened by lifting to the ceiling—when we did that, the mountains seemed right outside. What a bonus! I truly felt like Heidi, the Swiss girl, in this unreal-looking room, our home for the night. Never would I be so close to the mountains as I was in Chan-drakot.

On a resting platform near the lodge a young Tibetan from near Mustang had his wares for sale. His English was excellent because he had gone to three schools for Tibetans in India, but he had to go back home because his parents were in a "pitiable state." He was selling teacups with silver, articles one uses around the house like needle cases, bell-metal bowls from Dolpo, fossils in black geodes. I wished I could have bought something to help him—it was impossible, riding Raja.

We walked to another lodge for our supper. After one hour our meal was finally prepared and served: rice, dhal, vegetable, and hot lemon tea, which was always delicious. One Nepalese man was standing around listening to us talk; I finally asked him his name and what his work was. He told us he came near us to hear English spoken so he could improve his English. He was one of the seven local teachers for the 300 children: 80 girls and 220 boys. It was his room Aru and I were using that night. What a coincidence since we were teachers too. (How I wished I had left him five rupees for the use of his "air"-conditioned room.)

It was extremely cold as we walked back to our own lodge. Fred lent me his modern space-age blanket, five layers of insulation. On each side was a layer of aluminum foil and a layer of protective plastic, one side was shiny, the other blue. I was warm all night because of that blanket. Imagine, being in the most primitive room possible and using a late spin-off blanket from the space age. Wonders never cease! In the distance children were singing to the accompaniment of a drum. What a delicious way to go to sleep in this faraway corner of the Himalayas at 5700 feet. Good night!

I was awakened at 1:30 A.M. by a loud crunching sound. I said aloud, "Is there a rat in the room?" but Aru was fast asleep, so I used the torch (flashlight) and shined the light everywhere to see if some creature was there. With so many cracks anything could have come in. My torch revealed no moving object but the loud crunching sound was still there, so I assumed a buffalo or stray animal had gotten into the pen below us, where our four ponies were. Then I saw the torchlight of our guide shine around the pen. One pony had gotten away from his post, and the guide had to find him. Quiet came and so did more sleep.

At the crack of dawn we unhooked the wooden slats, opened the window, and in front of us was the most beautiful sight—the Annapurna peaks with no cloud cover. The sky turned from pale pink, rose, lilac, light purple, and finally the white snow-covered peaks against the blue sky . . . the Himalayas in all their majesty right outside our strange little window! All the aches and pains of riding the pony vanished. A moment of pure beauty—those moments don't last long. Soon the clouds came and took away that glimpse of heaven we had briefly experienced. That was why I had ridden a pony for two days to find, not the pot of gold at the end of the rainbow, but the peaks of the Himalayas! Success.

Reality told us it was time to rise and begin our preparations for the day. The only water came from a faucet attached to a spring—ice cold. There was no toilet anywhere except a spot in a grassy area or field. Somehow, we performed these morning duties without too many people watching us. Breakfast was eggs, pan cornbread (sometimes called Tibetan bread), with our own cheese, honey, and hot tea. I was sorry to leave this place knowing it was the remotest I would ever be from my kind of environment.

As we retraced our route back to Lumle, we met a mule caravan, each loaded with various provisions. The two lead mules or ponies always wore a colored plume of yak hair and many bells around their necks; a woven carpet piece on each forehead. They carry nothing—they move fast and the rest follow them. We had to stop because of the huge caravan coming down our narrow path. I counted them as they went by—ninety-six mules. Imagine! I had read about this kind of transportation but never ever thought I would actually see it.

After they passed we continued our trek to Lumle and were happy to see the mother and son again at their lodge. Because we liked them so much we stopped for another breakfast, took more photos with them, and enjoyed the valley view far below. Any day I would go back to visit Lumle and its precious little village and friendly inhabitants.

As I met women along the route I would say "Namaste" to each one. Without fail, each woman returned my greeting (that is what "Namaste" means). Often they were carrying bags on their backs, sometimes a baby, but usually they held their hands together in front of their face with fingertips touching as they said "Namaste." Once I saw a man with a huge basket of eggs; another time it was a man with many rolls of fabric on his back. The only way to get merchandise to the villages was for man or animal to carry it. No wheels had ever touched the stony uneven path. These people may not have much in the way of comfort and their work must have been hard but they seemed happy and contented with their lot in life.

As we neared Naudanda we found many children just getting out of school (Friday was a half-day). The little boy who called me Grandmother at the lodge before, saw me and ran beside Raja all the way back to the lodge. I was afraid some boys would get too close to Raja and scare him—that never occurred. I had given that boy one rupee for a pen and he took out his new pen to show me. Yes, a friend for life. It was good to arrive back at our hotel. Hot lemon tea made me feel more human as we waited for lunch in the courtyard, looking at the mountain peaks across a deep valley with terraces for farming. Fred figured out from the scale on a map that the peaks must be twelve miles away as the crow flies. A nap in the afternoon was most welcome. Aru was exhausted because she had been walking two days and now had a blister on her heel as well as a swollen hand and hurt elbow. In spite of her problems she had been a good sport without complaining.

The weather was good every day—warm with a cool breeze. I wore a "long-john" top, a pullover, a corduroy *kurta,* and my poncho in early morning; the layered look. Later I would take off the poncho and sling it over my Tibetan bag containing my camera, binoculars, a small money purse, and toilet paper just in case. I had chosen the correct clothes for this adventure. Slacks were a must when riding a pony.

Who were these six people who were sharing a four-day trek in Nepal? This was what I found out:

Name	Occupation	Nationality	Age	Religion
Sangpo	guide	Sherpa, Nepal	20	Buddhist
Shreeman	porter	Gurka, Nepal	28	Hindu
Aru	accountant	Indian	30s	Christian
Tashi	artist	Tibetan	25	Buddhist
Fred	science teacher	American	61	Quaker
Lou	music teacher	American	58	Christian

Again, supper was at 7 P.M. in the downstairs room but this time we ate by kerosene lamps suspended from the ceiling. Two young Englishmen told us they were musicians, a violinist and violist who had worked in Australia for the last year. One read a book but the other talked with us as we watched the sunset on the mountain peaks changing colors from the red-pink glows fading into the grey-blues . . . then darkness . . . vivid stars and familiar constellations . . . and sleep in air with no air pollution.

Our Sherpa guide, Sangpo, told Tashi we should begin our last day's trek as early as possible. We decided to be on the road at 8 A.M. We rose at dawn and saw a spectacular sunrise, but it was soon muted and the magic moment had disappeared. Even though breakfast had been ordered early it arrived late, because of only two burners using wood chips and sticks. Porridge, eggs, milk tea, and Tibetan bread was quickly eaten. I counted the people watching me get on the wall and then on Raja—twenty-five children, youths, and older men and women. What a sendoff I received from the villagers. My special friend was right there, so I let him hold my bag with camera and binoculars while I mounted Raja. I am sure he felt a special pride in that small gesture. With hand waves and good-byes, we all set off on the narrow path through Naudanda and turned on a dusty road bending around a hill.

There were farm houses on both sides of the path, very well kept. For a half-day we traveled on a smooth path, then came to the end of the ridge and had to descend those 2000 feet again, although we were on a different trail. For two evenings the conversation had been, "How will Lou get down those 2000 feet?" The Sherpa said he could carry me; Tashi said he would carry me; they thought some coolies might be there to carry me. All the while I knew I would get down on my own, with Tashi's help. This time there were no steps. One could not possibly ride a pony going down such a steep slope with rocks and boulders strewn everywhichway, as before. So off the pony and with Tashi by my side we slowly proceeded down the treacherous track. Women walking toward us would ask Tashi what had happened to me. I told him to tell them the truth, but he said they would not understand the word *polio*, so he made up stories about how I had fallen off the pony or whatever. The last woman said, after asking Tashi about me, "If she can't walk very well, she can't ride a horse." He answered, "She can ride a horse very well." At one point a native on his pony jumped from rock to rock very fast, zigging and zagging as though he were on level ground. My heart almost skipped a beat as I watched this man maneuver his steed so beautifully and easily. What a moment!

After three hours and several rest stops we arrived at the bottom. I was surprised I didn't feel exhausted. After another rest we were on the tarmac at the edge of Pokhara, back in "civilization" again. A bell sounded behind me and a bicycle sped passed, a car honked letting me know they were passing, a garden tractor pulling a loaded trailer made much noise as it chugged by. For a moment I wished I were still "up there" in the land of people walking, mule trains with tinkling bells, and the clip-clop of Raja's hooves on the stony path. Then I realized that this, down here, was *my* world. Already the four days seemed like a dream, but my aching muscles told me it had been real. As Raja took me into Pokhara I was very thankful I had had no mishap, had traveled with three excellent travelers and good friends, a fine guide and porter. The pony trek had been a success—a special, once-in-a-life time adventure in the Himalayas.

29

Change of Plans, Spring 1982

I had enjoyed the winter vacation of 1982 so very much—the company and visit of my dear Japanese friend, Mary Hotta, in Delhi and Jaipur; the pony trek in Nepal with three dear friends; and the arrival of another friend, Eva Felde, from Heidelberg, Germany, teaching days. After a few days in Delhi showing Eva the sights, we taxied to Woodstock together. I had stacks of mail to read since I had been gone for two months. What should I find among the letters but one from a man I had dated in New York; he moved to Florida and I moved to India. Now he said he wanted to get reacquainted! I must say that was one of the biggest surprises in my whole life. He also told me about the difficult time getting my address (he only knew my last name as ''Golden,'' and not my maiden name of ''Nelson''). After some time and many wrong bits of information, he wrote a letter to ''The Resident on Three Pine Farm, Eagle Grove, Iowa.'' My sister-in-law, Irma, who now lived in our large family home (when my father passed away in 1968, Mom had exchanged houses with Bob and Irma's smaller home on the farm), answered the letter and gave him two addresses in India—the Methodist Guest House where I often stayed when in Delhi, and the Woodstock School. He wrote two letters, one to each place . . . the letter to the guest house never arrived. I soon answered his letter from the Woodstock School and our correspondence began.

We decided we should meet again, so during my summer break from teaching, I flew to Iowa to attend my niece Melissa's wedding outside on the lawn at the farm. How happy I was to be able to share that moment in her life. The following week Sam flew to Iowa, where we visited all my brothers and sister's homes and their families as we got reacquainted. After much thought and discussion I would go back to Woodstock for one more semester, then fly to Miami where we would get married. (Yes, plans *do* change as life goes on year after year.)

That semester was very busy with teaching and getting ready to leave—making purchases of Indian items I felt I wanted in my new environment in Florida; getting rid of things that others at school could use; many farewell parties, etc. I was co-chairman of the social committee, which meant planning a staff banquet for the end of the semester.

We chose "Christmas Around the World" as the theme, because we had staff from so many countries. Those from that country decorated that table. Our nurse was from Burma, so she decorated it with lighted pagodas; several were from Australia and they used seashells and sand (December 25 is summer there); South India had typical decorations from there, and North India had another type. That banquet turned out to be absolutely beautiful as well as each table having authentic decorations. Guests could sit at any table they wanted. I chose to sit at the Burma table, a country I wanted to visit but hadn't yet. I also asked a good teacher friend, Dan Lacy, to announce my engagement (others knew I was leaving but they didn't know why). He made the unexpected remarks after which everyone came to congratulate me and wish me well.

A few months later I received the following from Hugh Bradby, Woodstock vice principal:

> Resolution of Appreciation which the Board passed pertaining to LouCelle.
> LouCelle Golden spent five years with us at Woodstock. She came to us with a wealth of teaching experience almost unparallelled in a new teacher at this school, having taught in Germany and Japan as well as the United States. This experience stood her in good stead as she knew exactly what results she wanted from her students and the best methods to achieve these results. Her pupils responded with the affection and respect which students everywhere accord to a teacher who has consistently high standards and who insists on these standards being met. But Lou had a soft heart also. She was the life and soul of social life in the Quad, and proved herself a much-loved friend to many people inside and outside of the Woodstock Community. It was highly appropriate that, in a year which saw three other marriages among staff members half her age, Lou should have left us to get married to a long-standing friend in Florida. We wish Lou and her husband all the best as they embark together on this exciting new phase of their lives. Please let us know when you will be bringing your husband out on the pilgrimage to Woodstock.

So ended my life of teaching music for thirty-eight years in various countries . . . and the beginning of my retirement years with a husband named Samuel Fertik.

VIII
RETIREMENT AND TRAVELS
(1983–)

Share our Happiness

Samuel Fertik and LouCelle Golden
are happy to let you know that we were
married on January 10, 1983 in Miami,
and will be living at 3101 N. Country Club Dr. Apt 202
Miami, Florida, 33180.
Phone: 305/935-0421

Summer on the road

Winter in Florida

30

Marriage and Travels

Sam and I were married in Miami on January 10, 1983. I was so happy my sister, Carol and her daughter, Jean were present for the simple ceremony. Sam's good friend, David Glickman was his best man. Sam already owned a condo in an eight-story building in a beautiful area called Aventura with two golf courses, trees, lawns, flowers, and small ponds. Every time we came in the entrance gate I couldn't believe I was part of this—and retired.

Sam had been the manager of the graphic arts department of a large company in New York City; in Florida he continued his love of art through the Miami Art League, where he also was editor of their monthly newsletter and one of their officers. He had been in the Navy in the 1940s and participated in D-Day on the battleship USS *Texas*. He had a son, Bill, and three grandchildren—Joshua, Lily, and Michael. We got to know Lily very well because she attended college in Fort Lauderdale, and we saw her very often. (She always calls me "Grandma," the only person who uses that—it's good to hear that term of endearment.)

He enjoyed traveling too, so we purchased a twenty-one foot Winnebago motor home traveling the United States and Canada for five summers, always stopping in the Midwest to visit my family. The first summer I found out my mother was seriously ill at the nursing home in Iowa, so we hurried there to be with her. By this time she couldn't talk, but I knew she had been waiting for me to arrive before she died. I spent a day with her and was there when she breathed her last breath. I was so glad I had made it home to be with her—she had always been there for me during my struggles and triumphs.

We continued to travel and see the world:

1985: A three-week tour took us to China, including a four-day Yangtzee River trip in the Three Gorges. Of course, we climbed the Great Wall—and so much more. I had always wanted to visit China because our Iowa neighbor to the north of our farm, Daniel Nelson—no relation—was shingling his house in 1890 when he got the "call from God" to be a missionary in China. I felt if he could go to China, sometime during my lifetime, I would also go. Our tour even included the area where he spent his life. (Yes, dreams do come true.)

1988: We spent two months in India and Nepal and made that pilgrimage to the Woodstock School to introduce Sam to my friends there. We visited my Tibetan "family" in Kathmandu, Nepal, also.

1990: Eighty-one relatives flew to Norway for a family reunion for three days with two hundred Norwegian relatives. Everyone stayed in the home of a relative during that reunion. We had tours of the area where Grandma Laura had lived near Stavanger, and visited the house where Grandpa Lewis lived near Haugesund—and saw the glass pane where he had scratched "Lauritz"—before leaving for American in 1886. The following two weeks some had tours around Norway while others continued seeing relatives. This great reunion happened because of the *Larson-Jotten Family* book my mother and I put together in 1972!

1992: Sam and I celebrated the five-hundredth anniversary of Columbus discovering America on a fifty-two day cruise through the Panama Canal—then circumnavigated South America., We experienced a terrible storm before entering the Straits of Magellan where a piano tipped over, two thousand eggs broke, the breakfast buffet tables collapsed, etc. We had never experienced anything like it before and had to stay in our beds for twelve hours until it finished. The day was cold and clear when we circled Cape Horn, a desolate and lonely island. It was good to have seen it so near Antarctica . . . where I never expect to travel.

At Punta Tombo, on the southern coast of Argentina, we visited the vast rookery and breeding grounds of the magellanic penguins braying as they waddled around—what a special experience! Later that day we visited a typical Welsh town, Gaiman, where traditional Welsh tea was served with sandwiches, cakes, and cookies as we listened to an a capella choir sing Welsh songs. It was hard to believe that such refined singing could be produced in empty windswept Patagonia.

On this trip Sam liked Santiago de Chile best; I liked Buenos Aires, Argentina, where we enjoyed a gaucho fiesta on the pampas; we saw Evita Peron's tomb in Recoleta Cemetery, and much more.

1993: A Black Sea cruise took us to Odessa, Ukraine, from where Sam's parents had left as small children. We saw nothing of their area but got a feel for present-day Odessa. In Yalta, it was too far for me to walk from the bus to the palace where Stalin, Churchill, and FDR had met at the end of World War II, so that dream remains unfulfilled.

1995: After visiting family in the Midwest, we left our car with nephew Jim in Minneapolis and flew to Vancouver, where we began our cruise on the Alaska Inland Passage, stopping at Ketchikan, Juneau, Skagway, Sitka, Seward, with tours of the highlights at each town. The scenery was breathtaking and grand, with mountains, glaciers, ice floes, birds and animals, and sunny days. A bus took us to Anchorage, then to Denali Park, where we were overnight . . . a six-hour bus tour of the park where we saw Mount McKinley (now called Mount Denaldi) the entire day—a real miracle. The McKinley Explorer train took us to Fairbanks for a three-day bed-and-breakfast home stay. Here we met an Athabascan Indian woman, Lilly Pitka, from Fort Yukon, who was staying at the same home. I interviewed the eighty-three-year-old woman, who told me about her life as a child when her family spent the summers at fish camps and the winter trapping animals. She was fourteen years old when she did the exquisite beadwork on a moosehide velvet jacket that is now on exhibit at the Alaska Museum. Sam and I were invited to go with her to the airport when she left for Fort Yukon. One flies there or goes by boat; there are no roads.

Alaska is so interesting and different from the "Lower 48." I was happy to revisit the state and saw many changes—my first visit was in 1961.

1996: We had a world trip by plane and cruise ship, taking the section of the cruise called "Ancient Trade Routes of the East." After flying to Hong Kong we began our cruise and were soon in Vietnam for two days. Sam explored Thailand while I flew to Burma (Myanmar) with a small group from our ship. I had wanted to visit the country ever since high school when I heard the song, "On the road to Mandalay where the flying fishes play, and the sun comes up like thunder out of China cross the bay." I found the country beautiful, with gentle people, but I also learned more about the Nobel Peace Prize winner in 1991, Aung San Suu Kyi, who had been under house arrest for several years because of her nonviolent struggle for democracy and human rights. We drove by her home but our guide told us we couldn't stop. Apparently things were not as "gentle" as they appeared. Rangoon (Yangon) was a bustling town, while Mandalay, farther to the north, seemed untouched by such progress. . . . I liked the old look. I couldn't go in any temples or pagodas because one must take off socks and shoes. The pagodas were often gold-leaf–covered and shone brightly in the sunshine. We went into a gold shop were two men were hammering gold bars to make into thin strips.

When I passed in front of the girl at a table with gold leaf, she stood up and placed gold leaf on my right wrist. It was as though I was getting a special gift from Burma because of my lifelong dream!

The cruise ship went through the Suez Canal; stopped in Egypt where we saw the pyramids near Cairo; went on the "Lawrence of Arabia's Wadi Rum" trip, driving across the desert in an open Jeep, stopping at Bedouins' tents . . . a rough ride. Because one engine broke on the ship, we didn't get to stop at Djibouti, or Goa, India; because of terrorists we couldn't stop at Sri Lanka or Israel—four real disappointments. We flew back to Miami from Athens—yes, it WAS a trip around the world!

Between those longer trips we often went on seven- or ten-day cruises in the Caribbean. One cruise was on a Russian ship to Central America, which we enjoyed because of the different customs and food on board. For "senior citizens" a cruise seems to be the best way to travel now—less unpacking, all needs are provided on the ship, and a good way to make new friends.

Do I have any regrets of places I have not visited or people I have not met? Of course I do. How I want to spend a night or two in a yurt (nomad's tent) in Mongolia; I want to see St. Basil's Cathedral in Red Square in Moscow and somewhere in Russia hear hours and hours of the Russian religious music; I want to visit the fifth Scandinavian country, Iceland; and I still want to see a tiger in the wild. People? I wish I had met Albert Schweitzer, who saved organs from destruction in churches in Europe, was a doctor in Africa—his philosophy was "Reverence for Life." President Franklin Roosevelt, in spite of his polio problems, was a four-term president, and my inspiration. I never saw the great musician and conductor Arturo Toscanini. I could go on, but why think of the things I have not done? I have been blessed from the beginning to the present decade with a multitude of opportunities in music, travels, and friendships!

Aboard the Air France Flight from New Delhi to Paris—1988

Sam and I boarded the Air France flight at the New Delhi airport and sat in the first row seats in tourist class with the movie screen right above us. In the next two seats were two older women from India wearing gray flecked Punjabi outfits (loose long pants gathered at the ankles and tops which came below the hips) and new large shawls pulled over their heads. From the moment they fumbled with seatbelts and had no idea how they fastened I knew I would help guide them into the technicalities of the twentieth-century. I got the seatbelt fastened around the woman next to me; she tried to help her friend but to no avail, so I stretched across and somehow got it fastened. I tried to say a few words in Hindi but that was not their Indian language, so we used another language—smiles and hand movements.

After some time the trays of food were placed in front of us. I could tell they hadn't a clue about getting the utensils out of the plastic bag, fruit juice out of the small container, or the plastic off the top of the salad and entree. I opened the oil and vinegar dressing and poured it over their salads. They tasted it but made a face which showed they didn't like it. Tea and coffee came later; they both took tea; however, one of them accidentally spilled it on the tray, her clothes, and even her sandals, which she had taken off. She did the best she could to wipe it up. Finally, the meal was over, the lights were put out, and the movie began—right in front of our faces. The woman next to me indicated I should fix the headphones so she could hear and watch. The other one was fast asleep with the shawl completely covering her head. I watched the expression on the face of my seat companion as she watched the movie. For the entire movie she didn't take her eyes off the screen. Was it her first? What intrigued her?

Night and quiet came to all the passengers aboard. I got up and went to the restroom and when I returned to my seat, they both indicated they also wanted to go. I took them, one at a time. First I showed her how to lock the door but when she went inside she didn't lock it. I stood outside so she wouldn't be disturbed. She then said the word *pani* (water), so I showed her the faucets in the sink, the soap, the towel, and where to discard it. She washed her hands, then cupped them and filled them with water and began to drink. I shook my head and said, "No," and she spit it out. She returned to her seat and I fastened her seat belt. The other woman got up after I unbuckled her seat belt. This time I lifted up the lid of the toilet so she would know what to do. We got back to our seats and more sleep—but never for long. A steward brought the immigration forms to fill out before landing in Paris. I took out my passport and completed my form. Through motions I asked for their passports. The woman in the far seat handed hers to me and I wrote down what it said: her name; born—Lahore, Pakistan (it was an Indian passport) in 1924; occupation—housewife; identifying marks—"dark hair turning gray."

331

The woman next to me never gave me her passport, so I assumed someone else on the plane had it. I asked them where they were going and they said, "Glasgow."

How I wished we had a common language and I could have learned about their lives, their families, their folklore, their dreams, their knowledge about living. They had so much they could have shared with me. Instead the woman beside me looked me in the eye and chuckled—a kind of laugh that told me we had shared much and in that sharing we had a good time together. Her eyes were sparkling brightly, her skin was dark, and she had broken and missing teeth when she smiled.

When the plane landed and it was time to part, she put out her hand and shook mine with her strong, firm handshake. I gently touched her on the shoulder but felt like giving her a big hug. She put her feet into her sandals, picked up a large plastic sack with odds and ends, and was gone.

Imagine not being able to read a word or signs, not knowing how to use our Western twentieth-century items, yet they had the courage to leave their little village and fly to another country and century. What brave women!

I felt a real kinship to those women, because forty years ago, I, too, had embarked on my first trip away from my country, and my life was never the same again. That was when I truly began to *live*. I hope they felt the same way.

31

A Strong Stand on Education

Each Thursday from 10–12 A.M. a person (usually a former English teacher) came to our condo and gave a book review for those who were interested in our building. She was hired by the Dade County Education Department. For two months I had been attending the interesting sessions. Today was registration day for the new semester and I gladly went. Sam had painted the signs for our building bulletin board announcing the registration. As I arrived in our community room a paper was given to me to sign, write down my birthday but not the year, as well as my Social Security number. Then I visited with an interesting woman from our condo.

When the session began, the woman in charge of the book review announced, "You know you have signed a paper which says you do not have a high school diploma." I couldn't believe my ears! I asked her what she meant. She explained that if we didn't sign that paper as a non-diploma person, we would be charged $102.00 per semester; otherwise it was free. She then explained that the Florida legislature had passed a bill the last day of the session without reading the numerous pages. As she was talking I became more troubled and asked more questions. Finally, I said, "I had no idea about this and I want that paper back which I just signed. I didn't know I had to lie to get into this course. I have been a teacher for thirty-eight years with a master's degree [I should have added that I had many more hours above it] and at the present time I have an exhibition about Tibetans, their paintings and artifacts, at the Coral Gables branch library. There is no way I can continue in this group." I took the paper and stalked out of the room.

As I walked to my condo I thought about my family and stories I had heard about my father's family. In 1872 Oliver and Nels Nelson and their bulldog left Wisconsin, where they lived, for Colorado, where they hoped to move the following year; however, when they got to Fort Dodge, Iowa, one of their horses died so they could go no farther. They both worked hard to earn enough money to buy another horse and settled on land in Humboldt County near Fort Dodge. They began to break up the land, haul lumber, and build a small house. Then they returned to Dodgeville, Wisconsin, for the winter. In the spring of 1873 they and their mother, Ragnild, and her two daughters, Emily and Jane, and the dog started out in a covered wagon along with friends in two other covered wagons. They all got to the Mississippi River, where they waited for the ferry to take them across. They had let the bulldog out and he was not there when the ferry arrived, so they left without him. Many weeks later, the dog arrived alone 100 miles west of the Mississippi River at their new home in Humboldt County. He had been there the year before. What a reunion that must have been!

In the 1970s my mother and I had traveled to Dodgeville to try to find out more information about my father's family. At the courthouse we found the Deed Record of their farm between Oliver (my father's father), the sisters Emily and Jane, Nels the brother, and Ragnal Haldorsdatter Nelson, born 1812, widow, the heirs at law of Ole Nelson, deceased. The comment beside said: "This is her (Ragnal's) sign—X." What a surprise to learn that my great-grandmother could not write her own name and had to use an "X."

My father wanted to become a coach but was needed on the farm, so he never fulfilled his dream; all five in his family graduated from high school. Those in my mother's family had more than a high school education. Most had a college degree. Two were teachers, one taught piano, one a clerk, one was in social work, two were farmers, one a lawyer, one a dentist. The children of those nine became doctors, teachers, nurses, beauticians, a retired lieutenant in the air force, a nursing home administrator, and successful farmers. How could I possibly deny my heritage?

In my own family, education was not discussed per se; it was just expected for each of us five to become educated. My parents were proud that each of us received a college degree. They never took out insurance policies—our education was our "insurance policy."

My siblings and their children had degrees and worked in various disciplines.

Albin   Doctor of Veterinary Medicine
          1. James   Ph.D. in chemistry; law degree
                       Intellectual Property Attorney
          2. Linda   Music degree; nursing degree
          3. Richard   Dentist

Robert   Math and Physics degrees (master's degree in math)
Computer and math high school teacher
1. Gregory   Computer systems analyst
2. Rebecca Dentist
Lieutenant in the U.S. Dental Corp—5 years
Civilian contract dentist for Navy—4 years
3. Melissa   Music degree (master of arts in piano)
Music teacher
4. Timothy Aerospace engineer
5. Jennifer Lab technician

Carol   Speech and drama major; art minor degree
Substitute teacher in many subjects
1. Barbara English major degree
Bookkeeper
2. Donald   Animal Science degree
Cattle Superintendent on Oxley Hereford Ranch
3. Ronald   Animal Science and Agriculture Economics degree
Crop Superintendent on Oxley Hereford Ranch
4. Mark   Animal Science degree
Rancher on his wife's family ranch, which he is buying
5. Jean   Office management and business degree
(She bungee-jumped in New Zealand while on an interim college course)
Service parts sales representative

Orin   Agronomy degree
Administrator of nursing home
1. David   Psychiatric treatment worker
2. Nancy   Social work degree
Activity outreach—community life
3. Clark   German and Norwegian degree (master's degree)
Distance learning teacher of German for the Denver public schools

I have always been so pleased and proud of my nieces and nephews with their interest in education and all their hobbies. It was because of them I would write my life story so they would know where "Auntie Lou" was when she was not at home. All these thoughts went through

335

my head—there was no way I could deny my educational qualifications, so much a part of my Norwegian heritage—our family heritage. And so I walked out of that session on ''book reviews'' where I would have to lie.

32

My Iowa Home—Three Pine Farm, 1993

I was sitting on the bed in what used to be ''my'' room in August, 1993, looking out the two east windows at the fields beyond. The wind was blowing so hard the short soybean plants lay flat by the force. There had been too much rain . . . and large black patches appeared where water had been standing too long. On the front lawn the flag pole stood empty—no one lived in the house now to take care of it. The lightning and thunder seemed far away; one-half hour ago they were directly above with the dark, threatening clouds. Inside the nearly empty house some buckets were placed in strategic spots to catch the rainwater that came from cracks in the roof. It was the beautiful home built in 1922 and where I grew up. It was seventy-one years old and beginning to show its age.

There were memories in every nook and cranny from five of us living there. When my father died, my mother exchanged houses with her son, Bob, and his family of five—Mom moved to their smaller house on our farm. Now, twenty-five years later, they had all left after filling the home with all their activities of growing up. We were trying to take care of the tangible memories stored in the attic. My niece, Becky, and I looked in boxes that contained letters and postcards dating back in 1914; one box contained my mother's essays and papers from her Jewell College days; a garment bag of clothes had belonged to Grandma Larson in the 1900s. I found drawings of birds, trees, and butterflies and reports from 1937 when I was in sixth grade; another box contained letters and scrapbooks from my teaching job in Manson, 1946–1949. Becky checked over her brother's and sister's boxes and found dolls, GI Joe's, stuffed animals, a box of her mother Irma's early school papers. What does one do with family memories? It is very difficult to throw away memories.

Boxes, large and small, new ones and battered ones, some covered with dust, tucked under beams or near the windows were next to parts of beds or piles of magazines. The large attic had never been an organized place. When Aunt Lyda moved to California she stored dressers, etc. there; Grandma Larson lived at our house for her last ten years and had many things there; it was a catchall for several generations.

I was privileged to help with the task along with other family members and the children who diligently carried the boxes down two flights of stairs for sorting and discarding.

I found these special pieces of family memories:

The letter from my father asking my mother to marry him, from 1916.

Grandpa Oliver's journal he started in January, 1900, the new century. He was fifty years at that time. He kept daily notes for six months. What a treat to read about the past and our "roots."

My five-year diary given me by my mother in 1937. I wrote every day during my high school years and one college year—'37, '38, '39, '40, '41. What memories those pages gave me.

Mother kept scrapbooks on all important events and people; consequently there were scrapbooks on Lindbergh, Dionne quints, World War II, movie stars, political figures, community affairs, on and on.

Letters from relatives in Norway from before World War II, during that war, and after—most written in Norwegian. Mother could write Norwegian, so she wrote for her mother, Grandma Laura.

Aunt Lue, Mother's sister, had gone with Grandpa Lewis to Norway in 1914. We found a letter to Grandma saying she had seen the sled dogs, the sled and tent used by Amundsen at the Pole. What a thrill that must have been for a fourteen-year-old girl.

Grandma Laura's ninetieth birthday cards and letters from family and friends. How we hated to throw that box away.

My parents, Albin and Tillie, anniversary decorations and cards for both their twenty-fifth and fiftieth, from 1942 and 1967.

Brother Bob's string bass he loved so much. When he was in the army in 1946 the folks had a chance to sell it and wrote Bob in Italy to get his permission. He wrote back, "No, that is just like a member of the family."

Uncle LeRoy's letters from the army, most of them censored, then photostatted (small copies). Once he wrote he was stationed in a place having the same name as one of his nephews. Much time was spent on that riddle but someone figured out it was nephew Orin—he was stationed in Oran.

Tintypes of great-grandparents—very large ones. These were used when Mom and I wrote our family genealogy book in 1972.

Bibles in Norwegian, some large and some small . . . a few in English.

Books from country school; college text books, paper back books and *National Geographic* magazines—there were many decades of those, which took us to faraway places.
Old clothes, sometimes used for dress-up and pretend by grandchildren.
A large wooden box containing Japanese umbrellas of various sizes, kimonos, and many types of their footwear, from my two years in Japan. I got them for my "show and tell" and gave them to grand-nieces for playtime.

The family home was sold in 1994. The buyers were my brother Bob's youngest daughter, Jennifer, and her husband, Denis, and two children. How fortunate it is still in the family. The farmland was sold in 1996—to a Nelson cousin who added it to his many acres near our farm. Memories of that era are all I have left; I *really* am now living beyond the fields!

IX
EPILOGUE

Traveling carries with it the problem of being at home everywhere and yet nowhere, for wherever one is, some part of oneself remains on another continent.

—Margot Fonteyn, English ballerina

Tributes

In 1975 I was listed in *International Who's Who in Music and Musician's Directory,* printed in Cambridge, England.

* * *

In 1994 I received a letter from Gerald J. "Sam" Berry, Ph.D., Lieutenant Colonel, U.S. Army Retired. He had been my student in Heidelberg, Germany, in 1957. This is his letter:

Dear Miss Nelson,

Although I know you're Mrs. Fertik now I guess I will always think of you as Miss Nelson. I am Sam Berry, Class of 1957, Heidelberg American High School. Recently during a church service, our minister asked if we could each identify one teacher during our school years who most influenced us. Then he asked if we had ever taken the time to tell them. As I thought back through my high school and college years, the name that came to the top of my list was you.

I have never spent any time professionally in music but I've enjoyed singing in church choirs and small groups ever since I left Heidelberg HS. My sister, Patricia, did become a music teacher and is still teaching music in the King William County School, Virginia system. She also remembers you fondly. My daughter, Susan, now sings in the church choir with me.

I've read your bio from our Alumni letters and envy your experiences with Tibetans, etc. I spent time in Okinawa (2 years), Viet Nam (2 years), and Germany (6 years) as the result of military service (30 years, retired in September of '90). One of my last assignments was as the Chief of Staff of the Heidelberg Military Community; I was a frequent "guest" in the schools. While at the reunion in D.C. last month your name came up during our reminiscing about the best part of high school.

Thank you for the influence you had on my life and I wish you all the best in yours.

Sincerely,
Sam

It is always good to hear that one's efforts while teaching were lifelong influences—that is the purpose, especially in art and music. I surely enjoyed thirty-eight years of dedicated and talented students, such as Sam, in the various schools on our earth. I thank them for all the beauty and harmony they gave back to me!

* * *

Certificate

In Recognition of the vital support given by LOU CELLE NELSON FERTIK
in preserving the history of the American Overseas Schools
as a CHARTER MEMBER of
The American Overseas Schools
Historical Society, Inc.
In witness thereof the Board of Directors of this Corporation have here-
unto subscribed their names to be affixed at Litchfield Park, Arizona this
31st day of December, 1996.

* * *

"Tillie Award"

The first "Tillie Award" was given to LouCelle Nelson Fertik at the Larson-Jotten reunion on July 20, 1997, in Eagle Grove, Iowa, attended by eighteen Norwegian relatives and American relatives totaling 197. The award was for her collaboration with her mother, Tillie Larson Nelson, on the *Larson-Jotten Family Genealogy,* published in 1972, twenty-five years ago. (Because of that book many Norwegian relatives have visited American relatives and attended our reunions. It has been a bridge between those in Norway and those in America.)

Countries I Have Visited (1948–1998)

North America
Alaska
Canada
Mexico
United States

Central America
Belize
Costa Rica
Honduras
Nicaragua
Panama

Caribbean
Bahamas
Barbados
Cayman Islands
Dominica
Dominican Republic
Grenada & Seps.
Jamaica
Martinique
Netherlands Antilles
Puerto Rico
St. Kitts
Trinidad
Virgin Islands, American

South America
Argentina
Brazil
Chile
French Guiana
Uruguay
Venezuela

Pacific Ocean
Australia
Fiji Islands
Hawaiian Islands
New Zealand
Papua New Guinea
Ryukyu Islands (Okinawa)

Africa
Angola
Botswana
Egypt
Kenya
Lesotho
South Africa
Swaziland
Tanzania
Uganda
Zambia
Zimbabwe

Europe & Mediterranean
Austria
Balearic Islands
Belgium
Bosnia & Herzegovina (Sarajevo)
Bulgaria
Croatia (Zagreb, Dubrovnik)
Denmark
England
Finland
France
Germany
Greece
Hungary

Ireland (Eire)
Ireland, Northern
Italy
Luxembourg
Monaco
Netherlands
Norway
Poland
Portugal
Scotland
Spain
Sweden
Switzerland
Turkey in Europe (Istanbul)
Ukraine
Vatican City
Wales

Near East
Dubai
Iran
Israel
Jordan
Kuwait
Lebanon
Syria

Asia
Bhutan
China, People's Republic
China, Republic of Taiwan
Hong Kong
India
Japan
Kashmir
Korea, South
Lesser Sunda Islands (Bali)
Macao
Malaysia (Kuala Lumpur)
Myanmar (Burma)
Nepal
Pakistan
Philippines
Sabah (North Borneo)
Sarawak
Singapore
Sri Lanka (Ceylon)
Thailand
Turkey in Asia
Vietnam

Uncle LeRoy's Letter about Dr. Sabin, 1993

We received this letter from Uncle LeRoy about Dr. Albert Sabin regarding the polio vaccine. It needs to be included in my autobiography.

28 June 1993

My Dear Lou and Sam—

As a 39-year member of Rotary I have been enthused about the many projects, mostly international, but none compare with the Polio Plus initiated in the early '80's. To me it is the most noble effort for world good that could be chosen. The credit really goes to Dr. Albert Sabin and his development of oral vaccine. The "Rotarian" issue carried the news of his death earlier this year. To me it brought sadness as well as a very happy memory.

Let me explain: In the early '70's I served on the Legislative Council of the American Dental Association. We had an annual agenda of a 2–3 day seminar in Washington, D.C. Our purpose was to contact our own Senators and Congressman but more importantly to contact each member of both Senate and House Health Committees. Our wonderfully staffed Washington office made all arrangements. Our purpose was to express appreciation for their support of our magnificent Research Activity at Bethesda, Maryland and "lobby" for continued and increased support. On this occasion everywhere we went we encountered three rather desolate looking characters (scientists). Hollywood would describe them as serious looking, bearded, ill-fitting clothes with baggy trousers. As I was the Chairman of our Council, I engaged them in conversation and learned the identity was Dr. Albert Sabin and two colleagues; that they were in need of funds to continue the work in Oral Vaccine; that they were under constant criticism from AMA alleging their work with live virus was dangerous, etc. Most of all their work was done outside of U.S.—Poland, Russia, Mexico, and a couple of other South American countries. I invited them to join us which they did, as well as attending a couple evening receptions we had scheduled. I followed later his contribution making possible the Polio Plus Campaign. When he was to be given Rotary's high award at the International Convention in Birmingham, England, I decided to be there (also it's only a short hop to Stavanger). The next year, 1985, the International Convention was held in Kansas City and Dr. Sabin gave his acceptance

347

speech. I was there, too, and had a visit with him recalling the episode in Washington, D.C.

What a gifted man—to think of it—a few drops of oral vaccine giving immunity! A real blessing. I have the very highest regard for Dr. Sabin and his achievements! Another example of a foreign-born contributor to our society. He tells of his uncle providing for his education and enrolling him in dentistry in New York University; after two years he transferred to medicine. Lucky for all!!

I must apologize for this long story. I guess I just wanted to share the details of an unforgettable experience. Thanks for reading it.

> My very best to you both,
> With love,
> Uncle LeRoy

Post-Polio Syndrome

Polio had left its mark on me when I had the disease at age seven; however, it never interfered with my life. Then in the middle of the 1980's my left foot began to give me problems; it had always been the weaker leg. A doctor suggested I get a plastic brace, which I did. It seemed to help, a little. Short articles appeared in newspapers about "post-polio syndrome" but no one knew much about it—including the doctors. Ten years later I had to get a plastic brace for the right leg. I also use a cane outside the condo. Weakness and fatigue are also part of the problem. Yes, polio problems had reared their ugly head again with the passing of years.

More and more Post-Polio Associations have organized, including an excellent one in South Florida. I attend the meetings held once a month with a variety of programs such as support sessions; Legislative actions and effects on us; long-term care; pain/post-polio syndrome; a picnic in a park and a holiday party. It is good to get to know the others who are as surprised as I am at what had happened to polio victims in our later years.

Now, I am more thankful than ever that I began to travel when I was young; accepting the challenges and opportunities as they arrived and fulfilling my dreams along the way. Believe me, post-polio syndrome slows one. But it hasn't stopped me yet, and I pray it never will!